# THE ALPINE JOURNAL

D0539321

## 1995

1. Baffin Island: the West Face of Mount Asgard. (*Paul Pritchard*) (p47)

# THE
# ALPINE JOURNAL

## 1995

### The Journal of the Alpine Club

A record of mountain adventure
and scientific observation

Supported by the
MOUNT EVEREST FOUNDATION

Volume 100
No 344

Edited by Johanna Merz

Assistant Editors:
Roy Ruddle and Geoffrey Templeman

THE
ALPINE
CLUB

THE
ERNEST
PRESS

THE ALPINE JOURNAL 1995
Volume 100 No 344

Address all editorial communications to the Hon Editor:
Mrs J Merz, 14 Whitefield Close, Putney, London SW15 3SS

Address all sales and distribution communications to:
Cordee, 3a De Montfort Street, Leicester LE1 7HD

Back numbers:
Apply to the Alpine Club, 55 Charlotte Road, London, EC2A 3QT
or, for 1969 to date, apply to Cordee, as above.

First published in 1995 jointly by the Alpine Club and the Ernest Press
Typesetting by Johanna Merz
Disc translation and repro by Westec
Printed in Great Britain by St Edmundsbury Press Ltd,
Bury St Edmunds, Suffolk


A CIP catalogue record for this book is
available from the British Library

ISBN 0 948153 41 5

The Alpine Club                                    The Ernest Press
London                                             Glasgow

# Foreword

This is the 100th volume of the *Alpine Journal*. The first 100 years of the Alpine Club were celebrated 38 years ago with the *Alpine Centenary 1857-1957,* and naturally enough that volume concentrated on the history of the Club rather than of the *Alpine Journal,* even though these have always been closely interlinked. The first *AJ* appeared in March 1863, having been preceded by three volumes of *Peaks, Passes and Glaciers.* Since then, successive volumes of the *AJ* have not always appeared in exact synchronisation with the passage of the years. But there is a resonance about 'the 100th volume' which seems to demand something special. By a happy coincidence the 60th anniversary of the 1935 Everest Reconnaissance falls this year, and to mark the event Charles Warren has kindly released extracts from his previously unpublished diary of that expedition.

*AJ100* also celebrates the first British/Irish ascent of Everest from the north, with Dawson Stelfox's vivid evocation of his experiences on the North Ridge in 1993, together with John Tinker's no less gripping story of the second British ascent from the north only a few months later. From time to time, a combination of factors (such as the advent of easy travel and the evolution of new mountaineering techniques and equipment) results in a great leap forward into previously impossible realms of achievement. The two articles on Everest from the north reflect such an advance, as does Jonathan Pratt's report of his ascent of K2 with Daniel Mazur. And Paul Pritchard's remarkable story of his lengthy struggle, with three others, on the West Face of Mount Asgard shows how the limits of climbing aspiration are continually being pushed forward.

The 100th volume coincides with the 40th anniversary of the first ascent of Kangchenjunga. Some of the members of Charles Evans's 1955 expedition returned to the mountain this year, and a special Kangchenjunga evening was held at the Alpine Club. These events will be reported in next year's volume. Meanwhile, many achievements described in *AJ100* – such as Robert New's descent of Lowe's Gully on Mount Kinabalu in Malaysia and Evelio Echevarría's peak-bagging exploits in Bolivia – demonstrate that exploration and adventure are still possible in this shrinking world.

Christopher Russell has now contributed his 25th article entitled 'One Hundred Years Ago'. Always impeccably researched and accompanied by carefully chosen photographs, this fascinating series offers far more than a bare recital of facts. With his annual presentation of both the great events and the small byways of mountaineering history, Christopher has helped to keep us in touch with the achievements and traditions of our past.

In the *Alpine Centenary 1857-1957* John Hunt gave a prophetic warning:

> As increasing numbers look for outlets among the hills, from the
> growing artificiality of civilisation, there is a tendency, slight as yet
> but noticeable, to translate to this realm of lasting values some of the
> false values from the cities ... From the wisdom of experience it is
> possible to see clearly the importance of preserving the spirit of
> adventure in the future, yet of keeping that spirit free and objective,
> uncoloured by the prowess of individuals, still less of the nations
> which breed them. Provided that the danger is seen and the balance
> maintained, then the future of mountaineering is bright.
>
> *From 'After a Hundred Years'*

In recent years, some of our older members who read those words back
in 1957 may have felt disappointed to see that balance not always being
maintained. But John Hunt also expressed the hope: 'that such barriers
as the Iron Curtain will now be lowered for mountaineers who live on
either side of them.' With Russia and Central Asia rapidly becoming our new
playground, his wish is being amply fulfilled. Moreover, the recent joint
Indian–British expeditions (including the one described by Chris Bonington
and Paul Nunn in this volume) have shown what can be achieved through
international co-operation, rather than competition.

For a perceptive analysis of the state of mountaineering in 1995, I warmly
recommend Ed Douglas's article, 'Protect and Survive', in this volume.
Ed shows how widespread concern about the environment is affecting
both the ethics and the direction of our sport. On the vexed question of
bolts, the letter to Doug Scott from Etienne Gross, Editor of *Die Alpen*, is
also highly significant.

Looking ahead, I hope that the *Alpine Journal* will continue to give a
comprehensive picture of current activity in the mountains, together with a
sensitive awareness of the effects of change on the mountain environment.
I hope, too, that the AJ will always, in the future as in the past, provide a
vehicle for historical research and scientific investigation, a forum for
debate and an outlet for all that is best in mountain literature.

I am grateful to the Mount Everest Foundation for its generous support,
and to José Luis Bermúdez, Ted Hatch, Peter Hodgkiss, Roy Ruddle,
John Slee-Smith, Geoffrey Templeman and Michael Ward for much valuable help during the past year. Finally, I sincerely thank all the members of
the Alpine Club, and also a few non-members, who have contributed to
this 100th volume of the *Alpine Journal*.

*Johanna Merz*

# Contents

Contributions from:
*José Luis Bermúdez, H Adams Carter, Chris Cheeseman, Lindsay Griffin, Tony Howard, Harish Kapadia, Paul Knott, Paul Nunn, Józef Nyka, Bill O'Connor and Simon Richardson.*

## MAPS AND DIAGRAMS
Maps 2-5, 9-10, 13, 14  compiled and drawn by Ted Hatch

**Maps and Diagrams**

\*    *The diagram of K2 is based on a drawing by Jim Curran, by permission.*

# Illustrations

*Appearing between pages 84 and 85*

*Appearing between pages 116 and 117*

# Everest from the North

'We are going to sail to the top this time and God with us – or stamp to the top with our teeth in the wind.'

*George Leigh Mallory*
*Letter to Tom Longstaff, 1924*

## CHARLES WARREN

# Everest 1935: The Forgotten Adventure

*(Plate 5)*

As the only surviving member of Eric Shipton's reconnaissance expedition to Mount Everest in 1935, I have allowed myself to be persuaded
by Michael Ward that I ought to put on record my memories of that expedition, which never got the publicity it deserved. It seemed at the outset to
have a not unreasonable chance of success on the mountain, but my diary
notes show that the monsoon season was unsuitable and that we suffered
from many altitude-related health problems. Moreover, without the help
of oxygen we probably had little real prospect of pulling off 'the mountaineering coup of all time'. However, we carried out valuable survey
work and made first ascents of Kharta Phu, Kharta Changri and many
other peaks above 20,000ft.

I think it was early in 1935 that Shipton asked me if I would join his
proposed reconnaissance to Everest that year. He explained that we would
not be expected to climb the mountain itself because it would be too late in
the season to do that. The purposes of the expedition would be threefold:
firstly, to examine snow conditions during the monsoon period; secondly,
to carry out a professional survey of the environs of Everest under
Michael Spender; and thirdly, to test potential newcomers for an all-out
attempt to climb the mountain in 1936. Having already proved, in 1933,
that I could go high in the Himalaya, I was invited, I liked to think, primarily
as a mountaineer rather than as a doctor.

In those days we travelled out to India by sea and it took us a month to
get there, passing through Egypt where some of us climbed the Great Pyramid. At Darjeeling we recruited porters at the Planters' Club and it was
here that the great Tenzing was engaged to come with us. At the age of 21
he was our youngest Sherpa. Our party then passed through Kalimpong
and the lovely foothills to Gangtok, where we were hospitably received by
the Maharaja of Sikkim, before making our way up the beautiful Teesta
valley to the Kongra La pass. Instead of going into Tibet by the traditional
route via the Chumbi valley in Bhutan, we went straight up through Sikkim
– a better and more direct way. However, once over the Kongra La pass
into Tibet, Eric decided not to continue north to rejoin the old route at
Kampa Zong but to turn west to the village of Sar, with a view to acclimatising while exploring and climbing in the Nyonno Ri range.

My diary takes up the story; I like the diary to speak for itself because it
reveals exactly what I did and felt at the time.

3

**9th June**
Langmu. Up and away by 7.30 am. The village managed to provide one
pony – a lazy little mare – which [Dan] Bryant and I shared. The transport
went well and we reached Sar by 11.30 am and found the others all packing up in preparation for early start in the morning. Far too much of a
rush. I have just had time to collect together some dressings and medicines
for the mountain parties.

Tilman, [Edwin] Kempson and I are to rush at Nyonno Ri, and hope to
get up it. I could not help thinking that inspection from a distance would
have been a wise preliminary measure and certainly not a waste of time.

Later in the afternoon I went with Karma Paul [interpreter] to visit a
man who was reported to be very ill up in one of the houses in the village.
We walked right round the base of Sar, which is indeed a striking place,
before we reached the house of the sick man whom we found squatting in
the usual dark hovel. He was very breathless and it only took a short time
to observe that he was suffering from heart failure. I gave what advice I
could and his son returned with us to the camp for the medicine with which
we were to treat the poor man's condition so inadequately.

Sar consists of two portions: the ruins of the old fort walls, so solid when
compared to the loosely flung together houses which form the newer village. The old part was apparently destroyed over a century ago by the
Nepalese. The old ruins rise magnificently from the rocks on which they
are built and are so perfectly suited to the starkness of their surroundings.

**10th June**
Up early. I kept on being held up in my arrangements by the advent of
various sick from the village. There was a man who was reputed to have
malaria. I also saw a small girl with phlebitis.

Away at last at 8 am. Struck a path which conducted one gently up the
hillside towards the snout of a glacier flowing east off the Nyonno Ri
group of peaks, and here in a little green dell at the very snout of the glacier
was a pretty gompa. We flung [ourselves] down on the lovely green turf
and soon the men had brought us chang from the monastery. I cannot
imagine a lovelier spot for a camp.

During the last half hour of the advance I was most definitely affected by
the altitude: very breathless on the slightest slope and that feeling of loss of
power in the limbs just as if one had got out of a sick-bed after being confined there by illness for a long time. At 2.30 pm we pitched camp beside a
small lake in the moraine-covered glacier at an altitude of about 18,000';
a most attractive site with the highest peak of Nyonno Ri standing guard
over us threateningly.

**11th June**
Woke up at 5 am. Red sky with long cloudy streamers coming from the
south. A little later some sleet. Got going at 7 am and advanced up the

moraine. Soon came to a glacier lake into which an ice fall broke off abruptly. It was up the line of this glacier and ice fall that we hoped to go. The upper part of the route to my mind looked impracticable.

Party broke up. Tilman and Angtharkay went to make a way through the ice fall, Edwin and I set off to climb a peak of about 19,700', above camp, with a view to getting a better idea of the lie of the land. This proved infinitely worthwhile. On the summit we spent an uncomfortable time taking angles and photographs with the theodolite. An exasperating game waiting for the mountain to come clear of mist. Reached the summit at 1.30 pm.

Quickly made camp and found that Tilman had crossed the lower ice fall but found the upper one impracticable.

### 12th June

Set out to reach the glacier coming from between Eric [Shipton]'s peak and Nyonno Ri which we had seen yesterday from our observation peak. First part of walk up some easy old moraine heaps. Perfect morning and, as we mounted, all the peaks of the main range stood out in the clear air. A few plants between the rocks made life more tolerable during the last and more arduous part of the march: a lovely little magenta primula and a tiny blue star of a flower attracted my attention.

At 1.30 pm we were up on the glacier and the men had set to work to hack out a platform for the tents on the moraine. Tilman very weak and feeling unhappy. Very tired myself but not feeling ill, just weak in the leg muscles. Retired to sleep for a couple of hours and was much refreshed. Pretty certain we can reach the col tomorrow but very uncertain about the possibility of climbing the mountain.

### 13th June

Started at 8 am for the col. Very slow, and everyone feeling the effects of the altitude. Snow on glacier particularly unpleasant: little pinnacles 1 ft high on a base of dry glacier. At the start of the final slope to the col Tilman had to go back. We advanced slowly, the snow conditions becoming more and more exhausting. Eventually I went right through into a crevasse which, after I had extricated myself, proved on inspection to extend almost indefinitely in both directions. We halted, exhausted.

It was decided that a course close to the rocks would be the best one to take, but we all felt much too exhausted to tackle it today. On the way back to our camp we climbed up on to a small moraine peninsula on the left bank of the glacier and set up the theodolite, taking a round of angles on the distant giants which were clearly visible in a cloudless sky.

### 14th June

Slept well last night. Started at 7.30 and moved much more easily and rapidly towards the col. Tilman slightly weak, but beyond being a little short-winded on the uphill bits I was feeling very fit and going well, quite different to yesterday.

We made for the snow where it abuts against the rocks and worked a way up this until we could get onto rocks and climb 50' to the col. The snow was considerably crevassed at this place, but the crevasses were easy to see and to avoid falling into although on the descent I did go into one up to the waist.

The col on its westerly slopes consisted of a precipitous gully so that a descent from it on that side was impossible. We had to content ourselves with a return whence we had come. Before leaving, the theodolite was set up and a round of angles and photographs was taken.

Camp was regained at noon and Angtharkay was despatched to send up the other porters to carry down our camp. We ourselves set off an hour later and after walking well past the lake at the foot of the glacier began to fear that we had missed the porters' camp. However, we eventually recognised Angtharkay's footprints and continued our way over the next rise, from which we at once spotted their tent in a little mossy hollow in the moraine heaps.

Lying full length in the afternoon sun on the grass of this sheltered spot will remain longer in my memory as one of life's more enjoyable moments than all the excitement of climbing to the col.

## 15th June
Uncertain of our objective on setting out, but making for south Sar glacier. After examining the route from a distance we decided to make a short day of it. Found a delightful hollow with a lake in the moraine and settled down to camp here at 10 am.

## 16th June
Carried camp up a stony gully and along the ridge until a suitable site was found some 1 hour short of the col. The men levelled out two platforms for the tents, and we are very comfortable here. Rest of day spent lounging about camp. Tomorrow we hope to climb the south peak of Nyanno Ri. From here it looks absurdly near. It should go if we can get over a somewhat forbidding rock step in the lower section.

## 17th June
Slept fairly well. Got started at 7 am. Tilman led up the glacier and took us straight to the col. Surprising views down the other side which is quite precipitous. Did not waste time but moved on up from here over a snowy hump in the ridge towards the rocky obstacle. The rocks were slabby but we mounted by a gully which was full of loose stuff with comparative ease. In attempting to make an exit onto the ridge, Tilman upset some large blocks which descended upon the party. We all fled for shelter and fortunately nobody was struck, but it was a near shave. After this I led through

to the right and came out onto the ridge. Above the rock section we tried the snow on the crest but it soon became icy and so we took to the rocks just below the ridge.

I had to cut 2 dozen steps down to the rocks in fairly hard ice and was completely exhausted, with cramplike pain in the arm at the end of it. Tilman took the lead and we mounted by the rocks for as long as possible but eventually had to come out onto the snow crest and cut many steps in steep hard snow. Above this it was a question of mixed rock and ice work, usually pretty steep and trying.

At 12 noon we gained the prominent point on one peak, about 21,600', which almost seems to constitute a separate mountain: the true summit was some 200' above and a considerable distance away from us, yet with a difficult section of ridge connecting us with it. We all decided that any attempt to reach it would so exhaust the party that the day might end in disaster. Our mid-summit was a somewhat narrow snow pyramid. We sat for nearly ½ hour enjoying the tremendous scenery on all sides of us. It was perfectly warm in the sun and one might almost have been on an Alpine peak.

On the ascent, for one moment the clouds to the west parted and we got our first glimpse of Everest which looked quite unimposing at 30 miles distance. The descent was accomplished without event and we reached camp again at 3 pm.

**18th June**
Went up to the col again this morning and spent an hour up there taking angles on peaks and panoramic photographs. The weather is definitely more unsettled: there were heavy cumulus clouds coming up from the south early and by the time we had regained camp at 10 am it was snowing. We found the rest of the troops there with tea ready prepared for us.

**19th June**
Got started by 6 am. The idea was to continue survey work, but the mists were on the hills early today and it was snowing gently most of the time; in fact it looks as though the monsoon has arrived.

Returned in the direction of Sar by emerging from our last valley and crossing towards the mouth of its northerly neighbour where we found the camp which the men had moved down for us at about 1.30. Pretty tired after a fairly strenuous walk with much up and down hill work in it.

[There is a gap here in my diary while we were travelling between Sar and Rongbuk and not actually mountaineering.]

**8th July**
Last night we camped ½ hour beyond Camp 2 on moraine in the midst of East Rongbuk ice pinnacles. There was a lovely view of Kellas peak as

one looked down the trough in the glacier between the ice pinnacles. We got going at about 9 o'clock and, for the first few hours of the stage, I was able to walk in my shirt-sleeves so warm was the sun.

Towards 2 pm a few monsoon clouds began to pile up towards the north and behind the mountains to the south, but the weather remained good throughout the day. We spent some little time clambering over and between the ice pinnacles in order to make our way to the great moraine trough in the centre of the glacier where the route lies. At one point we were stopped by a little glacier lake. Shipton and Tilman tried to circumvent this obstacle and in the process Bill went right into the icy water up to his neck. He was fished out, having lost his ice axe, and made a rapid change into some dry clothes. The axe was lost for good and all in spite of prolonged fishing operations. Eventually another route, involving a little descent of an ice wall, down which the loads had to be lowered, was found which brought us into the trough.

The trough is quite remarkable. It is a strip of moraine which runs for several miles between an avenue of ice pinnacles some 25'-30' high. It provided an easy highway up the glacier. As we advanced, the trough steepened and became shallower and more narrow. Eventually we climbed out onto the smooth surface of the upper part of the glacier where the going was good. There was a thin layer of firm snow, not more than 2-3 inches deep, on what was to all intents and purposes dry glacier. Here Eric raced ahead; it was easy to see that he was the man who had been high before. It seemed a long way round the corner to Camp 3, but the going was good and eventually we reached the moraine heap which forms the camp site. Bill, Edwin and Edmund [Wigram] were pretty tired on arrival, particularly Edmund whose frightful paroxysmal cough (almost like whooping cough) was a continual reproach to the doctor as he came up the glacier.

**9th July**
Did not sleep well until the early morning but was quite warm. Decided to move camp some 1 hour further up the glacier. We set off about 9.30 am. There was some monsoon cloud blowing up from the south, but at first I walked in my shirt-sleeves. I was a little way ahead of the others, and Eric had just sat down on a stone to rest. I saw a boot lying in the snow and a little ahead was a green mass which I took to be a tent left as a dump by the last expedition. I shouted to Eric as I advanced – hello! here is a perfectly good pair of boots and a tent; must be a dump. Then on approaching the green heap I got a bit of a shock to see that it was the body of a man lying huddled in the snow. At once the thought flashed into my mind – Maurice Wilson. I shouted to Eric – I say it's this fellow Wilson. Quite soon the rest of the party came up with us and we had to decide what to do.

The body was lying on its left side with the knees drawn up in an attitude of flexion. The first boot I had found some 10 yards down the slope, the second was lying near the man's feet. He was wearing a mauve pullover, grey flannel trousers with woollen vest and pants underneath. There was a stone near his left hand to which a guyline of a tent was attached. The torn remains of the tent was pulled out of the snow some few feet down the slope from him.

We wondered whether to tell the porters, but by this time they had come up to us and had seen what we had discovered. For the most part they took the matter very casually, except Jigmy who was sitting on one side during the unpleasant operation.

Before disturbing the body we searched in the snow for his notebook and other belongings. Eventually a lightweight rucksack was found along with a small Union Jack on which were signed the names of his girl friends, and most important of all his diary – an extraordinary documentary revelation of monomania and determination of purpose. It ended several days prior to his death with a statement that he was off to the North Col for the second time.

From his position I think that he must have died in his sleep in his tent of exhaustion and exposure, the tent having blown away at a later date. There are three curious points in connection with the tragedy. 1. No sleeping bag was to be found. 2. He was within 200 yards of the 1933 Everest food dump which he knew about since he had already made use of it. 3. He was within hailing distance of Camp 3 where Tewang was supposed to have been waiting for him.

After some discussion it was decided to bury him in a crevasse: the moraine was changing too rapidly for a surface burial there. So we wrapped him in his tent, and after cutting away the lip of a suitable crevasse, slid the body into the depths where it immediately disappeared from sight. We all raised our hats at the time and I think that everyone was rather upset over the business. I thought that I had grown immune to the sight of the dead, but somehow or other the circumstances and the fact that he was after all doing almost the same as ourselves seemed to bring his tragedy a little too near home.

We built a cairn at the spot where the body was found and that evening we read through his diary to try and find out some of the circumstances of his death.

The old food dump was discovered under some rocks some 200 yards further on and here we pitched our camp and revelled for half a day in the delights of jams, cakes, soups and such delicacies as Carlsbad plums from Fortnum and Mason until I for one felt almost sick at the sight of such abundance of food.

## 10th July

Went up to North Col and found a good route in steep but excellent snow conditions. Started to snow halfway up so porters became fed up and refused to go on higher; they just dumped their loads and laughed at us. There was no alternative but to go down. Eric justifiably annoyed at the attitude of the men: wondering whether to send them all down to Rongbuk. After a talk, however, the men were very repentant and said that they were willing to carry in the morning.

**11th July**
Again up to North Col. There has been a good deal of snow during the night which has obliterated our tracks. Eric led the men up to the crevasse which we reached yesterday and here they dumped the second relay of loads. I brought up the rear very slowly with Bill, Edmund and Edwin. Bill was completely done in and it is quite obvious that he will not get to the col just yet. Edmond's cough is frightful. Very hot and frightful glare which damages the face and lips greatly. Was in my shirt-sleeves most of the time. Began to cloud up on North Col towards midday. Back by 2 pm.

After some discussion it is decided that Eric, Edwin and self establish North Col camp with 10 porters tomorrow. Other two advised to stay at 3 and acclimatize better. Bill very annoyed because he is left with only 2 porters: Jigmy is sick and Nima has a headache. But still we must have the men up on North Col, and they would be much better resting for 2-3 days.

Jigmy obviously no good up at 3; has bronchitis and is feeling altitude very much; have advised him to go down to Rongbuk.

**12th July**
Set out to establish North Col. Snow still good and got half the loads up by mid-day. Only one steep bit where 2-3 steps had to be cut. Eric led up here. I brought up the second rope. Fine until about 3 pm when North Col in cloud. Half the food still to be fetched up from lower snow slopes.

**13th July**
Went down to the dump to shift up rest of the food with the fit porters. Upper part of route a little steep, but snow on the whole holding well. Personally slept well last night with the aid of Allonal. We are managing to get down nearly 5 oz of pemmican at night, but only with a struggle.

**14th July**
Off day on North Col. Warm sun up till about 11 am. Then cloud. Nothing to do but lie in sleeping-bag. Discussed plans a bit and argued about possibilities. Idea is for Eric and Edwin to make a 3-camp attack on the summit.

**15th July**
Much snow fall in night. Eric woke me at midnight to point out drift coming in at our door. Snow in boots and on sleeping-bags. The blizzard worried us considerably. Eric very cold all night which disturbed me too. Sun got onto our tents at 8 am and the snow drift began to melt off.

Everest dead white. Avalanches coming off the N face all night. Set off for a short ascent towards 5. Snow was pretty good but there was some new stuff. Edwin started to get some pains in the chest; he is looking very blue. I was going fairly well, though my toes were getting cold. N peak in cloud most of the time. We only went about 400' up the slope to see what the snow was like, then returned.

**16th July**
Heavy snow fall during the night. Lay awake listening to stuff coming off N face of mountain. We had decided to make a push for 5 in the morning – Edwin or I to stay up there with Eric according to how we were going – but on looking out of our tents the mountain was so obviously out of condition for several days that we decided to evacuate N col, leaving food and 2 tents up there. We were all rather worried as to what the slopes on the col would be like.

The views from the col this morning were the best we have had. Everything in white snow mantle with lovely fleecy clouds piling up behind almost every peak: Pumori to the west, Kharta Phu to the east, and Everest to the south.

Eventually set off about 9 o'clock in two ropes. Eric and Edwin, Edwin leading, with 5 porters went down first. I followed with a second string of 5 men. Angtharkay next to me. The first party had only gone a few yards down the slope when they got to a place where the surface snow had avalanched; they worked down this cleared surface but soon had to traverse beneath a plaque of unavalanched snow which was at least 1 yard deep. The snow on which they were traversing was good, but the whole party was exposed to the serious danger of the snow slope above them avalanching. I shouted to Edwin to know if I should take my men back, and without hesitation he said yes. However we waited on a safe surface,which had come off from top to bottom, until the others had crossed beneath the *mauvais pas* to a place of safety. Then we ran the gauntlet to reach the safety of an overhung crevasse. The whole descent was the most dangerous and unjustifiable thing that we could have done considering there was still 10 days' food up on the col and that we could have waited there for conditions to improve.

[Edwin Kempson wrote in his diary: 'I had been last on the lower rope and Charles was first on the second rope. I had entreated him to return and he most strongly agreed, but moral persuasion I suppose led him to come down all the same – and we reached the bottom safely. We had a colossal argument about the safety of the up and down route. Eric stoutly maintained that the former was the more dangerous.' Walt Unsworth commented in *Everest*: 'Shipton's argument was that if the place had already avalanched it was unlikely to do so again for some time – a nicety of judgement when twelve men's lives are at stake.']

Lower down the slopes two of my men deliberately unroped and started to run down on their own; the others tried to do a sitting glissade with distinct danger to the party below. I did my best to pull the party together, but I had not enough Hindustani to tick them off properly.

After glissading the last slope singly we reached our No 3 at noon, where we were let loose into the good things of the 1933 dump. Glorious to sleep on rock again.

**17th July**
Started at about 9 o'clock for the glacier bay west of Kharta Phu, taking with us 6 porters, all of whom are to return to No 3 after carrying up our equipment to the foot of the mountain. By 2 pm we had put up our tent in the little coomb which lies beneath the col to its north. The journey up the lateral glacier, after the crossing of the E.R.G. [East Rongbuk Glacier], was simplified by another typical trough on its true left bank. In the latter part of the journey there was a slightly troublesome schrund to cross. We are hoping to get started on the mountain at 6 am tomorrow.

**18th July**
Got away at 6 am after rather a miserable breakfast of tea, biscuits and jam. Very cold start.

At first mounted rapidly in good hard snow crust towards the col, but after ½ hours' going the slope steepened up and turned to ice. Eric spent nearly an hour cutting steps for about 100' onto the lower lip of a small schrund while Edwin and I stood and shivered in our steps below him. I remember watching the sunlight creeping up the slopes away on our left and wishing that it would soon hit us. Above this icy section the slope again became crusted and less steep. Here we came up into the sunshine and were able to stamp back some feeling into our numbed toes on a small outcrop of rocks whilst we admired the view to our east. Already there was cloud filling the valley, but several great peaks topped the white foam. The Kellas rock peak stood out fearfully pointed and forbidding in appearance. As there was still a chance of taking some angles and photographs from the summit we continued to shoulder our loads; easy scrambling, at first, but began getting very cold in the feet. Eric had to stop to take off his boots. Personally going well. Final section of ridge longer than it looked, and very narrow. A short section of rotten rock followed by a narrow snow crest.

Sat on summit for about ½ hour; not a bit cold. Much cloud about, but the mists varied frequently so we got splendid views of Everest and Makalu from time to time.

Down to the col again within an hour, then quickly down the snow slopes of the morning. At the ice steps went down one at a time held from above on the end of 100' rope, then untied and glissaded.

## 20th July
Off day at 2. Towards evening Edmund came complaining of toothache and a swelling in the mouth. It turned out to be an abscess arising from a dead tooth which I pulled for him under local anaesthesia.

## 21st July
Two parties of us start off for a camp near the snout of the little glacier which comes off the Kellas peak in a southerly direction. I am with Edwin and [Michael] Spender with the survey party. The others are out to climb the Kellas peak, all except Dan who was left to convalesce at 2.

We went over into the main trough which was followed down until we were opposite the first great tributary which comes into E.R.G. on its true right. Here we struck out of the trough towards the glacier right bank and had an amusing time picking a route through the ice towers and in crossing a glacier stream. Our camp is beside a delightful little lake at the snout of the above mentioned glacier. The Kellas peak party have camped near the screes 500' higher up.

## 22nd July
Away at 6 am with Spender to help him establish his stations, then on to climb 22,000er on ridge immediately to the east of Kellas. Saw the other party reach the col between us and Kellas, and a little later on saw them put up their tent near some rocks. Reached our summit about 11 am. Much more airy than anticipated. Shouted across to the others in their tent and had a reply; then descended to Spender in ½ hour. After this a glorious descent down scree slopes and the rest of the day spent in comfort at our lakeside camp ...

## 24th July
Up and away, with Da Kitar and Tenzing B. [Bhotia, later known as Norgay] carrying the theodolite and a little food, to climb the 22,000er above our camp and Spender's station.

I set a slanting course up steep but well frozen snow slopes so as to gain S ridge at a point just short of a conspicuous tower. Working in the shade until we came up on to the ridge, where we got the most perfect views we have yet had. The cloud bank was still low round the waists of the mountains so that we had clear views of Nyonno Ri, Makalu, and all the giant peaks as they rose from the foam. Kharta Changri, our next door neighbour, looked very fine, and we worked out a possible route for an attack on her in a few days' time.

¾ hour put us on the summit, a lovely little rocky table on which one could lie and sleep in the warm sun. We were surprisingly aloft on this unmarked summit, in fact we seemed to be not far short of our neighbour to the west and of Kellas peak.

Edwin set up the theodolite and took a round of photographs, whilst I traversed over to a lower summit and took sterios. We lay in the sun until the peaks clouded up and then quickly returned to camp.

## 25th July

We set off at about 11 am with Tenzing and Da Kitar. Very hot on glacier: I was going badly and feeling nauseated. About ¾ hour from camp vomited some pemmican which I had recently taken.

We pushed on round the corner into the next coomb where we decided to put a camp on some moraine in the middle of the glacier, lower than intended, and to have the camp moved up next day.

## 26th July

Our two men appeared at 8 am and we struck camp and advanced up the glacier, finding an easy route through the ice cliffs, until we had reached the flat shelf below the depression in the ridge and here we pitched camp. Tenzing and another are to come and fetch us down at 10 am in the morning. Glorious views of Everest and Makalu from the camp.

Food is not too plentiful, but we had pemmican for the evening meal to fall back upon.

## 27th July

Got the primus going at 5 am and got started at 6 am for Kharta Changri. Easy route up hard snow to the col, but feet got very cold. Above the col snow bad, but soon reached lowermost rocks and here halted. I took off my boots in order to thaw my toes; only half successful. Moved on again up ridge, snow and rock alternating. Preferred the rock where possible on account of cold feet and bad snow: we were kicking in up to our knees. Last two rises in ridge very steep snow and extremely exhausting. However, reached the summit, a sharp snow cone to which 3 ridges converge, at about 9.30 am. Poor view on account of mist. SE ridge from here seems to be impracticable.

The ascent of this fine looking mountain turned out to be remarkably free from technical difficulties.

*Envoi:*

This surely must have been one of the most *enjoyable* of all the expeditions to Mount Everest. It was small and achieved the objectives set for it at little cost. Not the least satisfying aspect of it was helping Michael Spender with his survey work, because this inevitably involved exploration and the ascent of unclimbed peaks. A new map of the Tibetan environs of Mount Everest was the outcome.

*Charles Warren*
*14 July 1994*

## DAWSON STELFOX

# Everest Calling

*(Plates 2–4, 6–11)*

I was on Croagh Patrick last week – Ireland's holiest mountain, climbed by thousands of pilgrims every July, many barefooted, many dragged up by will and faith after bodily powers fail. I followed the long ridge stretching westward to the Atlantic, the spectacular panorama of Clew Bay and Clare Island obscured by thick mist, but with the sun burning through from above. Voices came out of that mist, memories trapped by exhaustion were suddenly released and I was carried back to another mountain over a year ago when once again I was in thick mist on a long ridge, with sunshine above and a summit ahead – Everest or, more properly, Chomolungma. A mountain calling ... calling to me as much as Croagh Patrick calls to those barefooted pilgrims.

The muffled but insistent bleep of an electronic alarm stirred me from a restless stupor. It was 2am at 8300m. The torch flickered on, revealing frost caking the tent roof. I ventured a hand out and pulled the stove out of a sordid mess of half-cooked food and torn packages in the corner of the tent. Fingers seared to the freezing gas cylinder and jolted me awake, sending an icy shower of frost down my neck. I retreated into the depths of the bag and lay exhausted, shivering from cold and at what might be ahead. Outside, a lightning storm flashed over Nepal, thick cloud settled over Tibet. There was justification for staying in bed, for not going on. The weather was bad. We would have to go back.

> I can honestly say that I know of nothing ... which is so utterly exhausting or which calls for more determination than this hateful duty of high-altitude cooking ... Perhaps the most hateful part of the process is that some of the resultant mess must be eaten, and this in itself is only achieved by will power: there is but little desire to eat – sometimes indeed a sense of nausea at the bare idea ...[1]
>
> *Lt Col E F Norton, 1924*

It was 27 May 1993, nearly two months since we had arrived at Rongbuk on the north side of Everest. It had been two months of hard load carrying, struggling with altitude and weathering storms, but also with clear and windless days, achievement and satisfaction. As Frank Nugent and I lay huddled together in a tiny frozen tent at Camp 3, we were very conscious that this was our last chance of the summit. The yaks to take us home were due in a few days. The monsoon was already rushing up through India. With Robbie, Tony and Mick snapping at our heels, one day behind, ready to pick up the pieces or launch off our efforts for the top, this was our last and only chance.

From the warmth and security of my sleeping-bag I reconsidered. There was no wind. The forecast was good. We felt tolerably able to think and move. We could always turn back later, and there were Dermot's reassuring words on the radio ...

*... We will contribute any breath of strength behind your back that we can.*

The stove was lit and the feeble flame gave new life to our preparations. Slowly, laboriously, moving one at a time in the tiny tent, we got ready to leave. Half a cup of tepid tea, a mouthful of cake and some Complan. We planned to leave at 4am, but the hour slipped past and it was after 5 before we finally got out of our bags, forced on our bulky boots and gaiters and crawled out of the tent to a bitterly cold but perfectly still night. In a blinkered daze, daring not to think about the discomfort and menace of the situation, we set off upwards into the black night.

> Our pace was wretched. My ambition was to do twenty consecutive paces uphill without a pause to rest and pant, elbow on bent knee. Yet I never remember achieving it – thirteen was nearer the mark. Every five or ten minutes we had to sit down for a minute or two and we must have looked a sorry couple.[2]
>
> *Lt Col E F Norton, 1924*

Deep soft snow, a maze of ramps, gullies and unexpectedly steep rock. Torch beams casting for clues – shreds of old ropes here and there. Darkness dissolved, sun touched the summit and as we shivered on the cold northern flank, new life swept us, entranced by the glowing crest above ...

> The ground over which we started was easy but trying; scree, which slipped while we were trying to mount it, and rocks, which provided simple scrambling. It was intensely cold, but ahead of us we saw a patch of sunlight, and strained every nerve to reach this and get warm.[3]
>
> *T Howard Somervell, 1924*

**Radio conversation 8am:**
*... Dermot, we've reached the main ridge, just short of the First Step. Pretty hard going – up to our knees in soft snow, fairly tiring. We're carrying on anyway, but it looks like more of the same.*
*... Dawson, I've been climbing with you for years and I've never known you not to carry on and I know you will carry on and that Frank will carry on as well. Take plenty of rests and the day will change ... You've a long time ahead of you, so don't feel you have to make any decisions yet.*

Leaving the ridge we began to work out into the face. For the first few yards the going was sufficiently straightforward, but presently the general angle became much steeper, and our trials were accentuated by the fact that the stratification of the rocks was such that they shelved outward and downward, making the securing of adequate footholds difficult.[4]

*George Finch, 1922*

We teetered and slithered across those 'steeply sloping, evilly smooth slabs', now covered with a foot of powder snow obscuring any foothold. Easy ground became serious. The First Step loomed, towers of grey and brown rock. It all looked so complex; which way to go?

### Radio conversation 10am:

*... Hi Dermot ... The weather has picked up a bit – it's more pleasant up here now than it was earlier on.*

*... Dawson, we have sound, we have sight and some people think we even have colour. We can pick you out in the greatest of detail – we can see you moving, we can distinguish your limbs. We are extremely impressed by the speed you are going at ...*

*... Maybe you can tell us where we are then Dermot, 'cos we're not quite sure at the moment ...*

We were traversing under the First Step, on 'slabs of rock like tiles on a roof' covered in soft snow, waiting for the trigger to send them sliding down the north face below.

I found myself stepping from tile to tile, as it were, each tile sloping smoothly and steeply downwards; I began to feel that I was too much dependent on the mere friction of a boot nail on the slabs. It was not exactly difficult going, but it was a dangerous place for a single, unroped climber, as one slip would have sent me in all probability to the bottom of the mountain.[5]

*Lt Col E F Norton, at his high point 1924*

### Radio conversation 12 noon:

*... Dermot ... we are struggling, in very difficult conditions and the return journey is going to be very difficult as well – a lot of soft snow lying over slabs without any old fixed rope around ... we haven't made a decision on whether to press on ...*

*... Robbie here, Dawson, at the Chinese Camp 2 ... we'll be absolutely happy to do anything we can to help – if there's any possibility of us getting to and beyond Camp 3 it would be an absolute pleasure for us to help ...*

Arrived under the second step, they saw at once that, not only was the second step itself impossible from this side, but they could not even reach the foot of it. Above them rose the dark-grey precipice, smooth and holdless.[6]

*Hugh Ruttledge, 1933*

Seriousness and exposure rose up and overwhelmed us as we cautiously inched our way across the flank of the ridge. We tied on to our 6mm Kevlar rope and I led up an awkward ramp to a curious rock mushroom, a broad platform at 8680m and the shreds of a tent.

Frank followed, struggling with his breathing and for the first time looking seriously under strain. On the steeper ground he was gasping for air that wasn't there, disturbing his balance and concentration. He was concerned that he was nearing the edge of safe control. It was already obvious that we wouldn't make it to the top and back down before running out of oxygen and probably daylight. As we moved on across a narrow slabby ramp that turned the next pinnacle, Frank could see his control slipping away. He decided to turn back while he could still look after himself, rather than continue a bit further and be a liability to me. Central to his decision was not to hold me up, not to spoil my chances. He stayed to photograph me as I edged on towards the foot of the Second Step and then turned to begin a slow, cautious descent, without the elation of the summit to counter the weariness of being alone on such a vast and complicated mountain.

**Radio conversation 1pm:**
*... OK Dermot, some disappointing news, Frank has turned back about 10 or 15 minutes ago, over.*
*... Dawson, we accept that and sympathise with you for being on your own. We've had some conversation with Tony and Robbie and Mick a short while ago and they've put themselves in full support of your effort.*
*... Dermot, that's reassuring. Certainly I would like to go for the summit but I am going very slowly and I'll have to make a decision at some stage along the way, so anyway I'll carry on and I'll talk to you in a while.*
*... Dawson, do keep going for a while yet – conditions look good, you sound strong, we're terribly sorry you're on your own. Bear in mind the possibility of going down the south side.*
*... Dermot, that had crossed my mind but practicalities will ensue as always. I know you always accuse me of being too pragmatic, but there you go ...*
*... Dawson, take care, you're totally in control, your conversation is articulate, you're practically arguing with me and you've got a lot of movement in you yet.*

The Second Step – the psychological as well as the physical barrier, the gateway to the summit. Did Mallory and Irvine climb it in 1924? Did the Chinese climb it in 1960?

> Soon, all four of us reached the famous Second Step ... No wonder the British adventurers were stopped short here ... Near the top of the step a three metre high vertical rock slab suddenly stood in our way. Liu Lienman blazed the trail but failed in all his four attempts to open up a way ... Now he was completely exhausted. This made Xu Yin-hua impatient. He took off his heavy cramponned boots and thick woollen socks. Gripping the crevice with his hands and stepping on the rock surface with his

feet, he tried to climb up. But twice he failed and fell down. Then snow
began to swirl in the air, which made the climbing all the more difficult.
What was to be done? Turn back like the British climbers had done before? No! Certainly not! [7]

*Wang Fu-Chou and Xu Yin-hua, 1960*

They made the top, in the dark, but it was some years before the sceptical
West believed them, and then only with the evidence of Xu Yin-hua's frostbitten feet and harrowing story. The Chinese were back in 1975 and neatly
avoided a repetition of this by carrying up and placing a 20ft long aluminium ladder on the last part of the Step.

It's still there, precariously fixed, swinging wildly on loose pitons, but
even to reach the ladder is not easy. Strands of tattered rope lay down the
vertical buttress but to their left I climbed a short, chock-stoned and snow-
filled gully that led up to a series of ramps zigzagging up the crag to the
foot of the ladder. First oxygen bottle nearly empty now, but turned up
full, I gasped my way up, one rung at a time, body held flat against the
rungs to stop the swinging, eyes avoiding the protruding and vibrating pegs.

End of the ladder. Still steep. I sweep away the choking powder snow
and search for holds. A long step out right, a lunge forwards and I'm up,
gasping from an empty bottle and on easy ground. Change bottles ... mind
clears. Radio on and talk to Base Camp – Dermot, John, Richard, Lorna,
Kathy and Leslie huddled around the base set, willing me on ...

**Radio conversation 2pm:**
*... I'm just at the top of the Second Step – top of the ladder, which is fairly rickety,
and across now to the bottom of the third step.*
*... Dawson, no man at 28,000ft has a right to sound as fit, as well, as healthy and
as happy as that.*
*... Well I'm reasonably happy but I'm not too sure about fit and healthy, Dermot.*
*... Dawson, Richard here. That's tremendous – it sounds to me you're over a par-
ticular psychological watershed and its tremendous to hear you.*

Easy ground now, a vast boulder-strewn plateau. The afternoon cloud closes
in, a light breeze picks up and it begins to snow. Keeping well down from
the ridge to avoid the cornices, I plod on, searching out hard snow patches,
stumbling into drifted holes between the rocks. Down below, Robbie and
Tony had the same problem as they fought their way up to Camp 3 ...

**Radio conversation 3pm:**
*... Dermot here Robbie, come in.*
*... Dermot, it's snowing very heavily up here ... conditions here underfoot are terri-
ble – it's going to be really hard work for anyone in this ... I'd say Dawson is getting
the same snow as us, but there's no wind, so it is not prohibitive.*
*... The problem for Dawson is he has to return – he has only about 6 hours of
daylight left to get to the summit and return ...*

*... Dawson here, Dermot. I'm in the middle of good Scottish winter conditions at the moment.*
*... Dawson, those are the conditions that suit you best ...*

Across the top of the Great Couloir. Eyes straining through the cloud and snow for the route ahead up the summit tower. A steep rising traverse through rocks and onto the upper snowfield. Up a vertical windslab break line hoping the slope above is stable, out to the right onto more steep slabs. Wind rising, but not yet a serious problem.

> And wind on Everest is subtly demoralising. An upward step is no longer something interesting and worth doing, but something useless, and the final pyramid of rock, with its writhing plume of wind blown snow, the summit of Everest; it is the epitome of weariness.[8]
>
> *Frank Smythe, 1933*

### Radio conversation 4pm:

*... OK Dermot, I'm somewhere on the summit snowfield. I'm still quite low down on it but it's not too far I think.*
*... Dawson, you're there, you've got it done. It's only a question of pursuing it and fairly soon it will level out. Give us a word on what conditions are actually like ...*
*... Still in deep snow I'm afraid. The sun is breaking through the cloud, which makes it quite pleasant, but I can't really see very much ...*
*... Dawson it sounds as if you are very close and the conditions are not too miserable – you sound healthy and fit as well – watch out for cornices on the Kangshung side but I'm sure you're well able for that. You have it in the bag Dawson.*
*... It's not in the bag till I get down Dermot.*
*... We know that and we know that you always get down. Best of luck, we're behind you completely and the main thing is we have the utmost confidence in you.*
*... Thanks for that Dermot – hopefully next broadcast from the summit.*

Steep slabs forced me to the right towards the West Ridge, looking for a break in the steep buttress above. I felt a bit duped – no one had mentioned difficulties on the last bit. Was I in the right place? Should I have stayed on the snow to the left after all? A broad ramp above looked promising and a shred of old rope hanging uselessly on a rock step confirmed the line. The ramp led back left onto the summit ridge. I climbed through the cloud, the sun came out, the wind dropped. The climbing was absorbing; I swarmed up the last few steps and out onto the summit ridge and ... there it was, Kangshung face, topped by an aluminium pole.

> Somehow and for some reason I go on. I'm nowhere in particular. I'm just climbing automatically, instinctively. I don't expect it but suddenly it's there – the tripod, the blessing of proof, the curse of destruction on this perfect place of solitude.[9]
>
> *Reinhold Messner, 1980*

The North Ridge of Everest: Dawson Stelfox traversing towards the Second Step before making the first British/Irish ascent from the north on 27 May 1993. (*Frank Nugent*) (p15)

*Left*
3.  The crest of the North Ridge of Everest between the First and Second Steps. (*Dawson Stelfox*)  (p15)

*Below*
4.  The final few metres to the Summit. (*John Tinker*)  (p25)

I wandered up the last few yards to the top, the snow untracked and pristine on all sides, absorbing the beauty of the most extensive panorama on earth. The green jungles of Nepal to the south contrasting with the brown rolling barren hills of Tibet. Mountains from end to end – Kangchenjunga in the far east; the painful reminder of Manaslu marking the limit of visibility to the west. My eyes roamed the familiar peaks of Khumbu and finally, across the range and down to Rongbuk, down to Base Camp ... Everest calling Rongbuk ...

**Radio conversation 5.10pm:**
*... Dermot, the altimeter is reading 8848m and I'm sitting on the summit of the world.*
*... Dawson listen to me – you're the tallest man in the world ... and you've just made the first Irish ascent of Mount Everest and the first British ascent of the North Ridge – absolutely magnificent achievement Dawson – we're surrounded here by people – Irish, Nepalese and Tibetan, everyone offering congratulations.*
*... Dermot, I'm not going to say very much, but just that it's an honour to be sitting up here, and an honour to be given that possibility by everyone else on the team – and I'd like to think that I represent all the other climbers, all the other members of the expedition – Irish, Nepalese, Chinese, Tibetan and everyone back home as well. It's an absolute honour to be here – you're down in the cloud at the moment, I'm up above it and I've got the most magnificent panorama of all the big peaks of the Himalaya.*
*... Dawson, we won't forget Frank at this stage – we received a message ten minutes ago that Robby and Tony saw him approaching Camp 3 – going strongly and looked safe.*
*... I'm really glad Frank is safe – I only wish that he could be up here with me ... it's as much his achievement as mine me getting up here because there was a lot of teamwork in the early part of the day and I wouldn't have gone the whole day on my own.*
*... Dawson, we knew you would carry all our aspirations with you and would represent all of us and none would feel excluded when you stood on the summit and that's how we feel now.*
*... I'll just take a few photographs and I'll be on my way – I've got about 4 hours to dark and I think I'll just about make it, but I have a torch with me anyway so I might even make the last bit in the dark ... If I could just send a message home ... especially to Margaret, whose support has been an enormous help, but also to everyone back home who has helped in so many ways ... It is absolutely magnificent to feel that I am at the top of a pyramid of people from home and out here who have put me up on the top. I can't express it any more – I'm on my way down ...*

I thought of them all individually, strung out over the mountain, yet bound together invisibly and inextricably – Tony and Robbie slowly making their way up to Camp 3 to support Frank and me and make their own attempt the next day. Mick and Mike, who gave up their own chances to support mine. Dermot and Richard, now confined to illness but who played an instrumental role in the success by their early work and continued wisdom; to the support team – Nick, Rory and Stephen, now back home in Ireland but leaving a legacy of strong foundations behind; Kathy, John Bourke, Leslie and Lorna, all playing their part in forming and binding the strength of the team; Brian at Advanced Base Camp, and John Murray at the North Col, both hanging on grimly, stoically to capture the spirit of the expedition; our Nepali staff, the Tibetan yak herders and even the TMA officials; and Frank, now slowly making his way back to Camp 3, the driving force of undiminished commitment throughout.

But it was 5.30 and darkness would be on me by 9. I knew it would take me five or six hours to get back to camp, the last few inevitably without oxygen. Down the summit tower with two abseils over the rocksteps, carefully retrieving my precious 50m of 6mm rope. Across the broken spur to the snowfield. Slowly down the windslab break, then with more abandon, slithering down shallow gullies to the plateau. Cloud rolled in again and suddenly I was lost.

My tracks were filled with the afternoon snow. The featureless slope gave way to the vertical drop of the Second Step – only one way down – I had to find the top of the ladder. I dropped down lower – no, it couldn't be here ... laboriously back up again ... still couldn't find it ... back down again, lower this time ... getting steep ... hold on, this is serious ... feet sliding and scraping on thinly snow-covered slabs. Down below, Robbie saw me wandering around way off the line, but the radio was off and he could only watch.

STOP. Despair moving in with the fading light. Calm down ... think ... remember what it looked like when you pulled over the top of the Step ... much closer to the crest. Back up again, and there, barely discernible depressions in the fresh snow – my old tracks, leading to the ladder.

Abseil down past the ladder, back along the traverse to the old tent site and the rock mushroom. An awkward diagonal abseil down the full rope length. Oxygen gone now, darkness closing in. The radio an invaluable companion. I learnt that Frank was safely down to Camp 3, Tony and Robbie safely up there. Talking concentrated my mind, forcing me to think, avoiding automation. Down and round the First Step and in the last few minutes of daylight reached the top of the old ropes leading off the ridge, down the steep rockband above the tents.

Head torch on now in the gathering gloom, plunging down the morning's tracks, grateful now for the deep trench we had ploughed upwards. A light at the tent flashed; I flashed back. The tents seemed a long way down. An old rope lying slack in the snow pulled tight as I abseiled off, sending me slithering down a heart-stopping six feet ...

Off the ropes now, down through the deep snow and suddenly, there was Robbie, out to guide me in and envelope me in warmth, Frank and Tony brewing up in the tents. The day was over, 18 hours after leaving. I was back in Camp 3.

I slept fitfully, barely able to think about the summit – more concerned about getting enough to drink and getting down. Robbie and Tony left on their own attempt by 4am, but despite my excitement and concern I fell asleep until 7 when they reached the main ridge. In worsening weather we discussed their options and it was with a certain relief that they made what later proved to be the right decision and came down.

In the elation of getting back to the camp it was easy to forget that we were still at 8300m, out of oxygen, out of food, out of gas and out of energy. Ahead of us was a demanding descent in worsening weather and only the urgent need to get down out of the thickening snow and the rising wind kept us moving. Control is so easily lost, the body so frail. The desire to rest, maybe never to rise again, is almost irresistible. The mind wanders ...

Layers of mystery and tragedy are interwoven with the snows of the North Ridge. The ghosts of Boardman and Tasker haunt the pinnacles off to our right; Marty Hoey can be traced on the face to our left; many, many others are all around. In the distance, but feeling close to me now, are friends lost on other mountains. Far above us, the spirit of Irvine, and Mallory ... in at the start, there to the end.

> ... the entire summit ridge and the final peak of Everest were unveiled.
> My eyes became fixed on one tiny black spot silhouetted on a small snow-crest beneath a rock-step in the ridge; the black spot moved. Another
> black spot became apparent and moved up the snow to join the other on
> the crest. The first then approached the great rock-step and shortly emerged
> at the top; the second did likewise. Then the whole fascinating vision
> vanished, enveloped in cloud once more. [10]
>
> *Noel Odell, 1924*

**Summary**: On 27 May 1993 Dawson Stelfox reached the summit of Everest. Owing to his dual nationality, he had achieved both the first Irish ascent of the mountain and the first British ascent of the North Ridge.

**Expedition members**
*Climbers*: Dawson Stelfox, Frank Nugent, Dermot Somers, Mike Barry, Richard O'Neill Dean, Mick Murphy, Robbie Fenlon, Tony Burke.
*Support*: Leslie Lawrence, Nick Stevenson, John Bourke, Kathryn Fleming, Stephen Potts.
*Media*: Lorna Siggens, Rory McKee, John Murray, Brian Hayes.

**Note**: The full story of the expedition is told in Lorna Siggen's book *Everest Calling* (Mainstream 1993), including writing by Dermot Somers and Dawson Stelfox.

REFERENCES

1   E F Norton, *The Fight for Everest.* Arnold, 1925.
2   Ibid
3   T Howard Somervell, *After Everest.* Hodder & Stoughton, 1936.
4   George Finch, 'The tortures of Tantalus' in *The Assault on Mount Everest 1922,* Charles Bruce (ed). Arnold, 1923.
5   E F Norton, *The Fight for Everest.* Arnold, 1925.
6   Hugh Ruttledge, Everest 1933. Hodder & Stoughton, 1934.
7   Wang Fu-chou and Xu Yin-hua, 'How we climbed Chomolungma', in *Everest. The Best Writing and Pictures* (ed. Peter Gillman). Little Brown, 1993. The article was first published in English in *Mountain Craft,* summer 1961.
8   F S Smythe, *Camp Six.* Hodder & Stoughton, 1937.
9   Reinhold Messner, 'A partner in myself' in *Mountain,* July/August 1981.
10  Noel Odell, dispatch to *The Times,* written on 14 June 1924, as reported in *AJ36,* 223, 1924.

JONATHAN TINKER

# Climbing the North Ridge of Everest

(*Plates 4, 6–9*)

*In memory of Mark Miller, my friend and colleague. Mark should have shared this adventure, but he was on the ill-fated PIA jet which crashed near Kathmandu in September 1992. Our expedition to the North Ridge went ahead as planned, not as a memorial, but as a trip that Mark would have enjoyed participating in.*

After Mark's death I had eight months to prepare for the trip to Everest's North Ridge arranged by the commercial firm Out There Trekking (OTT). This was not a guided trip. It is worth making clear the distinction. A commercial expedition means that suitably qualified climbers pay for someone else to organise the expedition. There are many fine climbers in demanding jobs who do not have the time to undertake this time-consuming job but who wish to go to high altitude. The leader co-ordinates everything and may supply a 'backbone' of good climbers to help push the route. This style of climbing is not particularly new and there are several historical cases, from the Duke of Abruzzi to 'Everest the Hard Way', where wealthy individuals or employees of sponsor companies have gone along as climbers.

To be guided in an Alpine sense is, in my opinion, not possible on the highest mountains. Often the 'guide' (or leader) is in a different camp from the client, there is normally a much higher leader/client ratio than there is in the Alps, rescue can be at best a prolonged affair, and the weather and objective dangers are of a different order of magnitude. The bottom line on Everest is that one is operating on the border of what is possible, and that it is physically impossible (for instance) to carry a man down from the summit.

The North Ridge is a far tougher proposition than the South Col route. All the technical difficulties are concentrated in the summit day and, apart from Mallory and Irvine, many people have died, retreated or got lost in the bewildering maze of ledges, walls and snow patches above 8000m. We were working on a very tight budget and it was made clear that this was to be a traditional expedition, with success being defined by getting one man to the top, whether he be Westerner or Sherpa. Every member had two chances of success; either he would climb the mountain himself or he would be part of a successful expedition.

I assembled a team from the UK, France, Finland, Ireland and Australia. I added 'backbone' by inviting a couple of my friends from eastern Europe. George Kotov from Russia is an ex-speed climber who has made the first winter ascents of two 7000m peaks in the Pamirs, and who is OTT's main man in the former Soviet Union. Maciej Berbeka from Poland, one of the very best and strongest mountaineers in the world, has made the first winter ascents of Cho Oyu and Manaslu as well as a new route on Annapurna South Face, together with near misses on Broad Peak in winter and the South Face of Dhaulagiri. We had been together on K2 and Nanga Parbat, both in winter, and he is without a doubt the strongest partner I have had in the mountains. Another old friend, Jonny Muir from Australia, who reached the summit in 1988 via the South Col, came along with his wife Brigitte, hoping to make the first ascent from the North by a couple. But in many ways the most important members were my Sherpa group, 'the Kharikola posse' led by the workaholic Ang Rita, who were exceptionally competent and great company.

I had been on the North-East Ridge in 1985 and was pleased to be back. As Ang Rita said, 'It is a special place.' There were many changes. There were a few nuns and monks in the monastery. The Chinese had built a toilet block so much in the style of classic communist brutalism that no one dared enter. There were many other expeditions strewn about the plain. These varied greatly in strength. Apart from my own team, the only other group to reach the summit was a well-organised party of Koreans who put two men on the summit. Other teams were unlucky: Indians who had burned themselves out climbing in the monsoon, disorganised Spaniards who didn't have enough equipment to sustain a base camp, or bizarre Greeks who went home early after it had snowed for ten days. Probably the strongest trip of all was Ed Viesturs' solo expedition to the North Face. The strongest teams are not necessarily the biggest ones.

We were lucky with our timing. The monsoon petered out as we arrived at Base Camp. Advanced Base Camp and Camp 1 at the North Col were quickly established. One of my abiding memories of the trip was of Chris Brown, who farms near where I live in North Yorkshire, looking across the immense wall of the North Face and quietly shaking my hand and saying that he had dreamt of this moment for many years.

There are two main problems with the North Ridge. The North Col at 7000m is a spacious area with room for many tents. Above this there are very few suitable places to camp. The other great problem is the wind, which sweeps across the ridge from Nepal into Tibet. By a curious topographical or meteorological quirk, the wind can die down above 8000m. The ridge is broad and easy all the way to Camp 2, which we placed at about 7900m. It was a long way in the wind and stopped all but ourselves and the Koreans. Tents did not last long and no one spent a comfortable night there. Above the campsite the ground becomes more mixed and we fixed some rope ... then the trip changed completely.

On 4 October Dr Karl Henize collapsed at ABC. A former astronaut, he had come to Everest, with support from the American space agency NASA, to do some research. He was one of a group of four, including

Harry Taylor, who were involved in an attempt to break the world record high-altitude parachute jump. They were working as an independent group, sharing our facilities, but were not there to climb the mountain.

We put Karl on oxygen and took it in turns to carry him down the moraine. Four members stayed with him that night at the 6000m camp, taking turns to keep the Gamow bag (the equivalent of a decompression chamber) inflated. Karl died in the early hours of 5 October. Following his stated wishes, we buried him near where he died.

For me, this felt like the end of the expedition. We had all liked Karl in the short time we had known him and I would have been quite happy to call off the trip immediately. However, everyone else wished to continue and time was now getting very short. The yaks were due at ABC on 14 October. Camp 2 had been destroyed by the wind and consisted of little more than a dump of oxygen cylinders.

Maciej had gone very quiet, which I knew was a sign that he was getting ready for a big effort. His plan was simple but dangerous and physically very demanding. He would go from Camp 1 at 7000m straight up to put in Camp 3 and then climb the mountain the next day. We decided that Lama Sherpa would carry a load and return to the North Col, and that Lakpa Nuru Sherpa, who had summited via the South Col three times in the previous 18 months, would go to the top. I would go up in support the next day with Babu Chhire Sherpa.

Quite a lot of us were gathered at the North Col by the time Lama came down. He shared a tent with Babu and me. During the night he developed snow-blindness and we stayed up to feed him brews and administer first aid. It was clear and bitterly cold as a large group of us set off well before dawn. The climbing became a ruthless physical test. Jon and Brigitte were carrying a tent and stopped to erect it at about 7500m. Bruce Hubbard, a very strong climber, had to turn back at 7800m with freezing feet. Down-suited and goggled, we said goodbye in classically typical Scottish weather conditions. I wished he had the One Sport boots which Babu and I were wearing.

Above 8000m the wind started to die down. Babu and I slowed to a snail's pace. I was kept going by the fact that we were the only people who could help Maciej and Lakpa Nuru if anything went wrong. We staggered into the camp, a solitary tent perched on a promontory on a snow slope at 8150m, where we collapsed in a ruin of down and Gore-Tex. Plugged into oxygen for the first time, we quickly recovered. We knew from the radio that the first pair had reached the summit, and I was very relieved to see two tiny figures slowly picking their way down. Eventually they reached the tent, still on oxygen that made them look as if they had come from another world ... they had.

It was obvious that Maciej had pulled out all the stops. The Sherpas had not been too keen in bad weather at 7900m the previous day. 'Just 10 more minutes' had got the group to the top camp. The crest of the ridge leading to the First Step had looked 'too bloody far away'. They had traversed low and picked a way across the North Face and found a way directly up to the foot of the Second Step. This 'OTT deviation' was an inspired piece of super high-altitude climbing, achieved in the dark after completing the equivalent of a full-scale Alpine route the previous day.

The way was clear for Babu and me to have a go. My friends were safe and our cares had dropped away. Babu had already climbed Everest from the north and south and decided to sleep but not climb on oxygen. This would save cylinders for further attempts. Babu and I get on well, sharing the same sense of humour. He is about 5½ft tall and built, as a friend said, like a professional darts player. His profits from his expeditions go into building an enormous lodge in his village – a practical pension fund.

We started cooking at 11pm, aiming to get away by 2am.

'How are you feeling, Babu?'

'Great.' Babu always says he feels great.

The tent was being pushed by the wind, so we waited for an hour for it to die down a bit. One more tea and tsampa and we were ready to go. Outside the tent it was clear and cold. I felt optimistic.

'Let's do it, Babu.'

It was a privilege to watch a very talented climber fighting his way up a mountain. Some of the tracks were still visible in the light of our head torches as we switchbacked up the face. I had never used oxygen before and was amusing myself fiddling with the flow rates. On one very steep groove in the yellow rock band we came across ten metres of fixed rope left by Maciej and Lakpa. Otherwise we climbed unroped. As the sun rose, Everest cast an enormous shadow over Nepal. The Second Step lit up like the prow of a ship. Suddenly we came across a short line of steps from the Korean ascent a week earlier. We had joined the 'normal route'. We approached the Second Step, part of my mind thinking of Mallory and Irvine.

An easy rock slab, a little wall and a small snowpatch led to the famous Chinese ladder. I had been expecting a delapidated caving ladder and was relieved to see a solid metal structure that is likely to still be there in a hundred years. To the left was the crack that Xu Yin-hua had climbed in his socks in 1960. The wall was steep but covered in small holds. It is possible that Mallory and Irvine, using combined tactics, could have overcome this obstacle.

At the top of the Second Step I changed my oxygen cylinder. The ridge flattened out and we easily bypassed the so-called Third Step. We were at 8700m. My mask iced up and I ripped it away. We were getting hypoxic, but it never crossed my mind to dump the now useless oxygen cylinders. The internal dialogue of any climber on an interminable snow slope was the same as it had always been: ' ... Stay away from those cornices on the left ... I wonder what's round the corner ... Why not not take another step?', but I do remember feeling surprised that all this was happening to me.

We traversed to the right onto the North Face. Tricky mixed climbing, a bit of tatty rope and pitons. A couple of steps chopped in a bank of frozen gravel. Dawson had very helpfully supplied a detailed route description and had warned me about this section.

'Careful ... maybe Mallory and Irvine slipped off here.'

Suddenly we emerged onto the summit ridge, the summit obvious, perched on a great frozen wave of a cornice. Lots of energy now. It was 9.20am on the tabletop-sized summit. A couple of oxygen cylinders had been placed next to a strange tripod adorned with prayer flags. Babu added his and we thumped each other on the back. I pulled out our sponsors' logos and we took lots of photos. The world looked as beautiful as it should. I radioed down to ABC: 'This is for Mark.'

We felt great without oxygen. I remember thinking that I have felt more tired on top of Ben Nevis. But this burst of adrenalin was revealed as an illusion when we set off down. At the first outcrop, where we stopped to get a pocketful of rocks for the other team members, friends and family, we sat down and found it difficult to get up again.

Red lights started flashing. The wind was rising and the tracks were filling in rapidly. We were a long way from support. Descent became an ordeal as hypoxia and dehydration made their presence felt. Camp 3 appeared and we slowly staggered nearer. Descent was misery. As a team, we had made the first Polish and the second British ascent (or maybe the third ... ) of the North Ridge of Everest. Thanks to Maciej we had made a new variation on the North Ridge route. It was an almost super-human effort; back in ABC Maciej's eyes seemed to have changed colour. When he got back to Poland he had to go straight to hospital. His immune system had taken a battering. Karl had died. The cost had been too great.

**Summary**: An international expedition organised by Out There Trekking was successful on Everest in 1993. On 9 October Maciej Berbeka made the first Polish ascent of the North Ridge with Lakpa Nuru Sherpa and on 10 October Jonathan Tinker, expedition leader, made the second British ascent by the same route, with Babu Chhire Sherpa. Both parties used a variant, climbing further to the right and avoiding the First Step. There were 19 climbing members of the expedition, four high-altitude Sherpas and a research team from the American space agency NASA. Sadly, Dr Karl Henize, aged 66, a member of the research party, died at 6400m from high-altitude sickness.

## MICHAEL WARD
# The Height of Mount Everest

*(Plates 10, 11)*

*Recent expeditions to Everest from the north have contributed new material towards both the configuration of its summit and the exact calculation of its height .*

W hen the peak now called 'Everest' was first observed in 1847 by J W Armstrong of the Survey of India, it was labelled 'Peak b'. Situated about 70 miles west of Kangchenjunga, it looked undistinguished and was often nearly invisible, being overshadowed by Makalu (Peak XIII), a more dominant looking mountain when viewed from up to 200 miles to the south. However, rough calculations put the height of 'Peak b' at 28,800ft.[1] (See Fig 1)

Between 27 November 1849 and 17 January 1850 the same mountain, now called 'Peak h' and then 'Peak XV', was observed by J O Nicholson from six stations between 108 and 118 miles to the south on the plains of India using a 24-inch theodolite. Radhanath Sikhdar, the chief computer to Andrew Waugh who had succeeded George Everest as Superintendent of the Great Trigonometrical Survey, calculated the results. It was not until 1852 that the computations were sufficiently advanced to indicate that Peak XV was higher than any other known mountain. But it was only in 1856 that the individual readings of 28,990ft, 28,992ft, 28,998ft, 29,002ft, 29,005ft and 29,026ft were considered sufficiently reliable for the average height of 29,002ft to be recorded. This was due to atmospheric refraction which was still being investigated.[2,3] It was only then, some nine years after the 'discovery' of the peak in 1847, that it was considered a sufficiently reliable figure for Andrew Waugh to convey it to Sir Roderick Murchison, President of the Royal Geographical Society in London, as the correct height of Everest.[4] It was the world's highest mountain and, considering the distance from which these figures were computed, it is extraordinary how closely they approached the currently accepted height of 29,028ft (8848m).[2] Further observations were made between 1880 and 1902 from Darjeeling, and a height of 29,141ft (8882m) was calculated,[5] but this figure did not gain general acceptance.

With the opening of Nepal in 1950 surveyors were allowed to within 30-40 miles of Everest and a small Indian survey team reached Namche Bazar, 18 miles south of the mountain, in 1953. Between 1952 and 1954 a new and sophisticated survey network was set up by B L Gulatee, then in charge of the geodetic and research branch of the Survey of India. From the main network already established in India a chain of six quadrilateral figures went N towards the Himalaya, ending in an 8-sided figure. From points on

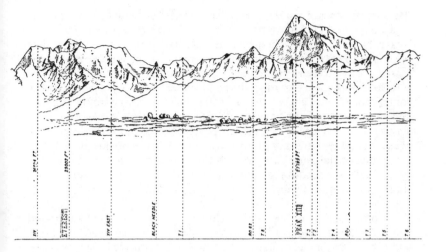

Fig 1  Everest and 'Peak XIII' from Bangura Trig. station
(Distance of Everest about 126 miles, and 'Peak XIII' about 118 miles.)

this, Everest was observed on numerous occasions at distances between 29 and 47 miles. Today's accepted position – latitude N 27° 59' 15.85"; longitude E 86° 55' 39.51", and altitude 29,028ft +/– 0.8ft (8848m) – is the result of this work. However, all the stations were grouped in an area S and SW of the mountain.[6]

In 1960 Chinese surveyors under Professor Wang Wenying covered the north side of Everest and accepted the 1954 Indian survey's position and height. It was on that expedition, on 25 May at 4.20am, that Wang Fu-chou, Kombu and Xu Yin-hua reached the summit – the first ascent from the north.

In 1975 the Chinese mounted a large combined scientific and mountaineering expedition to Everest. The Survey was brought a major step forward by putting a survey tripod as a target on the summit on 27 May. From 13 control points between 5600m and 6300m and between 7km and 12km from the summit, a height (excluding the thickness of the snow cover) of 29,029ft +/– 1.1ft (8848.13m) was computed, above the mean sea-level of the Yellow (China) Sea about 2000 miles away! It was also observed that Everest was rising at a mean rate of 0.15mm each year.[7]

In 1987 a re-examination of the height of Everest was made by an Italian party using global positioning systems (GPS) and electronic distance-measuring (EDM) lasers. These established conclusively that Everest was by a large margin the world's highest peak, with K2 (Mt Godwin-Austen) in the Karakoram the second highest at 28,250ft.

In 1991 Professor Roger Bilham of the Department of Geophysics of the University of Colorado at Boulder, whose main research interest was in the plate tectonics of the Nepal Himalaya, carried out a major repositioning of a number of GPS stations in Nepal. He set up four new stations at Lukla, Namche Bazar, Pheriche and Kala Pattar respectively, as well as one at the ruined Rongbuk monastery. His main finding was that the Everest massif seemed to be rising in one block rather than in segments.

In 1992 two prisms for the reflection of laser beams were placed on the summit on 12 May, a day when over 30 people crowded onto the summit, and measurements were made with EDM lasers from a new station at Thyangboche in Nepal by a small survey team backed by the Boston Science Museum and its honorary director Bradford Washburn and his wife.[8] In September of the same year, after prisms had been placed on the summit by the Italians, a Sino-Italian party measured the height of Everest from six stations, three in Tibet and three in Nepal, and each within 8 miles of the peak.

The official result of these Italian–Chinese surveys has recently appeared in a major article in *G P S World* by Georgio Poretti, Claudio Marchesini, and Alberto Beinat, all of Italy.[9] The new Everest altitude is reported to be 8848.65m. However, this new altitude for Everest is based on field work which assumes Everest's summit is bedrock – and that this bedrock was 2.55m below the snow surface of the summit at the end of September 1992. But an article by Bradford Washburn[10] on the configuration of the summit indicates that the new Italian altitude was in fact based on the very hard ice layer encountered by Todd Burleson, Peter Athans and Vernon Tejas when they were placing Washburn's laser prisms on the summit on 12 May 1992.

In 1993 Dawson Stelfox reached the summit from the north side[11] and took photographs of the First and Second Steps and their approaches. He also took one from the summit looking north-east (*Plate 11*). In this, the two-prism assembly of the 1992 (Washburn) party is shown clearly, whilst behind it is some equipment, left by the Italian party, which had apparently been blown over during the winter of 1992/93 and replaced by an unknown hand in the spring of 1993.

Another photo by Stelfox taken some yards from the summit looking south-west (*Plate 10*) shows an oxygen bottle and prayer flags visible in the snow about 12ft from the surface on the NE side of the mountain. Presumably these were originally left on the surface snow of the summit and were buried by successive snowfalls.

It seems from these photographs and other observations that extra snow is added to the summit during each monsoon; this settles and gets blown away by the ferocious winter winds, the height of Everest remaining much the same.

Winds of 165mph from the west-south-west were recorded by Washburn in his Learjet in December 1984 when he flew over Everest at 39,000ft. The direction of this prevailing wind, which is parallel to the NE ridge and at right angles to the ridge between the south and main summit, probably explains why there appear to be no cornices reported on the NE ridge overlooking the Kangshung face, whilst there are large ones on the ridge between the south and main summits overhanging this face.

This recent work emphasises how accurate were the observations and calculations of the many British and Indian surveyors in the past who worked under poor conditions and with much less sophisticated equipment than is available today. Their work was most aptly and correctly named 'The Great Trigonometrical Survey'.

REFERENCES

1   L A Waddell, *Among the Himalayas*. Constable/Westminster, 355, 1899.
2   P V Angus-Leppan, 'The Height of Mount Everest' in *Survey Review, Vol 26*, 367-395, 1982.
3   B L Gulatee, 'Mount Everest – its Height and Name' in *Himalayan Journal 17*, 131-142, 1952.
4   A S Waugh, letter in *Proceedings of the Royal Geographical Society 1*, 345-347, 1855-57.
5   J De Graaf-Hunter, 'The Height of Mount Everest' in *Geographical Journal 121, Part I*, 21-27, 1955.
6   B L Gulatee, 'The Height of Mount Everest: A New Determination. (1952-54)' in *Survey of India, Technical Paper No 8*, 1954.
7   L Donsheng, Y Jixiang, 'Scientific Surveys of the North slope of Mt Qomolangma' in *High Mountain Peaks in China*, People's Sports Publishing House of China, 1981.
8   Bradford Washburn, 'The Altitude and Position of Mount Everest' (unpublished), 1993.
9   G Poretti, C Marchesini, A Beinat, 'G P S Surveys Mount Everest' in *G P S World*, 33-36, October 1994.
10  Bradford Washburn, 'The Configuration of the Summit of Mount Everest' in *AAJ 1995*.
11  Dawson Stelfox, 'Everest Calling' in *AJ100*, 15-24, 1995.

ACKNOWLEDGEMENT

I would like to thank Bradford Washburn for his help in writing this article.

JEFF LONG
# Climbing in the Killing Fields

Shekar, a few klicks west of the dirt 'superhighway' to Lhasa, has been a classic jumping-off place for Everest expeditions since the days of George Mallory. Here, climbers can begin acclimatising to the Tibetan plateau before heading into Base Camp at 17,000ft. Trucks deposit inbound expeditions at a Chinese hotel or the more rustic 'guest-house', and there you sit for up to a week, listening to dogs barking and the wind blowing.

A favourite diversion is a day hike through the rubble of the old *dzong*, or fortress, that snakes up the hillside overlooking town. The ruins look long dead, ancient enough to match Mesa Verde or Chichén Itzá. But until just 35 years ago, Shekar Dzong housed thousands of Tibetan monks and served as a regional capital.

In 1959 the People's Liberation Army 'liberated' Tibet from itself. Since then, 1.2 million Tibetans – one in every six – have died under Chinese occupation. That compares almost exactly with what the Khmer Rouge left behind in Cambodia. But until the spring of 1993, when I made a detour through what has been dubbed 'The Killing Fields', the connection had never occurred to me. At first glance, the two countries seem worlds apart; the one tropical, populous, and internecine, the other chilly and pacifist. You detect epic tragedy in what remains: ghost villages laced with bones and land mines, monasteries like Shekar's reduced to rubble. But there's more to it than that. Both Tibet and Cambodia are Buddhist. Each had a population of 6 million ethnically homogenous people. And each lost a million or more people to regimes bearing radical Maoism and weaponry made in China. On the eve of elections, I toured Cambodia with a United Nations worker, and witnessed firsthand the grand, $3 billion attempt by the world community to lift a nation out of its own history. In Tibet I found the exact reverse – a nation abandoned to its circumstances. The principles of international law have been trumpeted in Cambodia, forgotten in Tibet. The Forbidden Kingdom may as well be invisible.

Anonymity comes naturally to Tibet. Scattered through Asia, Europe, and the United States, its 120,000 refugees have become a virtual cliché of exile. The Tibetans' code of non-violence has muted their rage, and the fact that China's invasion of Tibet occurred 40 years ago – in the wee hours of the Cold War – makes the Tibetans' loss appear almost obsolete. Progressive Chinese like to blame the murder and destruction in Tibet on the excesses of the Cultural Revolution a generation ago. But that sidesteps the issue of ongoing genocide. The massive resettlement into Tibet of racially pure Han Chinese – gulag prisoners, People's Liberation Army soldiers, registered workers, and 'floaters' – is rapidly finishing off what is left of the country.

This population transfer is the Middle Kingdom's version of old-fashioned Manifest Destiny. In Manchuria, where China's resettlement campaign began in the 19th century, there are now 75 million Chinese and fewer than 3 million Manchurians. Inner Mongolia, invaded in the 1950s, now numbers 8.5 million Chinese and 2.5 million Mongolians. And the Chinese are doing the same thing in Burma today. Population transfer steals jobs, food, and natural resources from the locals. In the name of progress and development, the tactic also turns the native people into an 'ethnic minority' in their own country.

Thanks to high-altitude cash subsidies, guaranteed jobs, and other incentives, more Han Chinese populate Tibet today than Tibetans. Chinese commonly refer to Tibetans as barbarians and dogs. Tibetans are pushed off their land to make way for development projects. Their culture and religion are being replaced by Chinese karaoke bars, concrete apartment complexes, and satellite dishes. Tibetan forests and mineral deposits are being stripped and shipped eastwards at a furious pace to build China's 'economic miracle'. Wildlife has been machine-gunned; the people have been communalised, tortured, executed, and marginalised.

At times it has seemed that climbers alone were detailing events within this remote nation. From Heinrich Harrer to John Ackerly (director of International Campaign for Tibet) to Galen Rowell, Annie Whitehouse, Doug Scott, and David Breashears, climbers have provided the outside world with some of the clearest accounts existing of Tibet's slow death. At the same time, however, mountaineers and trekkers need to acknowledge that our journeys into Tibet are helping to underwrite its death. Except for spontaneous donations to yak herders, pilgrims or monks we meet along the way, every penny of our money goes to the People's Republic of China (PRC) and helps pay for its illegal occupation of Tibet. Renting Everest and other peaks to climbers is one of the few ways that China can obtain valuable foreign currency in Tibet. The revenues can range in the hundreds of thousands, even millions of dollars per year, particularly when huge Japanese and Western groups come rolling through. That money directly subsidises Chinese settlers and the Chinese soldiers who imprison, torture, and kill dissenting Tibetans.

Here and there along the touristed stretches, mostly around Lhasa, the PRC has permitted a dozen or so monasteries, like the one at Shekar Dzong, to begin rebuilding. These are mere shells staffed by monks who are underpaid, overworked custodians designed to showcase China's so-called freedom of religion. In effect, China is cobbling together a quaint Disneyland for Western *dharna* bums, adventure travellers and mountaineers. Along with their foreign currency, travellers provide an audience for Chinese propaganda. As visitors to Tibet, where the genocide and artifice are safely tucked behind China's great wall of 'internal affairs', we tend to act as if Tibet were none of our business. The Chinese get our money *and* our compliance. That has to change.

The debate over our presence in Tibet – whether it does more harm than good – is long running. Some purists believe we have no business visiting

Tibet at all while the Chinese remain in control. Certainly there is power in the argument that we ought not to conduct business in Tibet (and that includes renting the Himalaya and contracting services) with the very people butchering it. On the other side of the coin are those who argue that politics, even genocide, have nothing to do with travel. They argue that world travellers – climbers, particularly – obey no borders. Their spirit is their passport. For these modern-day Ulysses, nothing transcends the freedom of the hills.

Maybe, once upon a time, ascent allowed climbers a fantasy land beyond ordinary responsibilities. If so, those times are gone. Himalayan mountaineers are no longer separate from what has become a global tourism industry. Worlds we climbers visit may be more extreme than the beaten path, but our actions still carry moral force. Whether we champion human rights or trade upon them or do nothing at all, we are making a choice. Even in the deepest Himalaya, our choices are our signature.

The exiled Dalai Lama has declared that tourists should visit his former homeland, the more the better. He requests just one thing in exchange: our voices. He asks us – climbers, trekkers, and Holiday Inn'ers alike – to bear witness, to speak honestly about what we see.

The burden, then, is on each of us to *see*. It means being informed and aware and not pretending that our mega-expeditions, our misinformation, and our cosiness with the Chinese Mountaineering Association have no real consequence.

At the top of Shekar Dzong, you emerge into a magical forest of hundreds of prayer flags. In the far distance, Everest blows its plume and several thousand feet below lies the town of Shekar, the Tibetan third of it whitewashed, the Chinese section cement gray. Remarkably, it's possible to feel a spirit of hope here. Even in this killed place, you can see that Tibet is not yet dead. If only a boycott of the Himalayan range could halt China's rape of Tibet. We could make our sacrifice, gain our merit, be done with it. It's not that easy. At present it seems more likely that our presence – informed and vocal – may contribute to some measure of independence upon the high plateau.

There are no easy rules to guide our conduct in these other killing fields. There are no free answers. But it is time that climbers take their presence in Tibet seriously. Whether we like it or not, one way or another, our mountain holidays are helping to shape that country's future.

**For more information contact:**
The International Campaign for Tibet
1518 K Street, NW, Suite 410
Washington. DC 20005
(202) 628-4123

*This article first appeared in the American magazine* CLIMBING *and is reproduced by kind permission of the Editor and the author.*

# Expeditions

JONATHAN PRATT

# Against the Odds

## The 1993 K2 West Ridge Expedition

*(Plates* 17–21)

N ine expeditions attempted K2 from Pakistan in 1993. All of these
ended up climbing on the Abruzzi ridge (or one of its variations);
our expedition was the one exception as we were on the other side of the
peak, attempting the second ascent of the West Ridge. With the Abruzzi
appearing overcrowded much of the time, we felt fortunate to have our side
of the mountain to ourselves.

British expeditions were the first to attempt the West Ridge: in 1978,
when Chris Bonington's expedition was discontinued after Nick Estcourt
was killed in an avalanche below Camp 2, and later, in 1980, when Doug
Scott's expedition reached a high point of about 7500m; both were abandoned before reaching the real difficulties. The West Ridge was finally
climbed in 1981 by a large Japanese team using high-altitude porters and
oxygen. There was a Spanish attempt in 1982 but no one had been on the
route in the intervening 11 years.

None of the climbers in our team was well known and, since our famous
predecessors had failed so low on the route, no one gave us much of a chance;
in fact both the Mount Everest Foundation and the British Mountaineering Council refused to endorse our expedition. Despite the lack of support
from Britain we still felt confident in our ability to succeed.

When we applied for a permit we tried to name our expedition 'The K2
West Ridge Expedition', but the Pakistan Ministry of Tourism rejected this,
saying 'Every expedition name must include the name of a country'. This
posed a slight problem as our team included five Britons, three Americans,
a Canadian, a Frenchman and an Irishman. We toyed with a few ideas but
in the end our official name became 'The UK/USA K2 Expedition'.

Once in Islamabad we cut through all the red tape in just a few hours and
should have been on the next plane to Skardu. Unfortunately an Indian
attack on the Siachen glacier caused the army to commandeer all the planes,
so we were forced to hire a bus and set off on the arduous journey to Skardu
by road. A day in Skardu to recover was enough, and we were soon hiking
up the Baltoro glacier accompanied by a small army of porters. The walk-
in was uneventful except for the wonderful weather, which only turned
nasty on the last day when we endured the unenviable experience of establishing Base Camp in a ferocious blizzard. Rather than place our Base Camp

on 'the Strip' with the other expeditions, we put our camp below the Gilkey Memorial in a better position for approaching the West Ridge.

It is the custom, on the death of a mountaineer, to place a dinner plate on the Gilkey Memorial, which commands a special but sobering position at the base of K2. As we arrived the first plate of the year was being attached. This was for a member of the Slovenian expedition who had died during a successful ascent of the Abruzzi Spur. We witnessed the sad procession, unaware that this would not be the last plate placed on the memorial that year.

But to us this seemed like another world and our camp was filled with optimism and excitement; after all the planning and anticipation we had finally arrived and were anxious to start climbing. There was, however, an unforeseen difficulty. We had expected a simple walk up the glacier to the foot of our climb; but the glacier was heavily crevassed and it took us several days to scout out a route through it. Instead of the anticipated short stroll to Advanced Base Camp, this complicated route took over six hours. Later we found a short-cut, but it was still a long slog.

These unanticipated difficulties, rather than dampening our spirits, inspired us with fresh determination and, aided by an unusual period of good weather, the entire team worked together on advancing the route. We made spectacular progress and within just seven days had established Camp 3 at 7100m on 8 July. But now the expected storms arrived and we retreated to Base Camp for a much needed rest.

Sadly, on our return, we found another plate attached to the memorial, this time honouring a Canadian who had died returning from the summit. Three successful ascents so early in the season showed that conditions on the Abruzzi were unusually favourable; however, the two accompanying deaths seemed to be an ominous warning.

Meanwhile, with the weather pinning us down in Base Camp, we pondered a little on our own climb. So far, our approach could best be described as a mad, chaotic charge up the mountain. We elected for a change of strategy: we got organised. We reverted to classic siege-style tactics and divided the group into three teams, each taking its turn at the front. Unfortunately this coincided with two weeks of bad weather and despite the leaders, commanding from the rear, urging the advance troops to face the blizzard bravely, only 200m headway was gained when Andy Mayers and Scott Darsney pushed ahead.

Finally this assault ended when Etienne Fine started to feel unwell in Camp 3 at 7100m. Since he had climbed this high a week before without problems, we did not, at first, consider altitude sickness and thought he had just overworked himself. Luckily our doctor, Andy Collins, was also at Camp 3 and diagnosed pulmonary oedema. Etienne was still capable of walking and we immediately descended. All was going well until suddenly he collapsed, murmuring incoherently. Andy took over and declared he must give him an injection of Dexamethazone. Etienne put up a spirited resistance, but he was soon overcome by weight of numbers, and the dose was duly administered somewhere in the proximity of his backside. Thus prodded into action, he shot off down the hill and was soon safely back in Base Camp.

After some rest Etienne appeared to be fully recovered and, after consulting all our doctors (three of them) and getting a second opinion from the other doctors on 'the Strip' (another three), he was pronounced fit to climb. We then held one of our few team meetings; Etienne declared that he wished to continue climbing and Andy Collins agreed to accompany him. We also decided on another change of strategy. When the expedition was in a state of chaos we had advanced 1700m in seven days. When we used organised siege tactics, we had advanced 200m in thirty days. We voted for chaos!

On 20 August the team rejoined the fray with renewed vigour, with Etienne and Andy bringing up the rear. Unfortunately Andy contracted a virus and was forced to descend, but Etienne decided to carry on alone. Meanwhile the team had established Camp 4 at 7600m and then descended, leaving myself and Dan Mazur to explore the route to 7800m. On returning to Camp 4 we found Etienne showing signs of oedema again and feeling quite weak. Although it was 5pm we decided to descend immediately. This critical decision probably saved his life, but the descent was a nightmare as Etienne mustered all his remaining strength to struggle down. The night was clear, which aided our descent, but in the bitter cold there was a serious risk of frostbite. The situation was not helped by a freak malfunction of our radio, which could transmit but not receive. With no radio contact and the rest of the team in Base Camp several days climb away, we could expect no help for some time.

Before us was a large snowfield followed by several steep rocky cliffs. Once we had reached the steep sections of the route we could lower Etienne on the rope, but before this we had to negotiate several long traverses, and crossing them was only possible if Etienne could walk, however shakily. Painfully we made progress down. Several times Etienne collapsed, gasping for breath, and only persistent cajoling would get him going again; but we kept moving.

Eventually, after hours of continuued effort, Etienne gave up, and no amount of persuasion could stir him; it seemed to be the end. We knew we could not move him, and could only wait beside him and watch him die. Fortunately we did have a small medical kit and, as a last resort, we decided to try and inject him with Dexamethazone – but the liquid was frozen solid. With our bare hands we fiddled with the needle and vial until our fingers were dangerously numb. Finally Dan lost patience and jabbed the syringe into Etienne anyway. Surprisingly, this affected a staggering spurt of energy from Etienne. We were going again.

But although Etienne was moving he was only semi-conscious. Remarkably, he was still able to climb across some very tricky ground.

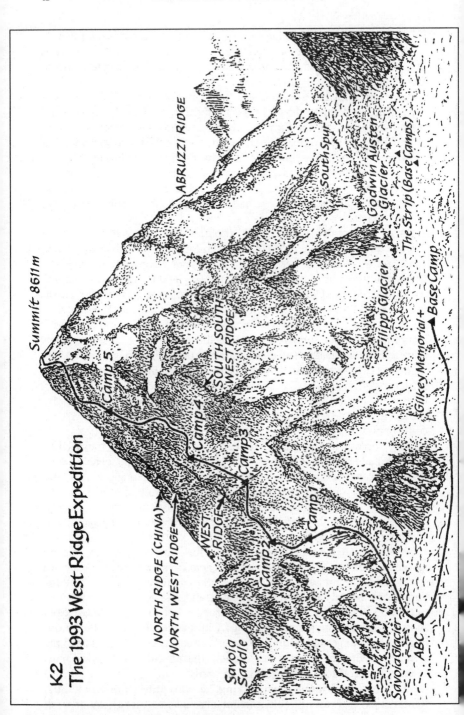

K2
The 1993 West Ridge Expedition

Summit 8611m

ABRUZZI RIDGE

NORTH RIDGE (CHINA)
NORTH WEST RIDGE

WEST RIDGE

Savoia Saddle

SOUTH SOUTH WEST RIDGE

South Spur

Camp 5
Camp 4
Camp 3
Camp 2
Camp 1
Camp 2

Godwin Austen Glacier
The Strip (Base Camps)
Filippi Glacier

Gilkey Memorial +
Base Camp

Savoia Glacier
ABC

Years of experience and his ingrained climbing ability must have carried him through. Once on steeper ground things got easier; Etienne was able to abseil and we made much faster progress, arriving in Camp 3 at 4am.

By the time daylight arrived we knew we were over the worst, but we were still at 7100m and had some difficult terrain to cover. Fortunately Etienne remained conscious and was able to continue under his own steam, even if slowly and with plenty of help. We spent that night in Camp 2 and next morning started to descend to Camp 1, when we met Jonathan Wakefield and John Arnold who, despite minimal information on the radio, had guessed the situation and come up to help. By this time, all three of us were extremely tired and meeting them was an immense relief. We had to wait the rest of the day in Camp 1 because of the danger of avalanches, but our descent that night was uneventful as, by now, Etienne was recovering and the rest of the team had arrived to help us.

In Base Camp, Etienne completely recovered from his oedema but all his toes were seriously frostbitten. An immediate evacuation was his only hope. After a couple of days of anxious waiting, we were relieved when the helicopter arrived and took Etienne to Skardu. Subsequently, back in France, he had to have all ten toes amputated.

While we were preoccupied with Etienne's rescue a terrible tragedy was happening on the Abruzzi: two Germans and a Swede had died descending from the summit. Now the mountain had claimed five lives, and it was an inescapable fact that every summit party had suffered a fatality: K2 was living up to its reputation.

Being somewhat isolated from the other expeditions, we were not affected by the prevailing feeling of despondency; rather we felt ready for the summit. We set off in poor weather, realising that it would take us five or six days to reach the top; hopefully by then conditions might have improved. Seven of us left camp together, but as we progressed some of our climbers started to drop out. Earlier, Andy Mayers had suffered frostbite on his hands, feet and nose; he bravely tried to continue but now he felt it would be too painful to go on. Then Scott Darsney suffered an attack of cerebral oedema and had to return, accompanied by John Arnold. That left four of us in Camp 4.

As we climbed up to make Camp 5 the weather started to deteriorate and Jonathan Wakefield decided to go down. The next day Andy Collins, Dan Mazur and myself continued up. Our plan was to try for the summit; but since an overnight bivvy seemed likely, we took a tent and stove but left our sleeping-bags behind. Our progress was hindered by technical climbing, and towards evening we reached a forbidding rock band at 8200m where we elected to stop for the night.

The next day dawned windy and cold, and optimistically we prepared ourselves for the summit. Andy and Dan crawled out of the tent and I was just putting my head through the door when I was rudely shoved back by the others scrambling to get back in. The shelter of the tent had fooled us:

the ferocity of the wind and its accompanying hail was unbearable. That day the quest for the summit was out of the question, so we waited in the hope of better conditions the next morning. With three of us in a small bivvy tent without sleeping-bags, we spent the day struggling with the constant cold, cramped conditions and thin air. Things did not improve as the temperature dropped sharply with the coming of night. We massaged each other's freezing feet, and stole a few hours' fitful sleep.

Unfortunately the next day proved worse than the previous one and after such a rough night we willingly admitted defeat and scurried back down the mountain. During this time Andy unwisely removed his gloves to adjust his crampons, and received frostbite on all his fingers. When we reached Base Camp he too took the helicopter out, but happily back in England he made a full recovery.

By now all the other expeditions had departed, leaving just Dan Mazur and myself at the base of K2. After nearly a month of perpetual storms we enjoyed a period of almost perfect weather. We were being lured back up the mountain before we had rested sufficiently from our recent spell at 8200m. We resisted the temptation; but after four days we could wait no longer. We were in a hurry, so we adopted a new strategy – continuous climbing; that is, climbing non-stop throughout the night and day until we reached the top. Thirty-six hours later we were back up at Camp 4, but now the clouds began to drift in and it started to snow. Rushing up the mountain didn't seem so important any more, so we stopped for the night.

During the next two days the weather deteriorated still further. However, this did not prevent us from climbing, and we moved up to our previous high point at 8200m, this time taking the precaution of bringing our sleeping-bags. After a comfortable night we woke at 3am. The air was completely still and the sky was awash with stars – conditions were perfect. We began preparing for the day ahead. Everything goes so slowly at this altitude that it was 7 o'clock by the time we were ready. When we left the tent the mountain was shrouded in cloud and it was snowing lightly.

Our first task was to penetrate the imposing 100m rock band immediately above us; slowly we made our way up it via a series of short ramps and tricky slabs. A narrow gully led through the top of the rocks onto the snow band that crosses the SW face at 8300m. Here we were met by a vicious wind which howled across the exposed face. Compared with the exhausting effort of gaining vertical height, it was easy work making the horizontal traverse across the face and we soon reached the SSW ridge, also known as the Magic Line. Here we received a nasty shock. We were faced with a towering rock cliff with no obvious line of weakness. After exploring the alternatives, a narrow chimney appeared to offer the only chance of success, but this started with 10 metres of blank wall. The bitter wind cut through to my very bones and threatened my resolve.

'It's getting late,' I said. 'Perhaps we should turn back.' Dan gave me an arched look as if to say 'These Englishmen, they will have their little jokes!'

Without a word he turned back to the cliff and was soon hammering in some pitons and starting to aid his way up. With each agonising move, he appeared to be on the point of falling off; just in time, he was able to pull up into the narrow chimney, which provided much easier climbing. On the other side of the ridge we were sheltered from the tearing wind and for a moment the clouds cleared, giving us a glimpse of the summit 300m above us. Our goal seemed so close, but we knew we still had a long struggle ahead. As we climbed the SSW ridge, we realised that if we continued we would be committed to spending the night out high on the mountain; but neither of us gave any hint of wanting to turn back. The climbing was steep, and made more difficult by loose rock cloaked in a light covering of powdery snow. This slowed us down considerably, but when we reached a simple snow slope the summit appeared within our grasp. But our hopes of summiting before nightfall were frustrated as we bogged down in a patch of bottomless snow. Realising that further effort was futile, we traversed over to the ridge and bypassed the snowfield on some rock slabs.

Returning to the ridge brought us into the full blast of the wind. As the clouds closed in again with the fall of night, we found shelter under an overhanging boulder. We rested for a while and pondered whether to bivouac here and go to the summit in the morning or continue to the top during the night. As the weather was getting worse by the minute, we decided to go for the summit while we still had a chance.

We left our packs at the bivvy and weaved our way up through the rocks onto the summit ridge. By now the weather was very bad and, as we climbed, clouds built up down below us. The wind gathered them up and sent them racing over us like ghostly horsemen; it was as though we were in a dream. We ignored it all and kept plodding relentlessly on and on. The great ridges of K2 dropped away from us on all sides, disappearing into the turmoil of the ever-changing clouds. Suddenly we were there; there was no more mountain above us; we were on the summit. It was one hour to midnight.

'Take a photo,' gasped Dan.

All through the trip people had been complaining that I did not take enough photos. 'Don't worry,' I assured them, 'I'll take the important one, the one on the top.' I reached for my camera – it wasn't there. I had left it in my pack. Dan glared at me. 'You idiot!' he said, and stumbled back down the ridge.

We had stayed on the summit for only a few seconds. Now getting down was all that was in our thoughts. Soon we were back at our overhanging rock, where we made another brew. It was tempting to sleep there for the night, but the noise of the wind was telling us not to delay. As we set off I became conscious of a mysterious being accompanying us. I could not see it, nor did it speak to me, but I could feel its presence; it was climbing with us as if part of our team. Almost immediately after leaving the bivouac we reached the steep rocks and had to start abseiling. We only had a meagre 15m of rope and a few pitons, so we had to make many short abseils and use natural anchors. Each time I looked for suitable anchor points, I consulted our 'presence', and mysteriously I would notice a placement for the rope. In this way the three of us slowly descended the rocks, making about 15 abseils in all.

Light came as an imperceptible warming glow in the swirling clouds; it was now that I noticed that the 'presence' was gone and also, more disconcertingly, that we were lost. We were on the top of an overhanging cliff which overlooked an easy-looking snow ramp. This was not the way we had come up, but we couldn't find our tracks nor recognise any familiar terrain. To abseil down the cliff would be irreversible, so if the snow ramp led to a dead end we would be in trouble; but looking in vain for our ascent route was using up our fast-ebbing strength. We decided to go for it. Fortunately the ramp led back to the crest of the ridge and we knew we were safe.

But our troubles were not yet over. Traversing back across the SW face was sheer misery as we now had the wind against us, which iced up our faces and penetrated to our very core. Equally discomforting, the snow conditions had worsened and we had to front point our way, fighting to keep balance in the buffeting wind. Eventually we regained our small tent at 3pm. We had been away from it for 32 hours.

It took us another three days of exhausting work to drag our weary bodies back to Base Camp. Knowing that five people had died descending K2 that year, and that the mountain could still spring a nasty surprise, we did not relax our guard until we were safely back in Base Camp. Well, we thought we were safe in Base Camp. There we found that we were not the only ones who had been experiencing an adventure. A large menacing sérac had detached itself and come crashing down as a huge avalanche sweeping past our camp. All our tents had been flattened and destroyed. Certain disaster was only averted by the fact that only one person, Captain Wasim, our liaison officer, was in camp at the time. His tent was sheltered behind some rocks and although it was ripped to pieces he was unharmed. We vowed to leave at the earliest opportunity; we were the only expedition to summit without suffering a fatality and we wanted to keep it that way.

One last plate was added to the Gilkey Memorial that summer. The plate honouring Al Rouse and Julie Tullis had been lost during the previous winter, so with the help of Captain Wasim we placed a new plate to their memory.

**Summary**: The 1993 UK/USA K2 Expedition made the second British ascent of K2, and the first British ascent of the West Ridge (second overall). Dan Mazur (USA) and Jonathan Pratt (UK) reached the summit on 2 September 1993. The other team members were Dr Andrew Collins (UK), Andrew Mayers (UK), Jonathan Wakefield (UK), Dean James (UK), Mike O'Shea (Eire), John Arnold (Canada), Etienne Fine (France), Scott Darsney (USA) and Greg Mortensen (USA).

## PAUL PRITCHARD
# Hammering the Anvil

*(Plate 1: Frontispiece)*

The six of us lay there curled up in agony, our shrunken stomachs paying for our hour of gluttony. We were back in town after three weeks of work and hardship in the mountains and it was all we could do to gorge, sleep and rest our cramping limbs. Now this may seem like a fitting end to an adventurous expedition but the truth of the matter was – we had not yet even got to the foot of our mountain.

In April through May, with Celia Bull and Steve Quinlan, I had cruised around the Utah desert climbing on those magnificent sandstone towers. And then to Yosemite where we climbed three routes on El Capitan, the final one being a new route: *'Adrift'*. That was excellent practice for what was to come. Celia then flew home and on 29 May Steve and I flew up to Baffin Island. Keith Jones, Simon Yates and Noel Craine came straight out from the UK and, after many letters and phone calls, here we all were grouped together shivering on the bleak airstrip of Pangnirtung. A local man took us by skidoo the 30 miles up the frozen fjord and dumped us and our one and a half tons of food (or 'bearded nonsense' as Keith would call our vegetarian fodder) and wall gear. We paid our driver and he disappeared over the white horizon. We milled around and scratched our heads. This was it – we had all studied, long and hard, Doug Scott's famous photos showing the mountain's overhanging profile. This was the beginning of a long-dreamed-of adventure: to attempt the West Face of Mount Asgard.

We ferried three loads each up the Weasel valley and then up the Caribou glacier. Thirty miles, fives times. This gave us an ideal opportunity to study the towering walls hereabouts. For two days we were stormed in on the Caribou col. It was horribly cold and three feet of snow fell around our tents. Then, after 16 days on foot and on ski, we established a Base Camp of sorts below Asgard's West Face. It looked terrifying, hoar-frosted, blank and sickeningly high.

Already we were worryingly low on food and had adopted a strict programme of rationing. After making two attempts on the approach slope to the face we decided it was far too dangerous owing to avalanche risk. We needed at least a week for the snow either to consolidate or slough off. We were therefore faced with a tricky decision. In a week we would be virtually out of food and Simon and Keith only had a couple of weeks left before they would have to fly home. We had all totally underestimated the seriousness of this venture and the time it would take. Eventually it was decided that we would all go back to 'Pang', put Simon and Keith on a plane and buy a stack more food for a big push. This was tough on them but inevitable in the circumstances. As we waded through the appallingly soft snow of the Parade glacier, we met a Catalonian called Jordi Tosas who had come to attempt a solo of Mount Friga. He wasn't having much fun alone, so we invited him to join us. On such a technical wall, one pitch a day can be good progress and we would find four a useful number to even out the workload and prevent conversation from stagnating.

On arrival back at the fjord head we found that the pack ice had broken up and it would be impossible to get a skidoo or a boat in to pick us up. So we walked, at first on an ice shelf and then through miles of Scottish bog. By the time we arrived in 'Pang' we had walked and skied almost 200 miles ... and so the feeding frenzy began. Then, with traumatised digestive systems, we said goodbye to the boys, shouldered our loads of the choicest junk food that Pangnirtung general store had to offer, and headed once more for the hills. This time a small boat managed to take us a fair way up the fjord. As we plodded back up the Weasel valley the weather gave us the worst it could – horizontal rain and torrential floods. This was the storm the elders had told us about: the almighty storm which heralds the coming of summer. But, even so, its attempts at halting progress compared favourably with all that Patagonia had thrown at us in previous years.

After 28 days we were once again below our face. The lower slope was still bad but we managed to fix it and get our gear to the foot of the rock, where we found the perfect site for Advanced Base Camp. A huge bergschrund ran the width of the face and was banked out with snow. We tunnelled into the outer rim to make an excellent three-roomed house only ten feet from the start of the route.

So on 30 June we at last began our climb. We had no difficulty in finding the route as there was only one feature rising from the snows on a mirror-smooth sheet of rock: a shallow, nearly blank groove with a poor nut placement at twelve feet. I attached an RP* to a ski pole and placed the nut. I hauled up and then, after a couple of minutes attempting to place a peg, the nut ripped and I landed flat on my back in the snow, much to the mirth of Doctor Craine. I eventually overcame this first crux (and got my own back) by standing on his head. Fantastic free climbing then followed up a sickle-shaped ramp; this led to an immense hollow flake which was impossible to protect even with our Camalot 4.* To stay safe, we climbed a difficult aid seam to the left and swung into the offending flake higher up. Even though the cold was often intense at certain times of the day, we managed to keep a pair climbing for 24 hours a day. The luxury of constant daylight meant that we could accomplish the climbing in fast time without the threat of benightment.

(* *An RP is a very small brass-headed nut. A Camalot is a piece of protection resembling a Friend but much bigger, for very wide cracks.*)

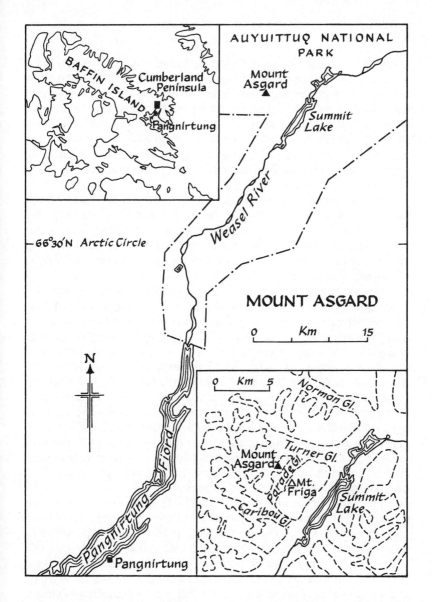

Even vague features were now sparse and from here on we were forced to wander left and right to hit the smallest groove or flake on which to fight for some height. The face steadily overhung and there were no ledges. Occasionally, when the rock was totally smooth and we couldn't make progress with skyhooks, copperheads or birdbeaks, we were forced to drill rivets. These rivets are bodyweight placements, being only ½ inch long and ¼ inch in diameter; over all, we used 34 of them. We also used twelve bolts at belays where it was not possible to arrange anything natural. Most E face El Capitan routes have over 200 holes.

After fixing eight pitches of very technical manoeuvres, we reached a small ledge where we mounted a portaledge camp. We hauled up bivvy gear and a 60-gallon barrel of water and set about the open snaking cornerline above. This corner was the biggest feature of the route. It was about three pitches long, all at A4, so it was not as easy as we had hoped! The rock was friable and often impossible to peg. Shift work was still in progress; usually Steve and I would go up for 15 to 20 hours and then, having had a good sleep, Jordi and Noel would come up and take over and it would be our turn to rest.

The corner faded in a sea of blank rock but 50ft out to the right a dyke of diorite struck a black line all the way to the decapitated summit. Our attempts at a huge pendulum failed owing to the steepness of the rock, but hooks, heads and rivets got us across. Seen from the glacier this dyke had been the basis for our line, but on closer acquaintance it turned out to be just a stain of terrible soft rock.

For the last month we had had the Auyuittuq National Park to ourselves but presently two more teams arrived to try our line. The Swiss team had, very sensibly, sent all their food in by skidoo in winter and then walked in over five days. And the American pair! As we lay snoozing at our ledge camp, the throbbing of rotor blades pierced the utter tranquillity and, at the very foot of the crag, out jumped Brad Jarret and his friend Chris. We shouted our hellos to each other and both teams started fixing further left.

We had now been on the route for ten days and we were virtually out of food again. The next day was 10 July and the last possible day we could top out and still make our flights. Up until this day we had just been plugging away and controlling our fear, never thinking of an end. But now urgency pushed its way in, like when your slide show is supposed to start in five minutes and you're stuck in a traffic jam! We were still on overhanging rock with no sign of a summit.

In the evening Steve and Jordi went up to do what we hoped would be the last 200ft overhanging pitch and at six the next morning Noel and I jugged up to join them. They had just finished and excitedly beckoned us up the ropes. They could see the top and the weather was holding good. We would go light and fast from here. Pitches of beautiful free climbing fell by, though some of the cracks were ice-choked. The hours also fell by and the team was becoming dangerously fatigued. The others had a chance to brew up and nap, while I slowly aided the penultimate pitch. Noel led through, pulled an overhang and clasped the summit with both hands. Unlike most mountains, there are no soul-destroying false summits on Asgard – you just slap the top and mantleshelf.

On top, after being crammed together for so many days, we each wandered in our own direction with our own thoughts. It was the moment which can only be tentatively imagined when planning an upcoming trip. It was 11pm. The sun was low and the hundreds of crimson peaks pointed long shadows to the east. We stayed and picnicked and then cautiously began the long descent down the route. Ten abseils got us to the portaledges at 4am. By now Steve and Jordi had been working for 36 hours. We were all shattered and began to let ourselves feel the pain in our swollen and bleeding hands. We washed down anti-inflammatory pills with sweet tea and slept for 12 hours. It was late afternoon before we began abseiling again and lowering all the kit, but by 10pm we had everything at the snow cave. We had left the face clean. We worked all night lowering the haul bags down the lower slope, on which there were sections of 70° water ice. The glacier was in appalling condition and we sank up to our thighs even on skis. At 7am we collapsed into our Base Camp tents, exhausted.

When we awoke the storm which had been brooding for two days looked about to burst. We hurriedly struck camp and headed out in the early evening. We could spot the Americans and the Swiss about two pitches up their chosen lines. Their routes looked blanker than ours and we guessed they would take more drilling. We shouted up encouragement and waded off down the Turner glacier chased by the boiling storm.

'Poor guys up there,' I thought, ' ... but they can handle it!'

None of us had ever travelled on such a dangerous glacier before; at one point Noel sank up to his waist in slush. Our packs weighed over a 100lbs and we almost wept with relief when we dropped them at the summit lake emergency shelter. It was 3am and almost dark for the first time in two months.

A two-day forced march got us down to the fjord head where we were met unexpectedly by our new Inuit friends from Pangnirtung out fishing in their boat. We got trapped in drift ice, but we didn't care! Everyone was laughing. When we finally made it to town it was a joy to see other people again going about their lives. The first Beluga whale of the season had just been caught and we joined in the celebrations; and we were treated to the finest salmon we had ever tasted (though we turned down the seal blubber). The Inuit showed us far more hospitality than we felt we deserved and when we finally boarded that little plane we left with fond memories.

**Summary**: The first ascent of the West Face of Mount Asgard was made by Noel Craine, Paul Pritchard, Steve Quinlan and Jordi Tosas. The route '*Hyperboria*' is 1000m (19 pitches), A4+, E4 6A. The summit was reached on 10 July 1994 after 11 days on the wall.

JULIE-ANN CLYMA

# Voyage to the Goddess

(*Plates 12–14*)

> ... from a distance of sixty miles we got our first good sight of the two peaks of Nanda Devi towering over their inviolate ramparts of ice ... We were now on the very threshold of the Himalaya and every day the scene became more impressive. Perhaps the finest march of all is that ... through the gorge of the Gori River, roaring down white from the Milam glaciers ... In the recesses between the cliffs were thickets of Himalayan oak, trees of rhododendron and box, with stands of dwarf bamboo. On the crags above were *thar*, short-horned, long-haired wild goats, desperate climbers and lovers of precipices ... Flights of entrancing butterflies thronged our path.
>
> Tom Longstaff, *This My Voyage*

Nanda Devi – the Goddess – has long provided a challenge to enthral the mountaineer. Described as 'the most romantic mountain in the world, surrounded by legend of inaccessibility', since the turn of the century she drew the attention of some of Britain's finest climbers including Graham, Ruttledge, Longstaff, Shipton and Tilman. Repeated approaches over a period of 50 years were required before even a route to the foot of the mountain could be forced. The Rishi Ganga, an obstacle equal to the mountain itself, provided a way into the Nanda Devi Sanctuary from the west, for the first ascent of the main summit in 1936.

For a younger generation of climbers it is not just the difficulty of the terrain that has made the Sanctuary inaccessible. In 1982 the Nanda Devi area was closed for environmental reasons resulting in a total loss of access to a large number of important and historical peaks. However, in 1993 my husband Roger and I learnt that the 'inner line' that marks the restricted area close to India's sensitive border with Tibet was to be relaxed making it possible once more to reach the eastern rim of the Sanctuary by an approach from the Milam valley.

Prior to the closure of the border in the 1970s, the Milam valley was the main link between India and western Tibet (three routes lead to the Tibetan markets of Gyanima and Taklakot). Our research showed that the Pachu Gad, one of the side valleys from the Milam valley, had probably not been visited by a mountaineering party since 1905 when Dr Tom Longstaff tried to reach the Sanctuary from the east. With the two Brocherel brothers, Longstaff climbed out of the Pachu Gad by crossing a pass at

5. Kharta Changri, 7056m. The first ascent was made by Charles Warren and Edwin Kempson during the 1935 Everest Reconnaissance Expedition. (*Charles Warren*) (p3)

6.   Everest from Base Camp. The North Ridge is the left skyline.
     (*Dawson Stelfox*) (p15)

7.   The final slopes of the North Col, with the North Ridge behind.
     (*Dawson Stelfox*) (p15)

8. The Chinese ladder on the Second Step. (*John Tinker*) (p25 )

9. The Second Step and Summit catch the morning sun.
   (*John Tinker*) (p25)

10. The Summit of Everest looking SW, 27 May 1993. An oxygen bottle
    and prayer flags can be seen about 12ft from the surface on the
    NE side of the mountain. (*Dawson Stelfox*) (p15, p30)

The Summit of Everest looking NE, 27 May 1993. In the foreground is a two-prism assembly left by Todd Burleson on 15 May 1992 at the request of Bradford Washburn. Behind it is some equipment left by an Italian survey team on 30 September 1992. (*Dawson Stelfox*) (p15, p30)

12. Nanda Devi East seen from the Panchu glacier. The South Ridge rises steeply on the left-hand skyline. (*Julie-Ann Clyma*) (p52)

Traversing a gendarme on the South Ridge of Nanda Devi East.
The South Ridge of Nanda Devi is in the background. (*Roger Payne*) (p52)

Julie-Ann Clyma approaching the summit of Nanda Devi East at 4.30pm,
6 October 1994, having made the first female and first alpine-style ascent.
Nanda Kot in the background. (*Roger Payne*) (p52)

15. The Indian British Kinnaur Expedition 1994. The N face of Rangrik Rang, 6553m,
seen from Camp 1. The first ascent was made on 20 June by the NE ridge
(left skyline). (*Harish Kapadia*) (p57)

16. Manirang, 6593m, seen from Mane Village, Spiti. The third ascent was made
on 10 July by the SW ridge. (*Harish Kapadia*) (p65)

*c*5300m on the ridge between Nanda Devi East (7434m) and Nanda Lapak (5782m) and descended into the Lawan valley. Longstaff and the Brocherels went on to become the first to see into the Inner Sanctuary when they reached the col on the south ridge of Nanda Devi East (Longstaff's Col *c*5910m) and climbed the first obstacles of the ridge before turning back. They then almost reached the summit of Nanda Khot 6861m and left the area by an intrepid first crossing of the Shalang and Poting glaciers. All these excursions were completed in a very lightweight style with the minimum of support. Finding great inspiration in Longstaff's lightweight exploration of the area, the possibility of using the pass at *c*5300m to reach the unclimbed NE ridge of Nanda Devi East seemed a challenging possibility for a team of two climbing in alpine style.

Nanda Devi East was first climbed in 1939 by a Polish expedition that followed Longstaff's route to the S ridge. Other ascents of the S ridge were made by parties based within the Sanctuary in 1951 (French), 1975 (Indian–French) and 1976 (Indian–Japanese). In the post-monsoon season of 1991 an Indian–Russian expedition with 32 climbers repeated the Polish approach from the Lawan valley (they reported fixing 9000ft of rope and fourteen members reaching the summit). A year later an Indian Border Security Force also repeated the climb, as did a large Spanish expedition in the pre-monsoon season of 1994.

The approach to the mountain from Munsiari along the Milam valley and Gori rivers proved every bit as spectacular and beautiful as Longstaff had described, and the four-day walk brought us to an excellent Base Camp site in Alpine-like meadows in the Pachu valley on 12 September. Having established ourselves in the valley, our efforts to reach the NE ridge of the mountain were somewhat short-lived. The route to the pass that Longstaff had reached on snow in 1905 was completely bare. Our attempt to climb to the pass was made in miserable conditions: low cloud, rain, steep mud, unstable scree, loose rock towers, and the rattle and hum of stonefall. We reached *c*5200m beneath a final steep loose wall before deciding to turn back. After a reconnaissance of other options from the Pachu valley it soon became clear that our only hope of climbing Nanda Devi East in the conditions would be by moving around to the Lawan valley.

It was not until 21 September that everything was at the new Base Camp site. Up until this point we had slept no higher than 4200m and we now had only 17 days before having to start the walk out. We decided to spend 4-5 days on an acclimatisation trip, and then make an attempt on the summit. We looked again at a possible route to the NE ridge from this valley, but the dry conditions and the added threat of sérac fall made us turn our attention to the S ridge. Once again, we found ourselves travelling in Longstaff's footsteps. Already on the S ridge was an Indian–American expedition of eight members that was coming to an end having reached a high point of around 6200m, and a Spanish expedition that was load-carrying to Longstaff's Col. Both teams were using fixed rope.

Having moved up to Advanced Base at c4700m for a night, we made a pre-dawn start next morning, and decided to climb an independent line to the left of the route fixed by the other teams. Just as on the Pachu side, there was no usable snow low down on the mountain, making it necessary to climb a rock rib to reach Longstaff's Col. Although the rock was very loose in places our route gave some enjoyable pitches before returning to the crest of the rib at an easy section to join the line being used by the other teams. A snow patch at c5500m provided a tent site and our first proper night on the mountain.

Next day we moved up to Longstaff's Col and continued along the Pinnacles. The first two towers were bare of snow, exposing loose rock and rubble, but a snow patch on top of the third Pinnacle provided an excellent site for a single tent and our second night on the mountain. The next section of the ridge was steeper, but at last gave some reasonable quality snow and steep rock steps, with inspiring views into the Inner Sanctuary. This third day on the mountain saw us reaching the American team's high camp at c6100m.

The following day we left our tent, and climbed as high as we could in order to check out the upper part of the route for our summit bid. The climbing involved further absorbing rock and snow steps and then gave way at c6200m to an elegant, corniced arête. It was a great pleasure to step out on unspoiled territory, away from the old fixed rope that littered the lower section of the climb, and to be totally alone on the mountain The snow arête soon merged into a wide and windswept shelf that presented obvious potential for a further campsite. Above this shelf a mixed face led to the next section of the ridge. We climbed up to c6700m before turning back owing to the strong cold wind that had begun to blow from the Sanctuary. It was clear from our exploration that a number of lines would be possible on this face and that at its top at c6900m there might be potential for a further camp site. Happy with this reconnaissance we sped back to our tent. Leaving our tent behind at 6100m and our stove and pans at Longstaff's Col, we descended next morning to Base Camp.

With time extremely limited before the porters were due to return on 8 October, it was only possible to take two rest days – although 'rest' was rather a misnomer for, like the Americans, we were taken aback by the amount of rubbish left in the Base Camp area. We spent a day shovelling up debris and burning or burying as much as possible.

On 1 October at 5.30am we left the site of Advanced Base Camp for our tent at 6100m, which we reached almost 12 long hours later at 5pm. Having made such a big height gain (1400m) in one push with heavy sacks we decided to take a rest day on the 2nd. We enjoyed a long sleep but in the afternoon experienced a period of heavier snowfall and spectacular peals of thunder. We became fearful that we had missed the best window of weather and might now be defeated on our summit bid. However, the morning of the 3rd dawned clear, although extremely cold and windy. We finally set off at 10am along the ridge. It was hard going on the steeper rock steps with heavy sacks, but we made steady progress and reached a good campsite beside the Spanish at *c*6500m on the plateau by early afternoon. Unfortunately a terrific storm blew up, and we were soon enveloped in driven snow and strong winds as we struggled to get the tent up. We eventually crawled into the tent around 3.30pm and spent a miserable afternoon trying to dry out our equipment.

It seemed that in each day the window of calm conditions was shrinking. The strong overnight winds on the mountain were not abating until later and later in the morning, while the afternoon storms were moving in earlier each day and becoming more intense. It seemed prudent, before making our summit bid, to try to move our tent higher.

Meanwhile, the Spanish announced that they were going for the top the following day from the Plateau. At midnight they woke us up as they set about preparing to depart. The wind was howling and the temperature was bitter; in our minds this was no time to be going up. We settled back down, with thoughts of another rest day in mind, but got little rest until 4am when the Spanish finally departed. By 10am the wind had dropped and we spent the next few hours drying out equipment and eating as much as possible in preparation for moving up the next day. We saw the Spanish reach about 6900m but, fearful of frostbite, they descended and decided their expedition was at an end. In the afternoon the valleys to the east of the mountain were again shrouded in cloud, and there was more snowfall. We had another bad night owing to strong winds, but the morning of the 5th dawned clear and by 10am the wind had dropped, so we set off.

The climbing on the face proved to be very enjoyable with good snow and lots of interest provided by weaving in and out of rock bands. All except one short 25m pitch was climbed moving together, and by 3pm in deteriorating weather we reached the cornice of the upper ridge. We traversed for 100m or so until just above us we could see the prominent black rock marking *c*7000m. In the poor conditions our only choice was to start levelling out a tent platform in the steep slope dropping down from the cornice to the plateau below. The night was appalling. Both of us developed altitude headaches and the strong winds seemed as if they would flatten the tent. A further complication was the huge volume of powder snow being deposited inside our protective snow walls, making it necessary to shovel out the entrance of the tent every hour or so.

Waking from a light doze to the early morning sun was a great relief, but on our exposed perch the wind howled. It was a miserable process gearing up inside our small tent – first frost, then condensation rained down. The effort of wriggling into wind suits and pulling on boots saw us gasping for breath with heads pounding. It was not until 9.30am that we stepped outside. The view before us was inspiring, as the horizon was clear and the way to the top obvious. Taking turns in deep snow, we set off along the corniced ridge.

The wind had us labouring in our steps, but within a couple of hours we had reached the first major obstacle: a steep wall. The way through this barrier, with its complex array of rock buttresses and snow couloirs and slopes, was not immediately clear. However, continuing close to the edge of the ridge seemed the most obvious thing to do, and soon we were launched on short pitches of ice interspersed with awkward rock steps. Three pitches saw us through this and then we were back on the sharply defined crest. The climbing moved from one side to another, skirting rock obstacles and providing exhilarating climbing over the outrageous exposure to the valley floors on either side. The desperate cold meant that it was not possible to stop even for a moment to pull out water bottles or food. Despite our continuous progress, it was close to 3.30pm before we reached a further steep wall that we sincerely hoped would soon lead to the summit. Mindful of our stretched state and the usual afternoon storms, we pondered the climbing ahead. While part of us urged the need to go down quickly, the desire to finish what we had started was great. Uncertain that we could climb the most direct route up the wall, instead we skirted around to the Sanctuary side of the mountain. While this proved initially straightforward, it left us facing a final precarious pitch up steep loose rock slabs. However, having overcome this last obstacle and regained the ridge crest, only another 100m of almost flat ground lay between us and the final rock outcrop.

We reached the summit of Nanda Devi East at 5pm just as the sun was dipping behind storm clouds. Snow was pluming off the top of the main summit but the sky was clear and from our vantage point we could see across to the summit of Nanda Kot and to the horizon in every direction.

The descent was long and tiring and not without incident when an abseil point almost failed. We spent one more night at 6900m, descending through the next day and night to reach Base Camp just four hours before the porters arrived on the 8th. Our brief moments on the summit had been bliss although we were acutely aware of our exposed position, without any chance of outside help if things went wrong. In our solitude we were conscious of those who had pioneered the way before us. We had climbed in the best style we could and felt that our lightweight ascent had been a fitting conclusion to the voyage that Tom Longstaff had embarked upon nearly 90 years before. Our feelings could perhaps best be described in the words of Eric Shipton : ' ... in the sanctuary of the Blessed Goddess we had found the lasting peace which is the reward of those who seek to know high mountain places'.

**Summary**: In September-October 1994 Julie-Ann Clyma and Roger Payne attempted a new route on the NW ridge of Nanda Devi East (7434m). When this proved impracticable they moved to the S ridge and, on 6 October, made the first British/New Zealand ascent of the route, the first ascent of the mountain by a woman and the first ascent in alpine style.

CHRIS BONINGTON

# A Truly Joint Venture

## The Indian British Kinnaur Expedition 1994

*(Plates 22–24 and front cover)*

The mountain towered over the end of the valley, higher than anything around it, big and complex, with corniced ridges stretching down to outlying peaks. Clouds played hide and seek around the cluster of summits, concealing then revealing. We gazed through binoculars, got out our telephoto lenses, excited and relieved at last to be seeing our objective. Until this moment when we breasted the shoulder, our mountain had just been a spot height on a map – Point 6553 – it didn't even have a name. But it was the highest peak in the Tirung Gad range in southern Kinnaur, an area that had only recently been opened to climbers and in which only two peaks had been climbed – Jokanden (6473m) and Phawarang (6349m). We had not even been able to obtain a photograph of our objective but to me this was an attraction, for it added to that sense of exploration that is the essence of mountain adventure.

There are very few areas left that are so relatively untouched. The 8000 metre peaks are beginning to resemble the mountains of the Alps, with networks of routes up them and base camps reminiscent of Snell's Field in Chamonix. The climbs are challenging and the crowded base camps have their social charm, but that delicious sense of surprise engendered by the unknown is lost.

Our expedition numbered eleven climbers from India and Britain with Harish Kapadia and myself as joint leaders. It was a formula that Harish had tried with great success on four previous occasions with various British groups. In 1985 Jim Fotheringham, a Greenland veteran, had been a member of the first joint expedition to Rimo in the East Karakoram, while Paul Nunn had been to Chong Kumdan, in the same area, in 1991. Graham Little and I had been with Harish in 1992 on Panch Chuli, when between us we made six first ascents. That year we had also had our share of narrow escapes, with Stephen Venables falling 80 metres and badly damaging his knee, while I went for an involuntary 150-metre slide down steep snow.

We were following the same well-tried procedure, the British members joining Harish and the Indian team in their home town of Bombay, travelling by train through Delhi to Kalka, and then up the winding rack railway to the old Indian summer capital of Shimla. Harish, a cloth merchant by profession and editor of the *Himalayan Journal*, has a passion for railways and plans his expeditions accordingly. In Bombay we had savoured the local cuisine – another passion – and had sampled his training routine. This consists of a brisk early morning walk round the Bombay race track followed by a series of energetic sun salutes, a stretching yoga exercise. There aren't many crags near Bombay.

A bus had met us at Shimla and taken us up the Sutlej valley – a deep gash through the Himalaya that now resembles a gigantic building site with a series of huge hydroelectric projects being built, with accompanying new towns and potential industry. We stopped on the way at the headquarters of the Indo-Tibetan Border Police. They were warmly hospitable but the following morning our host, Mahendra Singh, who had led the expedition that made the first ascent of Panch Chuli II, had some bad news. He showed us the map of the area – not even our liaison officer was allowed to carry one – and with a slight smile, pointed to the valley that reached around the northern flank of the mountain and which probably gave the easiest approach.

'You can't go up that,' he told us. 'It's too close to the Tibetan border. Anyway there are plenty of ways up this.' He indicated a tightly contoured wall that seemed to guard the western approach. 'People of your experience should have no trouble at all.'

Was there a slight edge in his comment? We didn't take it up. Surely we would find a reasonable route up one of the two valleys that were open to us. Following the Sutlej, with exciting glimpses of snow peaks at the head of side valleys, we swung onto a track that wound its way up to the village of Thangi at the foot of the Tirung Gad. This was the roadhead where we were to collect donkeys to carry our gear up to Base Camp. Kinnaur is both Buddhist and Hindu, the two religions interweaving with Hindu temples and Buddhist Gompas set alongside each other. The attractive villages of stone and timber houses, roofed with huge slates, cluster among terraced orchards of apple and apricot, and huge cedar trees cover the steep slopes of the foothills. Since the area had only just opened up to tourism, the local people still regarded visitors with a friendly curiosity.

We set out from Thangi on 3 June and at the end of our first day camped below some superb 1000m high granite cliffs – pathside cragging to equal anything in the Alps. It took us three leisured days walking up the Tirung Gad to reach the shoulder just short of the village of Charang where we had the first glimpse of our mountain. It looked complex and challenging. That night we stopped at Rangrik Tungma, a little monastery just beyond Charang at the foot of the valley leading up towards our objective.

The Gompa, a solid square building with tiny windows, was reputed to have been built by a god in a single night some 700 years ago. The walls of the main chamber, lit by a fluorescent light powered from solar panels, were filled with statues and murals of reincarnate lamas, Buddhas and guardian spirits. It had a feeling of great peace and sanctity. This was a Tantric monastery dedicated to the female embodiment of the Buddha and was therefore cared for by nuns. They were a cheerful, down-to-earth lot who gave us plenty of practical advice: to take it steady, to be patient and, on a very specific level, to accept that the best route up the mountain was by the valley that was denied to us. They warned us that the approach from the west was guarded by huge walls swept by avalanche. We decided, there-fore, to make a recce before committing ourselves to a base camp.

Graham Little, who works for the Ordnance Survey and has a feeling for maps, opted to look at the Racho Khad, convinced that this was where the route lay. Meanwhile, Jim Fotheringham, Muslim Contractor, Paul Nunn and I decided to try to find a breach in the walls above the Racho Thach glacier and gain access to a high plateau from which we could climb not only Point 6553, but also several other smaller peaks for which we had permission. This would enable us to adopt the same strategy as previous Kapadia expeditions, when, after establishing a common Base Camp, the team had split into small groups tackling various different objectives, and climbing alpine-style in the purest sense.

A 1½ hour walk took us to the proposed site of our Base Camp at the confluence of the Racho Thach and Racho Khad glaciers. It was an idyllic spot – a summer yak pasture nestling among moraine ridges and boulders at a height of 4170m. We walked on up the valley, surprised by just how far the glaciers had receded. The snout was around 4700m, a clear indica-tion of how low is the precipitation of snow in this area. But the view of the wall guarding the way onto the plateau was increasingly worrying. We reached a moraine ridge at approximately 5000m on the south side of the glacier from which we had a clear view of most of the approach. A mas-sive sérac broke off from the wall opposite, falling clear for about 500m and then bursting in a huge cloud of particles to sweep across the glacier. There seemed no safe route from this side. We returned despondent, to find a relaxed and happy Graham at Base Camp. With Divyesh Muni and Jim Lowther, he had reached a similar height up the Racho Khad and had confirmed his interpretation of the map. A steep but climbable headwall led to a ridge stretching towards the summit.

We had a feasible route for Point 6553, but this was the only one. The entire team were going to have to concentrate on the one line – a lot of people and different styles of climbing. Harish and the Indians worked a capsule system, moving *en masse* from Base Camp upwards, using some fixed rope when necessary and taking with them some of their high-alti-tude porters. The British members of the team were committed to climb-ing in three pairs. I teamed up with my regular partner Jim Fotheringham. Graham Little, with whom I had climbed on Panch Chuli in 1992 and in Greenland in 1993, teamed with Jim Lowther, another Greenland hand. The final pair were both well-known members of the Sheffield mafia: Jim Curran, who was making a film, and Paul Nunn, President of the British Mountaineering Council. For good measure, Harish's wife Geeta and Geoff Birtles, editor of *High* magazine, were trekking with us to Base Camp.

Graham and I imagined the expedition would work out in a similar way to our previous trips, with the various pairs doing their own thing; but Fotheringham and Nunn, both of whom had climbed with Harish before, envisaged and welcomed a more communal effort. And that is how it ended up: a varied group going for a single route.

Our expedition was certainly multi-faceted, with a fanatical bridge school (Birtles, Bonington, Contractor, Little and Lowther), a cricket team (all the Indians, most of our porters, Birtles, Curran and Lowther), and a 'pujah' group, led by Kapadia and Fotheringham (known as Lama Sahib), but keenly followed by myself and other members of the team. (A 'pujah' is a Buddhist or Hindu religious ceremony and we held one at every opportunity.) There was even a computer game team, led by Bonington but supported by Muni and Fotheringham, who fought out a complex game called Strategic Conquest. In between all these activities we found time to climb and were going to have to meld into a cohesive team.

We all moved up to Base Camp on 7 June, our little donkeys following a path carved out of the packed mud and snow patches of the moraine. A very rough cricket pitch was set out and we held a pujah in the warm light of the afternoon sun around a little altar we built above our camp. Smoke from a sweet-smelling fire of juniper swirled in the sunlight, while the less religious (or was it superstitious?) played cricket below. I gazed into the drifting smoke and tried to visualise our team as an harmonious whole.

The following day we made a reconnaissance, carrying loads up to the site of our proposed Advanced Base at 4870m in the Racho Khad. I had a severe attack of bronchitis and therefore stayed, sick and frustrated, down at base. Everyone returned that night enthusing about the view and the route. Harish was still thinking in terms of an alternative line the Indians might take, finding a way onto the SW ridge of our objective.

Two days later the entire team moved up to Advanced Base. I was still feeling ill and wondering if I would ever catch up with them when the weather broke. It reminded me of my experience on Kongur, when a combination of powerful antibiotics and a spell of bad weather had enabled me to overcome an attack of pneumonia and get back in synch with the team. The same thing happened now. The entire team, less Graham and Jim Lowther, came back down the next day. Three days of bad weather let me throw off the infection and we all returned to Advanced Base to find Graham and Jim still there, although they had carried their tent and food to the foot of the face between snow showers.

We were still very much separate groups with separate ideas. The days spent up at Advanced Base had inevitably meant that Graham and Jim had formed their own plans and perhaps had a feeling of slight self-righteousness that they were sticking it out at the sharp end while everyone else had fled the mountain. We, on the other hand, thought they were eating into rations to no great avail. It was the classic division of an expedition into groups, each convinced of its own virtue.

Graham and Jim were planning to move up to a camp below the headwall that afternoon. To me it seemed high time we tried to integrate their effort with the rest of the expedition. At the same time, Harish had sent out a recce comprising Pasang Bodh and Prakash, his two very accomplished Manali porters, to investigate the alternative SW ridge approach. They had drawn a blank, so it was now obvious that we were all going to be on the same route.

With a large group going for the same climb it made sense to fix-rope the steep headwall leading to the col. The following morning, Lowther, Little, Divyesh and Pasang set out from Advanced Base Camp to start work on the headwall. We ended up spending three days fixing it, each day with a different group. Graham Little started it off with a tensed single run-out of some 75m up frighteningly unconsolidated snow, while Jim Fotheringham and I had a superb morning finishing the route off and reaching the col on 17 June. The route to the headwall was complicated by a combination of steep unconsolidated snow and shattered rock. The latter provided the only remotely secure anchors and therefore the line picked its way from rock island to island in a convoluted diagonal.

The view from the col was both magnificent and daunting. The NE ridge started in a steep triangular face of snow leading up to what appeared to be a pinnacle, although we knew from what we had seen from below that this was just a bend and flattening in the angle. From there it curled round into a corniced sweep towards what we hoped was the summit. We would need at least one more camp before making a bid for the top. Looking to the north, we could gaze over the mountains of Tibet stretching into the far distance, while to the east was the Garhwal with a dramatic pointed peak dominating all around it – surely it must be Kamet (7755m), first climbed by Frank Smythe and party in 1931.

Fothers and I were in a state of excited elation when we got back to camp, to find most of the team waiting for us. Little and Lowther had slipped back to Advanced Base for a rest but had returned that morning and were packed ready to move up to the col that night and go for the top the following night. Fothers and I certainly couldn't have done this; it had been a long day and we needed a rest. I had mixed feelings, partly wanting to be in on the first summit bid, and partly surprised and disappointed that we were still operating as separate pairs rather than merging into a single team. After some discussion we reached a reasonable compromise. Harish had already decided that Divyesh, Muslim Contractor and Pasang Bodh would represent the Indian part of the team, whilst all six Britons wanted to go. Graham agreed to delay his departure until early next morning and just move up to the col, followed by the others. They would spend the night on the col and then the next day move up to a camp on the ridge. Fothers and I could have a rest day and then in a single push catch them up at the ridge camp and the entire team, in the best Russian style, could go for the summit together.

Harish came up to Advanced Base that night, and the following day the three of us lazed in the sun, cooked and ate and watched the rest of the team slowly climbing the fixed ropes to the col. Next morning, feeling fit and rested after our lazy day, Fothers and I quickly followed up the fixed ropes in the shade of early dawn, had breakfast on the col and caught up with the others about halfway up the steep wall leading to the crest of the ridge. Little and Lowther had opted to climb through the previous night, and we could just see their tent, a little blue patch dug into the cornice.

It was late afternoon by the time we joined them and had dug out platforms for our tents in the steep snow. At 6000m it was a superb camp site with views that stretched in the west to the mountains of Kulu, through Spiti and Tibet to the peaks of Gangotri in the east. We could identify Thalay Sagar and Kedarnath Dome. We settled down for the night and I woke up at two, called out to the others and started brewing. The Little and Lowther team were away first, closely followed by Fothers and myself. Jim Curran had been agonising about whether he should go with us or not, worried not so much for himself but that he might slow us up. He set out but after one rope length decided to return to the camp. Paul Nunn hitched onto Muslim Contractor and continued up the tracks.

It was snow all the way – not very steep, but nerve racking – with a few inches of unconsolidated snow on ice threatening a constant risk of avalanche. There was an ice step halfway up – only grade 3, perhaps not even that, yet it felt serious at that altitude. Lowther and Little broke trail practically all the way. At one stage Fothers and I caught up while the lead team was resting; we offered to do our bit out in front, but Lowther was soon on Fother's heels, like a keen young Labrador pup, and Fothers gracefully waved him past. At that point we decided we might as well have a really good rest and let Divyesh and Pasang Bodh move through as well.

The summit seemed a long way off, and yet the peaks around us were slowly dropping away. Point 6447, for which we had permission, was now level with us although the only way we could have reached it was by crossing our present objective. Suddenly, from what seemed far above, Jim Lowther let out a shout. He was there, on the very top of our mountain. About half an hour later Fothers and I had caught up and pulled over the brow. It was an improbable summit. There hadn't been a single ledge or flat space all the way from the col and yet here on top there was a level space twenty metres across – a perfect camp site. Not only that, by a little rock outcrop to one side there was even a pool of melt water. Graham, the resourceful, had brought up a gas stove and the makings for tea. It was already purring away. Fothers and I, totally improvident, had only a bar of chocolate left between us, and were really grateful for that mug of hot tea.

To the south big thunderheads were massing over the foothills, a tidal wave of cloud was engulfing the Gangotri, but we were in the warm afternoon sun. It was as magnificent a panorama as any I have seen from the summit of a mountain, even from those that were very much higher.

Our expedition had been successful, the more so since eight of us had reached the top together and through that process had coalesced from a loose collection of pairs and groups to become a truly joint expedition. Moreover, we had enjoyed the stimulus of a type of mountain exploration that must soon be gone for ever, as every nook and corner of the world's mountains are discovered.

We called our mountain Rangrik Rang, after the little monastery at its foot. The monastery almost certainly was built by the hand of man; the mountain could well have been fashioned by the Gods.

## Summary
The Indian British Kinnaur Expedition 1994 visited the Tirung valley, Kinnaur, from 3rd to 26th June, and made two first ascents. Part of the team went on to climb Manirang in Spiti and other peaks. (See 'Manirang' on the following page.)

**The Team:**
*Co-leaders*: Chris Bonington and Harish Kapadia
*Members*:: Muslim Contractor, Jim Curran, Jim Fotheringham, Vijay Kothari, Graham Little, Jim Lowther, Kaivan Mistry, Divyesh Muni, Paul Nunn and Joginder Singh Gulia (Laison Officer).
*Supported By:* Pasang Bodh, Harsingh (Sr.), Prakash Chand, Khubram, Suratram, Harsingh (Jr.), Kesar Singh (Sr. and Jr.), Dewan Singh and Nima Bahadur.

**The first ascent of Rangrik Rang, 6553m**, was made on 20 June via the NE ridge by Pasang Bodh, Chris Bonington, Muslim Contractor, Jim Fotheringham, Graham Little, Jim Lowther, Divyesh Muni, Paul Nunn.

**Other peaks climbed:**  Mangla, 5800m: the first ascent was made on 19 June via the NW ridge by Harish Kapadia, Kaivan Mistry and Prakash Chand. Kunda, 5240m, was climbed on 20 June via the S ridge by Harish Kapadia. Kimshu, 5850m, was attempted on 20 June via the N ridge, when Kaivan Mistry, Prakash Chand and Khubram reached 5780m.

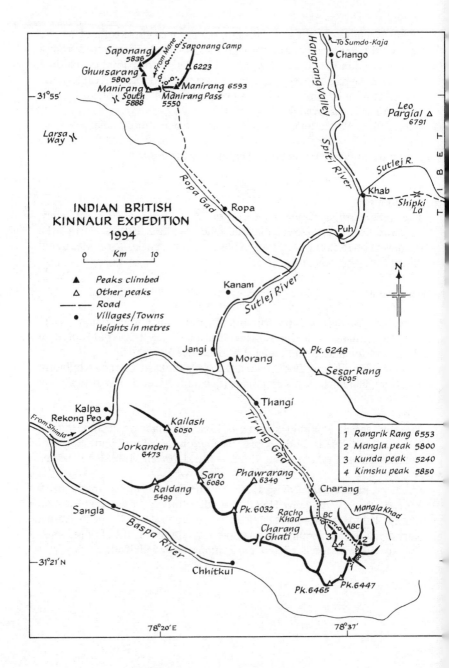

Saponang 5836
From Mane
Saponang Camp
6223
Ghunsarang 5800
Manirang 6593
Manirang South 5888
Manirang Pass 5550
To Sumdo-Kaja
Chango
Hangrang Valley
Leo Pargial 6791
31°55'
Larsa Way
Spiti River
Sutlej R.
Khab
Shipki La
TIBET
Ropa Gad
Ropa
Puh

INDIAN BRITISH
KINNAUR EXPEDITION
1994

0        Km        10

▲   Peaks climbed
△   Other peaks
—   Road
•   Villages/Towns
    Heights in metres

Kanam
Sutlej River
N

Jangi
Morang
Pk. 6248
Sesar Rang 6095
Thangi

Kalpa
Rekong Peo
From Shimla
Kailash 6050
Jorkanden 6473
Tirung Gad

1  Rangrik Rang 6553
2  Mangla peak   5800
3  Kunda peak    5240
4  Kimshu peak   5850

Saro 6080
Phawrarang 6349
Charang
Mangla Khad
Raldang 5499
Pk. 6032
Racho Khad
BC
ABC
Sangla
Baspa River
Charang Ghati
3   4
2
31°21'N
Chhitkul
Pk. 6465
Pk. 6447

78°20'E                    78°37'

PAUL NUNN

# Manirang, 6593m

*(Plates 25, 26)*

The exploration in East Kinnaur was the first stage of the Indian–British expedition in June–July 1994. As the monsoon advanced, a second foray, planned for a 'rump' of climbers in rain-shadowed trans-Himalayan Spiti, had Manirang as its main objective. Manirang peak (6593m) had been climbed twice before, first by South Africans Dr and Mrs J de V Graaf with Pasang Dawa Lama and Tashi Sherpa in 1952, and secondly, in September 1988, by an Indian Parachute Regiment expedition led by Lt Col Balwant Sandhu who made the first ascent of Changabang with Chris Bonington in 1974.

On 29 June 1994, when Chris and the rest of the British team trundled off in a pick-up through the deodars towards Shimla and home, Jim Curran and I stayed behind at the 'Director's rest-house', perched above the remains of the old Hindustan–Tibet road at Kalpa. We were all tired and monsoon clouds rolled up from the south-east behind the Jorkanden range across the Sutlej river. The dampening air weighed down our spirits but our hopes resided in the legendary aridity of Spiti.

Harish Kapadia, Jim Curran and I spent two days securing foreigner's entry permits for East Spiti. One could understand stony resistance among officials as we trailed an American Buddhist ranter from one dark administrative corner to another. After years wandering the east seeking enlightenment, he had become a mantra of complaint. Jim and I were allowed just 14 days in the 'inner line' area. Anyway, we were booked on the plane from Delhi to London on 18 July.

On 1st July we were off, one jeep with Harish, myself and most of the Indian climbers to see Kanam monastery where, high above the Sutlej, the Hungarian scholar of Tibetan, Csoma de Koros, stayed in his cell for many years in the late 18th century translating Tibetan manuscripts. Far below, in the gorge, Vijay Kothari, Jim and the equipment had gone direct in two jeeps with half a dozen porters. After midday we spiralled down the steep track back to the main road and followed, entombed in the savage rock gorge of the Sutlej, with occasional glimpses from rock galleries into the world above. After a stop at Poo military cantonment for a late lunch, a notable moment was a sighting of the great rock peak Reo Pargial, a close neighbour of Leo Pargial (6791m) climbed by Charles Warren and Marco Pallis in 1933. Theirs appears to have been the last significant foreign climbing expedition to East Kinnaur, if we forget occasional travellers, like Heinrich Harrer and Peter Aufschneiter escaping the prisoner-of-war camp at Dehra Dun to 'Seven Years in Tibet' during the Second World War.

Near the Pargials the Sutlej river veers 20km east towards Gartok and sources not far from Mount Kailas in Tibet. The Spiti river turns NW and a new road follows, chiselled and blasted for miles through dizzy rock walls. Some hours after entering Spiti we caught up with the other two jeeps as a fierce sidestream swept the road. One had a holed diesel supply from driving too fast through dangerous water. A bus waited beyond the obstacles. Equipment and porters were transhipped, leaving the crippled jeep and driver with diesel pipe first-aid to get him back. Jim was relieved to escape from this youthful driving maestro. It was 10.30pm when we reached journey's end, sleeping out at a sprawling village by the road below Daudhar monastery. A magical large beer after the exhausting journey brought immediate extinction.

Early next morning Vijay found a lorry to get us to the wire jula crossing the Spiti to Mane village at 3600m. A new bridge was still in construction. Before the heat escalated and within an hour of our arrival we and the baggage crossed the Spiti river, balanced in a hanging box across the flood. A juicy and last mango breakfast was fuel for a steep climb into the idyllic village in search of Muslim Contractor, who had disappeared earlier to forage for transport. Donkeys brayed seductively in the distance all day but failed to materialise.

I explored up the steep dry path towards Manirang. When I got back to Mane, where local dignitary Mr V Kumar accommodated us royally in his fine house, Jim admitted that a nasty bruise on one foot made walking impossible. He was forced to stay in Mane with Mr Kumar, to recuperate and catch up later. There was so little time that the expedition had to keep moving to have any chance. A forlorn Jim was left behind and I set off with his film camera in my load, trying to fathom a two-minute 6am seminar.

We climbed to a milky lake, passed a few yaks and after lunch skirted high slopes above a dismal gorge to Saponang at 4500m. Early on 4 July in poor weather we crossed the river to the true left bank of the rocky nullah leading towards the Manirang La. The path was faint after about a decade of abandonment as a trade route. It crossed screes, nullahs and limestone ribs, and the donkeys only managed two short, steep, half-loaded carries. Heavy rain fell as we reached a barren sloping stony camp at 4840m. Easier ground opened beyond, but the donkeymen went home, leaving us in the rain with a mound of gear and food and as yet no base camp.

On 5 July Muslim Contractor and I found a good site at 5360m, not far below the Manirang pass (5550m). A pleasant if stony place, it had a good glacial water supply and surreal arid peaks around. Meanwhile, to our relief and delight, Jim arrived, his heavy gear carried by a young porter. His foot had improved, cured by huge meals, rest and watching Navratilova's tenth Wimbledon final on satellite TV!

On 6 July Muslim, Divyesh and Harish, supported by Khubram and Suratram, found a camp site used by the 1988 party at 5700m and fixed rope on a short bare ice section that barred the route above. A wholesale move to Camp 1 followed, and on the 8th Contractor, Curran, Kapadia, Muni and I, with Kaivan and Khubram in support, climbed a couloir to the NW ridge of the mountain and set up Camp 2 in a sheltered hollow behind a looming limestone tower at about 6050m. The short stages allowed us to move when the snow was firm, and to shelter during the afternoon storms. The camp provided spectacular views north into Spiti, across the grim expanse of the NW face of Manirang, and south into Kinnaur.

Monsoon influences had now strengthened. Each afternoon brought snow, hail and rain, accompanied by pyrotechnics. Despite Spiti's dry weather, Manirang, poised above the Ropa valley in Kinnaur to the south-east and, at 6593m, the highest peak in its range, was an attraction to unwelcome meteorological intrusions. This explains the lushness of Mane village to the north-west, fed fresh water from the divide amidst a desert environment. Fortunately for us, the skies cleared and frost returned at night, so mornings favoured climbing and urgency where thunder had roared the night before.

Two possible climbing days remained on July 9th and 10th. Our Inner Line passes expired on the 14th, the expedition was due in Delhi soon after, and Vijay was already primed to summon the donkeys.

On 9 July Jim set off first up the ridge at about 5.30am, followed by me, with Contractor, Kapadia and Muni not far behind. Above a slabby tower the medium-angled snow ridge concealed a sting. A 350m section comprised hard, brittle ice. Five people, with two ropes between them, were not going to succeed. It had been supposed an easy peak, though quite why we were never sure.

First, Harish and Muslim saw the inevitable. After three rope lengths scratching precariously at merciless hard ice surfaces, so did we. Much disappointed, we retreated to the haven of Camp 2, repeating the experience of Colonel Sandhu's parachutists. In September 1988 they retreated hereabouts on their first attempt after fixing five ropes. Next day they fixed two more and got seven climbers of their 30-strong party to the top in fiercely cold conditions.

A council of war reached hard decisions. Muslim, Harish and Jim volunteered to descend, leaving Divyesh and me to try again, with seven ice screws, five rock pegs, two ropes, one day's food, and one day of expedition left. To encourage us, it began to snow at about 2pm and went on until evening, followed by lightning flashing from dusk to dawn. Full of doubts, we brewed tea from 3am and left at 4.30 on a suddenly glorious bright morning.

Good fortune indeed! The thinnest of new snow layers had frozen onto the bare ice slope. Divyesh went first, planting his crampons edge-on in a series of steep diagonals. The ferrule of the ice axe barely penetrated

A slip would be lethal as we soloed, but speed was essential for success. Well acclimatised, there were only brief pauses as we proceeded in steady rhythm, taking care especially at each turn of the diagonal when a slip would have been easiest. Before 8am we were at the base of the summit rocks.

Divyesh now led two full rope lengths up steep insecure snow and ice, on the very edge of a north face plunging a few thousand feet into Spiti, and belayed on two rock pitons barely penetrating the bad rock. Sun touched us from the right and the final mixed ground began to unfreeze. I led the last 100m of steep, loose boulders and snow, trying to hold the mountain together with hands, knees and feet, and fearful of dislodging stones on Divyesh below. One pitch had no belay; another finished with a perfect piton, a landmark for return. Then the angle eased, a few steps, and I was on the long narrow snow summit at 9.45am.

Within a few minutes Divyesh's grin bisected his face and said it all. An accountant from Bombay, at 29 he had already been on many Himalayan expeditions, climbed Kamet, survived an accident with his climbing wife, and now had added two more summits to his tally. The panorama was perfect through 360 degrees. We tried to look everywhere at once. As J de V Graaf recorded after his first ascent:

> ManiKang [sic] dominates all this region ... This is the only peak that I have climbed where the views of Tibet are truly uninterrupted and so spectacular. The vast plains, separated by isolated mountain chains, contrast sharply with the crowds of snowy peaks which I have generally been used to.

While the view of Tibet from the north side of Everest may be more spectacular, the pivotal view which Manirang provides is outstanding, from Rangrik Rang and its neighbours to the east, distant Garhwal, then up past Reo and Leo Pargial and Tibetan borders in the north, to the Spiti valley, Lahul and the 'rear' of Kulu, finishing with Jorkanden and Kalpa in the south. We photographed, tried to make the self-timer work, did modest flag waving, ate a little, drank water bottles near dry. A walnut, gift from a Lama, stayed on the summit, and crumbs for the birds.

By 11am clouds massed in the south and capped the highest peaks, creeping in sinister shrouds over the Pargials. A teeter down unstable steepening slopes to a solid piton began the descent. But abseils were irritatingly slow. Each one involved getting the ropes straight down totally loose rock, descending without kicking off rockfalls, and teasing the ropes free through suspended masonry without unleashing a bombardment. Once, too optimistic, the rope would not reach a piton left in place. Divyesh fixed one of our two remaining pitons at foot level. As he picked his way down on the abseil, I knew he did not trust it. Nor did I, but there was no better placement, and I was glad to reach the next anchor and see the rope sliding freely down the ice towards me. Lower still, a last old 'Cassin' piton, two inches in, just allowed our rope to reach the top of the ice field by 2pm.

The névé snow surface layer had been transformed. A brief experiment proved that to reverse the next 350m of climbing would be too dangerous – at every step our crampons balled up and threatened to trip us. So we abseiled straight down 300m, sacrificing six ice-screws, while a stiff SE wind blew clouds of new snow across the slope; but we did not pause to get out our jackets. Divyesh went first and fixed the screw while I pulled the ropes and fed them down, in a steady, well-ordered operation. A few football-sized stones crashed past. The snow slopes below, at a slightly easier angle, still crampon-balled and tripped. We finally reached camp at 4.15pm, quickly abandoning our intention of descending further that evening – the snow was too horrible, the likelihood of a slip too great.

The late-day storm was slight on 10 July, the night cold and starry. Rising before dawn, we were met by Kaivan and Suratram at the camp below and were back at base by 9am. Furious packing was under way, and the porters had already ferried equipment down to the donkey pick-up point. After breakfast Divyesh, Jim and I followed to the point where the donkeys were expected. When they did not come, Jim continued towards Mane village. Divyesh, Suratram and I baked on the scree for several hours, waiting. By afternoon we decided to descend to Saponang, leaving Suratram in charge of the gear, to meet the donkey train wading the stream an hour below. The two herders were driving the donkeys while riding two huge yaks, having been dislodged from sleep a few hours earlier by a warlike Curran. Towards 6pm the loaded mules returned to Saponang and with no further delay set off towards Mane. This was going to be some day!

It was a strange journey, mostly done in pitch darkness, crossing rivers, traversing rocky slopes and eventually descending the steepest direct path to Mane village towards 11pm. Suratram almost walked off into space and everybody was stumbling tired following the donkeys into the blackness. At last Vijay flashed a torch anxiously from the village, guiding us into Mr Kumar's house and a huge meal. Lullabies proved unnecessary.

Meanwhile, starting the same day, Harish, Kaivan, Muslim and the three Harsinghs crossed the little-used Manirang col and began a final adventure descending the Ropa valley. Kaivan had already made first ascents of Saponang (5836m) by the N ridge with Khubram and Suratram on 9 July, and of Ghunsarang (5800m) by its E ridge (with Suratram) on the 10th. This followed earlier investigations with Vijay Kothari.

On 13 July we all reassembled at the rest-house at Kalpa and repacked for the long return journey. Harish and Co had suffered a difficult journey down the Ropa valley, a nightmare drive with a drunken driver and the dire loss of Harish's rucksack when equipment tumbled off a taxi in the dark near Rekong Peo. We were so tired, the expedition so successful, that it was hard to find adequate things to say, though we had a long journey to Delhi in which to say them.

The expedition had other causes for satisfaction. All rubbish had been burned or removed, waste glass was pulverised and disposed of. Few tins were taken in the first place and none were left. Tins left by others were cleared where possible, as at Saponang. Jim Curran's filming went well. What more could we expect?

**Summary**: During the second stage of the Indian British Kinnaur Expedition, Paul Nunn and Divyesh Muni made the third ascent of Manirang (6593m) on 10 July 1994, supported by Muslim Contractor, Jim Curran and Harish Kapadia who reached 6300m on 9 July.

Other peaks climbed were Saponang (5836m) by Kaivan Mistry, Khubram and Suratram via the N ridge on 9 July, and Ghunsarang (5800m) by Kaivan Mistry and Suratram via the E ridge on 10 July. Both climbs were first ascents. In addition, the Manirang Pass (5550m) was crossed on 11 July to Ropa in three days by Harish Kapadia, Muslim Contractor and Kaivan Mistry.

BIBLIOGRAPHY

Harish Kapadia, *High Himalaya. Unknown Valleys.* 1st edition Indus 1993, revised edition 1994.
C Bonington and H Kapadia, Report: 'The Indian British Kinnaur Expedition 1994', July 1994.
S C Bajpai, *Kinnaur, a Restricted Land in the Himalaya*, 1991.
G Lloyd (ed), *Lahul-Spiti. A Forbidden Land in the Himalayas*, 1987.
A Gerard, *Account of Koonawur in the Himalaya*, Madden 1841, reprint 1993.
H Harrer, *Seven Years in Tibet*, Hart-Davis 1953.
M Pallis, *Peaks and Lamas*, Cassell 1939, new edition 1948.
M Devjani and Lt Col B S Sandhu, 'Manirang 1988' in *Himalayan Journal 45*, 190-194,1987-88.
J de V Graaf, 'ManiKang' in *Mountain World*, 345-347, 1954

ACKNOWLEDGEMENTS

I would like to express our special thanks to financial sponsors Duncan Sperry and VeriFone in Britain and Godrej in India, and to key equipment sponsor Berghaus Ltd

## ALAN HINKES

# The North Side of K2

*(Plates 27–32)*

The north (Chinese) side of K2 is one of the most remote places on our planet. Sir Francis Younghusband, allegedly the first European to see the north side of K2 in 1887, was impressed. In *Wonders of the Himalaya* he described his first sight of the mountain: 'There before me was a peak of almost perfect proportion, clothed in a glittering mantle of pure white snow and ice for thousands of feet, and standing up head and shoulders above all the mountains round ... The sight of that tremendous mountain, so massive, so firm and strong, so lofty, and so spotlessly and dazzlingly pure and white, necessarily left an impression which has lasted through life.' At that time Younghusband was a lieutenant making a remarkable epic journey from China to the Indian Subcontinent. Fifty years later, Shipton and Tilman made a similar journey which Shipton described in his book *Blank on the Map*.

Even today, just getting to this part of the Karakoram is an adventure in itself, and when I was invited to join the Reebok K2 expedition I had a good idea of the rigours I would be letting myself in for. Expeditions to K2 normally start in Pakistan; those aiming for the north side of the mountain travel up the Karakoram Highway and over the Kunjerab Pass to Kashgar in the Xinjiang Province of China.

We had a different plan. Our team of six climbers – Adrian Burgess, Alan Burgess, Brad Johnson, Paul Moores, Mark Wilford and myself – met in Kathmandu. Here we arranged for five Sherpa friends to take our expedition equipment overland through Tibet to the road head, a PLA outpost called Maza, in the wilds of Xinjiang. This would take the Sherpas about two weeks. Meanwhile, we six climbers flew anti-clockwise through China. This was not as simple, safe, easy or pleasant as it sounds. The flights were Kathmandu–Lhasa–Chengdu–Urumchi–Kashgar. Flying in China is an experience to be missed; our Sherpas definitely had the safest deal. We were glad to get onto the dusty roads and tracks which cross the edge of the Takla Makan desert, as we headed for the rendezvous with our Sherpas.

I had left Britain in late April, but it was early May before I arrived alongside the Yarkand river with 47 camels, 5 donkeys, 3 sheep, 4 goats, a few chickens and the rest of the team, heading to Base Camp. I felt as if I had been transported back in time for, apart from our bright modern trekking clothes and blue barrels on some of the camels, the scene looked as if it had not changed since Younghusband's day. For the first two days, we wandered down a track the Chinese had built in the 1960s. Soon we were heading deep into the high-altitude desert of the Karakoram. After crossing the Aghil Pass, we dropped down to the notorious Shaksgam river. At this time of the year it is a meandering stream in a vast, flat pebble-filled valley, flanked with 200ft vertical mudcliff walls. Getting down to the river is only possible in certain places. We found a narrow gully – probably the one Younghusband used in 1887 – and nicknamed it the 'Younghusband Slot'. It was only wide enough for us and the donkeys – the camels had to make a wide detour. We knew that the Shaksgam had a fearsome reputation for flooding in the summer, the whole valley floor becoming covered by the roaring river. On our return journey in August the experience of crossing this raging torrent was terrifying. Seemingly at the mercy of the camels and the torrents, crossing and re-crossing the swollen icy waters of the Shaksgam on camels is not fun, but fear.

After seven days walking in with the camel-train, we unloaded our equipment near the K2 river issuing from the snout of the K2 glacier, close to the spot that Younghusband called Suget Jangal in 1887. This site is around 3850m and we now had three weeks' hard graft carrying loads up the K2 glacier to establish an Advanced Base Camp below the mountain at 5000m on the moraine-covered ice.

It was 31 May before we could establish this high Base Camp but it was still bitterly cold. The ice on K2 was the winter variety, green, iron-hard and brittle as glass. Our initial aim was to set up and stock a Camp 2 at around 6800m. Working mostly in three pairs, we fixed rope up to Camp 1 at around 6000m, using the camp as a springboard for fixing rope to Camp 2.

This season the weather was generally good – at times too good, the heat causing a risk of serious stonefall. Early on we had a 10-day spell of bad weather and were trapped at Base Camp in Arctic-like blizzards. There is not much to do on a strip of moraine at 5000m waiting for the weather to improve. As well as reading, sleeping, writing and eating, we made some home-brew. When the weather finally cleared we watched several huge avalanches coming off K2. One particularly large one engulfed Base Camp. Luckily, most of its energy was already expended and the experience was only like being in a blizzard for 15 minutes.

I had a close shave one evening at Camp 1, when I was lying on top of my sleeping-bag in my underwear. I heard the characteristic rumble and roar of an avalanche. At first I ignored it ... just another avalanche, I thought. Almost immediately it got louder, and as I knew it was a big one I made a move for my camera. At that same instant I realised that this avalanche had my name on it. I dived out of the tent and clung desperately to the vertical ice wall and fixed rope at the back of the ledge. But the force of the avalanche was sucking me off the ledge and I was drowning under the wet mass. The tent was flattened under 6ft of snow and ice blocks; I was lucky to be alive, though unable to move, buried thigh deep in the snow which had set like concrete. This was serious, as I was clad only in my underwear and all my equipment was buried in the tent, which luckily had not actually been swept away. Fortunately Aid and Al had escaped the avalanche and were able to dig me out and retrieve my boots and clothes from the tent before I developed frostbite or hypothermia. I was lucky, for if the avalanche had struck ten minutes later, I would probably have been in my sleeping-bag and unable to dive out of the tent quickly enough to escape being fatally buried under blocks of snow and ice.

After that experience, I never used Camp 1 again and always went directly from Base Camp at 5000m to Camp 2 at around 6800m. This nearly 2000m trip took around six to ten hours depending on conditions. The tent at Camp 2 was perched on a tiny snow ledge with a 2000m drop to the K2 glacier straight out of the door. The way ahead to Camp 3 at 7500m was over mixed ground, with some rocky sections of about Scottish II/III.

Paul, Alan and Mark now decided to leave. It is not easy to split an expedition in totalitarian China, with its strict regulations, but they got out. Aid and Brad decided to climb a peak (P 5540) above Base Camp instead of going back on K2. But there were now enough tents, food, sleeping-bags and rope at Camp 2 for six people and it seemed a shame to let that all go to waste; so, being a 'waste not, want not' Yorkshireman, I decided to go up alone to Camp 2 and try for the top.

At about the same time a Spanish expedition arrived and I shared a tent with some of them for three nights. I spent another eleven nights, mostly alone, above Camp 2 at 6800m trying for the top. I didn't want to go back down to Base Camp, which would involve the long haul back up and across what we called the 'Second Icefield' just below Camp 2. This was racked with stonefall, particularly in the afternoons, and was quite a dangerous place. I sat out bad weather spells cramped into what was now a broken tent at Camp 2. At least there was plenty of gas and food and even a book which I read very slowly. Although I was now well acclimatised, I realised it was only a question of time before I would start deteriorating through staying too high for too long.

After ten days above 6800m, I reached the site of Camp 4, with only just enough room for a tent, on a rock eyrie overlooking the final hanging glacier and a 'snowplod' to the top. The climbing between Camps 3 and 4 was steep rock, in places perhaps V Diff or Severe, but it is hard to judge at 8000m. Here at Camp 4 (8000m-8100m), two of the Spaniards squashed into my two-man tent. The weather seemed set fair and early the next morning all three of us set off, unroped, up the hanging snowfield. There was quite a tricky loose rock traverse to begin with and then a steepish section of plodding through some séracs. The weather remained good and clear, with a 'China wind' blowing. No doubt conditions on the Pakistan side were perfect. But even though the weather was good, I became increasingly concerned about the avalanche risk. Strong winds had built up dangerous and unstable conditions and I was scared that the slope would slip. Large patches of windslab snow were breaking away around our footsteps.

I had been away from Britain about three months now and had reached around $c$8250-8300m, perhaps only six hours from the summit – but I decided to turn back. The two Spaniards went on a little further; then they too turned back after wasting time and energy getting themselves out of a crevasse.

As I started descending, I realised that I was burned out and that I had to go back to Base Camp for a rest before I could try again. At Camp 2 food was getting low anyway. But I needed to spend another night there on my way down. It was one of the worst nights of my life, as I constantly needed to dig out the tent to prevent it being engulfed by spindrift which was rapidly setting like concrete.

When I finally reached Base Camp, I was quite debilitated and in dire need of a rest. I had not totally ruled out another go on the hill, but Aid had brought the leaving date forward by three weeks and the camels were waiting at low Base Camp. I had no choice but to go down the K2 glacier and trek out with the camels.

'*C'est la vie,*' I thought! Still, I can go back; the mountain will always be there. Four of the Spaniards summited as I trekked out. Sadly, one died on the descent and one suffered serious frostbite resulting in amputations.

**Summary:** The 1994 Anglo-American Reebok K2 Expedition spent four months, from May to August, attempting K2 from the North (Chinese) side. The members of the expedition were Alan Hinkes and Paul Moores (UK), Alan Burgess (Canada), Adrian Burgess, Brad Johnson and Mark Wilford (US). After three members of the expedition had left, Aid Burgess and Brad Johnson climbed a peak (P 5540) above Base Camp, while Alan Hinkes, climbing alone, reached a high point of $c$8250-8300m. However, he decided to retreat owing to dangerous windslab conditions, shortage of food and exhaustion.

JULIAN FREEMAN-ATTWOOD

# Antarctica: Voyage of the *Pelagic*

*(Plates 49–51)*

An interest in using boats to get to a chosen mountain or region stem-
med from my becoming part owner of Tilman's last Bristol Channel
Pilot Cutter *Baroque*. Built in 1902, the poor old boat got a ferocious battering at the hands of Tilman, especially on a successful voyage to circumnavigate Spitzbergen Island, sailing within 600 nautical miles of the Pole
itself. Holed by floes and bergy bits, it was all the crew could do to keep
her afloat as far as Iceland where a mutiny occurred and the Skipper was
persuaded to pay their air fares home. He alone was willing to continue
across the north Atlantic in October, one of the windier months. On his
return with the boat the following year, Tilman sold the vessel to a friend
of mine and that is how I came to own my share. A taste for heavy weather
was imposed on me when I was caught out in the 1979 Fastnet race which
sank 18 boats and killed as many sailors. The Pilot Cutter, being a deep-
draughted vessel, found it no problem, and whilst she leaked like a basket,
I have always believed Tilman was right in choosing this type of boat for
stability in big seas.

However, I no longer had a share in *Baroque* and my first visit to Antarctic waters was by courtesy of *HMS Endurance*, the naval ice patrol vessel
which in 1989 dropped me on the island of South Georgia along with
Stephen Venables, Lindsay Griffin, Brian Davidson and cameraman Kees
t'Hooft. After being buffeted around the place by incessant hurricanes and
ending up in a snow cave of impressive proportions for 23 days, we finally
knocked off the two unclimbed peaks of Mt Carse and Mt Kling in the last
36 hours. [*AJ96*, 1-7, 1991] We had all been greatly impressed by the prolific wildlife and grandiose mountains and I was determined one day to go
further south to the continent itself.

To that end I was fortunate in making friends with a mariner and boat
owner with a prodigious *cv*. Skip Novak had captained no fewer than four
Whitbread Round the World races before finally building his own boat
with the assistance of a friend, Hamish Laird. The secret of the *Pelagic*
was its seven-ton lifting keel, enabling it to get into shallow water anchorages out of danger from the bigger icebergs. It had a Bermuda rig with
extremely strong running gear and a steel hull, ideal for work around Chile,
Tierra del Fuego and Antarctica. Skip visited me in Shropshire armed
with some slides of Grade V ice-climbing from the deck of the boat, and

I was salivating instantly. It turned out there were two berths available on the boat for January/February 1994 and, through a fortuitous meeting with Matt Dickinson at the Alpine Club symposium at Plas y Brenin, we decided to make a film. Matt had indeed already been the producer of our South Georgia film. Also on board would be two French climbers, Denis Ducroz and Chantal Mauduit, plus an Israeli climber, Doron Errel. Chantal had just climbed K2 without oxygen, becoming only the second woman to achieve it after Julie Tullis, and Doron was the only one of his countrymen to have climbed Everest. They were making the first ever Antarctic film for Israeli television.

On 9 January 1994 we found ourselves in Ushuaia (Tierra del Fuego), the most southerly town in the world, and cast off the following day heading for the infamous Cape Horn and all points south. The plan was to sail the 600 miles across the Drake Passage, the section of ocean between South America and Antarctica, and then on 300 miles down the W side of the peninsula to Crystal Sound. The whole peninsula and coastal islands comprise a labyrinth of fine peaks, iced from sea to summit and up to 9500ft high. Whilst the rock is not so good, there are some exceptionally fine couloir lines and, in the south, some fairly sound granite. The further south you travel the greater the percentage of good weather, dominated by the 'Polar high', as opposed to the endless succession of lows in the South Shetlands to the north of the peninsula.

Some 200 miles south of Cape Horn we hit a severe gale force 9 (gusting storm 10) which forced us to heave to for 36 hours in impressive seas. Heaving-up over the lee rail and elsewhere was also a common pastime at this point, reminding me of Harvey Pirie on the Scotia 1902 expedition whose diary entry for Nov 9th simply read 'sick and miserable' and for Nov 10th 'very sick and very miserable'. The strongly built 55ft *Pelagic* took it all in her stride.

After being forced to the SE with fully reefed main and staysail in continuing strong south-westerlies, we sighted Smith Island on a rare and perfect sixth day out. Mts Foster, Pisgah, and Christi are still unclimbed despite Tilman's interest and a more recent attempt by a forces team who were dropped by the *Endurance* the year after our South Georgia trip. They had extremely bad weather and bad luck, having spent nearly three months on Smith Island to no avail. But what a worthwhile target it looked and quite unlike the uninteresting snow dome I had thought it was.

Abeam with Brabant Island was the start of the Gerlache Straits (named after the captain of the *Belgica*, beset for the winter in 1899). Fantastic mountains of impressive size presented themselves both on the peninsula and on Brabant Island. Most of the peaks on the latter were mopped up by Chris Furze's joint services expedition in the mid-1980s.

We then motor-sailed into the Neumayer Channel between Wiencke Island and Anvers Island with the intention of returning to climb there later but for now continuing through the majestic Lemaire Channel,

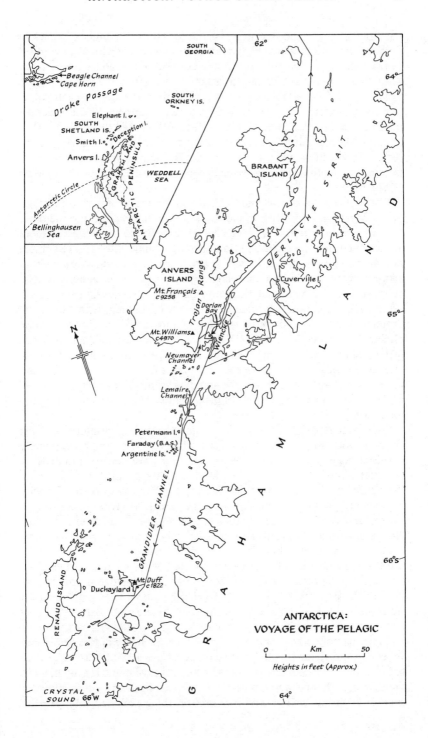

ANTARCTICA:
VOYAGE OF THE PELAGIC

0          Km          50

*Heights in feet (Approx.)*

past the Peterman and Argentine Islands into the Grandidier Channel, at the southern end of which lies Crystal Sound with a wealth of unclimbed peaks. This year, though, it was not to be. We were unable to force a way through the heavy pack ice, and great tabular bergs from the Bellingshausen Sea completely barred the way south as far as the horizon. After extricating ourselves from this labyrinth we settled for a preliminary 1822ft peak on a little mountain island called 'Duchaylard'. We named this peak Mt Duff after the fine plum duffs consumed almost continuously by Tilman and the recipe for which we were as yet ignorant of, despite much amusing conjecture. In a south-facing bay, we made what may have been the first landing on the island.

The plan was that Novak and I would try the S face direct, with Matt and Frank McDermot (an Irish friend of Skip's) on the E ridge and the other four on a ski tour to the W ridge. Novak and I began our climb at about 4pm, which may seem an odd time to start a climb until you remember that at midnight in that latitude it is still possible to read a book without artificial light. Getting over the bergschrund proved an exceptionally difficult task requiring a point of aid in horrible fathomless sugary snow conditions. There followed six pitches of steep ice-climbing, with little good protection, as it was not really cold enough to provide it. Most of these pitches were in the Scottish III/IV bracket. I remember feeling immensely privileged and excited being high on a face in such a monumentally desolate area. It was as if the rest of the world was a figment of the imagination rather than a reality. I suppose the grandeur of the ocean was responsible for this illusion as much as the endless peninsula ice cap and intriguing mountains.

When we were only three pitches from the top, bad visibility and mist swept in, with the prospect of a descent off an unknown and exceptionally corniced ridge. Furthermore, the ice conditions were sugary and the only reasonable protection was from snow stakes. We decided to begin a precarious string of abseils, eventually landing tired but happy on the S glacier after some 14 hours. Happily, the W ridge party got to within 10 metres of the top and verified the treacherous double-corniced conditions. At least Novak and I had got in some steep, satisfying and somewhat technical Antarctic climbing to put us in the mood for greater things.

Extricating ourselves from the bay, now full of ice, we had to steer quite far west to get around the Crystal Sound pack, and headed north towards the British Antarctic Survey (BAS) base at Faraday. They made us most welcome and force fed us with gin and tonic by the pint. Better still, they had a recipe for plum duff plus the one ingredient we didn't have for such a pudding, namely suet. For those Tilman fans, the noble duff is something venerable and apparently to be eaten on one's knees. Matt turned his culinary skill to it with admirable results while later, when I tried my hand in the Lemaire Channel and omitted to put a pleat in the tin foil to allow for expansion during two hours of steaming, the thing exploded, taking up the entire volume of the steamer and nearly making it as far as the cabin walls. A fierce look from the captain presaged a keel hauling.

We anchored at Dorian Bay on Wiencke Island about 10 miles across from the mighty 9258ft Mt Français on Anvers Island. This is the peninsula's highest peak and towers over all else, rather as Mt Paget does on South Georgia. We had our eye on a shapely-looking Anvers Island outlier called Mt Williams, named after the ship of that name used by William Smith (of Smith Island) and later chartered by Bransfield. First we had to contend with seven days of vicious gales. In fact we were not far off losing the boat one night when anchors and warps dragged. Putting on wet suits and up to our necks in freezing water, it finally took four hours to secure the vessel which listed violently when hit by the huge gusts. Even the Adélie penguins had been silenced.

Finally the weather did clear and we had fine views of the Trojan range and Mt Williams. Hamish motored us across the Neumayer channel to drop us at the only possible landing place on the calving ice front, with one week's emergency rations, fuel and a radio with which we could contact him after the climb, as he would have to take *Pelagic* back across the channel to Dorian Bay, the one safe anchorage in the area. Matt, armed with 16mm film gear, Skip, Frank and myself planned to climb as two pairs, with the two French and Doron climbing as a separate trio. I had liked the look of the E ridge of the 4970ft mountain, but the lower sections looked hard and although it would probably go, the weather window was unlikely to exceed 36 hours. So we all opted for a route to the north – a tricky mixed section leading to a possibly somewhat unsafe easy central glacier, with again some harder climbing on the upper 1500ft. Only those who have climbed mountains literally from sea level can appreciate just how spectacular even a five or six thousand foot peak can look and, in Antarctica, how severe it can feel. All of us approached on skis except Matt and me who had snow shoes. This was not due to some Captain Scott type aversion to skis, but simply that excess baggage charges on the plane to Ushuaia had disallowed it. Anyway, the approach was short.

The lower section involved mixed Scottish Grade III climbing for 1000ft with one quite hard pitch of Grade IV expertly led by Chantal and up which the skis were hauled on jumars for the central glacier. This central section was threatened for some of its length from high on the right and ease of mind was not assisted by the thundering and thuds of ice calving into the Neumayer Channel below. On certain steep sugar snow sections Matt and I smugly overtook the skiers; step kicking in our snow shoes we were able to go straight up where the others were forced into long zigzags. At about 1500ft from the top, skis and snow shoes were cached and crampons again donned for some spectacular climbing through ice towers and crevasses. One tower gave a pitch of Scottish IV which, on arrival at its summit, was found to be entirely detached from the remainder of the icefall. A long and protectionless upper 700ft of 45° to 50° sugary ice and snow required a general mountaineering steadiness and gave little hope of effective axe braking in the event of a slip. We pulled over a lip onto the N ridge and got the most spectacular views across the West Anvers Island ice piedmont. The summit ridge was a delight with great vistas opening up before us and later, from the summit, in a biting wind but perfect light at sunset, more superb views, the best we had even seen, showed up all the way south to Duchaylard Island, plus 150 miles of the Antarctic peninsula and plateau. To the immediate north lay the now not so dominant but grandiose Mt Français.

After half an hour of midnight filming, a twilight descent of down-climbing and abseils got us to the lower mixed section beneath the central glacier. A long abseil landed us in a 350ft 45° gully. I was halfway, carefully down-climbing, when a shout from above made me look up to see the wide and seemingly slow motion of a big and hitherto unheard avalanche descending inexorably onto us. Somehow, in the space of five seconds or so, I managed to move quickly to the left but lost footing, cartwheeled once, ice axe braked and got my head down, feeling quite certain that my (and everyone else's) time was up. The speed of the thing allowed no time for fear, only for action or inaction with hope. In fact we only had the dying front of a huge avalanche that had come from a sérac fall above the middle section of our climb. It had wiped out our route of one hour before and the scar of it could easily be seen from the boat five miles away. As everything was dying down I made the mistake of looking up and instantly received a golf ball-sized piece of blue ice in the right eye. I literally thought my eye had come out of its socket as there had been a blinding flash, momentarily nothing, and then a gradual regaining of blurred vision and some blood from the surrounding cut. Happily, the others were all unscathed – we had been fortunate indeed. My eye, by great good luck, returned to normal in a few days. Abseiling the last two pitches we gained the lower glacier and made it back to the landing place for a radio call to Hamish. We had been on the move for nearly 26 hours and already a few clouds were moving in. Hamish had seen us on the summit the previous evening through binoculars and now motored across immediately for a pick-up.

Climbing Mt Williams was a particularly fine moment for Matt Dickinson whose father attempted the peak unsuccessfully in the mid-1950s when working from *HMS Protector* on the then hydrographic survey of the area. Furthermore, Matt took much fine film footage which is likely to be edited into a TV documentary film.

Two days later *Pelagic* headed north into the Gerlache Straits for some beautiful encounters with 50-ton humpback whales. They seemed particularly interested in Hamish playing his clarinet and came right up to the boat to investigate. We moved on to Deception Island, in the South Shetland group, which is a partly active volcano with a flooded caldera 4-5 miles across. You sail through the one opening in the crater wall, called Neptune's Bellows, to enter a wierd moonscape of black ash covering permanent ice. Fierce katabatic winds are a feature of this rather gruesome island and indeed an eruption in 1969 demolished a Chilean base and part of a British one.

A further week across the Drake and a near knockdown by violent 'willywaws' in the Beagle Channel completed nearly 2000 miles under sail. It had been a memorable and happy trip to one of the wildest places on earth.

**Summary**: The members of the *Pelagic* expedition, January-February 1994, sailed in the 55ft cutter of that name 1000 miles from Tierra del Fuego to the Antarctic peninsula.

*Team members*
Skip Novak (captain of the *Pelagic* and veteran of the Whitbread Round the World race), Julian Freeman-Attwood, Matt Dickinson (film cameraman), Hamish Laird and Frank McDermot. Also aboard were Denis Ducroz (French guide and film maker), Chantal Mauduit (2nd woman to climb K2 without oxygen) and Doron Errel from Israel.

*Peaks climbed:*
First ascent of the c1822ft peak, named Mt Duff, on Duchaylard Island.
First ascent of the c4970ft Mt Williams on Anvers Island.
Cuverville Island was visited and the volcanic Deception Island in the South Shetland group.

## MARIAN ELMES
# Hills, Horses and Hunger

### The 1994 Anglo-Russian Expedition
### to the Tien Shan Mountains of Kyrgyzstan

Three years ago, I was fortunate enough to visit the Asan region of western Kyrgyzstan when this area had only just been opened up to Westerners. The quality of the scenery and the climbing, as well as the friendliness and warmth of the local shepherds, had greatly impressed me. Memories of those soaring rock faces, impressive snow peaks and horse tours with friendly yak-herders were constantly in my mind through the next two summer seasons, in the sub-Arctic Siberian Urals and the more familiar Bregaglia Alps.

Through the friendship I had developed with an English-speaking Russian, I was able to realise my fantasies of returning to Soviet Central Asia in the summer of 1994. The trip could not be organised without a great many problems along the way, since good relations with the West have barely been established in these areas and they are only just beginning to provide tourist facilities. Moreover, it wasn't easy to find a like-minded team of explorers. So many climbers seem to be content with easy options, and reasonably so given the usual shortage of funds, limited holiday time and family commitments. However, by Easter five others had agreed to join me, drawn from the ranks of the Alpine Club, the Fell and Rock Climbing Club and Chester Mountaineering Club.

Despite many last-minute problems with visas and travel arrangements, we eventually got ourselves to Alma Ata and thence to Lake Issyk-Kul on a minibus arranged by Dostuck Trekking of Bishkek. We stayed overnight at the lakeside camp there and enjoyed an idyllic swim at dawn, with peaks all around us seeming to float on the early morning mist. A jolting two-day truck-ride got us into the area we had been looking forward to visiting, and we set up Base Camp at 3400m in a broad grassy valley on the north side of a range of snowy peaks rising to 5000m. Herds of glossy-coated, well-bred horses, as well as sheep and little black yaks, grazed all around.

We had taken goods to trade with the local shepherds, who were mostly interested in ropes and basic foodstuffs, so we didn't go short of fresh meat, though our fuel (petrol and camping gaz) and most of our food ran a bit short, and at the end of the trip we were almost reduced to burning yak dung to boil up our last few grains of buckwheat. I lost a stone in weight – unwillingly, since I was skinny to begin with; but the lack of fat and milk products in our diet must have been the main cause. Unusually, the people in our valley were not milking the mares or yaks, and were pretty lean and hungry themselves.

The nine summits climbed by expedition members were all virgin peaks, as the area had not been visited before by climbing or trekking groups. The rock was mostly limestone and somewhat dubious in quality, except for the glacier-worn valley sides where good routes could have been enjoyed for their own sake; but they looked unpromising higher up, so we left them alone. Our climbs were a mixture of scree and ridge and snow. The snow consistency was mixed too, with some good ice on the SW faces in the early morning and waist-deep crud on the other faces. There was also a peculiar breakable crust with big holes underneath, together with enormous crevasses.

After some initial forays up various nearby valleys and low peaks to get an idea of the layout of the area, we launched ourselves on a peak-bagging spree, tackling first the easiest-looking options in the area, and saving up the nearest big summit for the end of the trip in the hope that the whole team might ascend it together. Sadly, this was not to be, since several members of the expedition had severe problems with acclimatisation.

The most obvious and attractive summit in the area, standing high above its satellites and presenting ranks of ferocious séracs on most sides, was a mountain we called (rather unimaginatively) 'Three Crevasse Peak'. I set off from Base Camp with Phil and Mike at first light one morning, up one of those interminable ridges of steep scree and loose rock, which we believed would connect eventually with the upper snow slopes and crevassed faces of our peak. Seven kilometres later, after various excursions around gendarmes and along ibex trails, we descended a chimney onto the snow. It was soft and fresh and deep – and it balled up our crampons at every single step; but there was good ice underneath and several steep front-pointing sections to overcome before the final knife-edged snow arête. On the summit we enjoyed breath-taking views of the wide open spaces of central Kyrgyzstan, stretching a hundred miles east to the high snows of the Inylchek glacier ranges gleaming in the midday sun.

The descent was much enlivened by a joint decision (in keeping with the best traditions of the Alpine Club) to perform a sort of kamikaze dive off the ridge down a scree gully that looked as if it might run out safely onto the glacier far below. Needless to say it didn't, and the vertical iced-up waterfall halfway down had to be duly overcome by abseils and some intricate manoeuvring. Soaked with icy water, we raced down the final screes to the afternoon sunshine, and a wonderfully vivid emerald green lake at the foot of the glacier where I indulged once more in my passion for skinny-dipping. (There weren't many days when I didn't find a glacial pool or river to swim in, having been trained in Siberia!) Just beyond the lake, a yak and her calf grazed among blue trumpet gentians and edelweiss.

Some of the most striking memories of this trip came from the last few days, when we borrowed horses from the local shepherds and went trekking round into the next valley. The etherial quality of the evening sunlight across the vast plains and distant mountain ranges, combined with the tremendous welcome we received from local nomads along the way, was unforgettable. Though I am no novice to riding, I found the experience totally hair-raising – struggling across boulder-fields, cliffs, ravines and near-vertical screes – all the while clinging on to our guide for dear life, on his pony's bouncing rump! We had to share horses, as a stallion had made off with our two best mares.

On the final night we partied with the shepherds in one of their summer yurts (they winter down in the Karakol valley). Later, I found myself galloping off in the moonlight with a drunken shepherd hanging round my neck, the fiery pony leaping streams and marmot holes, with wild Asian songs drifting across the valley. Fortunately I succeeded in locating the whereabouts of Base Camp in the gloom and unshipped from the pony just in time!

**Summary**:  In the summer of 1994 the Anglo-Russian Expedition to the Tien Shan spent a month in the Khrebet Borkoldoy range.

*Team members*:  Phil Bartlett, Marian Elmes, Larry Hooton, Nadia Lukina, Alan Martley, Jane Sanderson, together with five members from Russia/ Kazakhstan/Kyrgyzstan.  Helpers  included a cook, a doctor, a Chinese-speaking liaison officer and a masseur/radio operator.

*Peaks climbed*:  Mike Parsons, Phil Bartlett, Marian Elmes and Larry Hooton between them climbed nine virgin peaks  at 4500-5000m, including 'Three Crevasse Peak', *c*5000m.

7.  The 1993 K2 West Ridge Expedition.  The West Face of K2.
    (*Jonathan Wakefield*)  (p39)

18.　Jonathan Pratt and Dan Mazur between Camps 2 and 3 (at about 6700m). (*Jonathan Wakefield*) (p39)

19.　Camp 2, at 6600m, after a heavy snowfall. (*Jonathan Wakefield*) (p39)

0. Jonathan Pratt (L) and Andy Collins setting up Camp 3 at 7100m.
   (*Dan Mazur*)  (p39)

1. Jonathan Pratt digging a platform for Camp 5 at 8100m.
   (*Jonathan Wakefield*)  (p39)

22. The Indian British Kinnaur Expedition. Advanced Base Camp below Rangrik Rang, 6553m. The summit route followed the L skyline. (*Chris Bonington*) (p57)

23. The climbing team. *Clockwise from R*: Jim Lowther, Muslim Contractor, Jim Curran, Chris Bonington, Harish Kapadia, Vijay Kothari, Paul Nunn, Graham Little, Kaivan Mistry, Joginder Singh Gulia (liaison officer), Jim Fotheringham, Divyesh Muni. (*Chris Bonington*) (p57)

24. Rangrik Rang, 6553m. Jim Fotheringham on the fixed ropes between Camps 1 and 2. (*Chris Bonington*) (p57)

25. Reo Pargial (Purgyil), 6816m, the southern of the Pargials climbed in 1991. The highest peak of Himachal Pradesh, it rises above the Sutlej river at Shipkila. (*Paul Nunn*) (p65)

26. Paul Nunn on the summit of Manirang, 6593m. (*Paul Nunn*) (p65)

27. The North Ridge of K2: séracs above the bergschrund. (*Alan Hinkes*) (p71)

28. Digging out a shelf for Camp 1 at 6000m. The tent was later flattened by an avalanche. (*Alan Hinkes*) (p71)

9. At 6800m – the view from Camp 2 towards China, the K2 glacier below. (*Alan Hinkes*) (p71)

. At 8100m – looking back towards Camp 4 and a 3000m drop below the tent to the K2 glacier. (*Alan Hinkes*) (p71)

31. K2, the North Ridge. (*Alan Hinkes*) (p71)

32. Crossing the raging Shaksgam on the trek out. (*Alan Hinkes*) (p71)

JOSÉ LUIS BERMÚDEZ
# Crab Crawl on the Bezingi Wall

*(Plates 33, 34)*

'You may bivouac here,' said the saturnine Yuri Saratov, pointing his finger somewhere to the leftmost end of the long panoramic photo of the Bezingi Wall. He looked hard at us and walked about four paces to his right: 'Next bivouac,' he commented, pointing straight in front of him. Then, in case we hadn't got the message, he swung his arm back to the left and intoned: 'No bivouacs from Shkhara Main to Shkhara West.' By his standards he was being rather chirpy. Saratov's usual reaction to a proposed route was to pore over his prized collection of photos and point out the noted accident blackspots of the last thirty years. 'Any questions?' he asked, after informing us that the control time was eight days. We had none. 'You will take radio,' he commanded. We didn't have the heart to argue. It was, after all, the Russian way. Our call sign was Saturn 28.

We were there because I had found myself in the peculiar position of being a modest, although published, authority on an area I had never visited, or even gone near – the Central Caucasus. When the peer pressure became intolerable I finally decided to investigate my own description of the Caucasus as a natural playground for the adventurous climber, combining the grandeur of the Himalaya with the accessibility and technical challenge of the Alps, etc, etc. One of my worries was how awful it would be to flog all the way there only to discover 600 miles of snow-covered slag heaps crawling with trigger-happy Chechens. But the main worry was that the routes I was thinking of doing there looked dangerous. Particularly the grand traverse of the Bezingi Wall.

The Bezingi Wall is the show-piece of the Central Caucasus. It is an enormous north-facing wall, 15 or so kilometres long with 7 peaks and 11 summits, the highest of them over 5000m and rising 2000m above the glacier. Looking at it from the valley the eye is met with a vast swathe of improbably balanced séracs and the odd few islands of rotting rock. The good thing about the traverse is that it goes right over the top, neatly avoiding the conspicuous objective danger. The bad thing about it is that once on it there's only one place to get off, and even from 2000m below it was clear that there was mile after mile of gently overhanging cornice. The Bezingi Wall is the first thing the weather hits after roaring across the plains of Georgia, and the ridge has weird and wonderful features to prove it. The traverse of the Bezingi Wall was the route to do, as I had written in several places. I was particularly keen on it because I've always preferred climbing sideways to climbing upwards, despite the common prejudice to the contrary. Eventually I managed to persuade Neil Wilson, of Scullomie, near Tongue, to overcome his natural disinclination to climb outside Scotland. The Central Caucasus was just the thing for Neil, who was looking for new challenges now that he was running out of Munroes.

Our first attempt was short and sweet. Leaving the delightful Austrian bivouac in a Caucasian drizzle reminiscent of Scotland we found ourselves some hours later in a storm battling up the unpleasant ice of the Cockin couloir to meet the NE ridge of Shkhara. The ice was hard and progress slow. We were both reminded how much we hated 50° ice. A pitch below the bivvy site one of the bolts on my ice axe head fell out, creating the droopy pick familiar to owners of Mountain Technology Vertiges. The storm was still raging as we pitched the tent. We decided that we hated the Cockin couloir so much that we would press on anyway with three axes. The next morning we duly did, but failed to get very far. One of Neil's claims to fame is starring in a phenomenally expensive rescue on Ben Nevis when he was avalanched off the top of the Orion Face and broke a leg falling the full length of the rope. This made him rather sensitive to the presence of windslab and when the ridge started cracking and rolling, a few pitches further on the next morning, he refused to continue.

The retreat took a while, with the weather gradually improving the further we got from our high point. Just as we climbed the moraine to the Austrian Bivouac the clouds parted and a rosy sunset settled over the Bezingi Wall. It was clear we would have to make another attempt. But we were running out of time and still short of an ice axe. We would only have a chance to finish the route by leaving at the latest the morning after next. The only solution was for one of us to make a desperate trip to Camp Bezingi and back the next day. I was chosen. The round trip only took 10 hours of flogging up and down the character-building Bezingi glacier. At the Camp a helpful man welded my ice axe back together in a brutally effective manner. I don't think I'll ever have trouble from it again. Neil spent the day watching all the windslab fall off the ridge, or so he hoped.

We set off again at one the next morning. This time the weather was fine and we made good progress, although we were both quite tired. We bivvied on the NE ridge, a long way above our previous site. It was a perfect bivvy site, large and flat. It was a while before we saw another one of those. The next day was a short one. We pressed on up the magnificently corniced ridge to the summit (5200m), where we enjoyed the first of several extremely chilly and extremely scenic bivvies, looking out to the north across the whole of the Central Caucasus, and to the south over a remarkably lush Georgia. The contrast between the two sides of the wall was striking. Georgia has trees and fields and villages. Russia has glaciers and moraine. But the good thing about the Russian side, apart from the pork fat at Camp Bezingi, is that they don't shoot foreigners there.

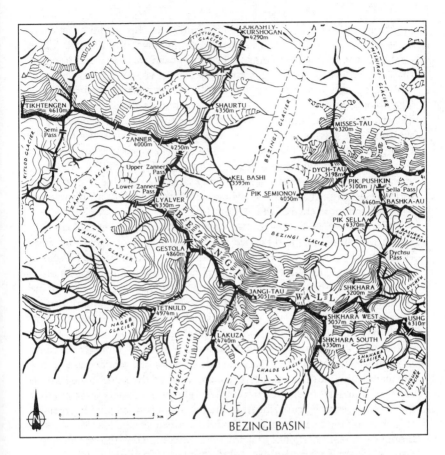

BEZINGI BASIN

A whaleback ridge descended westwards from the summit of Shkhara. We thought it was great. Unfortunately we could only gambol down it for 200m before the serious business of climbing sideways started. The ridge narrowed to a corniced crest, falling away steeply on both sides. We frontpointed sideways just below the crest, moving together on very insecure ice. Most of the time we stayed on the Georgian side, but occasionally we crossed the cornice and shifted operations into Russia to avoid some particularly foul stretches of ice. It was a rather peculiar feeling, teetering like a crab for hour after hour above a 2000m drop. But we were making good time and just managed to beat the evening storm to a plateau where we bivvied, somewhere near the West Peak of Shkhara.

But the good times couldn't last for ever. On day 4 we set out just after dawn. The cloud had come down, as it often did, but we followed the crest of the ridge in a generally westward direction. The ice was awful but we had got used to it by now, and breezed along. But after 30 minutes or so the topography of the ridge started to get more complicated, with ridges appearing off to the side. We hadn't bargained for this, and the last thing we wanted to do was charge off down the wrong ridge into Georgia. All we could do was take regular compass bearings, head westward and hope for the best. We were using Neil's compass, since I've never been very sure which bit points where, until it occurred to us that it might not be working. The obvious answer was to get mine out and double check, and so we did. Unfortunately, as it was being extracted from the top of my pack, the case with my sun glasses also emerged and bounced off down the face into Georgia. I was extremely annoyed, since they were prescription Raybans that had cost a fair whack. And then it hit me that neither of us had brought spares, in a stupid attempt to keep the rucksacks manageable. We were in a serious mess, with guaranteed snowblindness in the middle of a long traverse. This was incompetence of the highest order.

Things got worse. Even with two compasses to point us in the right direction we still got lost and headed off down the wrong ridge in the mist. Realising our mistake we retraced our steps back up to the ridge. The cloud refused to lift. Every time it looked as if a gap was opening up one of us would belt up to the top of the ridge, taking a gamble on falling through the cornice, and hoping that we would see some familiar landmark on the Russian side. Inevitably the gap closed before we had a chance to look through it. So we sidepointed sideways hoping that we would at least find somewhere flat enough to bivvy. Nowhere appeared. Eventually we came to what we later worked out was the first of the seven gendarmes that are the technical crux of the route. The clean crest of the ridge turned into a series of pinnacles of shattered rock. We didn't immediately work out that this was the seventh gendarme (they are confusingly numbered in reverse). It looked too big and complicated to be described as a gendarme. We still thought it a real possibility that we were on completely the wrong ridge. For some bizarre reason we decided to abseil into a couloir between two of the pinnacles to see if we could work round at a lower level. This was a mistake. Just as the second man was down the wind got up and it started hailing. Stones came flying down from the pinnacles above, and little avalanches started running down. Neil's Scottish training came in handy here, as he teetered back up the snow-covered slabs we had just foolishly abseiled down.

The weather was getting even worse. There wasn't much daylight left, and we clearly needed to bivvy. We poked hopefully at a few heaps of snow on the pinnacles that looked as if they might become snow holes, but they all fell apart to reveal huge drops down to the Bezingi glacier. Then I suddenly remembered falling into a crevasse not long before the pinnacles. Perhaps it could be expanded into a snow hole. The hole I'd left was still there and Neil disappeared into it to start excavating. I waited outside, listening to him getting down to work. The crevasse was about 15 feet below the crest of the ridge. After a few minutes he popped his head out to announce that we had a home for the night. It appeared to be an intercontinental crevasse stretching from Asian Georgia to European Russia. We didn't investigate too far, but it did look as if that part of the Bezingi Wall was honeycombed with interconnecting layers of air. It was certainly very draughty.

Things weren't looking good. We were stranded in a storm in a crevasse halfway between the summits of Shkhara and Jangi-Tau. Since Shkhara West we had been going more or less steadily downhill, and we didn't fancy reversing the route. Ahead of us lay the seven gendarmes that were supposed to be the hardest part of the traverse. There was a storm raging outside and, to cap it all, I was swiftly going snowblind after a day without sunglasses. We settled down for a cold and miserable night beneath the drip of meltwater.

The next morning things had picked up slightly. The storm had cleared and we could see the way ahead. Or rather, Neil could. I couldn't see a thing. My glasses were covered with sticking plaster leaving just a slit in the middle in a vain attempt to recreate the Rayban effect. We set off across the gendarmes. It wasn't entirely clear where the number seven came from. It seemed to be either one very big gendarme about a kilometre and a half long, or hundreds of little ones. It would have been very good fun if I had been able to see anything, but it turned out rather awkward, not least since we had to pitch everything. Neil went in front to do the route finding and talked me past the (to him) obvious cornices and treacherous snow-covered slabs. I followed instructions. This was all very well moving up the gendarmes, but rather traumatic coming down the other side when it was my turn at the sharp end of the rope, particularly since I had had to take a triple helping of dihydrocodeine to alleviate the pain in my eyes.

Progress was excruciatingly slow on day five. We didn't make it through the gendarmes but bivvied at the first flat place we found. I dosed my eyes that night with amethocaine and by the morning I could see again. The weather held and we were reasonably optimistic about finishing the route. After the last gendarme it was a quick plod from the Sandro Saddle up to Jangi East (5030m), across to Main and then West Jangi (5051m), over the gendarmes of the Saw of Katyn-Tau, and then Katyn-Tau itself (4970m) to the Katyn Plateau, which we had been told was magnificently flat and wide, and then over three progressively smaller summits to reach the Zanner Pass. Three days from the Sandro Saddle, we had been told. We had done the hard bits. It was just a question of hanging on for the rest of the route.

But day six didn't go well. We were still moving at a snail's pace. Neil had given me his sun-glasses and was now paying the price by slowly going snowblind himself. The previous five days had taken their toll. It took the whole day to get to the Sandro saddle. Just before the final gendarme I slipped on a particularly brittle and horrible ice traverse. Neil's ice axe belay pulled out, but he managed to hold the fall before we both went flying into Georgia.

In a moment our attitude to the climb changed completely. From having our sights fixed on the Zanner Pass we went instantly to the decision to bale out at the earliest opportunity. It was clear that the odds were on another stupid mistake from one or the other of us, and it wasn't clear that the route was worth it. Fortunately we were within striking distance of the one point on the whole ridge from which retreat is feasible – the NE ridge of Jangi East, which we had already ascended as a prudent training climb.

That night we bivouacked on the Sandro Saddle. There was some brief talk of going on, but it didn't last for long. The usual afternoon snowfall turned into a thunderstorm, the first we had experienced on the traverse. The Bezingi Wall is the highest and most obvious feature in the area, and the top of it was a scary place to be when there was lightning flying about all over the place. Mackerel skies suggested that the bad weather would last. The final straw came when we worked out what day it was and realised that our flight to Moscow was leaving in three days time. Even if we finished the route in three days we would have had to walk through the night back to Camp Bezingi to make it to Mineralnye Vodye in time. That wasn't feasible. The fleshpots of Camp Bezingi were starting to look tempting, and the next morning we succumbed at dawn. We arrived back at the Austrian Bivouac just after ten that evening. Anti-climactic of course, but still rather a relief. Our 'controller' and other Russian friends were pleased to see us, which was quite surprising since we both looked awful.

One can always tell how much of an epic one has had by how long the resolution never to leave the ground again lasts. This time it was nearly three days. Perhaps it wasn't so bad after all. In fact we probably quite enjoyed it. The Bezingi glacier was the best place to climb I've ever been to. But I would advise anybody planning a visit there not to underestimate the routes. It's not the Himalaya, but it's certainly not the Alps!

**Summary**: The Bezingi region in the Central Caucasus was visited this summer by José Luis Bermúdez and Neil Wilson. Their principal objective was the first British traverse of the Bezingi Wall from Shkhara to Lyalver. A combination of bad weather, sickness and incompetence forced them off the route after seven days. They climbed the hardest and most serious section of the traverse from Shkhara to East Jangi Tau, which is graded at Russian 5B. They felt that this equated to ED1/2, despite being technically far easier than any equivalently graded route in the Alps.

They also climbed the Cockin route on Jangi Tau, down which they later retreated (Russian 4B, Alpine D sup) and the traverse from Pik Warsaw to Pik Sella (Russian 3A, Alpine AD).

# Africa's Mountains

HAMISH M BROWN

# Opportunities in the Western Atlas

High in the Western Atlas lies the 'Lost World' Tichka plateau. It is not so much a plateau as the hollow head of the Oued (river) Nfis, its many joining streams coming together in meadows yellow with thousands of tiny hoop-petticoat daffodils – a magic sort of place, made doubly so by its rim of peaks whose outer edges fall in cliffs or steep valleys for thousands of feet. The peaks carry snow till well into spring and make an improbable backcloth to the romantic walled city of Taroudant in the Souss plain, just 50 miles inland from Agadir.

The Oued Nfis which drains this special place runs through evergreen oak forest, granite gorges, romantic villages and thuya forest down to Ijoukak on the Marrakech–Tizi n' Test–Taroudant road, then wends on, eastwards still, for another 20 miles to Ouirgane where eventually it breaks out onto the Haouz plain, west of Marrakech. Looking south from Marrakech the view is to Jbel Toubkal, 4167m, the highest summit in North Africa. A party of us who have roamed all these areas fulfilled a dream and made a ten-day trek from the Tichka plateau to Toubkal.

Though I had been wandering about the Atlas ranges for over 20 years I was late in discovering the special qualities of the Western Atlas. (Everyone heads for the Toubkal massif, as they do for Snowdon or Ben Nevis or Mont Blanc.) Aziz, a mountain man working in Taroudant, kept saying I must go up with him and see the Tichka plateau and its approach valleys. Eventually I did – and have been back every year for the last decade. I have a permanent base with Mohammed and his family above Imlil, the nascent 'Chamonix' of the Atlas.

In 1991 a party of us, primarily looking for mountain flowers (far more dangerous than climbing!), made the first descent of the Nfis with local Berbers. They didn't know if mules could get through, so it was quite an adventure for them; but if the Nfis 'went' then a Tichka to Toubkal super-walk would be a practical reality. The following year it was proved so – and great fun, for the activity itself, the superb scenery, and the lively lads who carried our gear on the six mules, cooked tasty local dishes for us, baked bread on hot stones, provided ceilidhs at the nightly bonfires and generally enlivened every mile of the way. We were thoroughly spoilt! In return we gave Aziz and his assistant Ali their first days of tuition with crampons and ice axes. We were also training two of them as guides; for Aziz and Mohammed were keen to organise treks for small groups of British – a modest economical input, not mass exploitation. Not another Toubkal! They were also determined to respect the local traditions and culture, and all junk carried in is carried out. Since the idea for such a project came from *them*, I became a willing partner in its implementation.

These people were wonderful to work with: Aziz with his charming kids; Ali, young and keen, a born mountaineer; Hussein, the big, jovial, efficient cook; young Mustapha on his first assignment; Mustapha's old father whose house we lived in at Tagmout. We shopped in the local *souk* (market), used local muleteers and made many local contacts. It was a great joy and a great privilege to meet such people.

We flew to Marrakech and then drove to Taroudant over the Tizi-n-Test road, thus bisecting the walking route at one place. This was historically Goundafa (*Lords of the Atlas*) country and of the reforming 12th century Berber Almohad dynasty, which ended with an empire stretching from the Sahara through half of Spain, begun by the Oued Nfis.

From drizzly London to supper under the stars on a square in Taroudant is quite a contrast; and so was the approach to the mountains next day. This was a five-hour haul by *camionette* (pick-up), starting in argan and palm country and ending among green terraces, flowers, and walnuts in new leaf. A traditional meal (and mint tea) in a traditional house displaced London even further!

The Upper Medlawa must be one of the most beautiful mountain valleys anywhere: an amazing greenness set among basically desert mountains ringed with stark peaks. Starting from Tagmout, the morning walk was shady but in the afternoon we ground our way up endless zigzags to the Tizi n' Targa (*c*2920m), the first pass onto the top end of the Tichka plateau. A band of snow gave the mules some trouble. A week earlier the *tizi* (pass) would have been impossible. That day and the next were spent 'Munro-bagging': climbing several of the 3000m peaks on the plateau rim and being mightily impressed at the rock and mixed climbing that lies untried so far. Imaradene, 3351m, was the highest but Ras Moulay Ali, 3349m, and the ridge westwards ('The Ridge of a Hundred Peaks') offered alpine opportunities we could not tackle then.

Bitter, unseasonable winds made life difficult for the less well equipped Berbers (we're slowly scrounging gear for them – contributions welcome!) so we walked right down the plateau the next day for a delectable riverside camp in the Tiziatin forest where the barren backcloth is given a soft pile of evergreen oak. A mixture of forest and granite gorges took us a day's march to the first village, Agadir, where our muleteers provided a fantastic entertainment that had the whole village crowding courtyard and rooftops to enjoy the music and dancing. In contrast, the day after linked village after village of local architectural interest, crowded with shy, beautiful children and women in colourful garments. We swam too and stayed overnight at Souk Sebt ('the Saturday market village') before thuya and juniper forest eventually led us to a village near the Tizi n' Test road. Here Aziz's muleteers turned for home in the Medlawa and Mohammed's muleteers were waiting for the rest of the trek to Imlil and Toubkal.

A day by the enlarged river Nfis took us to Ijoukak, a posting stage on the motor road, where the always different, always good eating was maintained. Hussein provided *tagines* (slow-cooked casserole-like dishes) with tasty fresh vegetables, spices, herbs and some meat or side dish. We took along plenty of dried fruits too. Moroccan food is a topic in itself. Another treat was a small *hammam* (sauna), which removed the dust and sweat of days.

A series of splendid passes under the snowy vastness of Tazharhart led us to Imlil and Mohammed's house. A whole day was spent regaining all the height we had lost, to the Tizi n' Iguidi, *c*2150m, and a bivouac by the first torrent beyond. Big, spacious country led to the Tizi n' Ouarhou and a descent into gorges again for a camp by the river. The Tizi Mzic, 2489m, leads directly over to Imlil (1670m) and is the real ending but we explored an alternative further north, trackless and rough, descending from the Tizi Oudite at 2219m. Mohammed's house overlooks Imlil – a welcome gîte with showers and lights provided by solar panels.

We went up to the slum of the Neltner hut (3200m). People were sleeping on and under the table and the exterior surrounds were hardly pleasant. We arrived with a thunderstorm. There was no way novices Aziz and Ali could cope with the conditions, so most of us (having been up Toubkal already) came back down. By setting off at 1.30am, the keen were able to crampon all the way up and stood on the top of North Africa to watch the dawn: the dream climax end to a dream trek.

To compress the Tichka to Toubkal trek description as I have done gives it a simplistic flavour perhaps. The country itself is tough and complex, maps near-impossible to obtain, while coping with transport and buying food offers a minefield for the uninitiated. Morocco is a fantastic cultural shock. Because of our contacts with Aziz, Ali, Hussein, Mohammed and the rest, it was as memorable an experience as any we had known – and, between us, our party had ranged over most of the mountain areas of the world. These are the intangibles that make something special.

Aziz and Mohammed now hope to offer their services in organising similar treks for English-speaking groups only. It seems a long way from the time Aziz interrupted my work (writing) at Taroudant with his plea 'Come and see my country!' From his dream has evolved this joint venture.

*Anyone interested in making this Tichka to Toubkal trek is welcome to get in touch. The best times to go are May, June, September, October. The Tichka plateau is worth visiting at any time, offering winter climbing from February to April and rock-climbing all the year round. Aziz, in Taroudant, can tailor superb below-the-snowline wanderings in spring and autumn. Mohammed can do the same at the Imlil-Toubkal end. I can sometimes help with supplying maps, now virtually unobtainable.*

### Useful addresses:
*Hamish Brown, Atlas Mountains Information Services (AMIS), 21 Carlin Craig, Kinghorn, Fife KY3 9RX. Tel 0592-890422. Please send SAE.*
*Tali Abd el Aziz, B.P. 132, Taroudant, Morocco. Tel 010-212-885-3501*
*Aït Idir Mohammed, B.P. 26, Asni, par Marrakech, Morrocco*
*Hotel Ali, rue Moulay Ismaïl, Marrakech, Morrocco. Tel 010-212-04-449-79*

MICHAEL PEYRON

# Middle Atlas Berber Poetry

The Atlas mountains of Morocco constitute a vast, varied and complex highland mass, one of the most extensive in Africa – also, one of the most lived in. Its Berber inhabitants, known among themselves as *imazighen,* are a thrifty, hardy and highly likeable people. Having often visited and stayed with these mountaineers, and taught myself *tamazight,* or Berber, I have endeavoured, over the years, to collect a comprehensive sample of their oral literature, including their poetry.

The purpose of this article is to give a brief introduction to the poetic production of a linguistic area embracing most of the Middle Atlas, together with a chunk of the Eastern High Atlas. This region contains some of the highest summits in Morocco, snow-capped from October to May, including Jbel el 'Ayyachi (3727m), Ma'asker (3265m) and Bu Iblan (3192m). There are also vast plateaux, frequented every summer by transhumant shepherds with tents, deep gorges and mercurial torrents fed by snow-melt. The best grazing is on upland meadows called *ilmuten,* often in the vicinity of pristine, monkey-haunted cedar forests. After a short, hot summer the herdsmen and their charges regain either fortified villages, called *igherman,* or semi-dispersed village clusters, where other activities, chiefly agriculture and woodcutting, are concentrated. Once the harvest is in, there are collective marriage ceremonies (*timghriwin*), after which all and sundry hunker down to see the winter through. Owing to centuries of abuse and misuse, however, with overgrazing, 'slash and burn', and a high soil erosion factor, coupled with the effects of a semi-arid, intensely continental climate, entire ecosystems are now under threat. Likewise, given the intrusion of the transistor radio, television, mopeds, canned goods and plastic, a whole culture is at risk.

Unsurprisingly, life in such a harsh environment tends to be tough. And yet the Berbers bear up bravely in the face of adversity. Attachment to their roots, together with their proverbial resilience in the face of outside interference, has so far guaranteed their survival. Poetry, produced with instrumental accompaniment, singing and dancing, is arguably the most visible feature of their culture. It is also an excellent way of letting off steam. Hence, apart from set occasions such as weddings, circumcisions, return from pilgrimage and official, or national, celebrations, Middle Atlas Berbers organise several impromptu song-and-dance sessions throughout the year. Participants are members of the village youth association, or *l'amt,* and things get under way on the village square after dark on a moonlit night, to the accompaniment of drum and fiddle or lute. Dancing usually takes place near a fire, useful for tightening up the skin of a drum, and young girls, sometimes reinforced by widows and divorced women, join in. The most widespread form is known as *ahidus*, with the dancers swaying, side-stepping, hand-clapping in line. The corpus of songs consists mostly of unrhymed couplets, called *izlan*, featuring assonance and alliteration.

Apart from the dancing, attention is mainly focused on the skill, or otherwise, demonstrated by the chief singer, or improviser (*anechchad*) who is supposed to give a flawless performance, especially if a rival bard is on the scene. The dancers are expected to provide back-up vocals throughout, which makes the whole experience a somewhat exhausting one. Despite close proximity of members of the opposite sex, participants are honour bound to respect certain rules of propriety. Although the singing invariably highlights the theme of spurned or unrequited love, the highly coded language remains essentially correct despite oblique allusions to sex, usually by means of symbols known to the community but unintelligible to outsiders. Furthermore, the dimension conjured up by these sung poems is both imaginary and idealised, the moral being that, through dancing and singing about these matters, participants can work off a possible surfeit of sexual frustration.

The main preoccupation in these songs is to honour the tryst with one's lover who lives far away, on the other side of the hill. The meeting-place will be in the densely-wooded area (*'ari*), or close to the mountain peaks which are constantly referred to and perceived as the ideal love-making environment. Apart from parents or rivals, the usual factors that thwart lovers are natural phenomena such as snowfall, a river in spate, or sheer physical distance. Readers will observe how down-to-earth some couplets are, contrasting with slightly more sophisticated efforts, running to several hemistiches, when lovers' quarrels and final partings are evoked. Throughout this poetry there runs a passionate streak, a blind adherence to the code of honour, to the given word, that is one of the main aspects of the Berbers' make-up.

FURTHER READING

Michael Peyron, *Great Atlas Traverse, Morocco*, 2 volumes. West Col Productions, 1989/90.

**On Middle Atlas Berber poetry:**
Michael Peyron, *"Isaffen Ghbanin" (Rivières Profondes)*. Wallada, Casablanca, 1994.

# Middle Atlas Berber poetry
collected and translated by Michael Peyron between 1981 and 1991

Weep not! Snow has fallen in the hills,
The passes are closed; your lover cannot travel!

\* \* \*

Greetings lofty mountain, and you,
   o countenances sweet!
On this day was written that we were to meet!

\* \* \*

Come and rest in the shade, let me quench your thirst,
Shelter by my side from the sun's burning rays,
Comfort and solace will I provide, whatever the price!

\* \* \*

O sage, read well your book of magic arts,
Charge the highest fee, but of this passion rid me!
Bow down, o mountain, may you through a miracle
Become a plain, that my beloved I may see again!

\* \* \*

Could I but enter the forest,
In the company of wild beasts,
And there sojourn with my beloved,
Safely hidden from prying eyes!

\* \* \*

Now you cloak me in the thickest of vapours,
   now the clouds
Do float away;  o mist, I am indeed your mountain!

\* \* \*

Should you hear overhead the raven's croak,
Will be but me reminding you, o beloved,
Of the promise that you failed to keep!

Mother, by the mountains I do swear: sleep I cannot!
By all that is Holy, God has inflicted upon me
    an incurable disease!
Had a bullet wounded me, a remedy would find;
Had a loved one died, consolation would seek
    through weeping;
My beloved, however, did slightingly ignore me!

* * *

Be downcast, o traitorous eyes,
You who did delude my heart!
Should the westerlies blow,
My tent's crossbeam would tremble!
Have I strength to climb the hill
Beyond which sojourns my sweetheart?
Would that she were beside me,
On this our parting day!

* * *

Like the venerable eagle,
Would that I could wheel aloft on broad pinions;
Yet my strength fails me,
My heart yearns for the topmost peaks!

* * *

Sit down and gaze at the night sky,
Until the stars do emerge;
He whom you seek exists not!

* * *

Have long neglected to replenish my foothill store-house,
Who knows when the snows will force me to seek
    refuge there!

* * *

Life is like unto a piece of carrion!
God gave it the semblance of a gazelle grazing
    on the mountainslope;
Down into the plain the hunter pursues her,
And when his time is come, Fate whisks him away!

PAUL CLARKE

# Mount Kenya's Diamond Couloir

*(Plate: back cover)*

'Hold,' I shouted, as I fell into space and the rope went tight. We were on Mount Kenya's Diamond Couloir. This was the apex of my climbing ambitions, but I was two metres up (with three hundred and ninety-eight to go) and not doing well. Ulf was suspended from an ice screw and I wondered how secure it was.

The Diamond Couloir is the ice-filled gully that runs straight up to the gap between Nelion and Batian (5199m), Mount Kenya's twin summits. It is perhaps the finest line on any big mountain in the world. This was a practice for our attempt the next morning. Practice is hard to come by for Kenyan-based ice climbers. The Diamond Couloir requires 400m of climbing, and takes about 12 hours. But to walk in, acclimatise to altitude, climb, descend and walk out, you have to allow a week.

I regained the ice, and had another go. The first pitch is nearly vertical, and the ice thin. The recession of the glaciers following climate changes means that there is hardly enough ice at the bottom these days. A slight corner held the best ice, and the difficulty was twisting from right to left on exiting from its top. On my first attempt I had swung out of balance, and so into space. On my second, I was more careful. I made it to easier ground. But it was still steep and I was panting hard at over 4500m.

'What happened?' Ulf asked, but before I could answer, we were hit by a massive spindrift avalanche. It was like having a stream of sugar poured over my head, only much colder. I was in a precarious position, and holding tight onto my ice axes. Ulf grabbed my hood and pulled it over my head. After 10 minutes the avalanche eased to the point we could move. It was midday and they were going to get more frequent. We slid down the ropes to the foot of the climb, and then descended 200m to the bottom of the Lower Darwin glacier. I was exhausted and sat down and nibbled chocolate.

'Do you think we can make it?' I asked Ulf, thinking retreat might be prudent.

'Well I'm feeling strong, and we can only try; I'm happy to lead all the hard bits,' Ulf, a 6ft 4in Swede, declared. Then, to prove the point: 'I don't think I have had enough exercise for today,' he announced, and set off up for a tour of the glacier.

Ever since I came to live in Kenya in 1985 the Diamond Couloir has been top of my list of climbs to do, although at grade VI (UIAA) it was intimidatingly hard for me and I kept on putting it off. But seeing it again on a recent walking trip had rekindled my enthusiasm and I had picked on Ulf as the strongest climber I know. And being from Sweden, he was familiar with ice. I had asked him one regular Tuesday evening, at the Mountain Club of Kenya's bar, if he was game. To my later horror, he simply said 'Why not?' Having about ten months to wait for the season gave me rather too long to contemplate the wisdom of my ambitions.

From the foot of the glacier, we retreated our way down 200m over boulders to the Black Hole bivvy. The Black Hole is a large overhanging rock, with stone walls to create some shelter. At the foot of a glacier, it is cold. With about 60cm of headroom, it is also uncomfortable. It was our bedroom for the night.

Reveille was at 2.30am but it took nearly two hours to brew up, have breakfast, brew again, and pack. We clambered over the boulders by the light of our head torches and sat down at the foot of the glacier to put on our crampons. Ulf was ready first.

'I'll go up and sort the ropes out,' he announced, as he set off up the glacier.

By the time I caught up and Ulf was ready to climb, dawn was coming. Ulf set off up the first pitch. Soon he reached the awkward bit where I had fallen off. He clipped the rope into an ice screw, made a move up and fell off.

'Hold!' he exclaimed. 'Hell, this is hard!'

He was still cold and not moving well. The fall had left him in a horizontal position held by the rope, facing up with his crampons in the ice. He set about disentangling himself, and then continued up.

With the benefit of the previous day's experience, I managed to follow up without any further mishap. We carried on for several more pitches before stopping for some blueberry soup from our thermos. The trouble with getting up at 2.30am is that breakfast does not go down well. Blueberry soup is a popular Swedish brew guaranteed to revive on all occasions. As often with good food on extreme safaris, it sounds revolting contemplated in Nairobi before or afterwards, but at the time it seemed indispensable.

Ahead loomed the headwall – the crux of the Diamond Couloir. Nearly vertical, it comes near the top when you are committed.

'Does it look possible do you think?' Ulf asked, while we had our brew.

'Well, that's for you to decide,' I said, thankful that Ulf was proving such a determined companion. It looked nasty.

I led a steep pitch to the foot of the headwall. I was on the right-hand side of the gully. I banged a piton into a crack in the rock with my ice hammer, tied myself to it, and brought Ulf up. A piton, rather than an ice screw, was reassuring before the headwall.

'Well led,' commented Ulf. My confidence was growing slowly, and I began to feel that we might make it.

I handed over some gear to Ulf, triple checked that everything was secure, and he led off. It was slow work, Ulf putting in an ice screw every two metres. After about seven metres he disappeared around a corner. The mist had come in and I started to feel very alone. A lot of spindrift started to fall on me from above, and I had to constantly clear it from the rope. A long delay followed while Ulf secured himself, and I started shivering violently.

There was a shout to continue. I was too cold to be terrified as I tentatively pulled up onto the headwall. It looks vertical; it feels vertical. It is in fact about 85°. That five degrees off vertical gives just enough room for you to stand in balance over the front points of your crampons. I reached up high with one ice axe, and swung it into the ice. The ice here was good and it gave a firm placement the first time. I swung the other. It held too. Then, hanging back on the handles of the axes, I pulled my way up the wall, kicking in firmly with my crampons until my hands were level with my chest. Then came the hardest bit. Hugging the wall so I was in balance, I gingerly freed the right ice axe. At this point it was hard not to swing away from the wall and lose contact. Two swings of the ice axe secured another good placement, and I repeated the whole manoeuvre. A further repetition brought me to Ulf's first ice screw. I hung on with one ice axe, while using the pick from the other to wind out the screw.

I carried on, only to be hit by another spindrift avalanche. I closed my eyes and hugged the wall, hoping that most of it would spill over my back. It was impossible to move. Standing on front points places a great strain on your calf muscles, and hanging on the ice axes puts a great strain on your arms. I started to lose strength. I managed to clip a sling from my harness into the loop at the bottom of the ice axe. I hung there, 300 metres beneath me, suspended in my harness tied to an ice axe with its pick one centimetre into the ice, and waited for the avalanche to pass. After five minutes I could move again. Another two metres took me to an awkward step around a rock, and a few moves sideways across the top of the wall I had come up brought me to the edge of easier ground. I dared for the first time to look down. The mist cleared a little and I could see the whole climb dropping away below. The situation was superb. I continued quickly now to reach Ulf.

The headwall continued above. Ulf had spent all his nerves on the first part, and went on, putting in ice screws every one or two metres. His concentration on this task made him oblivious to progress, for after about 15 minutes he looked down to me and exclaimed 'Christ, is that all I have done.'

But the angle soon eased off, and Ulf found himself on the lip of the Diamond Glacier, the one that hangs beneath Nelion and Batian. I followed onto the wall. As soon as I reached the steepest part another avalanche hit.

I was stuck for what seemed like 15 minutes and got fearsomely cold. I wondered if I would ever move again that day.

Finally the avalanche eased and, wiping the snow from under my glasses, I joined Ulf. The glacier is about four rope lengths high. It is steep but not hard. By now we were completely exhausted. I led up to a convenient stopping point and told Ulf I would bring him up. 'But there is still plenty of rope to go,' he replied sternly. I struggled on. The snow was soft, which made it hard work. After every ten steps I had to pause for a minute to regain my breath. Slowly we gained the Gate of the Mists, the notch between the two peaks. We paused to finish the blueberry soup. One short ice pitch up the north side of Nelion and a scramble brought us to the summit. It was 7pm and dark. Every move took all our mental concentration to summon up the effort.

On top of Nelion is a small hut, wide enough for four people to lie down and high enough to sit up. It is made of sheet metal with a foam-lined floor. Ian Howell, in a remarkable effort in 1970, made it in his back garden and had it parachuted onto the Lewis glacier. He then made 13 solo ascents to Nelion, each with a part of the hut on his back, and assembled it on top.

We stumbled into it. It was warmer than the Black Hole bivvy – thank God, because to save weight we had carried no spare clothing. The altitude destroys your appetite and we nibbled a few biscuits. My petrol stove would only splutter. Ulf drifted in and out of sleep, while I struggled to stay awake long enough to make a series of brews. It was after 10 before I allowed myself to sleep.

The next day we slowly stirred ourselves and abseiled off. The way was plastered with snow, and we had to be very careful. We reached our hut in the Mackinder Valley at 5pm. Ulf went ahead to our porters to announce our return, and they brought over the gear they had picked up after our bivouac in the Black Hole.

The last day. Ulf had been keen to get up at six and off the mountain, but half an hour after the alarm there was no sign of life from his sleeping-bag. Exhaustion had finally caught up with him.

We were back among the amazing vegetation of East Africa's high mountains. As we set off on the three-hour walk down, the land of rock and ice disappeared from view and the moorland gave way to giant heath. A final half-hour through hagenia forest brought us to the road-head carpark.

We were prepared for a need to celebrate. Ulf had brought some caviar, I some champagne. It was drizzling. We walked to an open wooden shelter and popped the cork, pouring some for the porters. After the only ascent of the couloir that season, it was hard not to feel a little smug. I raised my glass to Mike (porter's fee £2.50 per day).

'I bet you have never had this before.'

'Actually we have it all the time.'

**Summary**: An ascent of the Diamond Couloir on Mt Kenya by Ulf Carlsson and Paul Clarke in September 1992. Grade: Scottish V or UIAA VI. The ascent took 14 hours, with 8 days on the mountain to walk in, acclimatise, do a warm-up climb of Point Peter, climb and walk out.

JOHN TEMPLE

# Ancient and Modern:
# Some East African Mountain Myths

The Golden Age in the Alps and the founding of the Alpine Club came about, in part, owing to the release of middle-class capital, time and energy when, in mid-nineteenth century Britain, keeping a mistress ceased to be socially acceptable. At least that is the myth disseminated by Ronald W Clark in his history of climbing *Men, Myths and Mountains*. His invention of such an improbable scenario perhaps reflects the lack of legends available when he was trying to make the text fit the title. So far as East Africa is concerned, there is no shortage of what might be termed 'genuine' myths. These go back at least as far as Ptolemy and the Mountains of the Moon. If we accept that the snowy equatorial headsprings of the Nile are not an Arabic addition to Ptolemy's text, how did he get the Ruwenzori right? A pure invention, a truly random guess, is highly improbable. Perhaps the flooding of the Nile suggested to the Greeks an analogy with the snow-fed spring floods of their own country. This would make the possibility of equatorial snow mountains a more acceptable concept. The conclusion that someone from the classical world actually penetrated the heart of Africa 2000 years before Stanley, and either saw the glaciated mountains or heard of them from local people, derives from other information on the region subsequently shown to be correct. Pygmies still live at the foot of the Mountains of the Moon. Each of the two headstreams of the White Nile passes through a large lake. Ptolemy placed these lakes some 10° too far south, a pardonable error on the part of his informant who probably felt as if he had travelled the extra 1000km that this represents!

It is instructive, at this point, to quote Baron von Müller writing in the *Geographical Journal* in 1850:

> In the land of the Bari Negroes, under 4°10'N ... the inhabitants say that the river proceeds from the country, Ajan, 30 days' journey to the south, where it flows in four streams from a high mountain ... The Bhar el Abied [White Nile] comes from a high mountain the top of which is quite white ...

Thirty days' journey would represent a distance of about 450km. This approximates to the distance von Müller was from the Ruwenzori. In the Little Ice Age of the mid-nineteenth century the snowfields would have been more conspicuous than they are today. A group of traders from Egypt, enjoying some immunity to tropical diseases, could have reached the same place 2000 years earlier and collected relevant information. They would not have faced any greater difficulties; indeed, the disruption of the large-scale slave trade of the 1800s will have ensured that von Müller needed the firearms his predecessors lacked. The greatest improbability would seem not to be that the journey was made in the years before the birth of Christ but that any echo of it has survived.

A more substantial record exists in the case of Kilimanjaro. Diogenes, a Greek trader along the Arabian coasts, was blown southwards to make a landfall on the eastern coast of Africa presumed to be in the vicinity of Dar es Salaam. From there he claimed to have travelled inland for 25 days and to have reached lakes and a snow mountain he believed was the source of the Nile. Kilimanjaro is the only snow mountain likely to have been reached in the time available; to its west lie several substantial lakes. Ptolemy or his copyists merged this new information with the earlier report and interpolated a mountain range – the Luna Montes.

Thereafter, the Mountains of the Moon occupied several positions on the map of Africa. For some nineteenth century geographers they formed the eastern end of the fabulous Kong Mountains. This 5000km range spanned Africa along 7°N, reportedly reaching the snowline for much of that distance. It is a sad loss for African alpinism that no one since Burton has been able to find them. Livingstone was convinced that Ptolemy had been correct in locating them at 12°S. He died, wasted by malaria and malnutrition, drained by tropical ulcers, dysentery and ruptured piles, trying to persuade himself that the hills which rose a few metres above the stinking swamps were the mountains at the source of the Nile.

Dr Charles Beke, an early traveller in the Ethiopian Highlands, showed commendable originality when, ignoring precedent, he rotated the range through 90° so that it ran north–south from Ethiopia to Kilimanjaro. His readiness to adjust the location of the Mountains of the Moon to accord with any new information that became available earned him little credit. Cooley, the archetypal armchair geographer, said of him: ' ... Whether inland or on the coast wherever his hovering theories alight for a moment, there we have Ptolemy and the Mountains of the Moon.'

One of Beke's sources was Captain Short who claimed to have sailed a schooner some 400km up the river Jura, a river which proved unnavigable to von der Decken's steamboat some ten years later. Short reported seeing some distance to the west 'high mountains with white tops'. The site, according to the Survey of Kenya, is a vast plain. The mountains were at best a mirage enhanced perhaps by the use of the rum glass rather than the eye glass as an aid to vision.

At almost the same time, Krapf, the first European since Diogenes to penetrate the East African hinterland, had a brief sight of a genuine snow mountain. Mount Kenya was added to the already 'discovered' Kilimanjaro, which had been seen and reported by a white man, Rebmann, a year earlier compounding a controversy already blazing in journal correspondence columns. Several myths rose with the smoke. One extreme had the missionaries, Krapf and Rebmann, characterised as liars or purblind fools for suggesting that snow existed at the equator. At the other extreme, the membership of the Royal Geographical Society, from the comfort of armchairs in London, maliciously denigrated the reports of honest travellers.

The possibility of permanent snow on the equator was never seriously questioned. Reports by frostbitten conquistadors of the snowfields of the high Andes of Ecuador had been current since the early sixteenth century and confirmed by later travellers such as Humbolt. The unsettled question was whether the African mountains were high enough. Kilimanjaro would be about 6000m high if the descriptions of the extent of the snow were correct. At that height it should be visible to a sea-level observer more than 300km away, yet there were no reports of a sighting from Mombasa and the missionaries did not report seeing it until they had travelled inland for many days. The only estimate Krapf gave of its height was 'more than 12,500ft', an estimate which served to undermine rather than increase confidence.

The one genuine armchair geographer was the Irish scholar Cooley, who devoted his skills as a linguist and mathematician to the painstaking collation of geographical data from travellers from classical times to his own day. In the process he was acclaimed for exposing a fraud by a French explorer. This seems to have given him delusions of infallibility – a dangerous state of mind given the uncertain quality of much of the information he relied upon. In the context of East Africa he was on the record as maintaining that, while 'Kilimanjara' (as he called it) was the highest mountain in the area, its top was covered not by snow but by red cornelians! When the missionaries and later explorers reported snow, he pilloried them.

Keeping Cooley company were explorers such as Humbolt (briefly), Barth, Burton, and Livingstone himself. The two latter were careful, in public, to avoid outright denial, but both shared a burning ambition to be immortalised as the discoverer of the source of the Nile. Krapf's theory that the headstream would be found running NW from 'Mt Kenia' represented a threat, as he might then share the glory and attract the financial support that they themselves required.

Sir Roderick Murchison had no such inhibitions. As either the occupant of the Royal Geographical Society throne as President or the power behind it, he was the dispenser of financial support. Though he had never visited Africa, he was an eminent practical geographer and geologist. From the Peninsular under Wellington to the Urals as the Tsar's geologist, he had travelled widely in Europe. Initially he had accepted the existence of the snow mountains, but the case Cooley made against them led him to become an outspoken and influential sceptic. Apart from the vexed question of height there was the possibility, fostered by Livingstone, that the glittering summits might well be quartzite or some similar white rock. Partisans of the opposite persuasion had identified over a dozen 'snow mountains', some of which had already proven otherwise, undermining faith in any of them. None the less, virtually all those who expressed opinions at the RGS and in the press were supportive of the missionaries and the matter was closed by von der Decken's report on his expedition of 1861-62, though Livingstone and Cooley appear never to have conceded defeat.

The publication of *The Ice Cap* by the Mountain Club of East Africa in 1932 gave currency to a myth with apparently even older roots than the Mountains of the Moon. A Lutheran missionary, Dr Reusch, reported that while in Ethiopia he had been told that the crater of Kibo was the last resting place of Menelik I, the son of Solomon and Sheba. Returning from a campaign on his southern boundaries, the king had camped on the Saddle, the broad col between Kibo and Mawenzi. Like so many recent visitors in that high, bleak place, he felt old, tired of life and close to death. Despite suffering from the altitude, he carried on up next day, accompanied by his nobles and by slaves carrying his treasure. The nobles returned. Menelik, his slaves and his treasure remained in the crater.

The old Abyssinian soldiers and hunters who told Reusch this story seem to have displayed a very sophisticated knowledge of the topography of such a distant mountain. While it is possible that the legend is an authentic antique, the suspicion is that either the Ethiopian authorities circulated the story widely to give credence to territorial claims, or that the Rev Reusch had reverted to the habits of his exuberant youth as a Cossak Captain and was telling a good tale. Livingstone recorded that some Arabs believed that Kilimanjaro contained mummies, like the pyramids of Egypt, but Krapf, who spent four years in Ethiopia and spoke the language, made no mention of either legend in his *Travels*, despite a proprietory interest in Kilimanjaro.

The most recent myth to emerge dates from the centenary of the first ascent of Kilimanjaro. A Tanzanian paper published an interview with Jonas Louwa who had guided Meyer and Purtscheller on their successful climb. In common with the experience of many Africans in the colonial period, he seems to have been invisible to the Europeans, who make no mention of him. Louwa's claim cannot have been simply a matter of self-advertisement. After all, at the age of 120 years he could surely have enjoyed international celebrity as the oldest man in the world. To judge from the photo, in which he looks not a day over 70, he could easily have coped with the consequent fame.

Halford Mackinder, a man in whom great ability was harnessed to enormous ambition, envisaged Mount Kenya as a pedestal for self-advertisement. By being the first to stand on it he would come to the notice of a much wider public than the limited circle which knew him as a proselyting academic geographer. He had political ambitions and had stood for

Parliament within a year of returning from Africa. As a non-mountaineer he set out to create the myth that he was one. His expedition was an elegant piece of opportunism. The geologist Gregory's brilliant 'solo' effort in 1894 had established that there appeared to be a practicable ice route to the summit. (His judgement proved absolutely sound when, in 1950, Firmin and Bagenal made the first continuous ascent of the Southern Glaciers route, in effect following the footsteps of the Alpine guides César Ollier and Joseph Brocherel.) Freshfield, Mackinder's partner in what the old guard at the RGS dismissed as 'educational rioting', was uniquely qualified to advise on mountaineering matters. He probably directed Mackinder's attention to the necessity of professional help to make up for his lack of experience as a mountaineer. Mackinder had spent a single brief season in Zermatt, plodding up the Dom and some minor peaks behind a guide. By 1899 he was able to justify a sabbatical term which, combined with the long summer vacation, would give five months for the round trip. The Uganda Railway had reached what was to become Nairobi. His brother-in-law, Sidney Hinde, a senior administrator based in the Kenya Highlands, gave the expedition essential information, practical help and, above all, 'clout' in dealing with local difficulties. Curzon's friendship, dating from their undergraduate days, was exploited to get red tape cleared at the British end, while Campbell Hausburg, a second brother-in-law, was willing and able to finance the expedition.

There is little in Mackinder's later writings to indicate that he fully appreciated what a serious proposition Mount Kenya would prove to be. Once close enough to see the peak, Ollier can have had no such delusions. A native of Courmayeur, he must have been struck by similarities between the southern aspects of Mount Kenya and Mont Blanc. The latter is on a larger scale but they both display the same awesomely steep aiguilles, menacing séracs and complex arêtes. Rock with characteristics similar to Mont Blanc granite must have been a reassuring discovery.

Although Mackinder, in his published accounts, makes no reference to preliminary exploration, his guides had several days in which to make a determined attempt to find a way up the eastern side of Nelion's south ridge. Ollier's route is still essentially the same as today's *voie normale* – except for the misnamed Mackinder's Chimney. Its first ascent must have been too dramatic for Mackinder to have dismissed as one of the three *mauvais pas* he mentions in his diaries. Even today, armed with protection pegs, free of ice and cleared of loose rock, it fully deserves its grade IV. In 1929 it looked so daunting that Shipton and Wyn Harris were relieved to find an alternative round the corner. In 1899 it would have been intimidating, with abundant ice and an unprotected crux at the top – an overhanging scree-capped boulder. It was little wonder that Shipton and Harris were impressed by Mackinder's performance. Mackinder's guides had reconnoitred the route in the days prior to the first attempt on the summit.

The aid and comfort provided by a fixed rope and a top rope must have diminished Mackinder's appreciation of the route's severity and seriousness. There is evidence, however, that Mackinder, in his effort to extract the maximum credit from his own performance, deliberately set out to minimise the contribution of his guides. Methodical fieldworker that he was, he made notes during the climb. The detail recorded there differs from his subsequent written-up diary and both differ from his published accounts. The crucial sections date from the day of the ascent and the preceding days. The account in the *Geographical Journal* has César and Joseph 'defeated by the peak ... [They] had laboriously cut their way up the Darwin Glacier, and, bad weather intervening, could neither mount higher nor yet return by the dangerous way they had come. They managed, however, to effect a traverse to the south arête, and returned by the route which we had followed in the first attempt.'

The field-diary makes no mention of bad weather, though some afternoon hail would be normal and no more than a nuisance on an ice route. It describes how César and Joseph climbed the rib on the western side of the Upper Darwin Glacier, left a fixed rope when they descended and cut a line of steps to the south arête of Nelion. They were capable of continuing to the summit but did not do so because they were, after all, employed to take Mackinder there. They could also have used their ascent steps for the descent, but their plan was presumably to keep their employer off unprotect -able ice slopes as much as possible so that he could enjoy the security of the rock.

Returning to complete the ascent with their employer, they cut a line of 'bucket' steps slowly and laboriously up the Diamond Glacier. Ollier would have known that the time of greatest danger for the party would be the descent, when Mackinder's nerve would be tested by being forced to look into the abyss and when his tired legs would be least steady. Each large, secure step required 20 or 30 axe blows. This was energy well spent, but gave rise to yet another myth: the amazing hardness of equatorial ice. The nature of ice and the laws of physics do not change at the equator. The Diamond Glacier is neither steeper nor harder than the average hanging glacier. Exposed to the drop down the Diamond Couloir and at an altitude of 5000m, it is understandable that it should feel as if it were.

Denying Mackinder the credit he sought as a climber does not detract from his real achievement of seeing and seizing his chance and of finally getting to the top, his strength of character more than compensating for his limited experience. It is ironic that the recent publication of his book of the expedition has seen, with the help of his editor, the inflation of a further potentially damaging myth – that eight of his Zanzibari porters were executed. Fifty porters were contracted from the agents under explicit terms. These specified that for mutiny, a second attempted desertion, desertion with the theft of arms, striking an officer, or incitement to these offences, a summary punishment of thirty lashes could be administered. Execution was not an option. If eight porters were shot, self-defence would have been the only justification and and only credible if it had been reported to the authorities. The fifty surviving Zanzibaris could hardly be bribed or bullied into silence. The authorities in Kenya would not have been willing to connive in a cover-up. Mackinder had made himself very unpopular, forcing his party through over their objections and, as they had predicted, he had needed to be rescued. The expedition's supply problems and poor relationship with the Kikuyu chief Wangombe had resulted in the despatch of two armed relief columns – this at a time when they were already having to deal with a famine, a smallpox epidemic, the after-effects of a mutiny, the start of a rebellion and the threat of a Masai civil war. Mackinder's high-handed style in pursuit of an overtly recreational objective must have struck a discordant note on very taughtly stretched people. He deserved and would get no favours. If eight men had been executed he would undoubtedly have been called to account.

As conditions around Mount Kenya became more settled, the mythology of the African peoples was recorded. One feature was common to all. God – 'Ngai' – lived on Mount Kenya and did not welcome visitors. In Kikuyu tradition he had taken the founding father of the tribe to the top, shown him the wonderful forest land he was being given and where he would find a woman who would cultivate and populate it for him. The Masai version has their ancestor being given pasture land and cattle. Significantly, both tribes are, in terms of the millennia of human occupation of East Africa, relatively recent immigrants, their ancestors arriving probably within the last 500 years. The myth gives them some title to the land, a real 'moral high ground'. Only the vaguest stories are told of the people they displaced, who withdrew up the mountain. Names survive – Agumbo, Akiek, Memena – but little else. They are described as short in stature, often hairy hunters who lived in caves. In one tradition the last few survivors changed themselves into turacos – bright, noisy forest birds. Raymond Hook was convinced that a regular pattern of earth mounds in the vicinity of Urumandi marked their attempts at cultivation.

They had a supporting cast of mythical animals: the cheetah-like 'kitanga' of the forest and the hairy snake of alpine zones. There was an elephant (last reports were in the 1920s) with tusks so massive that they dragged on the ground. It presumably had to walk backwards to avoid snagging them in the bush. In the 1930s attention was focused on the 'maz roi', a sub-species of spotted lion, expensively and fruitlessly sought by Gandar-Dower. He did discover a lake at almost 4000m which he modestly named Lake Gandar. He was deprived of his memorial when the authorities, having had the Duchess of Gloucester's permission to honour the mountain with a lake called Alice, had failed to find another candidate.

A climbing exploit on Mount Kenya with mythical qualities involved a French expedition in 1952. *From Kenya to Kilimanjaro,* the book of the expedition, was devastatingly reviewed in both the *Alpine Journal* and the *Bulletin of the Mountain Club of Kenya*. The latter was waspish enough to elicit the threat of a libel action. The group had taken several days to get to the high point reached in one day by Harris and Shipton – a vertical ascent of about 200m. Their 'summit' party then spent most of a day pegging up a couple of pitches to the top of the wall which had turned Harris and Shipton back in 1929. Perhaps this triumph inspired the French party to superhuman efforts, because it apparently took them only from 4.30 to 5pm to get from there to the summit of Batian. They had already been on the go since 2am. The ground between them and Shipton's Notch on the summit ridge is not technical, but involved a height gain of about 100m and they claimed to have found some pitches of III and IV. From the Notch to the top required a further 100m of ascent and rather more than 100m in distance along a superb airy ridge. The climbing is not difficult but finding the easiest route is tricky. A party could be satisfied if it took them two hours from the top of the wall to the summit (Iain Allan's estimate of the time it took his party). A quarter of that time is just not credible. No summit pictures were produced, though they claimed to have reached the summit in daylight with a camera and a CAF flag to wave. The flag and a cache of pegs were later found at the top of the wall. There was no note left in the tobacco tin on the summit to show that they had been there. Their description of the climb gave no detail of any of the features of the route, but it did allow that ordinary climbers might take an hour over it. Altogether a very sorry tale.

Myths and legends continue to accrue to the mountains of East Africa. Few of them concern mountaineering; in these critical days, claims are subject to analysis which aborts otherwise promising myth material The local media, however, as witnessed by the case of Jonas the Centenarian, have no such inhibitions. With an often unsophisticated market to serve and with columns to fill, newspapers continue the time-honoured tradition of a good story taking precedence over probability. Moreover, the significance of the mountains in local culture stimulates the fantasies of would-be prophets. The several sole ascents of Nelion by the barefoot zealot Ephraim underline the power of religious belief.

ACKNOWLEDGEMENTS

I would like to record my appreciation of the help given me by the staff of the Royal Geographical Society Library where much of the above information was obtained. Other sources include the Alpine Club Library, the archives of Rhodes House, Oxford and Birmingham University.

PAUL CLARKE

# Mountain National Park Management in East Africa

(*Plate 52*)

In August 1991 President Yoweri Museveni of Uganda declared the Ruwenzori mountains a national park. Africa's third highest mountain thus joined the top two, Kilimanjaro and Mount Kenya, in having that status. This gives them the highest form of protection they can enjoy in their respective countries, but managing mountain national parks in East Africa is difficult. The organisations responsible are primarily concerned with wildlife, not mountains. Historically they have been underfunded and, on occasion, corrupt and incompetent. Most visitors are from Europe and North America and unfamiliar with local dangers – rapid ascent to high altitude, wild animals, impenetrable forest and shortage of water. Repeat usage by local residents is too small to foster lobby groups on management issues or much voluntary maintenance activities.

However, all three countries are making big efforts, with donor assistance, to improve their management of national parks. Kilimanjaro, Mount Kenya, and the Ruwenzori have been recent and early beneficiaries of a particular initiative: the preparation of a park management plan. Park plans are not new, but often they have not been realistic. This time much greater effort and resources have been put into their preparation. Kilimanjaro was the first of three of the pilot parks in Tanzania to have a plan prepared by a newly established planning unit, with assistance from a US National Park Service planner under the Tanzania National Parks Management Planning Project. Mount Kenya was the first national park for which Kenya Wildlife Service engaged an external consultant, and a plan for the Ruwenzori is currently under preparation. Funding for these plans came from: the Swedish International Development Agency, the World Conservation Union, the World Bank, the World Wide Fund for Nature (WWF) and the United States Agency for International Development (USAID). The western side of the Ruwenzori, in Zaire, have not fared so well – funding from the European Union was withdrawn in the early 1990s for political reasons.

The plans deal with the obvious mountain issues such as footpaths, huts, visitor numbers, visitor information, porters and guides, mountain rescue, rubbish, and campsites. But in Africa they have to consider a great deal more besides. All three mountains are surrounded by forests that are rich in wildlife and have smallholder farmers on their lower boundary. Forests have to be patrolled against poachers; farmers have to be protected from wildlife invading their farms, which means fencing. Elephants are abundant and on Kilimanjaro an effort is being made to keep wildlife corridors open so that they can migrate onto the open plains below. On Mount Kenya this is no longer possible, so populations will have to be monitored now that they are becoming compressed. Rare rhinos have to be protected. In Africa local communities expect to benefit from national parks, which usually means a portion of revenue is contributed to local development projects such as schools and dispensaries. Years of neglect mean that park offices and housing need rebuilding. Access roads, like that to Chogoria on Mount Kenya, are often in poor condition and need rebuilding. All this needs vehicles, plant, equipment and the people to manage and use them. As a result, only a small part of the plans is focused on items that are visible to the visiting mountaineer.

What will be visible to the mountaineer? In the Ruwenzori, the number of visitors on the Ugandan side has increased rapidly in recent years from nothing to 350 in 1988 to about 1700 in 1993. Ruwenzori Mountain Services (RMS) has, with USAID funding, built a bridge over the Bujuku river, developed a number of huts, and built a wooden footpath through the infamous Bigo Bog. Unfortunately the huts are small and not always adequate for the current level of visitors. The Bigo path is blending into the landscape with time but, with more expert technical advice, could probably have been laid more sensitively. RMS is basically a guide and porter operation descended from the porter operation used by the Mountain Club of Uganda in colonial times. Visitors are effectively required to take a porter each and a guide for the group. This is more than some hikers will want (exemptions need careful negotiation) but with a climbing trip requiring ten days, most mountaineers will require this level of back-up. RMS now offers guiding to the summit of the highest peak, Margherita, but with the first all-Ugandan ascent in the last five years, the quality of guiding on the peaks can be improved. The plan is still under preparation, and visitor services will be a major issue for it to tackle.

The Ruwenzori is the most extensive of the three massifs – it is a complete range. It is also the wettest, which means that the vegetation goes right up to the snowline and is very dense. Mount Kenya is drier and offers the best destination for technical mountaineers. The plan proposes that footpaths should be built up through the most eroded and vulnerable areas. There are already large commercial huts on the Sirimon and Naro Moru routes. The smaller old Mountain Club of Kenya huts are in poor repair and not viable. They will gradually be removed or become porters' shelters, with the aim of preserving the wilderness character of the Chogoria route by restricting it to campers. Austrian Hut will be retained. Almost all hikers keep to the three main routes, but in fact they are free to wander at will. There is plenty of scope for this once the visitor has got above the worst of the tussocks. Visitors are not allowed in alone (but solo climbing on the peaks is allowed) but are not required to take porters or guides. Kenya Wildlife Service is working with communities and porters' organisations to improve the quality of porter and guide services, which has been variable. A full-time mountain rescue team, capable of operating on the main peaks, is currently being trained. Campsites are being provided with pit latrines, and facilities on the Naro Moru route will be improved. Money has been allocated to improve the Chogoria route access road. Other access roads will be improved later, when and if money becomes available.

Mount Kenya attracts about 8,000 visitors a year. Kilimanjaro attracts about 12,000 by virtue of its status as Africa's highest mountain. Relatively easy access allows fast ascent, and with it altitude sickness. This makes it important to drink a lot of water, but there is none above 4,500m. The authorities have responded by making all parties take porters and guides and, more recently, they have to obtain them through a licensed tour operator. This situation has led to some very indifferent guiding. The standard service does an efficient job of getting visitors to Gilman's Point on the crater rim but there are many reports of visitors being discouraged, on some pretext, from going on to Uhuru Peak, the true summit.

The plan proposes that all summit-bound visitors are required to spend a minimum of six days on the mountain. The busy Marangu route will be limited to 10,500 visitors a year. Other routes will have much lower limits, need to be booked, and will be much more expensive. The Shira, Rongai, Machame and Umbwe trails will be 'up only' and the Mweka 'down only'. The attitude of the Tanzanian authorities is rather controlling, and the result is that, for adventurous souls who value the self-responsibility and sense of exploration that are the essence of the sport, Kili fails to provide a complete mountaineering experience. Other changes include closing the Shira road at 11,000ft, improving visitor facilities at the main Marangu gate, removing huts not on the Marangu route, and expanding Horombo hut to allow sufficient accommodation for visitors to spend a second night on the way up. A trail to Mawenzi Tarn from Horombo will provide an acclimatisation day trip and convenient access for climbers on Mawenzi Peak. The Marangu trail will be built up and realigned. Improvements will be made to mountain rescue equipment and sewage disposal equipment. Adventure activities such as parapente and mountain biking (but not mountaineering) will be banned.

Efficient management costs money, and the only sustainable source of income in a developing country is from park fees, which have risen sharply in recent years on all three mountains. The level of these fees may seem excessive for those used to free access to mountain areas in developed countries, but they are not unreasonable in terms of value for money. A more interesting question is whether they are put to good use. In 1991 revenue on Kilimanjaro was $1.75 million but expenditure on capital development and operations was only $0.39 million (although it is not clear whether this included centrally funded costs). This suggests that inadequate amounts were recycled back into the park. A surplus is sought to fund other of Tanzania's protected areas, many of which will never pay for themselves. One of the benefits of having a plan is that it helps make the case for adequate funding. With its plan fully implemented, Mount Kenya will cost about half a million dollars a year to run. Revenue for 1993/94 was expected to be roughly $275,000. The development of a lodge and game viewing circuits in the Sirimon forest area should increase the number of visitors substantially, and extra sources of revenue such as fishing and riding will be developed, but the park will at best break even. All fees will therefore go on park management. While some of the efforts are unseen by the mountaineer, a large proportion will be devoted to keeping access roads open, providing vehicles for park management, and training the mountain rescue team. The visitor in fact gets good value. The park staff dedicate themselves to their work despite ridiculously low pay.

Plans will, of course, amount to nothing unless they are properly implemented. This will depend on the parent institutions allocating adequate management and resources. These are improving rapidly, but there is still much to be done. The Ruwenzori were transferred from the Uganda Forest Department to Uganda National Parks (UNP) in 1991. The responsibilities of UNP and the Game Department will be merged into a newly formed Uganda Wildlife Authority in July 1996. This is being done with assistance primarily from USAID and the European Union. Unfortunately, however, Uganda has a current policy of decentralisation, and much responsibility will pass to weaker regional authorities from central government. Tanzania National Parks has always been a relatively autonomous and strong organisation. No major reforms are in hand but it is receiving steady assistance from British Overseas Development Administration, the African Wildlife Foundation, IUCN, the Frankfurt Zoological Society and WWF. The biggest changes have probably been in Kenya where responsibility was passed from the Wildlife Conservation and Management Department to the more autonomous Kenya Wildlife Service in 1990. Donors, who had previously overlooked WCMD, are ploughing several hundred million dollars into KWS. It will take a whole decade for all the changes needed to take place, and there are not only the mountain national parks to consider. But change definitely is happening.

The problems of management cannot detract from the fact that these mountains are unique places of exceptional beauty. They have as many visitors in a year as they probably would in a weekend if they were somehow relocated in the Lake District, management problems and all. In the words of Clive Ward in *Snowcaps on the Equator*: 'Once touched, these mountains are not something you can leave for ever and not return to.'

*Left*
33. The Central Caucasus: looking back along part of the Bezingi Wall. (*José Luis Bermúdez*) (p85)

*Below*
34. Neil Wilson somewhere among the gendarmes between Shkhara West and Jangi-Tau East. (*José Luis Bermúdez*) (p85)

35. The Corsican High Route: David Williams on Serra Tenda.
(*John Harding*) (p125)

36. Stephen Baker on Serra Tenda, Monte d'Oro behind. (*John Harding*) (p125)

7. The Corsican High Route: Patrick Fagan (R) and Rodney Franklin ascending Monte Rotondo, 2622m. (*John Harding*) (p125)

8. Paglia Orba, 2525m, from the ridge of Monte Cinto, 2706m. (*John Harding*) (p125)

*Left*
39. Contorted rock on the SE ridge of Paglia Orba. (*George Band*) (p131)

*Below*
40. The crenate ridge of Capo Tafonato. Note the famous hole which sometimes resembles a patch of snow. (*George Band*) (p131)

41. Cordillera de Potosí, Bolivia. The South Face of Cerro Cari Cari, 5040m, highest peak in the northern half of the Cordillera.
(*Evelio Echevarría*) (p162)

42.  Cordillera de Potosí, Bolivia.  Peaks of the Quimsa Condoriri group, SW side, with (R) Cerro Maucatambo, 4940m.  (*Evelio Echevarría*)  (p162)

43.  One of the small Samani lakes and the SW side of Cerro Mina Illimani, 5030m, in the background.  (*Evelio Echevarría*)  (p162)

4.  Henry Hoek, 1878-1951, was the first and main explorer of the Cordillera de Potosí.
    (*Reproduced by courtesy of Henry Hoek's stepson Peter Walluf of Frankfurt-am-Main*) (p162)

*Left*
45. Mount Trakora, *c*4800, in Irian Jaya
César Pérez de Tudela (barely visible
on the summit pyramid.
(*Jules Stewart*) (p156)

*Below*
46. Jules Stewart with Jayawijaya range
in the background. (*Jules Stewart*)
(p156)

GRAEME WATSON

# Tanzania's Other Mountains

(*Plates 53, 54*)

After years of stifling bureaucracy Tanzania's doors are opening to more and more visitors. The largest numbers of these are drawn to the major tourist circuit of Ngorongoro and Serengeti in the north of the country, but the greatest and most powerful draw has always been Kilimanjaro. The upside of this development is the improved communication and the greater ease of accessibility to Tanzania's other mountains. Yes, there *are* others apart from Kilimanjaro – a liberal sprinkling of ranges and isolated volcanoes split by the Rift Valley and dotted astride one of the most breathtaking and vast tracts of Africa that there is. This is the great sweep of mountains close to the Kenyan border which defines the perimeter of the Masai steppe. The northern mountains are reflected to the south by another crescent of high ground – the Southern Highlands. These start at Iringa and sweep southwards past the northern limits of Lake Malawi, crossing the bifurcation of the Rift Valley to follow its western arm to the shores of Lake Tanganyika.

Of the mountains to the north, Mt Meru (4566m) is the tallest and the most dramatic. This huge volcano is the fourth or fifth highest peak in Africa (the height of Ras Dashen in Ethiopia has not been established precisely enough to determine which of the two is the higher). Meru is a towering and impressively steep cone which sometimes supports a powdering of snow; its western wall was breached a quarter of a million years ago by a massive avalanche of liquid mud, exposing the crater floor and giving rise to an area of unusual and outstanding beauty which forms the basis of Arusha National Park.

Formerly climbed from Olkokola at the foot of its western slopes (a route which necessitated an ascent of over 2000m of steep volcanic scree), Mt Meru is now normally climbed in two to three days from the east. This marvellous hike, with stops at Miriakamba Hut and Saddle Hut, ascends through magnificent groves of hagenia forest to follow the sweeping crescent of the crater rim. The route affords superb views of the almost perfectly formed subsidiary ash cone in the centre of the crater and of the 2000m near-vertical ramparts of the wall behind it. The latter are unclimbable, as the volcanic rock is dangerously weak and comes away in the hands. The view from the summit extends hundreds of kilometres in all directions, but perhaps the most unforgettable sight from Meru is Kilimanjaro's ice cap in the setting sun.

Immediately to the north of Meru is the distinctively shaped hump of Longido (2629m). This massive inselberg of basement gneiss sports, on its western summit, a magnificent tooth of rock whose 1000ft face has attracted a modest number of ascents over the years. Thick thorn bushes and elephants are two of the hazards to be encountered on the ascent; but the upper ridgeline of this hill provides a vantage point 1500m above the vast reaches of the Masai plains and the hot alkaline wastes of Lake Natron in the floor of the Rift Valley to the west.

The area west and southwest of Meru, straddling the Rift Valley itself, is studded with isolated volcanic peaks and ranges of volcanic origin of all shapes and sizes. Sometimes referred to as the Great Cauldron Mountains, these are dominated by the Crater Highlands, a mass of high ground reaching over 3650m derived from eight interlocking volcanoes. The most prominent, though not the highest, of these is Ngorongoro, whose immense caldera of some 20km in diameter is the focal point of the Ngorongoro Conservation Area and of the northern Tanzania tourist circuit. Many who visit Ngorongoro, though impressed with its physical splendour, cannot help but be put off by the depredations of modern tourism and, in hurrying on, fail to explore and take advantage of some of the glorious and isolated mountain walking just off the beaten track to the north and south.

Crossing Ngorongoro Crater to the north one enters a high triangular plateau, described to the west and north by the two huge craters of Olmoti (3099m) and Embagai (3239m) and to the south-east by the towering peak of Loolmalassin, Tanzania's third highest mountain at 3665m. Much of the plateau is wide open grassland, populated by dignified and courteous Masai, who have yet to learn the demeaning ways associated with tourism. It is criss-crossed with cattle trails dating back thousands of years to earlier peoples. The upper slopes of Loolmalassin and Embagai are cloaked with a uniform cover of stunted heather. Walks to these peaks are long and exhilarating though water is scarce.

The views are vast and there is always the added excitement of coming across wildlife, either on foot or prowling close to one's tent while camped at night. Nothing can set nerves tingling quite like a lion's breath a foot or two from the flimsy canvas of a mountain tent! Not to be missed on such a visit is the crater of Embagai, a huge feature 7km in diameter and 1000m deep. At its floor is an emerald green alkaline lake, around whose edge one can wander in peaceful isolation. This marvellous walking country is only tarnished by Olmoti, whose similarly immense crater offers little except the frustration of bashing one's way across boggy tussock, or getting an equal battering from the dense heather and stinging-nettles which cover the crater rim.

Two other large mountains are situated south-west of Ngorongoro. Lemagrut (3132m), a fine mountain with grassy slopes and clumps of woodland, provides a vantage point over the Serengeti plains and the Olduvai gorge. It was volcanic ash from a minor volcano on Lamagrut's flanks

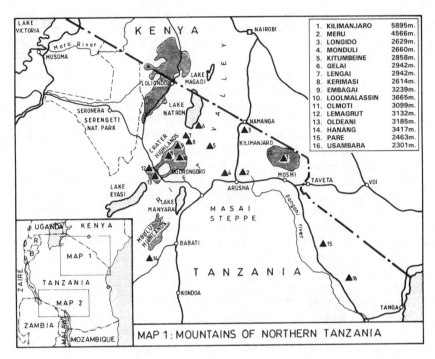

| 1. | KILIMANJARO | 5895m. |
|----|-------------|--------|
| 2. | MERU | 4566m. |
| 3. | LONGIDO | 2629m. |
| 4. | MONDULI | 2660m. |
| 5. | KITUMBEINE | 2858m. |
| 6. | GELAI | 2942m. |
| 7. | LENGAI | 2942m. |
| 8. | KERIMASI | 2614m. |
| 9. | EMBAGAI | 3239m. |
| 10. | LOOLMALASSIN | 3665m. |
| 11. | OLMOTI | 3099m. |
| 12. | LEMAGRUT | 3132m. |
| 13. | OLDEANI | 3185m. |
| 14. | HANANG | 3417m. |
| 15. | PARE | 2463m. |
| 16. | USAMBARA | 2301m. |

MAP 1 : MOUNTAINS OF NORTHERN TANZANIA

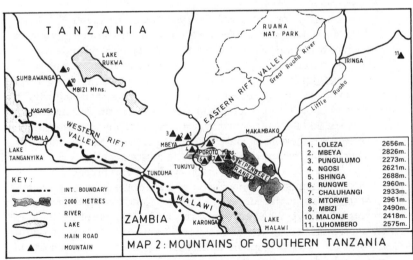

KEY:
INT. BOUNDARY
2000 METRES
RIVER
LAKE
MAIN ROAD
MOUNTAIN

| 1. | LOLEZA | 2656m. |
|----|--------|--------|
| 2. | MBEYA | 2826m. |
| 3. | PUNGULUMO | 2273m. |
| 4. | NGOSI | 2621m. |
| 5. | ISHINGA | 2688m. |
| 6. | RUNGWE | 2960m. |
| 7. | CHALUHANGI | 2933m. |
| 8. | MTORWE | 2961m. |
| 9. | MBIZI | 2490m. |
| 10. | MALONJE | 2418m. |
| 11. | LUHOMBERO | 2575m. |

MAP 2: MOUNTAINS OF SOUTHERN TANZANIA

which preserved the footprints of early hominids at Laetoli 3½ million years ago. Oldeani (3185m), a wetter and cloudier peak, supports a forbidding cover of bamboo and commands the landscape above Lake Eyasi.

To the north-east of the main massif are the two outliers of Kerimasi (2614m) and Ol Doinyo Lengai (2942m), the 'Mountain of God'. These are more recent arrivals on the scene, with Lengai still being active. Owing to its proximity to Lengai's dramatic crater, Kerimasi is more often than not ignored, though those who make the effort are rewarded with a fine hike some 1400m up its steep grassy slopes, usually from Loluni Crater to the north, and can enjoy a circuit of its wooded double crater.

Lengai to the north forms a near perfect cone. Its last major eruption was in 1967, but a minor eruption occurred in June 1993. Formerly climbed by ridges on its northern and eastern flanks, which necessitated some 2100m of relentless ascent, the mountain is now normally tackled from the north-west, where a vehicle can be driven to an elevation of 1400m, reducing the ascent to some 1500m. This shortened route allows time in the day to explore the crater, though there is a lot to be said for camping at the top overnight if possible. There is nearly always some minor action going on in the crater, with several subsidiary cones present on its floor. Some of these intermittently eject thin streamers of treacle black carbonalite lava, which oxidises and turns white after a few days. The views to the north from the summit over the crater to Lake Natron and westward over the Rift wall to the Crater Highlands are unsurpassable and the elixir of a potential eruption only serves to enhance them!

Located on the floor of the Rift Valley, between the Crater Highlands and Meru, are a number of other extinct or dormant volcanoes, the most prominent of which are Gelai (2942m), Kitumbeine (2858m) and Monduli (2660m). Both Gelai and Kitumbeine are huge mountains, towering above their surroundings and supporting upland islands of forest and permanent settlements. Walks up both these mountains are long and satisfying, though route-finding in the forest requires some care, and precautions need to be taken to avoid buffalo, which are numerous, and the stinging-nettles which must be amongst the densest and most vicious in the world. Monduli is a prominent forested beacon on the eastern Rift escarpment but its vegetation forms too dense a barrier for pleasurable walking. It is probably better to leave this mountain to the connoisseurs and concentrate on the pleasures of Tarosero to its immediate west. This is another mountain with fine open grassed ridges perched high above the parched plains of the Rift floor.

The most isolated of the Great Cauldron Mountains is Hanang, at 3417m Tanzania's fourth highest mountain. Located at the southern end of the Mbulu highlands in territory occupied by the Barabaig, a Cushitic people, Hanang has much of the feel of Meru about it, though on a slightly less immense scale. Approaching via Bahati and Katesh, the ascent is easiest from Gendabi to the west, or directly north up the rim of the crescent-shaped remnant of the crater wall from Katesh. A 1500m climb brings one to a marvellous serrated knife-edged ridgeline leading to the summit, with massive views over Lake Balangida and the Malbadow escarpment. As with their Ethiopian counterparts, mountain tops are holy places to the Barabaig and holy men will sometimes be encountered on the upper reaches of this mountain.

Other interesting ranges in the north of the country include the Pare and Usambara mountains between Kilimanjaro and the port of Tanga. Like Longido, these mountains are metamorphic in origin. The high rainfall they attract has encouraged fine stands of forest and the evolution over the ages of numerous endemic species of animal and plant life. (The original African violet grown in pots worldwide came from these mountains.) Sadly much of this is under threat as the fertility of the hills has attracted ever-increasing settlement over the years and they are now densely populated. Despite the human numbers, both mountain ranges have much to offer, including some of the prettiest and most spectacular scenery, as well as aggressively winding mountain access roads.

The best starting point for exploring the huge choice of mountains on offer in the south of the country is Mbeya, located at the point where the eastern and western arms of the Rift Valley diverge. Though similar in scale and with the same geological mix of metamorphic and volcanic rocks, the landscape here has a distinctly different feel to that of Northern Tanzania. This is partly due to the higher level of sedentary agriculture in the highlands, as opposed to the less obtrusive cattle keeping of the Masai pastoralists in the north. But it is probably more the result of the distinct changes in the seasons throughout the year. While the north generally enjoys two wet and two dry seasons each year, the south experiences one long wet season (November to April) and one long dry season. The contrast between the two seasons is marked, the wet season being typified by crystal clear views, muddy roads and difficult access, whilst the dry season comprises long, hot dusty days and culminates in huge grass fires whose clouds of smoke obscure the landscape and reduce everything to a grey haze. In between times the countryside is subject to marvellous changes of colour, the miombo woodlands of the plains turning like trees in a European autumn, whilst the flowers and purple grasses of the chilly uplands give them the feel of heather-clad Scottish highlands.

Forming a dramatic backdrop to the town of Mbeya is the Mbeya Range, rising to over 2700m. The peak immediately north of the town, Loleza (2656m), is now unfortunately surmounted by a radio repeater station and it is no longer possible to climb to its summit. However, there is some fine walking to be had on the upland grassland of its flanks within easy reach of the town. Mbeya peak (2826m) itself is some 6km to the west and can be approached either from the spectacular escarpment road to Chunya to the north, or by a more demanding hike from Mbalizi in the floor of the Rift to the south. From the summit the jagged ridgeline can be followed by eye to the lower summit of Pungalumo (2273m) at the end of the range, beyond which the glint of Lake Rukwa can sometimes be made out far away to the west. The Mbeya range provides marvellous ridge-top walking with ground orchids and other flowers underfoot. An eye has to be kept on the weather, however, as hailstorms can be sudden and violent.

Standing on the opposite side of the Rift Valley, south of Mbeya, are the Poroto Mountains and Kipengere Range. The former are generally forested volcanoes, whilst the latter is a huge area of frequently bleak moorland. Perhaps the most dramatic of the Porotos is Ngosi (2621m), a huge brooding mountain subject to some of Tanzania's heaviest rainfall and whose summit and crater are often enveloped in dense cloud. When this lifts, an eerily silent lake is revealed in the depths of the crater and the atmosphere is haunting.

South-east of Ngosi is another huge volcano, Rungwe (2960m), which occupies a great tract of forested land and dominates the staggering scenery of Unyakyusa at the northern end of Lake Malawi. It is a toss-up whether Rungwe or Mtorwe is the highest mountain in Southern Tanzania, though nominally Mtorwe (2961m), the highest point of the Kipengere range, is the higher by one metre. Together with Ishinga (2688m) and Chaluhangi (2933m), Mtorwe is located on the Elton Plateau, named after the explorer Frederick Elton who crossed the area in 1877. This huge expanse of rolling grassland is famous for the extraordinary variety of flowers which proliferate, particularly between October and April. The humped form of Chaluhangi is on the southern periphery of the plateau overlooking Lake Malawi, whilst Mtorwe and Ishinga tower above the headwaters of the Great Ruaha River and the Usangu plain.

West of Mbeya the long road can be followed to Sumbawanga located on the high plateau of the Mbizi Mountains sandwiched between Lakes Rukwa and Tanganyika. Surrounded by extensive forest, Mbizi peak (2490m) stands on the escarpment 1500m above the remote and mysterious Rukwa, whilst Malonje (2418m) is a lower and more accessible hump on the road south to Mpui.

Other fine ranges add to the huge variety of scenery and hiking potential to be found in Tanzania and these include the Nguru and Uluguru mountains, in the vicinity of Dodoma and Morogoro. On two other ranges, which have recently been declared wilderness national parks, only walking is allowed and no vehicles are permitted. Accessible only by lake steamer, the Makari mountains, on the shores of Lake Tanganyika, are the home of large numbers of chimpanzees, while Luhombero is a secluded and little visited massif south of the Ruaha gorge. Reaching these less accessible mountain areas can be a task requiring more than a little ingenuity, but the result may be the discovery of some marvellous unspoiled wilderness with the atmosphere and challenge of genuinely remote exploration.

# Granite Island

Here with a Loaf of Bread beneath the Bough,
A Flask of Wine, a Book of Verse – and Thou
 Beside me singing in the Wilderness –
And Wilderness is Paradise enow.

*Rubáiyat of Omar Khayyám of Naishápúr*
Translated by Edward FitzGerald

# Corsican Retrospective

*(Plates 35–38)*

It was with a fine sense of literary instinct that François Dévouassoud, Douglas Freshfield's lifelong guide and companion, pronounced of Corsica ' ... that when "le bon Dieu" was building the Alps, he must have had a bit left over and have thrown it down in the Mediterranean'.[1] Dévouassoud had recognised that, uniquely of the Mediterranean's islands, Corsica is *the* mountaineering playground for all seasons.

The island of Corsica, barely 183km long and 83km broad, rises like Venus from the sea to its 2706m culmination in Monte Cinto. Few travellers have not succumbed to Corsica's potent scenery and showered it with epithets – Ile de Beauté, the Scented Isle, the Mountain of the Sea, the Granite Island. Freshfield, the outstanding mountaineer/traveller of his day and no mean judge of scenery, knew of 'no region in Europe where within so small a space Nature takes so many different sublime or exquisite aspects'.[2] In summer its anchorages, coves and white sand beaches are the stuff of dreams. In winter its peaks are like diadems of pearls catching the rising sun. Corsica has a range of brilliantly coloured faces. Its abundant forests, exploited by seafaring nations from the Romans onwards, combine chestnut, oak, beech and, above all, the transcendental Corsican Pine, a monarch of European trees, which attains 700 years of age and over 50m in height. Equally characteristic is the impermeable jungle of shrubs, plants and herbs – arbutus, myrtle, cistus, rosemary, lavender and thyme – known as the 'maquis'. For long inviolate as a refuge of bandits, outlaws and Second World War resistance fighters (the 'Men of the Maquis') this matted aromatic growth is both a scourge and a challenge to all who stray off the beaten track. Stark and sheer above labyrinthine valleys and maquis-choked gorges rises Corsica's granite backbone – a twisting snake of rock crossed and recrossed by transverse ridges, buttressed by vertiginous walls and slabs crowned with aiguilles, gendarmes and obelisks. This is a country fit for heroes and a paradise for climbers.

Corsica's physical characteristics have moulded the mettle of its people and spawned a succession of larger-than-life, demi-mythical figures overladen with pride and ambition. Of this variegated cast of heretics, revolutionaries, idealists, irredentists, bandits, gangsters and soldiers, typical have been the likes of the patriot leader Pasquale Paoli, the murderer debaucher Miguel Manara (a historical Don Juan who adopted as his role model Molino's fictional anti-hero), the bandit Bellacoscia and, above all,

Napoleon Bonaparte, the quintessential Corsican, who recruited 43 of his generals and 10,000 soldiers from this his native island.

In classical times, Corsica was at the hub of a maritime trading cross-roads. The Pax Romana gave it seven never-to-be-repeated centuries of stability, when the vine, olive, cereals, irrigation, law, Latin and, latterly, the Christianity of the Old Testament prophets were introduced. But its subsequent history of invasion and resistance, the malign shadow of 'vendetta' and the inaccessibility of its interior, left Corsica to its own devices and made it something of a European *terra incognita*. Corsica's very existence barely touched British consciousness until 1765 when James Boswell became its first accredited British visitor. On this embellishment of his Grand Tour, Boswell's avowed object was to meet Pasquale Paoli, the charismatic statesman/general who led Corsica to 14 years of independence from Genoa between 1755 and 1769. To 18th century romantics, this tiny state was perceived as the embodiment of a political and social liberty that encompassed both classical republicanism and the ingenuousness of the innocent savage. Paoli himself remarked to Boswell that 'a man come from Corsica will be like a man come from the Antipodes'. Corsica marked a turning point in Boswell's life but, as an 18th century man of his time, he was more concerned with its people and politics than with its scenery. Yet within 30 years of Boswell's visit and a year before his death in 1795, the British came to Corsica to fight the French at the invitation of his hero Paoli. After the siege of Calvi, where Nelson lost an eye, Corsica became an Anglo-Corsican kingdom with a British Viceroy for two brief years before French reoccupation.

The actual unveiling of Corsica to the British travelling classes came 100 years after Boswell's visit through the works of an itinerant artist. Although popularly known for his Nonsense and Limericks (which have always confused the serious-minded picture-buying public), Edward Lear, influenced by Turner, Ruskin and John Martin, was arguably the outstanding topographical artist of his day. As a painter he was denied the recognition he craved in his day, but his journeys through harsh and unwelcoming country in the remoter corners of Europe, the Near East and India gave outlet to an adventurous and creative genius. Lear's 1868 visit to Corsica was effectively his swansong and his *Journal of a Landscape Painter in Corsica* the last and least successful of his many travel books. For all that, he always reckoned that this journey was 'worth any amount of expense and trouble'. Above all, his romantic landscape engravings convey, as none before or since have done, the 'grave hard splendour of the island untainted, then, by foreign ways; a place of untenanted wooded landscapes and brooding heights of rock and snow'.[3]

Two years before Lear's historic visit, Corsica had already been reconnoitred by a member of the Alpine Club. In 1866 the Rev W H Hawker arrived with a party which included five ladies and proceeded to climb Corsica's most beautiful peak – Monte d'Oro. Hawker's ascent was a British first but he formed a low opinion of the Corsican character which he considered compounded jealousy and ambition with vindictiveness. Fourteen years on, in 1880, Douglas Freshfield arrived with François Dévouassoud for the first of two visits. Freshfield's descriptions of Corsica's scenery, geography, history and its people are lyrical, perceptive and sympathetic. But essentially a mountain traveller rather than a cut and thrust climber, his Corsican peak bag was limited to Incudine and Rotondo in 1880 and Monte d'Oro in 1894. The first British ascent of Cinto had to wait until Frank Tuckett's 1883 visit with the artist E T Compton.

At this dawning stage in Corsica's climbing history, British attitudes to Corsica's mountains were cautious and condescending. Alpine Club member T G Ouston, who made the first British ascent of Paglia Orba in 1908, commented that Corsica 'appears to be treated by the British like a woman with a past ... interesting because fascinating, romantic and beautiful but otherwise to be left severely alone ... '. [4] It was left to the Australian brothers George and Max Finch with the Norwegian Alf Bryn to initiate the era of modern mountaineering. Their first complete traverses of Tafonato and the Cinque Frati were crowned by a daring ascent of Paglia Orba by its NE face in winter conditions in April 1909.[5] George Finch was later to become the first exponent of oxygen on Everest and a President of the Alpine Club. His Paglia Orba route remains a Corsican classic but, after his visit, Corsica's climbing history largely becomes a Continental catalogue.

Corsica's popularity with ramblers, roamers and rovers is a relatively recent phenomenon and a direct consequence of the creation in 1972 of the Parc Natural Regional de la Corse which covers over a third of the island. The aim of its founders was to revive districts where the old pastoral economy had declined as a result of depopulation and the conversion of winter pastures into farmland and vineyards. To reintroduce the traditional mountain life based on transhumance, sheepfolds and huts were rebuilt and communications between the inner and coastal island re-established. Tourism has many ugly faces but in Corsica it has been handled sympathetically and has rejuvenated the island's interior.

The thread which binds together so many of the Parc's component parts is the GR20 High Level Walking Route. This, an elaboration of an earlier route, runs some 200km from Calenzana to Porto Vecchio and has become the most popular and famous of its kind. With vertical intervals of 19,000m, the GR20 can either be done in 18-21 easy stages or as a stunt for fell-running freaks and fantasists bent on breaking 36, 24 or 12 hours to taste. I first visited Corsica in August 1986 with Roger Chorley, George Band and our respective families. On the GR20 we encountered Tilleke Naar, wife of Ronald Naar 'the flying Dutchman'. We had shared a hut on Mt Olympus with the Naars the previous year and back home I received an account of Ronnie's 1986 Corsican ski traverse characteristically described as ' ... one of the finest I have ever made ... the most difficult of its type for those in the know'.

Hype invariably sets middle-aged pulses racing so I hurriedly consulted Parmentier's oracular *Les Grands Raids à Ski* for elucidation. This revealed that ski routes across the island had preceded the creation of the GR20 itself. A local team had done the central section from Verghio to Vizzavona way back in 1960 and, seven years later, Jerome Pinoncely completed, solo, the first ski traverse of Corsica. Without the existence of huts, these were remarkable feats. Here surely was a *grand raid* for cognoscenti and connoisseurs. The line of the Corsican High Route on ski is self-selecting with little scope for deviation. Basically, you follow the GR20. South to north has to be the preferred line of march, for this way you progress inexorably towards that spectacular knot of peaks – Tafonato, Paglia Orba, Minuta and Cinto. These are Corsica's quintessential mountains whose attainment marks a crescendoing climax to the ski traverse of the Granite Island.

Where best to start and finish? The 'dream traverse' would run the gamut of the GR20 from Conca to Calenzana. But this would mean at least 16 stages and, given the unpredictability of snow cover, the weather's vicissitudes and the problems of reprovisioning *en route* without pre-arranged food caches, you might need three weeks to complete it. Altogether shorter, but dramatic and demanding, is the traverse of the northern section of the GR20 ending up at Asco or Calacuccia. Parmentier suggests seven days for the Bastelica to Asco traverse but to allow a mere 4-6 hours for the initial stage Bastelica to Vizzavona must be braggadocio. Naar's party took some 2½ days to negotiate this section, encountering problems galore on the steep, thickly forested slopes of the upper Gravona valley. Starting from Bastelica, a large village at the head of the Prunelli valley, there is the advantage of hotels and restaurants and the likely scalp of a popular Corsican classic, Monte Renoso at 2352m. But Bastelica is half a day from Ajaccio by public transport, well below the snowline at 770m, and some way off the GR20.

The logical start point for the northern traverse has to be Vizzavona, a hamlet with three hotels grown from the railway stop perched just below the 1163m Vizzavona pass that divides the massifs of Renoso and Oro. This pass forms a watershed between the westward-leading Gravona valley and the Tarvignano valley which inclines north to Corte, Corsica's ancient inland capital. Easily accessible by train from Ajaccio, Vizzavona is the GR20's natural break point.

My first attempt on the Corsican High Route in 1989 was frustrated by lack of snow. But 1994 was an outstanding snow year and on 26 February 1994, our party of six – Alpine Club to a man – having flown in from London the night before, waved down the 0800 hours Corte Express at an unofficial halt conveniently close to our Ajaccio hotel, to the irritation and incredulity of its indulgent driver. By 0930 we had alighted, located the GR20 and left behind us Vizzavona's sad, shuttered hotels which once welcomed Ajaccio's British community with log fires, ballroom dancing and skating on an ice rink set in a forest clearing. In summer, Vizzavona swarms with an international *mélange* of tourists and hikers. Now we had the path up the Agnone valley to ourselves. Our first stop was at the Cascade des Anglais, a spirited waterfall bounding down a succession of steps through polished granite, which recalled a dim memory of Victorian high days. Eight days later, in the bar of the Acqua Viva Hotel, Calacuccia, we were celebrating the end of our traverse under the baleful glare of a wildly mustachioed Bellacoscia photographed with his monstrous dog whose Tysonesque savagery put a price on its own grotesque head.

So what of this ski traverse which Naar described as 'the most difficult in Europe'? At first blush the whole venture had seemed wildly improbable but the route definitely goes. Besides, it is a wondrous thing of beauty tracing a firm but delicate line along the island's spine through clusters of spiky peaks crossed by porcupine ridges that fall and fade away on either side into hazy, impenetrable valleys running down to the sea. Atop this magical ridge, suspended between heaven and sky, with snow crystals glinting in the sun and the white-capped Alps and Apennines palely luminescent across the Mediterranean's blue gulf, we thought this 'paradise enow'.

But the route itself is unusual, complex and strenuous. Although Corsica's peaks are small by Alpine standards, they give an impression of height and have big vertical intervals. Whereas most Alpine routes run from col to col, traversing snowfields and glaciers, the Corsican High Route generally sticks to ridges. There are no glaciers but the terrain is broken and snow conditions variable. Progress is punctuated by a tiresome 'skins on, skins off' regime. Winter weather can be turbulent, with squalls coming in quickly and unexpectedly. Precipitation is higher than that of any part of south mainland France but, curiously, heavier on the eastern side of the island than the western. Thus, while a billowing cloud sea obliterated the eastern versant for the first four days of our traverse, the western was always clear and brilliantly illuminated by the winter sun.

Snowfall and snow cover are capricious. Proximity to the sea creates a hard, crusty surface névé before the sun gets to it. Thereafter, it soon turns to slush. On our traverse, snow lay thicker and longer on the northern slopes but was usually an unpredictable mishmash of crust and crumble. Some south-facing slopes, though well above the north snowline, were bone bare. But although mushy by afternoon, south-facing snow achieved a degree of consistency through freeze and thaw, and our best runs – Rotondo, Tozzu and outstandingly Cinto – were mainly on such slopes. Both Parmentier and Naar had their problems with the weather. Naar's party was delayed for three days by torrential red rain brought in from the Sahara by the Sirocco. Parmentier counsels as essential prerequisites for this route good navigation and Alpine competence. His own traverse of the Serra Tenda ridge was almost terminated by a windslab avalanche which landed him some way down the Manto Ravine. Storm or bad visibility would make route-finding mistakes serious – especially on the three key ridge passages, Onda to Pietra Piana, Pietra Piana to Manganu and the traverse of Monte Cinto. We were lucky in having only one bad weather day in eight. But that coincided with the critical passage of Pietra Piana to Manganu which, via a series of cols, culminates in the ascent of the SW ridge of the Punta ala Porta. This involved a snake-like progression, weaving through, or sidling along, a staircase studded with rock towers which emerged ghostly through the mist like ships' prows. In such conditions, to have reached the Brèche Capitello barely 4½ hours after leaving the Pietra Piana hut was a triumph of David Williams' navigational skills and the *tour de force* of our traverse.

The huts were a revelation and proved that humping fuel and cooking equipment over the entire route was a needless penance. All were equipped with the complete *batterie de cuisine* and gas cylinders. Solar panels provided instant electricity. But we had our problems. An older member almost parted with his hamstrings after accomplishing a geriatric splits in unyielding snow. Stephen Baker was reduced to a hospital case with torn ligaments after tripping over an inconvenient stone not far from the Col de Verghio.

Clear skies and panoramic mountainscapes set off by a Mediterranean backdrop usually marked our progress and the traverse of Monte Cinto justified Naar's description as 'one of the great ski climbs of Europe'. For the gluttons, the gastronomic high point coincided with our last day. Before catching the train back to Ajaccio, pause awhile at the Francardo's Auberge Casimir. There an eight-course lunch of immodest helpings awaits you with a wizened waiter of unexceptionable attentiveness.

**Summary**: Our northern Corsican ski traverse from Vizzavona to Calaccucia, probably a British first, was completed in seven stages between 26 February and 5 March 1994, with an extra day to climb Rotondo. Team members were Stephen Baker, Patrick Fagan, Rodney Franklin, John Harding, Rupert Hoare, David Williams, with Patrick Hemmerle in part. The stages of the traverse were: Vizzavona to Onda, Onda to Pietra Piana, Pietra Piana to Manganu, Manganu to Col de Verghio, Verghio to Ciottulu; Ciottulu to Tighiettu, and finally Tighiettu to Calaccucia.

*Peaks climbed*: Pinzi Corbini (2021m), Rotondo (2622m) with the zealots also bagging Manicca (2519m), Capu Tozzu (2007m), Paglia Orba (2525m) and Cinto (2706m).

REFERENCES

1   Douglas Freshfield, *Below the Snow Line*. Constable, 49, 1923.
2   Ibid, p70.
3   Dorothy Carrington, *Granite Island*. Longman, 1971.
4   T G Ouston, 'Nineteen Days in Corsica' in *AJ24*, 645, 1908-1909.
5   G I Finch, *The Making of a Mountaineer*. Arrowsmith, 33-39, 1924.

# Three Climbs in Corsica

*(Plates 39, 40)*

It was Willy Van Tellingen, a geologist, who first captivated me with the charm of Corsica, that scrub-covered granite island thrust up through the waters of the Mediterranean. I heard tell of a yachtsman, approaching through a thick coastal mist, who sniffed the scented wild herbs of the maquis before he ever saw the landfall. Willy's professor at Amsterdam used to assign each of his PhD students a few square miles of the island, leave them alone for two months, and then come out to examine them on their findings. Now in retirement, Willy has returned to pursue his profession as a hobby, using the latest radioactive dating techniques to address problems unsolved in his original thesis.

On the first of my five visits to the island we stayed in the tall shuttered house of an expatriate English writer. It was in a small hillside village just behind the Catholic church whose imposing façade overlooked the great sweep of the Bay of Calvi with its citadel where, according to local tradition, Columbus was born and where, two centuries ago in 1774, Nelson lost the sight of his famous eye, pierced by a splinter from a cannon-ball during the siege of Calvi.

The second time, we rented 'La Bergerie', a little stone-built house surrounded by vineyards, ancient olives and fruit trees on the coastal slopes. With the combination of French cuisine, local wine, fresh fruit and honey, we were hooked. As we sat in the shade of a mimosa tree, sipping our breakfast orange juice, an aged aircraft circling slowly above would suddenly eject a dozen tiny dots which blossomed into the parachutes of trainees from the nearby garrison of the Foreign Legion. In the evenings as they strolled off-duty in twos and threes through the streets of Calvi in their smart caps and beige uniforms, they added a *Beau Geste* atmosphere to the town. They were a reassuring counter to the very occasional terrorist incidents one read about in the press.

In July 1994 we rented La Bergerie again and invited friends to join us on all or part of the GR20, one of the best and technically most difficult of the 'Sentiers de Grande Randonnée', which follows the crest of the mountain chain forming the watershed almost the entire length of the island from Calanzana, near Calvi, in the north-west for 240km to Conca in the south-east. I was particularly attracted by three peaks, between 2000m and 2600m high, in the northern, most rugged part of the range: Paglia Orba, Capo Tafonato and Cinque Frati.

All three were climbed in a remarkable week in April 1909 by the Finch brothers, George and Maxwell, with their Norwegian friend Alf Bryn. They were then students in Zurich and chose Corsica as an ideal training ground for Himalayan exploration. In the Alps, a mistake or omission in food or equipment could be remedied by a quick dash to the valley, but in Corsica it would be necessary, as for a Himalayan expedition, to plan every detail in advance, and from the base onwards to rely entirely on their own resources. Their ascent of Paglia Orba by the NE face has become a classic of Corsican mountaineering. George Finch went on to reach over 27,000ft on Everest in 1922. As an experimental scientist, he pioneered the use of oxygen at high altitude and, rejecting the Norfolk jacket style Alpine clothing issued to the team, designed his own jacket from balloon cloth with a quilted lining filled with eider down – the prototype of today's duvet. Finch devoted a chapter to his Corsican climbs in *The Making of a Mountaineer.*

We chose to repeat their Paglia Orba route first. The key is the *Vire Finch* which is a ledge slanting across the otherwise sheer and vertical upper third of the NE face.In April, from their campsite across the valley near the Grotte des Anges, they could clearly see the ledge etched by the residual winter snow. The principal difficulty was to reach the lower northern end of the ledge; its far end joined the upper part of the SE ridge which led to the summit. To avoid losing altitude by having to descend into the valley, we chose a different route of approach which enabled us to stay overnight in the comfortable Refuge Mori, a gentle three-hour walk up from where we left our car at the horseshoe bend of the Fer à Cheval at Verghio. Unpacking our provisions at the hut, I was unable to find the half-bottle of 'Famous Grouse' we had intended for a nightcap. The guardian, observing my distress, disappeared into his private room and emerged to present us, much to our astonishment, with a quarter-full bottle of Scotch which someone had left behind. We slept well!

Leaving the hut next morning shortly after dawn, we contoured eastwards round the southern side of Paglia Orba. We crossed over the Foggiale shoulder and skirted beneath a series of confusing ridges descending from the summit. A peregrine dived towards two wild goats nibbling tussocks far below. Morning mist swirled round about us. It was difficult to discern the start of our route. According to our abridged English guidebook, we had first to cross over the SE ridge at a gap dominated by a large rock resembling the Sphinx. As the mists drifted and dissolved round the rock towers there seemed to be Sphinxes everywhere. We paused at a gap on one prominent ridge beyond which the main face seemed sheer into the distance. The Finch route must surely take this ridge, but we were uncertain. We decided to try climbing it anyway – a succession of towers with short sections of scrambling in between. Some towers we climbed direct, on others we took a line to the left.

We climbed as two pairs. I was roped to Dave Atchison, the youngest and fittest, who took the lead. Mike Westmacott and Peter Newman followed. The rock was generally good, coarse crystals of contorted porphyry. On one particularly exposed pitch – a rising traverse to the left – Dave spotted several pitons, so we were on somebody's route. It seemed quite difficult to me, well up in grade IV and harder than anything we had expected to find on the Finch route. Mike, our veteran of 69 years leading the second rope, admitted that he would have been loth to tackle it had not Dave already succeeded. Higher up, a vertical open corner seemed just as hard, particularly as I did not climb it very neatly and appreciated the reassurance of a tight rope.

Above us reared a vertical tower overhanging slightly at its base. It was composed of entirely different rock: a dark brown, almost black, chunky agglomerate with shallow depressions formed as if by a giant ice-cream scoop. It looked barely possible for anyone to move up from one scoop to the next; certainly not for me. The wall round to the right seemed equally unclimbable. Were we defeated? Could we even get off the ridge? I had no intention of reversing the previous pitches. What had other parties done at this point? Climbing down a few feet to the left, I spotted a tiny cairn; it was the key to an escape route down a gully to the screes below. Safely down, we looked back up at the succession of towers still to be climbed. Dejectedly, we worked back across to the Foggiale shoulder where we could see a sequence of cracks and chimneys leading more easily to the top. To restore our shattered pride, we took them and by 4pm we had reached the summit.

Great clouds were welling up from the west, obscuring the black outline of the Grande Barrière to the north which hid the Cirque de la Solitude, the most awe-inspiring part of the GR20. A wall creeper flew by, flicking its bright red wing patches. Dave descended a few feet and peered over the precipice of the E face. 'I can see where the Finch route started,' he said. 'By the side of that stream bed – not really a ridge at all. We didn't go nearly far enough around; we must have been on the south-east ridge.'

Back at our base we consulted the detailed French guidebook and confirmed that we had indeed climbed a large part of the SE ridge. We had been defeated – like most other parties – by the Tour Popoff, named in honour of a Latvian geologist who had made a special study of its curious pockmarks, or *tafoni*. Although the ridge was first climbed in 1932, the Tour Popoff was not scaled direct until 1962 by Kurt Diemberger.

As we descended by the normal route, on the western side, to the Col des Maures, we came face to face with the crenate ridge of the Capo Tafonato, first traversed by the Finch trio during their great week in April 1909, five years after the first ascent of its highest northern summit by Professor von Cube, one of the pioneers of Corsican mountaineering. It is a most striking peak, comprising a thin wedge of porphyry, oriented north-south, about 200m high and 600m in length. Astonishingly, at mid-height it is pierced by a huge crescent window some 20m across. Seen from afar, the hole with clouds behind it can easily be mistaken for a patch of winter snow.

The peak is a very popular and easy climb by a series of ledges slanting up from the col and skirting along the 'window sill' and around the north ridge, from where a short slab leads to the summit. We planned to do it the next day and it proved a delightful excursion after our exertions on Paglia Orba. We should have continued with the traverse, which involved a long rappel at the south end, but I felt lethargic and probably influenced my companions to agree that the exiguous north summit was sufficient. We lay there on a tangle of rope, basking in the sunshine. On the western slopes far below, the shadow of our peak was pierced by a shaft of sunlight shining through the crescent window. To the east we could just discern two climbers we had met earlier at the hut but who were now wedged securely in a shadowed vertical groove on the precipitous NW face of Paglia Orba. They were on *Surella d'Irlanda*, a grade VI route first climbed in 1980. We had the easy option, descending to our favourite plunge pool above the pine forest and the Cascade de Radule, and then under ominous lightning and thunder clouds just reaching our car as the first heavy raindrops splattered down.

A few days later, Hamish Nicol had completed his main objective of the holiday – walking the whole of the GR20 – and was ready for a final climb. We were now five. What could be more appropriate than the third of the Finch routes, the traverse of the Cinque Frati, a series of rock towers to the south of Monte Albano, resembling cowled monks in prayer, seen clearly in profile across the valley from Paglia Orba? This time, after a brief recce, we bivouacked by the riverside in the pinewoods by the Bergerie de Melarie. There were no sheep, but several wild pigs foraged amongst the pine cones. We were in position early, so we relaxed and bathed and read or lay on our backs on fallen tree-trunks, binoculars at hand, eyes searching the pine branches for a sight of the elusive Corsican nuthatch, unique to the island and distinguished from the normal species by a conspicuous white stripe above the eye. A golden eagle soared overhead as our spaghetti was cooking. We dined with a liberal ration of Scotch and turned in early. I lay in my sleeping-bag writing my diary to the sound of Hamish's snores.

Breakfast was enlivened by Peter proffering a bloody hand to Hamish, our doctor, for treatment. He had woken abruptly after midnight with the shock of finding his fingers in a pig's mouth! The pig was doubtless equally shocked. We hoped rabies would not develop before we were safely off the mountain.

We set off at 6.30am up a maquis-covered ravine to the base of the first of the Frati, following the bed of the gully to avoid the more impenetrable vegetation. Like taking snuff, one could pinch the leaves of wild thyme and rosemary and enjoy a noseful of scent. Having come up on the SW side, it took us 2½ hours to reach the roping-up point; once there, we realised we could probably have come more quickly up the SE slopes directly above the village of Calasima. I had taken notes from the French guidebook so, as instructed, encouraged Dave to lead up a long couloir, well visible from Calasima. It took him some time to get launched, so the other three, roped up and impatient to get going, selected a gully to the left. We didn't meet again until after the first summit; they got there first, but Hamish and I both insist we were on the correct route! At least ours followed the description rather well, avoiding an overhanging wall at mid-point by going up left and then back right by a tricky out-of-balance move. I was glad Dave was leading. The second tower was straightforward, and we roped down into the gap between it and the third Frati. This gave delightful climbing on compact slabs. At the same time we could see storm-clouds gathering from the west, with just an occasional few drops of rain. If the slabs became wet and slippery we would have to take especial care. The gap between the fourth and fifth towers, named the Coup de Sabre, was sheer and narrow and gave a sensational view to the west where black clouds were now obscuring Paglia Orba.

We just made it to the fifth and final tower with time for a quick snack before the heavens opened to the accompaniment of lightning and almost instantaneous thunder. We had to get off as quickly as possible and selected a long gully descending to the east. I had just completed a long rappel when a blinding flash struck us all; Hamish, still on the summit, was bowled over. The metal figure-of-eight descender in my hand became charged with electricity. I released it in shock. Had the current travelled down the wet rope? We were now drenched by the rain and moved on down as fast as we could. Looking back up, as we reached the lower slopes, the gullies between each of the Frati, which had previously been dry, were now like Yosemite waterfalls.

We pushed on down to the valley, getting separated from Peter who had taken a slightly different route towards the valley's main stream. That would now be impassable; crossing the various tributaries coming down from the Frati was exciting enough. We were concerned for Peter's safety. But all was well. After 2½ hours the rain stopped and by 7pm five bedraggled climbers straggled onto the main street of Calasima to face the bemused stares of villagers who were taking the evening air. They had seen us that morning in the initial couloir of the first of the Frati and were wondering how we had weathered the storm.

'Well,' said Hamish, taking off his helmet, climbing harness and soaking anorak. 'We have turned an adventure into an epic. Do you really think we should be doing this at our age?'

# Above and Below the Snow-line

### SNOW LEOPARD

She sloughed off her rucksack
and stood stilling her heart,
staring fiercely from this last
rise that was her journey's end.
She would take her time now.
Time was what he had given her.
Misted ridges rose like ghosts
towards their tombstone summits.
It was not as she expected –
so vast, so complex, so bright.
In this stark early light
the range was a wall of white
and blue, snow and shadow
that somewhere held him fast
in a slow echo of his fall
towards the glacier snout.

She would have to face the finding
of his axe, perhaps, even
his body resurfacing, some
future climbers' reluctant
photograph that would show
his scarf, perhaps, before they
rolled him into a crevasse
and turned towards their summit.
It had happened to others before.
Here it could not end for her.
Even the ice kept moving.
Even this morning she had seen
before sunrise, on the opposite
bank, a white on white shadow
she had not sought, and even now
dare not give a name.

*Terry Gifford*

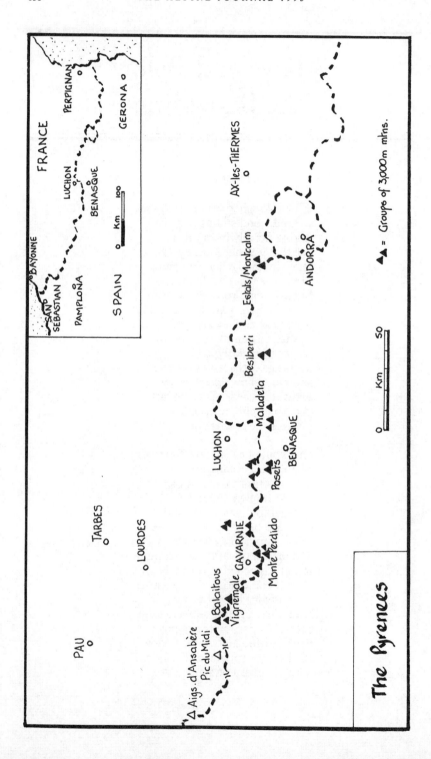

The Pyrenees

KEV REYNOLDS

# Pyrenees 3000

*(Plates 47, 48)*

In an age when the ultimate challenge for mountaineering list-tickers is the ascent of all fourteen 8000m giants of the Himalaya; when there are the continental Seven Summits as a secondary objective, and all the 4000m Alpine peaks have been climbed in a single season, the 3000m summits of the Pyrenees may seem rather tame by comparison.

Thank heaven for that!

Here are mountains and wild romantic landscapes of another order; peaks to enjoy for themselves, not to be assessed as collectable items like postage stamps or matchbox labels. The Pyrenees escape such attention because their mountains, ridges, aiguilles and faces remain largely unsung by activists beyond southern France and northern Spain; there are no reputations to be won or lost, and you can spend a whole summer of intense activity there and return home to be greeted by the bewildered indifference of one's peers. Mountaineering beyond the spotlight. Long may it last. Since there is nothing to suggest that increased height guarantees either routes of advanced difficulty or grace of form in mountain structure, in the Pyrenees as elsewhere some of the hardest climbs and most elegant outlines are to be found on peaks of modest growth; for example, the limestone aiguilles of Ansabère in the Cirque de Lescun at less than 2400m, or on the fine, shapely Pic du Midi d'Ossau at just 2885m – a true rock-climber's playground, if ever there was one.

The Pyrenees have little permanent snow and their glaciers are fast shrinking away. Few ice routes last much beyond Easter. But where snow and ice do remain as more than a daub of white in a shadowed gully, the mountains respond with a smile that attracts far-off.

The highest of all is Pico d'Aneto (Néthou to the French) at 3404m, the culminating point of the Maladeta massif just south of the frontier ridge, and separated from it by the flower-rich moat of the Esera valley in the central part of the range. From its summit a vast panorama is revealed. To the north, beyond the frontier crest, French foothills are awash with forest green. Out to the south successive sierras fade into the haze that hinders lowland Spain, while to east and west a jumble of peaks rise from barely-hinted valleys. Shapely peaks appear, like the double-pronged Forcanada, and large, sprawling blocks such as that of the Posets massif across the Esera to the west, where the range's second highest summit (Punta de Llardana) rises to 3375m. Defining peaks and summits is no easy matter, and the criteria for establishing a 3000m mountain is open to debate which goes beyond simple altitude measurement. In 1935 a list of just 41 summits was published in the journal of the *Unio Excursionista de Catalonia*. In 1968 that number was increased to 57; in 1977 it was 97, then 122! The Spaniards were particularly adept at finding 'new' tops for the list, and one could be forgiven for thinking that some major upheaval was going on in the Pyrenees as by leaps and bounds the total rose to 161, then fell to 153, then dropped further to 150.

In 1990 a new inventory was agreed by activists from both sides of the frontier, giving a total of no less than 278 tops. So, according to definition (and for the time being), the range boasts 129 principal peaks of 3000m or more, plus 67 secondary summits and 82 ridge projections. The majority will be found west of the Esera where they crowd along or near the frontier ridge, which mostly forms the watershed. There are exceptions to the rule, and some are so isolated from the main crest as to demand extensive forays from it. Most are ranged among massifs of considerable charm in which days of activity and scenic splendour underline the very essence of *Pyrénéisme*. But are they mountains to collect? Or mountains to admire? To my mind they are part of an overall landscape, and sometimes it's enough just to be there, moving aimlessly among and over them. But then, I never was strong on ambition.

Beginning in the west, the first to reach the 3000m mark is the Balaitous, a sturdy massif of grey granite bristling with ridges above small napkin glaciers. Found to the east of Pic du Midi d'Ossau, its southern flanks plunge to a barren Spanish valley via the Picos de Frondella, whose ridge is punctuated by a trio of listed summits. At 3144m the main peak of Balaitous was first climbed in 1825 by the military surveyors Peytier and Hossard, but details of their route were lost for decades, and even Charles Packe, that most thorough of all the early pioneers, did not know it had been climbed until, almost forty years later, he reached the summit and found a cairn already there.

South-south-east of Balaitous a clutch of summits top the magical 3000m mark. First the Picos de las Argulas with three peaks (Argulas, Algas and Garmo Negro), and the neighbouring Picos del Infernio (or Pics d'Enfer), lording it over a wild and stony region littered with tarns. These are all well within Spanish territory and accessible either by serpentine roads built to service hydro schemes above the Valle de Tena, or by long approach marches from the Marcadau valley in France. If one approaches from France, Cauterets is the nearest centre, but that is still a good two days' walk away. The best bet is to drive to Pont d'Espagne, then hike through the Marcadau valley and cross either Col de la Fache or the Port du Marcadau to gain this wilderness.

Col de la Fache is an easy saddle on the N ridge of the Grande Fache (3005m), surely one of the most accessible of all 3000m summits, being won by little more than a rough walk from the col. On 5 August each year a pilgrimage is held there in honour of all those who have died in the mountains. Though Grande Fache itself holds no great challenge, the country it surveys is second to none, the Marcadau especially forming a luxury of soft pasture, stony hidden corries and lots of twinkling tarns.

Seen peering over Col d'Arratille SE of the Marcadau's Refuge Wallon, the Clot de la Hount face of the Vignemale betrays none of the splendour of that mountain's great N face which soars out of the glacial plain of Oulettes de Gaube. Highest of all frontier peaks at 3298m, the Vignemale spawns the longest Pyrenean glacier which flows down its eastern flank and provides the most natural route of ascent, while rock-climbers have 800m or more of slab wall to play upon, or the classic Couloir de Gaube which gives out onto the glacier just below the summit.

Pique Longue is the crowning point, but there are other summits too: Pic du Clot de la Hount (3289m), Pointe Chausenque (3204m), Piton Carré (3197m) and the Petit Vignemale at 3032m, the latter reached by a short stroll from the Hourquette d'Ossoue which forms a convenient link between the Oulettes de Gaube and Bayssellance huts.

Continuing along the frontier ridge south-eastward, the neighbouring Pic de Cerbillona and Pic Central rise either side of Col Lady Lyster – named after Miss Anne Lister from Halifax who made the first tourist ascent of the Vignemale in 1838. Then come several 3000m ridge projections before rising to Pic de Montferrat (3219m), Grand Pic de Tapou (3150m) and Pic du Milieu (3130m) overlooking the deserted Ara valley which contains all the warm mystery of Spain.

The lower reaches of the Ara are accessible by vehicle – as long as you have no regard for your car's suspension. Napoleon had plans to force a road across the Port de Gavarnie (Port de Boucharo) and down through the Ara to gain access to the Ebro Basin, but his road-building plans here came to nought. However, a road exists today from Gavarnie on the French side to the col, where trippers and climbers leave their cars for a short walk round to the Refuge de la Brèche (Refuge des Sarradets). From here no less than a dozen 3000m summits may be tackled.

Most of these form the rim of the fabled Cirque de Gavarnie, from the easternmost Pic de Gabiétous (3031m) to the Grand Astazou (3071m) – a fabulous horseshoe that rises in several tiers, like a sliced simnel cake, out of the valley of the Gave de Pau. Climbers of modest ability can play daring games along the crest, left foot in France, right boot in Spain, leaving the cascade-dashed walls to those with greater ambition. In winter these walls come into their own as ice climbs of fluctuating appeal.

Pic du Marboré is the highest on the rim at 3248m, while running away from it to the south-east are the visually uninspiring Las Tres Sorores: Cylindre du Marboré, Monte Perdido (Mont Perdu) and Sum de Ramond. Of these Perdido (3355m) holds the most interest, not just because it is the third highest Pyrenean summit, but because of the beautiful ice-hung NE face tackled from the Balcon de Pineta overlooking the Pineta valley. The south-western side of Perdido blocks the head of the Arazas, the enchanting Ordesa canyon, while the last of the 3000m peaks here, Punta de las Olas, peers down on the deep and narrow slice of the Anisclo canyon – worth a day or two of anyone's time to explore.

The frontier crest moves on roughly eastwards from the Cirque de Gavarnie to form the Cirque de Estaubé, with peaks of 2800m plus, then, beginning at the modest Pic de Bouneu, a great ridge system sweeps round as the Cirque de Troumouse. This amphitheatre contains several tops over 3000m, the highest being Pic de la Munia at 3133m. Izard and marmot are kings here, while lammergeier cast dark cross-like shadows as they sail the thermals overhead.

This is very much 'cirque' country, for the south-eastern side of Pic de la Munia falls into the Cirque de Barrosa, while nearby Pic de Troumouse forms the lynchpin of both the Troumouse cirque and that of the Cirque de Barroude, the latter with a noteworthy wall rising from a teardrop of a lake accessible by a longish walk from Aragnouet in the Vallée d'Aure.

North of Barroude, and remote from the frontier ridge, the Réserve Naturelle de Néouvielle forms an adjunct to the Parc National des Pyrénées Occidentales. Although the hydro engineers have done more than their fair share of taming the Néouvielle region, it remains a superb area for trekking. There are numerous cols to cross, some wild and stony, others green and welcoming, that link tarn-bright valleys where a few huts provide an alternative to overnight camping.

As for mountains, the Néouvielle is not short of 'big' peaks, with thirteen claiming 3000m. Pic Long (3192m) is the highest, with a 600m N face rising from a small lake. Turon de Néouvielle was the first Pyrenean 3000er to be climbed (1787); Pic de Néouvielle was claimed in 1847 by De Chausenque, while Pic de Campbieil (3173m), neighbouring Pic Long to the south-east, demands little more than a long walk and scramble to reach the summit.

Trekkers tackling the classic Pyrenean High Route follow the frontier ridge eastwards from Barroude for two days before the next confrontation with a 3000m mountain. Along the way there are few nearby peaks, if any, that display charisma. That is not to suggest that the landscape is dull or uninteresting. The truth is, a vast sea of peaklets fills every horizon, while the valleys themselves tease with twists of silver and the only sounds that come drifting on a summer breeze are the occasional clatter of stones bouncing through a gully, and the far-off boom of a cascade. The world is just as nature intended.

The Vallé de Rioumajou has an appeal of remoteness. At its head a tight curve of ridges holds Spain at bay, but due east of the renovated Hospice de Rioumajou, Pic de Batoua (3034m) marks a resumption of lofty peaks, although offering little of note for the climber. The frontier ridge continues north-eastward to Pic de Guerreys, where the main crest and political boundary part company. The crest continues to the north where Pic de Lustou adds one more 3000m to the list, while the frontier dips south-eastward to Port de la Pez, then rises to another group of 3000m summits.

From each of these, as from the ridge itself, views south are dominated by the extensive block of the Posets massif, a great fortress of stone and screes, with dying glaciers dashed up high and jewel-like tarns cradled in the outstretched arms of this Pyrenean viceroy. Nine 'peaks' of the Posets massif are 3000ers, but for climbing interest attention is focused elsewhere. There are some charming glens fenced in by sturdy little spires. There are long arêtes to follow. There are secluded, sun-washed plateaux where streams meander out of late-spring snows, and high passes to draw the inquisitive wanderer.

Halkett, Redonnet and Pierre Barrau gained the 3375m summit of Posets in August 1856. Packe (AC Secretary 1870-71) was also attracted to the region and made a new route of his own by way of the then-formidable Glacier de Posets that today has almost completely disappeared. Packe's route is now taken as the *voie normale*, but the Ollivier guide details more than twenty ascent routes to the main peak, none of which is particularly difficult. Summit views are extensive and reckoned by many to be the best in all the Pyrenees, while the Estos valley that curves below the northern flanks of the massif, is one of the loveliest of all.

A long, steep haul up the northern hillside above the Estos hut leads to the Port d'Oo by which France is gained. From the Port the contrasting nature of the two sides of the Pyrenees is openly revealed; small glaciers on the French slopes, barren screes and dry rock on the Spanish. Gazing into France from the ridge, one is taken by an array of upthrusting peaks of considerable appeal: Pic des Gourgs Blanc nearby, Pic Gourdon and Spijoles, Pic Belloc, Grand Quayrat, Pic Lézat, Crabioules and Perdiguère. Deep below, in natural stony wells, turquoise lakes hold ice-floes often into September. This is a region worth spending time in, with climbs of quality in a magical setting. As for 3000m summits, there are no less than twenty principal peaks, and another 20 secondary summits to play upon.

The best approach to the Clarabide–Perdiguère massif is from Luchon via Lac d'Oo. Both the GR10 and a *variante* of the Pyrenean High Route make use of Refuge d'Espingo, so solitude is not to be expected there. A better bet is to take a small tent and find a secluded corner with a clear stream running and climbs almost from the doorway.

Luchon is accessible by train from Paris, making it a convenient point from which to strike south for the Maladeta massif, crossing the frontier ridge either at Col de la Glère, Port de Venasque or (a longer route) Port de la Picade. From either of these passes the Maladeta looks impressive: a huge block of mountain on the far side of the Esera valley with two shrinking glaciers draped against its north-facing slopes. Dividing the two glaciers is the long arête of the Cresta de los Portillones. Below the Cresta on its western side is the barn-like Renclusa hut, while Pico de Aneto rises high above its glacier on the eastern side. First climbed in 1842 by the Russian, Platon de Tchihatcheff, with Albert de Francqueville and the guides Argarot, Redonnet and Ursule, the standard route across the Portillone and Aneto glacier from the Renclusa hut takes about five hours.

But there's much more to the Maladeta than Aneto's crown. The western Maladeta ridge provides an enjoyable scramble over lots of minor summits and gendarmes, all at 3200m or more; there's the Tempestades crest stretching SE of Aneto, and the lovely firm granite of the Cresta de Salenques rising from the Col de Salenques to Pico Margalida. There are seventeen 3000ers and plenty of secondary peaks, and a long day's sport to be had in combining the great ridge systems of the whole massif in an outing that will have you gasping for liquid by the time you finish. South of Maladeta, and separated from it by the Vallhiverna, stands another 3000er, Pico de Vallibierna (3067m).

Above the Port de la Picada the frontier swings north, and only resumes its eastward trend along the northern wall of the Vall d'Aran, that Pyrenean anomaly being geographically French, but politically Spanish.

South of Vall d'Aran, and bordered on the west by the valley of the Rio Noguera Ribagorzana, is a wonderland of small granite peaks and an amazing collection of tarns. Some of these drain north to the Vall d'Aran; others feed streams that wash southward to the Noguera de Tor and Caldas de Bohi. At the head of romantic valley systems sheep graze in the shadow of dozens of attractive peaks. Hillwalkers with an eye for the country can dream up circuits of some of these peaks, with remote cols that overlook a true mountain wilderness, while there's enough rock sport to keep a climber happy through many a long summer's day.

Forming a lofty spine between the Noguera Ribagorzana and Noguera de Tor, the Besiberri massif seduces with lengthy ridge traverses, during which one can knit a choice selection of summits that look off to the Maladeta in one direction, and east towards the Encantados – Robin Fedden's *Enchanted Mountains*. The Besiberri claims five 3000ers, with a sixth rising east of the Cavallers dam (Punta Alta, 3014m).

It's a long trek east from the Besiberri massif to find the last of the 3000m peaks in the Pyrenees. It's a trek that goes out to the Vall d'Aran, then tackles several high passes round Mont Roig, crosses some challenging wild country, visits more tarns and, at last, cuts along the Vall Ferrera to the slopes of Pica d'Estats (3143m), the most cluttered summit of all, across which the Franco-Spanish border hiccups its silent way.

Estats is linked with Pic de Sottlo (3075m), which is also on the frontier ridge, and by a spur to Pic de Montcalm (3077m) towering over the forested tangle of valleys of Ariège. On the summit of Montcalm stands a large cairn, erected back in 1827 by Coroboef and Testu who first stood there and tried to unravel the geography of this delightful, yet still largely unworked range.

The Estats–Montcalm massif attracts more by its altitude than by any great mountaineering challenge or charisma. There are no rock climbs to speak of. The main summits are all accessible from Refugi de Vall Ferrera without much difficulty, while an opportunity to create some airy ridgewalks provides the proper focus for one's energies. However, the tangled, seemingly remote mountain landscape spread below and all around gives an impression of solitude.

Off to the east a corrugation of peak and ridge marks the rim of Andorra. Beyond that, various massifs hold their own individual appeal, rising and falling towards the Mediterranean. They may not claim any more 3000ers, but those who love mountains for what they are, and not what reputation has given them, who care more for time spent among them than as part of a 'ticking' campaign, will be well content. For every day spent among the hills is a day worth living.

ROBERT NEW

# Kinabalu: Summit of Borneo

*(Plates 55–59)*

Until this year, as a result of worldwide media attention, Mount Kinabalu was either largely unknown in the West or regarded as a fairly chunky but otherwise easy mountain of no particular interest to mountaineers. Few can now claim not to have heard of the mountain and, although their idea of Kinabalu has undoubtedly been modified by reportage often erring towards sensationalism, many are left not quite grasping what the mountain is really like.

Thinking back to my UK schooldays, neither geography nor history lessons had much, if anything, to say about Borneo. Except to know that it is the world's largest island, it remained something of an overlooked dark green spot on the world map that was far too backward and inconsequential to justify any study. It was only after a two-year spell in Uganda, during which the Ruwenzori mountains absorbed all my available leave, that wanderlust set me looking for jobs in the Far East. Hong Kong and Sabah seemed to be the only places requiring general practice surveyors in the mid-1970s. Hong Kong really didn't appeal (I have never been inspired to regard tall buildings as climbing challenges), but Sabah at least sounded different. First question: 'Are there any mountains there?' The answer was 'Well ... er ... yes, there is one mountain – but nothing very special.'

A check in the atlas showed Mount Kinabalu (pronounced Kinabaaloo) at 13,455ft – quite respectable really, considering it rises almost from sea-level. At not much less than either Mont Blanc or the Ruwenzori, it must surely offer some potential. So that settled the decision in favour of Sabah.

Tropical rain forest areas are not noted for their clear atmosphere and clouds generally gather after mid-morning. So one is very lucky to see the mountain when first arriving in Kota Kinabalu, the capital of Sabah (formerly known as Jesselton and North Borneo respectively). The early mornings are usually clear, however, and the mountain can be seen presiding over the comings and goings of everyday life, somewhat aloof and distant but ever present. This sight touches the soul, especially at sunrise when silhouetted against the morning sky its presence appears closer. Sometimes the mountain is seen even in the afternoon with its personality changing hour by hour, so that it almost takes on a character of its own in the minds of West Coast residents.

The first person to write in English about Mount Kinabalu was Alexander Dalrymple in 1769. The Idaan to which he refers are the Dusun of today who live on the lower slopes around Mount Kinabalu. He wrote:

> The Idaan have very many whimsical religious tenets; paradise is generally supposed to be a top of Keeney-Balloo ... guarded by a fiery dog who is a formidable opponent to the female sex; for, whenever any virgins come, he seizes them as his legal prize; but whatever women have been cohabited with in this world he considers as unworthy of his embrace and lets them pass.[1]

In 1922 another writer, Owen Rutter, observed:

> Mount Kinabalu is undoubtedly the most striking physical feature of North Borneo ... a landmark from afar; it rises sheer and wonderful above a thousand hills ... it is no wonder that natives hold it in veneration as the resting place of departed spirits and a dragon's home.[2]

Of course until Europeans started climbing the mountain the Dusun, although living up to about 6000ft, would have regarded the mountain peak as hostile. Early climbers had difficulty recruiting guides and porters because none had explored the mountain and all were petrified of the mountain spirits. The accounts of the early ascents show that non-Dusun porters had to be used and the Dusun guide bribed handsomely. Even then, long stops were required for religious rites and the guide refused to go above the tree line. After one of the early ascents an epidemic of illness in the villages was interpreted as retribution by the spirits for disturbing their peace, and the villagers were exceedingly hostile to visitors wishing to climb the mountain. Even the Chinese traders, going back to the beginning of the Ming dynasty, held Mount Kinabalu in awe. In China the most extravagant legends were accepted and it is possible that some of these spilled back into local folklore. Even today, despite knowledge and familiarity casting the old notions aside, the mountain is held in wide reverence and awe and largely regarded as the heavenly residence for the spirit world.

So why all this fuss? Most of Borneo rises only to about 3000ft, except for the Crocker range which rises to about 6000ft and stretches down almost the entire length of Borneo a little inland from the west coast. This entire area is covered with jungle except where placed under cultivation. Within the jungle is a world dominated by green shade with hardly ever a vista. Mount Kinabalu, rising to 13,455ft, is a complete contrast and it was perhaps that very contrast which led American aeroplanes flying over Sabah in the Second World War to report: 'Say, that God-dammed thing cannot be 13,000. Why that's nothing. It must be near as high as Mount Everest. These Borneo maps are all to hell anyway.'[3] By the end of that year all American war maps of Borneo were overstamped 19,000ft!

Kinabalu, even more than Mount Kenya and Kilimanjaro, positively forces itself on the conscience of its viewers. Moreover its open rock faces, distant panoramic views and occasional snow and ice contrast dramatically with the rest of Borneo, while unique flora and fauna provide excitement for scientists and fascination even for the casual visitor.

Kinabalu's special stature also arises from its unusual evolution. Although once regarded as a very ancient formation, it is now believed to be one of the youngest great mountains in the world. 'The whole structure has emerged, as granite through sandstone, in little more than a million years – mere child's play in geological time.' [4] This process is said to be still continuing at the rate of one fifth of an inch each year. The granite of Kinabalu is of course much harder than the sandstone of the Crocker range and accounts for the steep rock faces which surround the mountain and the numerous sharp peaks rising above the large summit plateau, which extends to about four square miles. Some of the flanks of the mountain form into ridges, the most prominent being to the south, east, north and north-west. Between the north and north-west ridges a deep cleft cuts into the mountain and its summit plateau, so dividing the plateau into two. The south ridge provides the easiest gradients and, because it also runs down to the Tenompok Pass over the Crocker range, this is the most accessible route on the mountain and provides today's standard summit trail.

The north and east slopes of the mountain fall to thick montane forest and primary jungle which extends for many miles before reaching villages and roads. Expeditions have had to choose between the easier terrain of the ridges, with no water, and the difficult terrain of the valleys with, if anything, too much water, and this side of the mountain remains a formidable challenge to expeditions.

Kinabalu was first climbed by Hugh Low in 1851. At that time, the journey to the base of the mountain from the coast was a much greater ordeal than climbing the mountain itself. Few today who leave their cars at 6500ft can possibly imagine what it was like to reach this point after walking for two weeks through the jungle. On his first expedition Low climbed to the col between Tunku Abdul Rahman Peak to the east and the Donkey's Ears to the west where there is a precipitous drop into the most impressive gully. This gully leads down into the main northwards cleft of the mountain, named after Low, while the impassive head of the gully into which Low looked is now called Commando Cauldron after a commando expedition which reconnoitred the area in December 1964. The col is now called Cauldron Gap. Low on finding a steep narrow ridge reported:

> On placing my breast against it and looking over the ridge, I gazed into a circular amphitheatre about 80 yards broad, the bottom of which from its great depth and my position overhanging it, was undiscernable, though I imagine I could see down two thousand feet.[5]

It is reported that after 'finishing an excellent bottle of madeira to Her Majesty's health' he left a note in the bottle and descended.[6] He reported being overtaken by 'Scotch mist' but possibly the excellent madeira contributed to that problem.

Ironically, although Low returned to climb the mountain twice in 1858, he never reached the summit and although his companion, Spencer St. John, climbed the peak immediately to the west of the summit to within 40ft, somehow the very much easier summit eluded him. From all available research, it appears that the first person to reach the true summit of Kinabalu was John Whitehead in 1888 on what is believed to have been the eleventh recorded expedition to climb the mountain.[7]

Other expeditions followed but during the first 100 years after Low made his inaugural climb in 1851 there were only 53 recorded visits made to the mountain. By modern standards, the early expeditions were amazing. The prize seems to go to Capt F C Learmouth who, accompanied by four others, and Wigson, a bull terrier that was probably the first and last dog to reach the summit, climbed the mountain in 1910 with over 100 porters. They certainly didn't stint on comfort and carried beds, mattresses, chairs, etc up the mountain. This expedition was in fact responsible for first establishing the height of the mountain at 13,455ft, and one of its members made a film of the expedition.[8]

Early expeditions also had to contend with elaborate religious ceremonies carried out by their guides and porters. There does not appear to have been any set pattern to these rites, and the number of chicken and other sacrifices that the expeditions were required to purchase seemed to grow year by year. Fortunately, with over 20,000 people climbing the mountain each year, these ceremonies have been dropped but the pay-off seems to be the Park requirement that all climbers hire Dusun guides who, for the pleasure of their company, charge RM40 per day (about £10).

There are now huts at four locations on the mountain. The lowest, known as Layang Layang Hut (formerly Carson's Camp), is positioned at about 8200ft and normally only takes a backpacking party about two hours to reach. This hut is strategically located on the lower border of the ultra basic rock zone so there is a significant change in the vegetation at this point. Accordingly, this hut is normally used only by scientists and park staff. The main base for climbers at the end of their first day's trek is at Panar Laban which is immediately below large rock slabs up which the summit route originally went. This base comprises two small aluminium huts at about 10,900ft and, more recently, the larger Gunting Lagadan Hut built almost adjoining. A little lower is the newest, Laban Rata Hut, at about 10,500ft, which boasts hot showers (if you are lucky) and a restaurant service.

The Panar Laban/Laban Rata huts accommodate about 150 people and despite the rarity of good sunrises most climbers make an early start to reach the summit at about 5.30am. The trail up to Panar Laban is an

7. North Face of the Vignemale, 3298m, seen from above the
Refuge des Oulettes. (*Kev Reynolds*) (p139)

8. The Besiberri peaks, seen to the west of Port de Colomers.
(*Kev Reynolds*) (p139)

49.  Antarctica:  the Towers of Cape Renard.
    (*Julian Freeman-Attwood*)  (p75)

0. Julian Freeman-Attwood on *Pelagic* with the Towers of Cape Renard beyond. (*Matt Dickinson*) (p75)

1. Skip Novak and Frank McDermot on the summit ridge of Mt Williams, *c*4970ft, with the Anvers Island ice piedmont down left. (*Julian Freeman-Attwood*) (p75)

52. Kilimanjaro from Amboseli National Park. The Kilimanjaro national park plan
aims to establish corridors to allow elephant to migrate from the plains
to the high montane forest. (*Paul Clarke*) (p113)

3. Mount Meru, Tanzania: view of crater from northern rim showing the summit, 4566m, and subsidiary ash cone. (*Graeme Watson*) (p117)

4. Tanzania: Kerimasi, 2614m, as seen from the summit of Lengai. (*Graeme Watson*) (p117)

55.  Mt Kinabalu, 4101m, Malaysia.  Steps on the standard trail to the summit.
     (*Robert New*)  (p145)

6. Low's Gully which falls over 900m from the summit plateau of Mt Kinabalu. (*Robert New*) (p150)

57. Young bracts at 12,500ft. Kinabalu Park protects and preserves the complete spread of plant life from lowland tropical forest to the limit of plant growth on the summit. (*Robert New*) (p145)

58. Mt Kinabalu: Dewali Pinnacles at sunset seen from the West Gurkha Hut. (*Robert New*) (p150)

59. West Gurkha Hut, 3840m, and Dewali Pinnacles. (*Robert New*) (p149)

almost unrelenting staircase through various types of montane forest. Above Panar Laban the terrain is more rocky and the vegetation is shrubby and starts thinning out. The first half mile is a series of wooden step-ladders which give way to a rocky trail leading to the top of the vegetation zone and the point where you climb on bare rock. From here the Park authority has secured fixed ropes all the way to the summit. On the steeper sections these are helpful but on much of the trail one simply walks along beside the rope which was placed after several people disappeared on the mountain without trace after missing the old cairns in bad weather.

At about 12,000ft one passes the Sayat-Sayat Hut which is a basic steel uniport shelter enjoying expansive views and a situation immediately below some of the summit pinnacles. This is a good base for climbing expeditions except for the fact that at about 4.30 every morning 150 people tramp by chattering away and wondering what the hut looks like inside. Dave Nichol, who wrote[9] about Kinabalu in the 1985 AJ, stayed here, but if you like late lie-ins, this is not for you.

The summit is in many ways the same anti-climax that so many summits offer today, with numerous mementoes left by proud climbers in the form of flags, inscribed plaques, notes in bottles and such-like, as well as film wrappers, sweet papers, tin cans, torn plastic macs, etc, etc. At sunrise you share the summit with 150 others, oblige a Japanese tour group by taking their photograph, blink at flash guns going off all around you and feel self-satisfied that you are amongst the few élite who have ever explored the other parts of this beautiful mountain. All this has inevitably given rise to the notion that Mount Kinabalu is an easy mountain. A notion which has caught some climbers off guard and has discouraged others from giving the mountain a second thought.

By half past six you are alone on the summit. The day's visitors are now racing down in a state of fulfilment, blissfully unaware that within an hour most of them will be suffering leg and knee pains the like of which they have never had before. Now you can enjoy the other, more real Mount Kinabalu: the magnificent rock peaks around you, the views over the entire north of Borneo and, for those used to living on the equator, the joy of a cool refreshing atmosphere. What you cannot fail to notice, however, is Low's Gully, the cleft that splits the mountain in two. You cannot see the bottom but you can see the steep rock sides dropping away unrelentingly into the invisible depths of the abyss – a sight that must have inspired every true climber who has ever climbed the mountain. From the summit, a short walk into the West Cwm area takes you to the West Gurkha Hut, a cosy little four-man hut encircled by granite peaks and pinnacles, except to the north-west where there is an expansive view to the coast. Built by the author in 1985 with the help of Gurkha soldiers stationed with the British garrison in Brunei at 12,600ft, this is a place where one can be at one with the mountain. It is the place for sunsets, meditation and as a base for climbing anywhere on the west plateau away from the crowds.

Some of the major peaks, of which there are about eleven, have easy ways up. Others, such as the Donkey's Ears, Dewali Pinnacles and King Edward Peak, require rock-climbing skills. But the Park authorities are always nervous about parties climbing any routes other than the standard trail. This nervousness arises because they have no mountain rescue service available, search and rescue being almost hopeless in jungle terrain. There is also the problem that international rings have been denuding some areas of the mountain of rare orchids and other plants.

To date, routes have been made down the full length of the East Ridge to Poring Hot Springs, up the NW flank by way of Marai Parai, up the Mesilau river to the East Plateau via the E ridge, up the Panataran river to North Peak and down Low's Gully to Kampung Melankap Kappa. There is also a route linking the East and West Plateaux. Unfortunately, relatively few climbing expeditions have left route descriptions behind and, of the 30 or so reports collected together so far, the actual descriptions are very poorly written and difficult to follow. When climbing, one comes across a lot of pitons and expansion bolts indicating earlier climbs, often by Japanese parties. Nonetheless, most of these have followed the easiest route to the top and there is an abundance of classic-looking lines still to be climbed. In particular, there is enormous scope to pioneer rock routes on the big faces that face into Low's Gully and on the steeper outer flanks of the mountain itself. With only a handful of people living in the area with more than a passing interest in rock climbing, new horizons in this aspect of the mountain will be very slow in emerging, especially so long as Mount Kinabalu suffers the 'only for tourists' tag.

The one event which may possibly change that is the unsuccessful and almost tragic British Army expedition which planned to make a first complete descent of Low's Gully. The attention given by the international press and television networks has now placed Mount Kinabalu within the knowledge of ordinary people throughout the world. With the writing of books and production of a film, this exposure will continue for a while yet. The bad aspect of all this is the sensationalism which has arisen in its wake. The good aspect is hopefully that some strong climbers will view Kinabalu as a mountain worthy of respect and deeper exploration.

Whatever routes may be completed in the future, Low's Gully must remain a special challenge. We all remember certain classic routes that we have done, such as routes along narrow arêtes in breathtaking positions. It is perhaps unusual to regard a gully as a classic route, but Low's Gully is such a major feature of Kinabalu that it must always tempt those in search of adventure. Indeed, the first article in the *AJ* about Kinabalu was an account of an expedition by Tony Smyth in 1958 which planned to ascend the mountain by way of the Panataran river and Low's Gully.[10]

For me, the most satisfying aspect of the route was the feeling of being totally engulfed by the mountain, the sheer majesty of the towering rock walls and the need to crick one's neck to view the high peaks. Nowhere else do you feel so vividly the full might of this magnificent mountain.

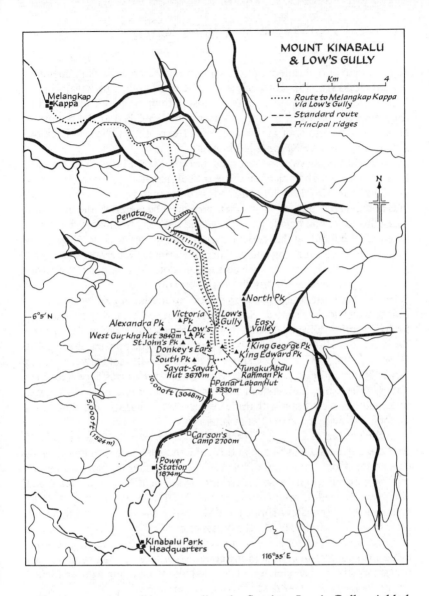

There are various claims regarding the first into Low's Gully. Added confusion arises because there is no precise definition of where the gully begins or ends. Some expeditions have even believed that Easy Valley, which gives access to the upper section of the gully, was the gully itself. We know that commandos abseiled into Commando Cauldron in 1964 and a report appeared in the *Alpine Journal* of a first ascent of 'the north face' which (since there *is* no north face) may be referring to climbs in the Commando Cauldron area.[11] Nonetheless, to most people standing on the summit it is the deeper gully below that which is Low's Gully proper. So far as can be ascertained, the first party to find a way into this lower section through the steep rock faces on either side was that of Pinfield, Brandi and

Alderhaden who abseiled into the gully on 6 March 1987 after spending several weeks searching for weaknesses in its surrounding rock walls. They identified a route requiring only an abseil down a face of about 300ft; they emerged through the vegetation into the river bed at the bottom at about midday, and after an hour or two of exploration climbed back out again using their abseil ropes left in place.

After that first known and recorded descent, Steve Pinfield was asked to lecture to the Sabah Society on the event but he hadn't taken many photographs. So in May 1988 he and I repeated the first descent with our cameras at the ready. Both of us felt that there must be a way off the mountain using this route and decided that we would have to give it a try. However, when climbing out on that trip it rained a little while I was standing in my jumars under an overhang and within a few minutes waterfalls were forming along the sides of the gully. There was no doubt that settled dry weather must be a prerequisite for any successful outcome.

1989 did not offer the needed dry period but in March 1990 we had a dry month which looked settled. So at the beginning of April we decided to go for it. Carrying 40lb packs with only the bare essentials we set off from the West Gurkha Hut intending to bivvy the night at the bottom of the gully. To get into the gully it is necessary first to climb to the col between Tunku Abdul Rahman Peak and King Edward Peak which gives access to Easy Valley. The Valley descends at various gradients, sometimes with scree-type material, sometimes with thick Leptospermum bushes, and sometimes in open slabs which extend to the gully rim.

At the bottom of Easy Valley the right side extends out to a small bluff overlooking the gully itself and at this point there is a large boulder the size of a house. This boulder has often provided bivvy sites for parties attempting the gully. From here we moved through vegetation into a stream bed which we needed to follow down to the abseil point on the lip. A short distance above this Steve slipped and slid down the water-smoothed rock almost out of control. He had the presence of mind to roll hard to the side and to catch hold of some vegetation with his hand. But the impact dislocated his shoulder and we had to retreat. Not feeling keen to carry two rucksacks all the way back up, I extracted all the climbing gear and left it under the house boulder ready for our next attempt.

In March the next year we again had a very dry spell and we decided to have another go. Getting into the gully was no great problem, although pulling our abseil ropes after us was a very committing moment. We slept that night on a rock in the middle of the river, at this time only a trickle. The next day we worked our way down the gully at a good pace, mostly jumping down from rock to rock but avoiding some big drops with detours through the dense vegetation to the side of the river bed. At one point we put in an abseil. It was clear that, while working your way down large river boulders on your bottom is fine for going down, the picture would be very different for anyone attempting to climb up.

At about 4pm we arrived at a point where the gully narrowed to a gorge about 25ft wide with sheer rock walls to either side, big rounded boulders in the river bed and a waterfall tumbling about 20ft to a lake stretching from wall to wall. A similar waterfall and lake could be seen 150 yards further down. It was immediately clear that this would be another totally committing move. Descent of the waterfall would commit us to the gorge with no obvious way out except on down an unknown number of further waterfalls. We decided we needed the night to ponder on this problem and camped right there.

The following morning we looked again at the problem and decided that we had neither the gear to tackle a succession of waterfalls nor possibly enough food, as we had only bargained for six days. The only other choice being to climb out of the gully, our attention turned to the gully sides above us. To the south the wall appeared steeper and more sparsely vegetated and, furthermore, the north wall would give access to the next tributary and thence to Melangkap Kappa, our intended destination. So we started climbing this wall at what seemed a promising point, quickly becoming entangled in almost vertical thick vegetation. A ledge seemed hopeful but after 100 yards this petered out on the blank face above the waterfall.

So we abseiled back into the river bed and started again. This time we reversed up the gully about 150 yards before taking to the wall. The going was hard with thick vegetation, often loose and sometimes overhanging, intermingled with prickly rattan. Gradually, as we rose and traversed west, the gradient eased until we thought we had climbed far enough and should start descending in order to reach the next valley.

But the aim of the expedition was to follow the river so, to keep weight down, we did not take water bottles. Now we had left the river we were parched dry. The terrain was difficult enough but thirst had the effect of creating far more stress and anxiety than the physical difficulties alone. So after a rest to try and make some saliva we descended about 150ft until the ground steepened to a point where, to proceed further, it would have to be an abseil. We were now above a lower section of the gully and could see more lakes and larger waterfalls below us. The options were to drop back into the gully, traverse west and up, or go straight up. It proved a difficult and crucial decision and we debated it for 20 minutes. The decision finally was to go up. The long pull-up, often hanging onto overhanging roots, was gruelling and my spirits were very low. Steve was fitter and did a good job egging me on. After what seemed an eternity, we hit a sharp ridge and collapsed for a rest.

We thought we had better eat something, but with no saliva how do you swallow? As I moved my jaw it squeaked and Steve's laughter didn't help much. He then said he thought he could see a footpath running along the ridge, but I pooh-poohed it as a small game trail of which there are always many in the jungle. He released his rucksack, got up and looked around. Then came a trimphant exclamation because he found an old sweet paper.

The lift in our spirits was immediate and somehow our parched throats mattered no more. The path was well cut, certainly not a native trail. The terrain was amazingly steep for a path of this sort and we figured it must be a British Army trail put in when they attempted to climb to the East Plateau from Camp Paradise near Kota Belud. A tree carved with '1990' confirmed this. After about 1½ hours the path dropped onto a small platform beside a river – a perfect camping spot by an idyllic river – just as the sun was going down. The toughest day of the expedition had come to an end. From here we followed the river downstream and then followed hunting trails to Melangkap Kappa which we reached in a further day and a half.

It was this route that the British Army training expedition that went so wrong planned to complete. They figured that, with more manpower and more gear, they should be able to overcome the last one mile or mile and a half of the gully to meet the main Panataran river. Ironically, it was just this combination of a large team carrying overweight packs that sowed the seeds of discontent and resulted in first the expedition splitting into two and then the weaker party reaching the end of its resources.

Too much has probably already been written about this expedition and undoubtedly various books and films are going to add to the confusion before all is done. I do not intend to add more fuel to the fire as I think most experienced mountaineers can read between the lines and make up their own minds as to what went wrong. My principal concern has been the response of the Park Authority in terms of their attitudes towards future expeditions to the remoter parts of the mountain. For the time being, it appears that the dreaded embargo on such expeditions will not occur, but no longer can they expect to be given access to the mountain without prior vetting of their plans and credentials.

The record time set by a Gurkha soldier for running to the summit of Kinabalu and back to the roadhead is about 2 hours 20 minutes. It is all too easy, given this knowledge, to regard Kinabalu as a mere afternoon stroll and write it off as of no account. This denies the fact that this is a great mountain with many moods and huge potential for new rock routes of a high order.

This mountain will always charm those who live in its shadow, just as Tom Harrison was charmed when he wrote about Kinabalu thus:

> ... here it stands, seemingly unshakeable, a mighty mountain. One hour it is there, the next nowhere – lost in the cloud world. Then there it is, safely back again at the first streak of day: that wonder lost twelve hours before, as the wet cold night clamped down across the moss forest. It is back, that incredible backdrop of teeth and fangs, gulley, precipice, cliff, plateau, gorge, peak, projectile, point – you name it, Kinabalu has it, up there above you, black and tense, looking as if forged in iron and dropped into place as a vast casting. Surely this is the most complete statement of 'I am a Mountain' made anywhere on this earth.[12]

## REFERENCES

1   Alexander Dalrymple, *A Plan for Extending the Commerce of this Kingdom and of the East India Company.* 1769.
2   Owen Rutter, *British North Borneo.* 1922.
3   Tom Harrison, World Within. 1959.
4   Tom Harrison, Chapter 1 of *Kinabalu Summit Borneo.* Sabah Society Monograph, 1978.
5   Hugh Low, *Kina-Below.* 1852.
6   David V Jenkins, Chapter 2 of *Kinabalu Summit of Borneo.* Sabah Society Monograph, 1978.
7   John Whitehead, *The Exploration of Kinabalu North Borneo.* 1893.
8   H W L Bunbury, 'The Ascent of Mount Kinabalu' in *British North Borneo Herald*, 1 September 1910.
9   Dave Nichol, 'Kinabalu – Northern Borneo' in *AJ90*, 187, 1985.
10  A J M Smyth, 'The Northern Approaches of Kinabalu' in *AJ63*, 27, 1958.
11  Notes in *AJ70*, 125, 1965.
12  Tom Harrison, Frontispiece to *Kinabalu Summit of Borneo.* Sabah Society Monograph, 1978.

**Note:** The Sabah Society Monograph entitled *Kinabalu Summit of Borneo*, published in 1978, is a comprehensive compendium of chapters covering all aspects of the mountain and is a particularly useful source of reference on natural history subjects. The first edition has long been out of print but a new, rewritten second edition, containing significant new material, is to be published during 1995.

JULES STEWART

# An Irian Jayan Adventure
## The first direct ascent of Mount Trikora

*(Plates 45, 46)*

Such is the madness of jet propulsion that a few days after sipping my last cappuccino in Notting Hill I found myself squatting beside a fire in a cave 11,000ft up in the New Guinea highlands next to a group of almost naked Yali hunters. My two climbing companions were tucked into their sleeping-bags on the spongy earth floor. Soon the Yalis began to drop off, snuggling up to one another higgledy-piggledy, like a litter of puppies.

The Yali elder, his bow and cluster of long arrows propped against the wall, kept a silent watch over the fire. They had largely ignored us since our arrival at the cave late that afternoon. Our porters, members of the rival Dani tribe, were now asleep at the far side of the cave. I excused myself, pressing my palms together under my chin, and as I eased into my sleeping-bag the Yali turned his face to me. Through the flickering shadows of the fire I saw a smile cross his lips. It was a warm, sincere and terrifying smile: his teeth were filed to neat little points. It wasn't the natives who were restless that night.

I had come to Irian Jaya, Indonesia's half of the island of New Guinea, with my Spanish climbing partners to log a first ascent of 16,000ft Mount Trikora, the summit of the Jawawijaya volcanic massif that bisects the island's swamplands and jungle on a west-east axis. Since the mountain was first claimed by a Dutch team in 1913, there have been half-a-dozen or so successful expeditions to Trikora. All of them have been via a relatively simple scramble up the W ridge, on which the most serious danger is hand lacerations from the jagged limestone rock. Our objective was a pure rock climb of the N face, which involves some 600ft of Spanish grade IV/IV+(D/TD) climbing to the ridge, a scramble to one of the nearby pyramids, all roughly about 200ft high, and an exposed climb to the summit.

The expedition was organised in Madrid and London over the course of a year. I was put in charge of logistics and my first startling discovery, thanks to the superb combined research material made available by the Alpine Club and the Royal Geographical Society, was that, contrary to what we had initially assumed, our mountain was not in Papua New Guinea.

My companions César Pérez de Tudela and Juan Luis Salcedo took on the more sobering task of raising sponsorship, which eventually was forthcoming from a Spanish sports shop chain. The excitement of entering one of the world's last largely unexplored territories began with a bumpy flight inland from the malaria-infested coastal capital of Jayapura to Wamena, the highland town that is the gateway to Baliem valley. Reminiscent of Conan Doyle's Lost World, the valley was discovered in 1938 by American adventurer Richard Archbold during a 14-month reconnaissance expedition in his Catalina flying boat. Today, Wamena is served by three daily 45-minute flights from Jayapura that disgorge an average of 1000 foreign visitors a month. Yet Wamena remains an oasis of rudimentary comfort within a territory where missionaries and the Indonesian army have made but a minor dent in a Stone Age culture. I glanced over the pilot's shoulder as the Twin Otter bounced through the mist-shrouded mountains on our approach to the valley. There were large blank tracts on his navigation chart marked 'relief data incomplete' and 'altitude undetermined', and it was comforting to note that he was not on automatic pilot.

The first sensation upon arriving in Wamena is one of welcome relief from the oppressive heat of Jakarta and Jayapura. The town nestles in the highlands at 5000ft and the climate is delightful and balsamic. Having escaped unbitten by mosquitoes on our one-night stopover on the coast, I was tempted to discard my Paludrine tablets.

Our Dani guide Joshua, who assured us he had disavowed the habits of his cannibal father, took his Roman Catholic upbringing seriously indeed: on our approach march to the mountain, we were invited to recite the Lord's Prayer three times a day as our fried rice and vegetables grew cold next to the fire.

Negotiations on the cost of our trek began over tea in Wamena's Baliem Cottages Hotel, Joshua crouched in a corner of the room, trimming his toenails with a machete. This hotel was a cluster of Dani-style circular thatched rooms, quite tidy and boasting *en suite* facilities, although familiarity with the siphonic cistern principle could be useful for prodding the loo into action.

I cast an apprehensive glance about, expecting Milton's 'at once came forth whatever creeps the ground' to materialise from the darker recesses of the room. In fact, during almost two weeks of tramping through the Baliem valley's wetlands and jungle, I did not spot a single creepy-crawly – a gratifying bonus for a pathological arachnophobe.

'Three thousand dollars,' Joshua said, in a characteristic display of good humour. It took us half an hour and a steady supply of Ducados cigarettes to talk him down to $1300 for the trek – including 14 porters and two Danis armed with bows and arrows to guard the sweet potatoes that make up the Danis' staple diet. Of this, $300 was earmarked for the local Indonesian police commandant as a 'thank you' for agreeing to issue our climbing permit, never before granted for a direct assault on Trikora. Needless to say, we never laid eyes on this document. We celebrated our last night in Wamena with a round of sweet tea, since the Baliem valley is a dry area. Having witnessed the drunken violence of Port Moresby's euphemistically-named 'Rascals' in neighbouring Papua New Guinea, I have nothing but praise for this policy.

The Indonesian government brochure on Irian Jaya promises a land of 'simple shocks', and we were not disappointed. During a rest stop on our first day, I found a chunk of what I took to be a paw-paw fruit lying next to a dwarf palm. Half of the fruit still clung strangely to the trunk like an enormous cyst. 'No good, no good!', cried Joshua, as I started to hack out a mouthful of the orange meat with my knife. The porters doubled up with laughter when I realised that what I had taken for dark seams of pips were pathways teeming with ants. The 'paw-paw' was a rotted ant-dwelling which Joshua demonstrated, by poking a hole in the crust with his machete, is repaired within minutes by a frantic swarm of the creatures: biting ants, as I later discovered when I stretched out on the grass for a siesta.

The Baliem valley offers the traveller pristine solitude. Often I would drop behind out of earshot of the porters to marvel at the eerie bog terrain where the marsh is at best ankle-deep, where low-lying clouds hide the hilltops on the horizon and deep jungle lies alongside the Dani hunting trails. At any moment I expected a brontosaurus to poke its head above the giant leaves of the banana trees. The only sound was the rhythmic suction of our boots; the ground never seemed to harden no matter how much altitude we gained. By the early evening it usually started to rain, but during most of the day the weather was idyllic for walking and we very quickly learned to tread on the drier mats of reeds.

Through a cleft in a rocky ridge we spotted the Baliem river which gives its name to the valley. A waterfall crashed down the hillside at an angle of 60°, and this would have to be negotiated to reach the valley floor. We began our descent behind the porters, grasping branches and bushes along the wall to keep from plunging headlong into the water. At one point, where the current rose to cover the narrow dirt track beside the waterfall, a network of notched fallen trunks had been laid zigzag across the cascade. It was a source of wonder to watch the Danis wrap their huge prehensile feet around the logs and scamper down with loads of sweet potatoes balanced on their backs. Unfortunately there was more to it than standing around and watching this display of agility. Juan Luis led the way, and upon placing his foot on the polished trunk he executed a spectacular pirouette which sent him tumbling about 20ft below onto a cluster of rocks and splintered branches. He emerged from the water very wet and bruised but he was not seriously injured, so we carried on.

A shattering cry went up later that afternoon as we plodded through the ooze of the valley. Instantly the rucksacks and food loads hit the ground and the porters sprinted off in pursuit of a tiny, almost imperceptible black speck on the horizon. They shouted wildly as they raced full tilt after their prey, and in a very short time returned with a spectacularly plumed bird of

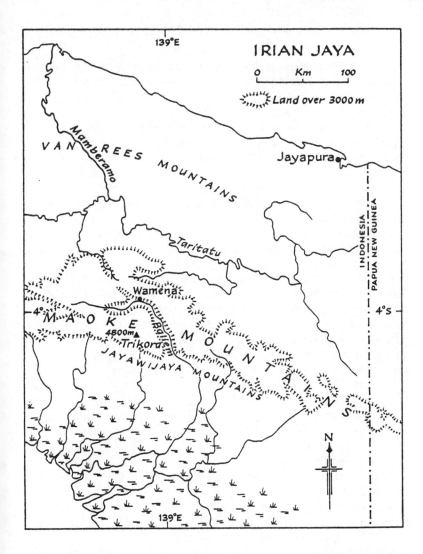

paradise in tow. This was thrust screeching into a cardboard box and became our mascot on the trek, to be carried back to Wamena and sold for its
highly-prized feathers.

We felt ourselves fortunate not to have encountered the most feared of
the Danis' hunting trophies, the cassowary. This ostrich-like bird has a
deceptively dull and passive appearance. To describe the damage it can
inflict with its huge clawed feet, Joshua took a small log which he stood on
end and split down the middle with a single sharp blow from his machete.
'Now two mans,' he said cheerfully.

It is in the bush that the Danis come into their own as the Melanesian
warriors who for millennia have survived on game and, occasionally, the

flesh of rival tribesmen. In Wamena those few who still refuse to wear the missionary sanctioned shorts and T-shirts make up an almost pathetic sight alongside the Indonesians from overcrowded Java who have flocked to Irian Jaya under the government's transmigration programme.

Joshua's Catholicism from time to time suffered a bit of slippage. On the night we spent in the cave he sacrificed a chicken for our evening meal as an offering for a safe climb. The chicken's blood was then drained into a plastic bowl emblazoned with a Batman mask and, to the delight of the porters, vanished in a huddle at the opposite end of the cave.

We later agreed that one of the most unnerving moments was the three-hour night march to the base of Trikora. Leaving the cave at 3am none of us was in a terribly hilarious mood as we trudged through the bog, the cold mud seeping into our boots despite Gore-Tex lining and gaiters. Isaiah, one of our Dani porters, had agreed to guide us to the base, provided we kitted him out with a pair of boots and I let him wear my red JB helmet. Having cleared the worst of the marsh, still following the beams of our head torches, we climbed a 600ft, 70° slope, grasping at mats of grass which Isaiah cheerfully assured us would support our weight. There were no clear patches of earth on this slope into which to dig our ski poles and I was convinced that the first handful of grass would come away at the slightest pressure and send me hurtling several hundred feet below.

The first light of dawn brought us to a vast moraine, where we exchanged our sodden trekking boots for sticky rubber and scrambled across the rocks to the base of the N face. It was then that Isaiah went ashen-faced: he had no notion that we had in mind a technical rock climb, believing that our objective was the classic ridge scramble.

'No good way, police come!'

He gesticulated wildly and crossed his wrists to indicate that handcuffs awaited us in the unlikely event we were to return alive.

'Man go up that way now two years,' he said, as he raised his arms above his head and let them fall dramatically to his side. 'Big fall down, head all broken, legs all broken, arms all broken.'

Isaiah was not exactly a font of encouragement. We never learned the definitive version, but it appears that an American – some say an Australian – had attempted a solo climb and had fallen to his death when a flake came away in his hand. The result was that a climbing permit, fictitious or genuine, will only authorise the standard ridge route.

Ignoring Isaiah's well-intended protestations, we roped up for what was to be some of the most exhilarating Dolomite-style climbing I have ever experienced. César took the lead towards a cleft which seemed to offer the best protection, but as the wall was pitted with superb chunky holds he opted to traverse left across the crack in search of a more challenging route.

'Maravilloso! Estupendo!' I heard him shout as he disappeared behind the cleft to set up our first belay. Juan Luis and I inched across the wall, which already offered exposure 100ft above the moraine. It was a sobering

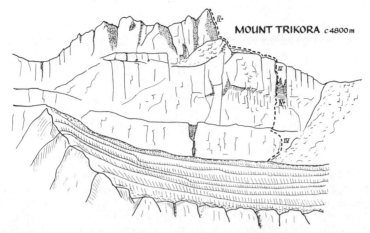

MOUNT TRIKORA *c* 4800 m

thought that, with an injured climber in tow, it would require at least a five or six-day hike to reach the nearest airstrip. With an immobilised victim, there was not the faintest chance of getting off the moraine without an airlift, assuming we had radio equipment and that a helicopter was available. Neither was the case. Two hours or so later we were on the ridge, congratulating ourselves on our effort. The several summit pyramids can only be reached by a ridge walk, as they are set back from the face itself. Each is 100 to 200ft high and Trikora's precise height is a matter of controversy. 4750m is the official figure, although our altimeter gave a reading of 4800m on the summit pyramid.

It was a windless and warm late afternoon three degrees south of the equator. With torturous thoughts of iced drinks topped with slices of lemon, we retraced out steps by some delicate down-climbing and three abseils to the moraine, where a much-relieved Isaiah greeted us with a broad grin and a handshake.

Apart from achieving a mountaineering first, our climb released César from the setback of a severe heart attack two years ago in the Khumbu Icefall on our Everest expedition in 1992. For Juan Luis, it proved that on an exposed, unclimbed face, adrenalin can be an effective antidote to the combined miseries of chronic diarrhoea and flu. For me, at nearly 52, it was reassuring to discover that I still retained some recently untapped resources of energy.

Our mountain climbed, we packed up our rucksacks and began the trek back to confront the culture shock of returning to the world of rail strikes and mortgage payments. As we retraced our steps across the vast soggy plain I remember thinking that this was the way it should be, with nothing to spend money on, no need to be entertained, and the only sound that of our boots sloshing through the wet grassland.

**Summary**: In June 1994 a British–Spanish expedition (Jules Stewart, César Pérez de Tudela and Juan Luis Salcedo) made the first direct ascent of Mount Trakora, *c*4800m, in Irian Jaya.

EVELIO ECHEVARRÍA

# Cordillera de Potosí, Bolivia

(*Plates 41–44*)

Papers of mountaineering interest about the Cordillera de Potosí are extremely few. There are two in English, one in Spanish and a handful in German. But all flowed from the pen of a single writer and all originated early this century. There also exist several very brief notes in geographical and scientific journals and that is all. This paper endeavours to bring up to date the available mountaineering information related to the Cordillera de Potosí, and also to describe my own exploration of the range.

## The city, the Silver Mountain and the range

To mountaineers Southern Bolivia is an unknown land; it is a high desert, nearly unpopulated. From its plateau of gravel and stones emerge a number of elevations that attain their highest point (c5900m) near the border with Argentina. But true mountain peaks are scarce, and few constitute even a small chain. Only east and south-east of the famed colonial city of Potosí there rises a strange, continuous mountain range with no official name. In 1903 alpinist Henry Hoek named it the Cordillera de Potosí. The inhabitants of the area use instead Cari Cari for its northern half and Andacaba for its southern half. The northern end of the range is located some 13km east of the colonial city itself, but the southern end cannot be seen from the city because the famous Cerro Rico ('Rich Hill') and some intervening ridges block the view in that direction.

The city of Potosí lies at 4060m and is the highest city in Bolivia. It is located within a basin protected by arid rolling hills and, to the east, by the Cerro Rico and the Cordillera de Potosí. Thus, in spite of its altitude it is not too cold. The city was famous for the copious silver that was mined in its Cerro Rico and it has been written that in the 1600s Potosí, then with 160,000 inhabitants, was the third largest city in the western world, after Paris and London. With its silver mines now depleted, the city can barely sustain a population of about 80,000. It is a decadent and depressing place, with only two or three fairly good hotels and not even as many acceptable restaurants. Still, historically speaking, it is one of the most famous cities in the world.

Like a gigantic brown-red anthill, the Cerro Rico de Potosí rears its conical shape 800m above the city to a height of 4824m. Its former names – Potocchi for the Indians and Cerro Rico for the Spaniards – are now no longer used: its official name is Cerro de Potosí. In the wet months (December to the end of April) the hill may occasionally appear dusted with snow, which fades away in a few hours. Once the city is left behind and the hill is seen from the plateau, it looks like a mere brown hump – a hill among many. Inevitably, a television antenna had to be erected upon its summit and a caretaker of the station inhabits a nearby cabin.

The dimensions of the Cordillera de Potosí are smaller than had previously been reported. It stretches in a N–S direction for about 25km and contains some 50 peaks rising above 4800m. The range is noticeably divided into two groups separated by a depression. The name Cari Cari, applied to the northern half, means, in Aimara, 'Man Man'; quite apt, since the rock peaks stand as rows of sentinels. This northern portion begins with a massif that contains some ten peaks between 4900m and 5040m lying west of the Huacani lakes. This section is some 13km due east of the Potosí city limits.

South of Cerro Cari Cari and of the Quimsa Condoriri massifs, the range continues with some 15 more peaks keeping within the same height limits. Conspicuous is the rock cone of Cerro Mina Illimani (5030m). Next to Cerro Jatún Casa (5023m) there is a crescent-shaped depression con-taining several lakes and lakelets; it is called the Jacha Molino Pampa and it is no less than 4300m above sea-level. South of it the second half of the range begins to rise, but the peaks now appear farther apart. Near the great lake of Tala Cocha several important heights rear their heads above the 5000m line, but the main southern group is found around the Andacaba mine. Here are the two highest peaks in the entire range: Cerro Macho ('male') de Andacaba, 5042m, and Cerro Cunurana ('Fat Snow'), 5056m. There is no permanent snow cover, though in normal years the range is covered with snow from December to the end of April. Water in the drier periods of the year is found in lakes and lagoons, which are abundant. Those situated on the north-western slopes have been supplying water to the city of Potosí and its mines since the late 1500s. All rivers which spring from the chain drain N and NE into the great Pilcomayo, or W and S into the Tumusla which, in turn, flows into the Pilcomayo.

There is little human or wildlife in the Cordillera de Potosí. There are no trees, bushes are stunted and only tuft grass abounds. During a two-week stay in the area the only signs of animal life I saw were a couple of wild ducks navigating in a high pond and a beautiful white falcon with black-rimmed wings flying at summit level. In the lower valleys there are small flocks of sheep and llama tended by their Indian owners who, whenever possible, avoid contact with strangers. No tourists or sportsmen are known to visit the range.

The penetration of the Cordillera de Potosí began early, with the exploit-ation of the Cerro de Potosí. There are many legends about the discovery of the Cerro's endowment of summit silver, but history relates that on 10 April 1545, Captain Johan de Villarroel, with several Spaniards and Indians, ascended the mountain to take possession of its contents. For a peak 17m higher than Mont Blanc, with permanent snow at the time, the Paleface smelled its riches; it was one more high summit to add to the impressive record of Spanish mountaineering that took place on the American continent between 1521 and the end of the colonial years around 1810.

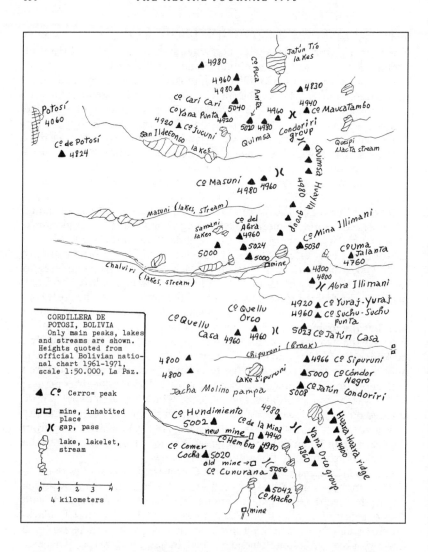

Potosí 4060

Cº de Potosí ▲ 4824

▲ 4980

4960 ▲
4980 ▲

Cº Cari Cari

CºYana Punta    5040

4920 ▲ Cºjucuni    4920

San Ildefonso lakes

Cºpuca Punta

Jatún Tío la Kes

▲ 4830

4940    Cº MaucaTambo

4960 ✕

5020  4980

Quimsa Condoriri group

Quespi Llacta stream

Quimsa Huayha

4980

Cº Masuni ▲ ▲
4980  4960

Masuni (lakes, stream)

Cº del Abra
▲ 4960

5024 ▲

samani lakes

5000 ▲

Chalviri (lakes, stream)

▲ 5000

mine

Cº Mina Illimani

▲5030

CºUma Jalanta
▲ 4760

▲ 4800
4800

)( Abra Illimani

CORDILLERA DE
POTOSÍ, BOLIVIA
Only main peaks, lakes
and streams are shown.
Heights quoted from
official Bolivian natio-
nal chart 1961-1971,
scale 1:50.000, La Paz.

▲ Cº Cerro= peak

□■ mine, inhabited
place
)( gap, pass

lake, lakelet,
stream

0   1   2   3   4
4 kilometers

CºQuellu Casa

Cº Quellu Orco

4920 ▲ Cº Yuraj-Yuraj
4960 ▲ Cº Suchu-Suchu Punta

4960 ▲   4960 )(   5023 Cº Jatún Casa

4800 ▲

4800 ▲

Chipuruni (Brook)

lake Sipuruni

Jacha Molino pampa

▲4966 Cº Sipuruni

▲5000 CºCóndor Negro

5008 Cº Jatún Condoriri

Cº Hundimiento
5002 ▲

new mine □
Cº Hembra □

Cº Comer
Cocha ▲5020

4980 ▲

Cº de la Mina
▲4940

4980 ▲

old mine →□

Cº Cunurana

▲5056

)( Yana Orco group    4860 ▲

Huara Huara ridge    ▲4900

▲5042
Cº Macho

□ mine

How many times the peak of Potosí had been ascended, we shall never know. How long ago it was! Two more centuries were to elapse before de Saussure's march to Mont Blanc. But it was certainly to exploit the silver that the Spaniards first entered the Cordillera de Potosí. It may have been from the summit of the Cerro itself that they had seen major lakes nestling in the nearby range. There are records dating back to the mid-1500s of *laguneros* (caretakers of lake dams) living in this area. These lakes seldom occur below 4200m and may even be found near the 4600m mark. But apart from their hydraulic engineering enterprises, the Spaniards appear to have left the Cordillera de Potosí alone.

## Mountaineering 1903-1985

The first mountaineer to penetrate the range was the German geologist, soldier, poet, skier and climber Henry Hoek. The son of a Dutchman and an Irishwoman, he was born at Davos in 1878 and died in Vaduz in 1951. He was a member of the German geological expedition of 1903 that surveyed southern Bolivia from the Argentine border to near La Paz and Cochabamba. All the publications mentioned at the beginning of this paper poured from his pen and to him we owe what mountaineering information existed up to the present. He belonged to that unique breed of mountaineers who cannot separate the physical effort demanded in climbing from the mental and spiritual experience. Herr Walter Kaltenegger described Hoek as 'certainly a great mountaineer in the old sense'. Hoek was also an accomplished writer and translator.

Having entered Bolivia through its bleak, stony southern plateau, Hoek and his companions were naturally surprised to behold in the distance a continuous rock range: ' ... a far stretching wall of mountains with striking, because individually formed, peaks ... an unknown ... unmarked mountain world.'

The expedition changed course, reached in November the Andacaba mine at the SW end of the range, and undertook some two weeks of studies and of climbing. Hoek and leader Gustav Steinmann ascended the Hembra ('female') of Andacaba. They were told at the mine that Indians had previously erected a cairn on the summit of this mineralised mountain (4980m). Then Hoek traversed alone to the summit of Anaroyo, highest peak in the entire range (today Cunurana, 5056m). It was when recalling that occasion that Hoek wrote a paragraph typical of him:

After I had exhausted the actual scientific interest of the view ... I was overcome by a feeling of absolute loneliness, such as I have never before experienced on any peak, not even in mid-winter, when all Nature is frozen into silence. Day was fast closing in. Everything in the clear distance became gradually merged into an undecided bluish-brown, an extraordinary mauve colour. In this lonely hour, when the very silence seemed audible, I lay there and listened to the far-away murmuring of the hurrying waters of the great European life-stream echoing in my mind. Many an image of home rose up from the sea of the past; but viewed from an altered stand-point the prospect also alters. I have come to think differently of many things out here, and to think consciously. In the silence, in the far off solitude, it often seems as if a quiet observer were concealed deep in your innermost being, noting your every thought, and you are conscious of this; and this observer forces his being into the most secret corners of your heart, and so on in an endless succession. Strange melancholy impressions are awakened by the bare dead landscape in whose centre you are absolutely alone with your thoughts.

After a short stay in the city of Potosí the Germans returned to the Cordillera. They accomplished its crossing at its waist by an ill-defined pass near the lake Mina Illimani and climbed a peaklet nearby. Hoek collected local names, prepared a good sketch-map (which, with the above quotation, appeared in *AJ23*, 20-26, 1906), took a few photographs and wrote several papers about his explorations (see Bibliography on page 172). If the name of any mountaineer is to be associated with the Cordillera de Potosí, it should be his.

As far as is known, at least from the mountaineering viewpoint, the range was thereafter left undisturbed. In late 1983 I said to myself that it had slept in solitude for too long and that its list of mountain ascents should be increased. Research in all likely areas, particularly scientific, could only disclose that the geologist Dr Manfred Wolf, of the German Democratic Republic, had published two papers on the metallogeny of the range. It seems that he ascended Hembra de Andacaba and may also have done other ascents in the southern end of the range. But that was all I was able to discover. Satisfied that I was to break new ground, I travelled to Bolivia in December 1983, at the beginning of the rainy season. I had taken for granted that the Potosí district was very dry, that climbing there would be possible any time of the year and that the only problem would be to find water. November of 1903 must have been a very dry month, or so it appears from Hoek's writings. Having arrived there 80 years and two weeks later, I found that things were very different. I only stayed in the area for a week, with nothing else to do but to behold the decadence of an imperial city and the fronts of dense rain-clouds pouring their content over the Cordillera. In 1985, wiser, I was back there in May. The weather was fairly good, even if sunny days were not really warm. The wind rose in the afternoons and nights were cold. But there was snow on the slopes facing the south and water was plentiful.

Transport was a problem. The charming tourism officials and the local wiseacres agreed that only an expensive private station-wagon could perhaps take me up dubious roads to near some high lake. I was fortunate in learning that the *laguneros* were AAPO people and thanks to this agency, the provincial water works, I was lucky to secure a ride in a lorry leaving for routine inspections of dams in the bigger lakes. The lorry left me at the Laguna (lake) Mina Illimani (*c*4400m), above which rose the imposing rock mass of Cerro Mina Illimani, 5040m (clearly, Hoek's 5300m Cerro San Fernando). Having obtained recent maps, I had already accepted that names and heights from the sketch drawn by Hoek in 1903 would no longer be valid. The charts issued in 1968 by the Instituto Geográfico Militar de Bolivia at a scale 1:50,000 showed different names and figures and, once I was on the terrain, they did make sense.

From the lake I headed for an obvious col to the north of it. I ascended the gap, dropped to the other side and camped by the small Samani lakes. Having acclimatised first in the streets of Potosí (4060m) I had no problem with the altitude. Not so with the weather. The morning had been brilliant, if rather cold, but by the time I reached the gap clouds began to appear and by evening I was experiencing the most sensational thunderstorm of my life. The very ground under the tent seemed to tremble with the explosions overhead. The heavy rain that followed was no doubt very much welcomed by the people of Potosí, who love to know that their mountain lakes are full to the brim.

On the following morning, 7 May, I resumed explorations. My intention was to begin where the Germans had left off in 1903, that is at the Mina Illimani pass. The gap I had crossed was clearly not the right one, since it was wide and easy, and the Germans had described theirs as not easy to locate and to cross. I retraced my steps to the col and from there I ascended a rock dome which I christened Cerro del Abra ('Gap Peak'), 4940m. Marching thereafter around the lake Mina Illimani, I headed for a lateral valley south of it where I camped by a small stream. On 8 May I attempted Cerro Yuraj Yuraj ('White-white'), assuming that from its top (4920m) I could obtain a sight of Hoek's pass, situated somewhere in those surroundings. The previous night had been very cold and windy and now, as I climbed the W gully of the peak, I was facing a wind of almost gale force. I climbed the SW or lower summit, but I knew that if I were to attempt to traverse the ridge to the main summit I would be blown from it. I descended to the camp.

The next day was warm, there was no wind and I anticipated a pleasant climb. I struck out for the big peak of Jatún Casa (5023m), whose red-brown rock pyramid glowed like a furnace at sunrise and at sunset. The mountain had very large boulders of sound rock, which called for upward pulling by sheer arm strength. On the summit I found, to my surprise, a very well-built cairn. I was soon to learn that the surveyors of the Instituto Geográfico Militar de Bolivia, when charting the range in 1956, had performed a number of ascents. For whatever reasons, when I visited the Institute's offices in La Paz, its personnel were not willing to disclose to me the names of the peaks that had been ascended, so for the time being I have to restrict the list of their ascents to what I myself was able to discover. The view from Jatún Casa, if not really attractive, was certainly the most extensive I had ever beheld. The bleak plateau of southern Bolivia stretched before me, with a number of semi-volcanic peaks rising above the brownish vastness. Conspicuous to the far south was Cerro Chorolque (5603m), said to have mines near its summit. The nearer landscape confirmed Hoek's opinion: the southern half of the Cordillera de Potosí was not as well populated by rock peaks as the northern half, or Cari Cari, was. There was snow only on the S face of the bigger peaks and none in the valleys. Lakes of varying sizes were seen everywhere. But I could not discern traces of Hoek's pass.

The following morning I was preparing to descend to Potosí to re-supply, when two Indians herding a couple of laden donkeys went past my camp by the stream. One was a young man and the other a much older woman, picturesquely attired in red, pink and blue-layered skirts. I was amused when the man, unceremoniously and without saying a word, examined and felt with his hands all my belongings, one by one. The woman stood silently watching. When they were about to leave I gave them a present of apples and oranges, which the highlanders greatly relish. The woman muttered a sort of Quechua *Oh la la*! and they were on their way. I watched them with great curiosity, wondering where they were heading for; I knew much too well that the end of the valley was enclosed by a ridge of very broken rock connecting Yuraj Yuraj with Jatún Casa. To my amazement I saw the two of them with their donkeys crawling and zigzagging up rocks and gullies until finally they reached the crest and disappeared. Only then did I realise that this was the pass which had made the 1903 Germans so apprehensive, but which they finally did cross.

Back in Potosí I learned that the AAPO engineers were sending another lorry, this time to the northernmost lakes, for another routine inspection. It was a unique chance to visit an area never seen before by any mountaineer, so I gratefully accepted their offer of a ride. Over a road of firm gravel, the lorry skirted slope after slope until it finally began to gain height when the road climbed up a narrow valley. At a string of lakes it came to a stop. I was surprised to see two other lorries there and a group of engineers and workers engaged in cleaning lake beds and repairing dams. Here at last I met a fellow mountaineer, something unheard of in the entire provincial department of Potosí (thrice the size of the Netherlands). Young and kind engineer Santos Vargas told me that, for purely sportive motives, he had climbed the highest peak in sight and the two descending northwards from it. Unfortunately I had arrived when he and his crew had to begin work, and thus I missed my only chance of a companion.

Alone, I headed for a gap at the end of the valley, located between a square rock peak to the left (east) and a row of other peaks to the right. I could see no snow, but I was now facing the barren and broken northern slopes of the range. By afternoon I had crossed the gap and gone down the other side, to the San Ildefonso valley, where I camped at around 4400m. The weather was very good now and remained so until my return to Potosí, but nights were getting increasingly colder (as the dry Bolivian winter progressed) and liquids that I kept inside the tent always froze solid at night. In the following days, 15 and 16 May, I ascended three peaks: first the truncated pyramid of '5020m' by its slightly exposed SW ridge. On its summit there was another military cairn, but since the peak had no known name I christened it Cerro Puca Punta ('Quechua' for red, Spanish for 'point', hybrid names being common in Bolivia). I then traversed north to the massive square block of Cerro Cari Cari (5040m). Once on the eastern slopes of the peak, in the last steep 50 metres, a long piece of blue string attracted my attention. It was a piece of fishing line left there by Vargas to mark his retreat at the trickier places. On the summit I found a roll of the same fishing line, Vargas's only momento of his visit, together with a well-built cairn with a metal disk affixed to it which read 'Instituto Geográfico Militar de Bolivia. 13 de marzo de 1956.' Mine was probably the third ascent. The next day I also ascended the N buttress of Cari Cari (c4920m), which I named Cerro Yana Punta, or 'Black Point'.

With this the fortnight I had allowed myself for my visit to the Potosí district came to an end. I returned to the imperial city, quite satisfied with the results of my modest expedition. It had yielded only two first ascents, but also the satisfaction of making first-hand contact with the manifestations of history, both in Potosí and in its Cordillera, and I had gathered practical information about a range that had gone unnoticed by mountaineers for more than 80 years.

## A traverse in 1993

There were times, in the past, when I used to wonder what the future held for the Cordillera de Potosí. Its peaks, albeit rocky in comparison with the other mountains of southern Bolivia, present only minor mountaineering problems. The range is therefore more suited to the high-level mountain traveller rather than the gymnast. With easy access and heights still within my capacity, the peaks of that Cordillera, which seemed to attract no one else in the world, were almost ideal for me, the more so considering that I had a rather heavy rucksack and 67 years of age to carry on my back!

When I arrived in Potosí in late April 1993, I felt quite depressed when I saw the brown cliffs above the city now devoid of snow. But Bolivia, like many other parts of the world, has been hit by the drought that began in 1987 and continues to the present. As for the city of Potosí itself, in comparison with 1985 it showed some improvements. There were two new hotels, one new restaurant and money could be exchanged easily. Tourism was evidently on the increase.

More realistic than on my previous visit, I visited the headquarters of the Andacaba mine, and its chief engineer, señor Luis Bottani, gave me a ride in his car to the mine itself, located at 4400m in the SW end of the range. From here I marched south to locate the old mine. It was abandoned. I crossed the ample saddle (c4500m) between Hembra de Andacaba and Cunurana and dropped down the other side into the Muyucocha valley. It was bleak and narrow, dotted with tarns and walled in on its E side by black cliffs. My stay in the Muyucocha was not very productive. The weather was changeable. It snowed repeatedly each day for periods of up to two hours and the wind persisted for most of the day. I found several abandoned miner's huts, which were excellent as shelters. Built of stone, they were ample and clean. I lodged in one of them for three days and managed to ascend Point 4940m, north of Hembra de Andacaba. I christened it Cerro de la Mina ('Mine Peak'), for it rose NE of the new Andacaba mine. From the top I traversed south to the summit of Hembra de Andacaba (4980m), which had a big cairn on it, evidence of several previous ascents. This mountain is rocky and steep, but not difficult. I also made several attempts on Cunurana, but the wind and sudden outbursts of hail and snow chased me down.

Since the weather was so unstable I judged it useless to prolong my stay in the southern portion of the range and I decided to carry out my project of traversing the major part from south to north. On 1st May I crossed the Casiri pass and went down into the Casiri valley. The unclimbed chain of the Huara Huara peaks (4900m), dark and sombre, looked very imposing to the east. Their W wall, which I was now facing, did not look feasible. I pressed on to the base of the Jatún Condoriri massif, where I hoped to do some climbing.

From a camp near the big Sipuruni Lake I climbed, on 3 May, black Point 5000m, north of Jatún Condoriri (5008m). It had a cairn on the top, probably built by surveyors, but since the mountain was unnamed I baptised it Cerro Cóndor Negro. The ridge to the summit of Jatún Condoriri looked too long and serrated, so instead I headed north to Point 4966m. Its summit had no traces of human visitors but I had noticed a small horseshoe-shaped construction just below it, so mine may have been a second ascent. All the same, the peak was unnamed. I christened it Cerro Sipuruni, after the lake it dominates. This system of placing camps anywhere and climbing what I wanted or what I could was very satisfying and, since I was alone and rarely saw traces of human life, it gave me a unique sense of ownership of the entire range.

As I continued to march northwards the weather gradually improved. On 4 May I didn't even wear a sweater. I crossed the rolling Jacha Molino Pampa and descended into a sheltered valley, called Chipuruni on the map. It was the pleasantest nook I had found in the range, with a wide brook and a few dwarf blue and yellow lupins here and there. The following day, my ninth in the range, I climbed the Jatún Cassa pass (c 4800m), thus connecting the southern half of the range I had just traversed with the area I had visited in 1985. From the pass I turned left (west) to ascend the rocks of an easy ridge peak, called on the map Cerro Quellu Orco ('Yellow Peak', 4960m), a first ascent. I was enjoying unusual warm, dry weather.

My next step was to ascend the Mina Illimani pass, from which I had a great view of my next goal, the northern half of the range. Several peaks of very striking outline hinted that I was in for a pleasant climbing campaign. But by that day I was quite spent. So I judged it better to abandon the traverse of the range, descend to Potosí for a rest and spend the rest of my allotted time climbing among the Cari Cari peaks. The return journey was known to me: the Mina Illimani, where two geologists gave me a ride in their station wagon, the dry San Ildefonso valley and finally the city itself.

On 10 May I returned to the range in very high spirits. In another mining vehicle I arrived at the same Lake San Ildefonso, this year reduced by drought to half its normal size. From its shores I marched up the valley, crossed the Quespi Llacta gap and descended east into the valley of the same name. I explored the peaks of the neighbourhood, noticing that cairns existed on the summits of two of them. I then headed for the Matterhorn-like Point 4940m, situated north of the gap. Since it did not look easy, I assumed that it would be a first ascent. It was not. Climbing over excellent rock, at times quite steep, I arrived on the summit and realised, to my astonishment, that it was a sanctuary. In front of a small cairn, two candles, one little plastic bag of coca leaves and two wine bottles were set out – clearly, an offering to a mountain divinity. A glance at the barren scenery around the mountain told the whole story. It was no doubt an offering to Pachamama, the Mother Earth of the descendants of the old Incadom, to request an end to the drought which had afflicted their land for so long.

I added a few stones to the cairn and placed into it a protected *gipfelbuch*, having also stated on it the name I had chosen for the peak:  Cerro Maucatambo. On the official Bolivian maps, Point 4940m bore no name; but in his writings Henry Hoek said that he had discovered the name of Maucatambo for 'the splendid rock mass' of that area. I also did something disgraceful. I took for myself some of the objects the hillmen had left for Pachamama. I took possession of the two small candles and the bag of coca leaves, with the innocent intention of donating these objects to the museum collection of my own mountain club. Now I know that I should not have done so.

I descended and slept in my small tent and the following day I moved to the Cari Caris, possessed by the same ambition that gnaws the heart of every peak-bagger. So far, the weather had been acceptable, but that night the wind rose and from then on it never relented.

Should mountaineers be superstitious? When one comes face to face with a firmly-established myth, what is one to do? Having read the excellent *Kulu and Lahul* by General C G Bruce (Arnold 1914), I wholly agree with him: myths, beliefs and superstitions are to be taken seriously and respectfully, even though one's first reaction may be incredulity or amusement. I had taken offerings which had been made to the Indian Mother Earth and for the rest of my expedition I paid the price. An unfinished programme was one part of it; unbearable weather was the other.

On 12 May I crossed three passes, traversing slopes horizontally in order to find a way to the N side of the Cari Caris. Throughout the day I was harassed by a devilish cold wind. Skies were grey and decidedly hostile. Once I had reached the third gap I realised that it would not pay to camp below it. The descent into the Jatún Tío valley would have meant a loss in height I was unwilling to make. I slowly retraced my way back to the San Ildefonso valley, where I camped on a small ledge protected from the persistent wind. The following day was equally unpleasant but I set out all the same for conical Cerro Jucuni (4920m). I had seen from below that it was crowned by a cairn; it was, however, my only chance of a short climb. When I reached the top the first thing that caught my attention was a big candle sticking out from the cairn itself. Another sanctuary, but this time I respected it and after depositing the usual summit register I hurried down. I arrived in my camp exhausted and numbed.

My stay in the Cordillera de Potosí had to be cut short. The winds were growing colder and stronger every day – proof that Pachamama was against me and I was not wanted there. From my tent, perched on the ledge, I could hear the mountain gods sounding the charge. That same morning I dismantled my camp and began a hurried descent. In the afternoon I was marching alongside the San Ildefonso Lake and before dark I was back in my hotel room.

Somewhat too soon, my Potosí adventures were at an end. Hoping to gain a last view of the range, I had reserved the afternoon before my departure from Potosí for a visit to a hill above a steep street end. The sky over the city was overcast and when I reached the viewpoint and searched for the peaks, nothing could be seen. A curtain of fog had solidly settled on the brownish foothills. I looked in amazement at the dismal scene and reflected how the steppe surrounding Potosí, now deprived of its unusual rocky crest and crown, looked very much a part of the Bolivian southern plateau. It seemed as if beyond the foothills there was only a void filled by swirling mist and fog. Nobody could have guessed that, somewhere behind the clouds, there rose a craggy, lonely mountain range.

ACKNOWLEDGEMENT

I am grateful to Mr Peter Walluf, who kindly lent me a photograph of his stepfather, the well-known climber and skier Henry Hoek. I located him by writing to the Postmaster in Vaduz, where Henry Hoek died, and asking if there were any 'Hoeks' in the city listings. The Postmaster gave me Peter Walluf's address in Frankfurt-am-Main (FRG) and enabled me to obtain, at last, a photo of an admired pioneer (*Plate 44*).

BIBLIOGRAPHY AND CARTOGRAPHY

The following bibliography is believed to be complete, but only the latest maps are recorded.

Luis Capoche, *Relación general de la villa imperial de Potosí*. Madrid: Biblioteca de Autores Españoles, 1957. (First published in 1585)
Henry Hoek, 'Explorations in Bolivia' in *Geographical Journal 25/5*, 498-513, 1905.
Henry Hoek, 'The Cordillera de Potosí' in *AJ23*, 19-30, 1906.
Henry Hoek, 'Bergfahrten in Bolivia' in *Zeitschrift*, Deutscher und Oesterreichischer Alpenverein 38, 121-148, 1907.
Henry Hoek, *Aus Bolivias Bergen*. Leipzig, F Brockhaus, 1927.
Henry Hoek, *Por las montañas de Bolivia*.
   Madrid, Bruno del Amo, editor, 1929.
Henry Hoek and Gustav Steinmann, 'Erlauterung zur Routenkarte der Expedition Steinmann, Hoek, v. Bistram in den Anden von Bolivien 1903-04' in *Pettermans Geographische Mitteilungen 52/1*, 1-13, 1906.
William Rudolph, 'The lakes of Potosí' in *Geographical Review* 26/4, 529-554, 1936.

**Maps:** Instituto Geográfico Militar de Bolivia, La Paz, *Hojas* (sheets) 6435-II (Potosí) and 6436-I (Puna), scale 1:50,000, 1968.

# Ski Mountaineering

## VADIM VASILJEV
# The Transpamirs Ski Expedition

*(Plates 61– 64)*

The Transpamirs Ski Expedition, which took two years to organise, aimed to break the stereotype of Russian winter ski expeditions.
These had often resembled a number of loops made by a hare over mid-
height mountain terrain. But, seriously, ski mountaineering in the Pamirs
presents some very complex problems and we were advised by old hands
not to attempt it. The highest mountains of the former Soviet Union are a
wild uninhabited land. Moreover, the Pamirs combine a large number of
climate zones, differently structured mountain ranges and a wide variety
of incredible natural objects such as the Sarez lake and the Fedchenko
glacier. In spite of these obstacles, we felt that we had the necessary training
and expertise to carry out our plan. The other three members of the team
were Ivan Zabello, Eugene Orlov and Leonid Skvortsov.

Ours was the first unsupported expedition to cross the Pamirs from the
SE to the NW – a distance of 480km. If you try to imagine spending 30
days as one of a small four-member group, at altitudes up to 6000m and
temperatures sometimes down to –34°C, with only 550 grams of dry food
per person per day, you will have some idea of the challenge we faced.

The expedition route started in the settlement of Murgab, situated on the
Eastern Pamirs plateau at an altitude of 3700m. After a two-day approach
through the Eastern Pshart valley, with its wide snow slopes resembling a
polar landscape, we surmounted the Ak-Tash pass (4200m) and started the
ten-day descent to our halfway point at the Bartang river gorge. The deep
snow, our huge backpack-plus-pulk weight of over 50kg and the problems
of high-altitude adaptation made the first part of the journey extremely
difficult. But fine weather and our tremendous enthusiasm gave us enough
motivation to attain the Ak-Tash pass and descend to the Western Pshart.

The Western Pshart river passes through a narrow gorge full of canyons,
some of which are unfrozen, and thick undergrowth. In some places the
bottom of the gorge was snowless, so that we could no longer pull the sleds
and had to backpack all our luggage. Twice we were unable to find a way
through along the side of the river and we had to wade along it, without
our boots, at temperatures of nearly –20°C. It took us three days to reach
the Murgab river which eventually flows into the 56km-long Sarez lake.
This lake appeared in 1911 after the massive Usoy collapse; it is one of the
most mysterious and unexplored places in the Pamirs. Even in summer
there is no easy way of reaching it. During the winter the lake is covered
with ice, which enabled us to cross it from east to west.

Surmounting the Usoy obstruction and the descent to the Bartang river were perhaps the hardest parts of the expedition. Without the use of the pulks and with no paths to guide us, there was no chance of travelling at more than 1.5km per hour. The terrible stony chaos of the Usoy obstruction, together with the almost impassable canyons of the Murgab, were a two-day ordeal. Moreover, there was no snow in the Bartang gorge (the largest gorge in the central Pamirs) so the next day we were again prevented from using our skis and pulks. At last, two days later, we were able to continue on skis, but now we faced a new hazard. Very heavy snow on the upper reaches of the Khavras-dara presented a real danger from avalanches. Twice we were pretty close to being caught, but thanks to our previous experience of avalanche-prone terrain we were able to avoid a disaster.

Thick fog, a head wind and a snowstorm didn't help us to ascend the Kholodny pass at 4600m. Sometimes we were forced to stop altogether while we waited for better weather, but finally we found ourselves on the saddle. After the descent to the Grum-Grzhimaylo glacier our speed was checked by its rough and ruptured surface; the need to use ropes in the icefalls slowed us down even more.

Two days later we were caught in a horrible three-day snowstorm at an altitude of 5300m. Thanks to the excellent construction of our tent we managed to maintain a good level of fitness throughout this unpleasant experience. The next day was sunny, with no wind and a temperature of −32°C. With renewed enthusiasm we set out on the ascent to the Zimovshikov pass at 5900m and by five o'clock we were setting up camp beyond the pass on the upper plateau of the Vitkovskogo glacier – one of the sources of the vast, 77km-long, Fedchenko glacier.

While descending the Fedchenko glacier to the Seldara river, we experienced the most dangerous incident of all. Three of the expedition members got stuck in crevasses down to a depth of 8m, when two huge snow bridges collapsed in front of them. Fortunately they were able to extricate themselves. Finally three giant icefalls were overcome without any further accidents. The last 80km of the route, which included the snow-free Seldara valley, the crossing of the Seldara river, the Tersagar pass (3600m) and the ice-covered Altyndara, took us three more days. The expedition arrived at the settlement of Daraut-Kurgan in the late evening of the thirtieth day.

It was now time to take stock of pluses and minuses. Our losses were few: one broken ski, one lost ski-pole, a few frostbitten areas of skin and a broken video camera. On the other hand, we had the great satisfaction of having achieved the first unsupported crossing of the Pamirs in winter.

**Summary**: Starting on 22 January 1994, the members of the Transpamirs Ski Expedition, Vadim Vasiljev (leader), Ivan Zabello, Eugene Orlov and Leonid Skvortsov, made the first unsupported crossing of the Pamirs, SE to NW, from Murgab to Daraut-Kurgan, a distance of 480km, in 30 days.

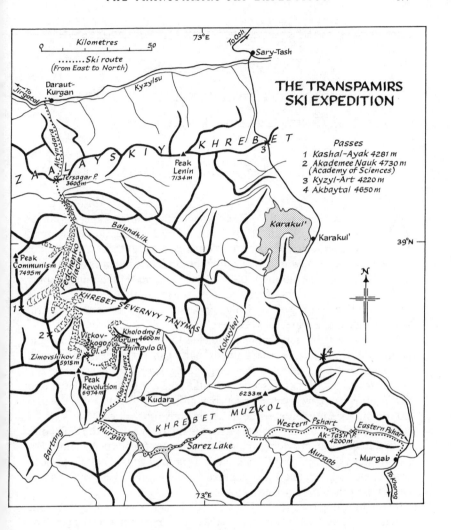

ACKNOWLEDGEMENTS

*I would like to thank the sponsors of the Transpamirs Ski Expedition: Malden Mills Industries Inc (USA), Apri Ltd, Equipment Ltd, SKF-Express, General Insurance Company, Northern Trade Bank (Russia). We are very grateful for their interest and support.*

Note: For further information, telephone or fax as follows:
0296-624-225 (UK) Att: Peak International
010-7-812-312-4128 Att: NERPA (Russia)

DAVID HAMILTON

# Almost a Russian Haute Route

## Central Caucasus Ski Traverse 1994

*(Plates 65–68)*

As the mist clears over the Stockji glacier the unmistakable outline of the Matterhorn begins to take shape. In the foreground four tired skiers make a slow descent towards Zermatt, thankful that the remainder of their journey is downhill. A day that began fourteen hours earlier with a pre-dawn start in chill mountain air ends in a brash neon-lit shopping mall. After the exertions of an eight-day, 100km journey from Chamonix there is little joy on arrival. Only sadness for what the once peaceful Alpine village of Zermatt has become.

Yet I felt satisfied for having completed the project in good time and good style. It was mid-February and my party had just made the first crossing of the season. The memories of grinding ascents and sweeping descents amidst breathtaking scenery would take a long time to fade; and few groups can have made this journey along 'the world's most popular ski mountaineering route' without meeting any other skiers.

For most ski mountaineers such a successful trip would be the high point of a winter season, providing entertaining tales for friends back home. For two members of this party it had been a training trip. The 'big project' which John Kentish and I had planned for the winter lay 3200km further east in the Russian Caucasus.

Three previous trips to the Caucasus had made me aware of the huge potential of this area for mountain adventures in summer or winter. The project which caught my attention was to open up a Caucasian high-level ski route through the highest part of the central Caucasus. Some research revealed that there had been little indigenous Russian ski mountaineering activity in this area and that obvious natural lines had never been attempted on skis. The best available maps were quite poor by western standards, but much better than those I had used while exploring remote ranges in Pakistan and China. My Russian friends in Moscow gave some helpful advice and I settled for a route which appeared to be very similar to the Alpine *haute route* in length and character. This involved skiing a little over 110km westwards from Vernhey Balkaria to the Elbrus end of the Baksan valley. The route would cross six high passes of 3400m-3900m and most of the skiing would be on glaciers above 2500m.

Even at the planning stage this Caucasian 'haute route' quickly revealed several important differences from its Alpine namesake. There were only two small emergency huts along the route, there were no possible resupply points and, once started, we would never be closer than 50km to any habitation. The most significant factor was that the route traversed close to the crest of the Caucasian ridge which marks the border between Georgia and Russia. Seventy per cent of the route was in Russia and thirty per cent in Georgia. The high mountain areas on either side of this frontier are uninhabited and would be deserted in winter. If all went well we would have no contact with the armed bandits currently ruling the Georgian district of Svanetia. However, if injury, starvation or storms forced us to descend into the Georgian sector our chances of survival were not good. My Russian friends assured me that we would all be robbed, arrested or shot!

Apart from these minor problems the plan looked a good one. The project, which I had only thought up in January, was set to run from mid-March to mid-April. John and I recruited two more team members: Mark Scarratt, who had been on Masherbrum with me in 1991, and Matthias Hammer, a German friend of his studying at Cambridge. I travelled out to Russia two weeks ahead of the others and managed to sneak some much-needed extra ski practice while running a touring programme for some British skiers in the Adyr Su valley, 25km from Elbrus.

The arrival of John, Mark and Matt at expedition HQ in Terskol coincided with a huge snowfall. We had a memorable day's skiing on the 800m north slope of Mount Cheget. This terrifying avalanche-prone slope of heavy powder was served by a rudimentary chair lift. The Russian skiers sensibly would not go near the north slope and stayed on the rutted 'pistes' of the mountain's east side. By the end of the morning we had each made three nerve-racking runs. Binoculars from the balcony of our hotel a few hours later revealed twelve sets of less than perfect 'S' tracks down the mountainside, liberally interspersed with erratic turns and large craters ... the Brits had arrived!

Ski-touring expeditions need to employ many varying tactics to address the problems of logistics. In alpine countries the excellent network of huts usually provides the answer. In polar regions the use of pulks enables groups to operate for considerable periods between resupply points. In Russia the problems were unique, but so was the solution. Our route was to involve more than a little technical climbing. This ruled out the use of pulks and meant that we would need to carry the necessary mountaineering equipment. We would be using tents most nights and needed full camping and cooking kit. It soon became apparent that we could not carry all of this in addition to food and fuel for twelve days. The 'Russian' solution to this dilemma was to hire a relatively inexpensive helicopter to pre-place three food dumps along the intended route. The plan was to carry all the climbing and camping equipment, and meet up with a food dump on every third day. This way our packs would only weigh 18-20 kilograms.

With all the preparations completed, the expedition finally got under way on 25 March. A 5½-hour drive through the dismal villages of Kabardino Balkaria brought us to the impressive limestone gorge of the Cherek Balkarski river which guards access to the isolated plain of Upper Balkaria. Igor the driver did a great job to coax the squat four-wheel drive bus along the deteriorating mountain track. Five miles beyond the last habitation, the road became impassable. It was time to pick up our ruck-sacks, shoulder our skis and start walking. The windswept path led through sparse forest towards mist-shrouded peaks in the far distance. The first wet snow lay on the ground at an altitude of 1700m. Darkness fell an hour before we reached our planned campsite at the junction of two rivers. Lit-tle did we realise that a pattern of long days and late arrivals had just been established.

The next day found us attempting to ski up a narrow gorge on steep slopes a few metres above a raging torrent of glacial meltwater. Progress through this hell of trees, bushes and rocks was so arduous that after 4½ hours of effort we had only covered three kilometres. By the afternoon the terrain improved and we were able to make better progress as we climbed onto the memorably named Dykh-Kotiu-Bugoisu glacier. Despite skiing now at over 2500m, the snow became wet and soft in the afternoon sun. Some very large and alarmingly fresh bear tracks in the snow added to our worries.

'Too cold by night and too hot by day' is a familiar problem faced by climbers in a variety of environments. This was our dilemma in the Cauca-sus. Awakening at 5am the next day, it took a superhuman effort in the cold blue light of dawn to melt snow, cook, eat, strike camp, and start ski-ing by 7.30am. For a few hours the skiing was enjoyable as we slowly gained height on our continuing westward journey. By mid-morning the sun's warming rays had ceased to be our welcomed friend and had become our hated enemy. Time was lost as we were forced to stop and strip off excess clothing. By the afternoon the snow had become so wet, heavy and sticky that progress was reduced to a frustrating crawl. Our skins con-stantly clogged up with damp snow as we inched forward beneath the mer-ciless glare of the sun.

But the day's ultimate frustration was to come from a different source. Our packs were as light as they would ever be, for we were carrying virtu-ally no food. On the evening of day three we were due to collect the first of the pre-placed food dumps. This had been left at the 'Austrian bivouac' at the eastern end of the great Bezingi glacier. As the evening sun dipped below the horizon these supplies were tantalisingly close, only two or three kilometres ahead. However, a tricky 3960m pass blocked the route. In the failing light I kicked steps up a steep gully just to the left of the lowest part of the ridge. The others waited 50m below as I fought to gain the crest of the ridge. From the top I could see the full panorama of the Bezingi Wall facing the isolated peak of Dych-Tau across the eastern arm of the Bezingi

63

50. The 1994 Anglo-Russian Expedition to the Tien Shan mountains of Kyrgyzstan: nine virgin peaks were climbed between 4500 and 5000m in the Central Tien Shan range. (*Marian Elmes*) (p 82)

69.   Sir Alfred Wills at 'The Eagle's Nest' in the 1870s.  (p207)

*Right*
70.  'The Eagle's Nest' as it is today.
     (*Trevor Braham*)  (p207)

*Below*
71.  'The Eagle's Nest' in 1877.  (p207)

72. Karabiner MC Greenland Expedition 1994. Descending from P. 2100m
(Peak 3) after making the first ascent. (*Jim Gregson*) (p183)

73. Looking NW over the Pourquoi-pas glacier. First ascents of six summits
along the ridge beyond the glacier were made by KMC team members.
(*Jim Gregson*) (p183)

glacier. I could just about ascertain the location of the bivouac hut and I could also see that it would be impossible to descend towards it from my present vantage point. The way ahead was barred by a huge ice cliff. It was dark as we retreated, dragging our exhausted bodies down unstable snow slopes for a few hundred metres to a point judged safe enough for a tent platform. It started to snow as we munched on leftover nuts and chocolate from lunch. It would not be entirely correct to state that up until now our luck had been good. But from this point on it got a great deal worse.

Crossing the Dykhnainsh Pass with our minimalist mountaineering rack was a precarious venture. Ultra lightweight equipment has much to recommend it as long as you never actually have to use it. With crampons marked 'not to be used for ice climbing' and a predominantly plastic ice axe, down-climbing a 200m ice wall was a nerve-racking process; and with only two ice screws being carried for a 12-day journey, using one to abseil the first bit of ice encountered was not an option. We had hoped for a short, easy day, crossing the pass and skiing down to the hut. It was not to be. The weather deteriorated; the wind increased, visibility worsened, more snow fell, and soon a full-scale storm enveloped us. Six hours after striking camp the small triangular shape of the 'Austrian bivouac' loomed out of the grey gloom. We squeezed in, glad to be out of the howling wind.

Our problems were just beginning. For although food and fuel were now plentiful Matt was ill. A renal infection from a previous expedition to Madagascar had flared up. To compound his problems, ill-fitting boots had given his feet bad blisters. Throughout the night the storm raging outside the hut continued. Driving spindrift managed to find its way inside, coating everything in a fine dusting of snow.

The following day was depressingly similar. Trapped in a space akin to the average garden shed, we ate chocolate, drank tea, and waited. The storm continued. Various options were discussed, but in the end there was no realistic alternative to abandoning the trip. Our lightweight philosophy had left little room for luxuries. However, Mark had sneaked along the ultimate extravagance – two-thirds of a book. The day was spent tearing *Bonfire of the Vanities* into smaller and smaller sections and passing them around. The four of us retreated into the world of Manhattan's shakers and movers, broken only by calls of nature which brought us back to the reality of our situation in the frozen wastes of Bezingi.

The weather seemed no better the next day, but the decision to abandon our trip and escape down the Bezingi valley had been made. Bidding our little hut farewell, we roped together and fought our way downhill through the deep, heavy fresh snow. It was one of the few times I have experienced a descent on skis which required more effort than most ascents. By early afternoon the weather had improved significantly. The sky cleared, revealing impressive views of Shkhara, Jangi-Tau, Katyn-Tau and Gestola – the fabled 'Bezingi Wall'. They were plastered with snow and every few minutes another huge avalanche would pour down in a thunderous roar.

Turning our backs on the great peaks we struck out towards the roadhead in the valley below. Ahead of us the view was blocked by a bank of low cloud which quickly rose to greet us, reducing visibility to a few metres. It was 7pm and dark by the time we had fought our way down the snout of the glacier and found a flat spot for the tents.

Plastic ski mountaineering boots are not designed for long walks on stony paths. Our feet were very unhappy after the 20km trek to the nearest village. The inhabitants were more than a little surprised to see four brightly clad foreigners, carrying skis and big rucksacks, limping out of the mountains. Our first priority was to eat a big meal that contained no freeze-dried ingredients. In vain we sought to buy some food. We had money: dollars, roubles and pounds. But the village had no food for sale! A large shop on the main square had 50m of empty shelf space. The owner held out his arms in resignation, looked to the sky, shrugged his shoulders and said 'Perestroika!'

I realised that there are a lot of differences between skiing in the Alps and in the Caucasus. Russia is not yet ready to welcome the hordes of recreational ski mountaineers who fill the Alpine valleys each spring. I even began to think that perhaps Zermatt is not such a bad place to end a ski tour after all.

**Summary**: In March 1994 four UK-based skiers attempted to traverse the highest section of the central Caucasus mountains. The proposed route of 110km ran east to west from Upper Balkaria to the Baksan valley. The trip was abandoned owing to bad weather and illness, with only one-third of the journey completed.

*Team members*: David Hamilton, Matthias Hammer, John Kentish, Mark Scarratt.

JIM GREGSON

# Probing the Pourquoi-Pas

## Karabiner Mountaineering Club Greenland Expedition 1994

*(Plates 72, 73)*

I deas for a return visit to Greenland were already in mind as I travelled home from my first trip to this exquisite Arctic playground. As
my local club, the Manchester-based Karabiner Mountaineering Club,
would reach its 50th year during 1994, it seemed fitting that a more unusual form of celebration of this anniversary should be undertaken – hence
for a group of us a Greenland expedition. Moreover, Greenland would be
especially appropriate because John Hunt, our Patron and past President,
had led an expedition to the Staunings Alps in NE Greenland in 1960 and
had climbed and named a peak in honour of the club.

Approximately mid-way between Mont Forel and Lake Fjord (Tugtilik),
where Gino Watkins was lost in 1932, the Pourquoi-pas glacier flows east
and west between Sekstjernen and the Glacier de France in latitude 66°N.
Intrigued by its querying name we planned to base our expedition there.

Our eight-person team, six men and two women, were flown from
Iceland and into the Pourquoi-pas using a chartered Twin Otter aircraft.
This charter was the major expense of the expedition, but the very spectacular flights into and out from the glacier were worth the cost. The little
aeroplane was stuffed with all our gear plus ourselves before skimming
across the fjords, glaciers and peaks north of Kulusuk island on Greenland's east coast. Touch-down on the ice was gentler than many a runway
landing. Thus on 23 July 1994 we arrived at our base camp location, 66°40'N,
35°49'W (as indicated on the aircraft GPS apparatus), just 30 hours after
leaving Heathrow airport. Our flight out was scheduled for 15 August, giving us 22 days to explore the area on skis and climb such peaks as we could.
After a day spent unpacking and sorting our equipment and food from the
freighted packages, we were keen to get started.

In the very early hours of 25 July we skied to the south side of the glacier
for a couple of hours to attempt a double-topped snow peak to open our
account. This went readily enough by an ice slope and a scramble along a
rocky crest to an untouched summit of *c*1500m. A first ascent for a first
climb was a good beginning. From this vantage point we tried to orientate
ourselves. The maps we had, at a scale of 1:250 000, showed some remarkable inaccuracies and we relied more on the aerial photographs we had
obtained from Copenhagen.

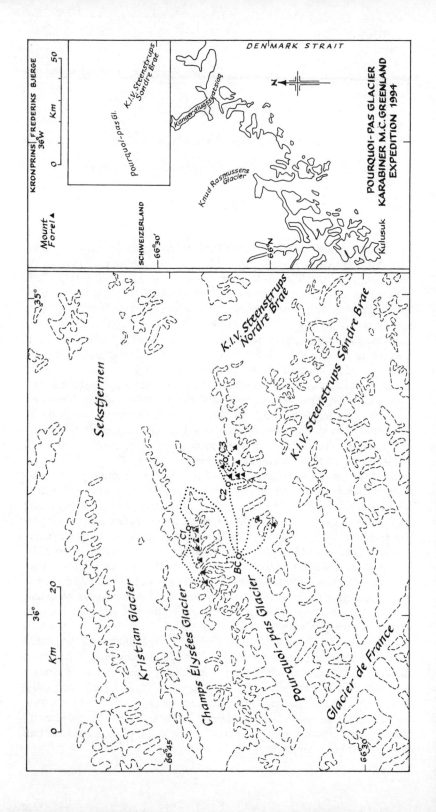

There were many attractive mountains all around us, and we laid plans to visit some of them by using additional camps. Accordingly, we loaded our pulks with supplies for eight days, storing the rest in a depot to leave behind. In the evening we pulled out of base, towing the pulks eastwards up the Pourquoi-pas *en route* for the next, higher-level glacier parallelling it to the north. From this time onwards we intended to adopt a 'night-for day' routine, skiing and climbing in the colder night-time hours and using the warmth of the days for cooking, eating and sleeping. There is, of course, no danger of benightment beyond the Arctic Circle at this time of the year. We were able to dispense with ropes for travel on the wide main glaciers throughout the period of the expedition, as the mostly level surfaces were generously snow-covered, so we avoided the hassles involved in trying to ski at a synchronised pace.

By midnight on this first journey we had pulled from the Pourquoi-pas over a broad saddle and headed down in the direction of Sekstjernen, a huge glacier basin lying to the east. In another 30 minutes we turned the toe of the last mountain ridge separating us from the steeper, higher glacier where we intended to place our camp. By 3am we decided that we had come far enough and on 27 July we set up our second camp ringed by inviting mountains. This site, at *c*1700m, was towards the southern side of a glacier rising to a watershed giving over to the Champs Elysées glacier.

In the following nights and days, we made climbs on seven more peaks and tops, all of them apparently first ascents. These varied in altitude between 2000m and 2200m, and were climbed by a mixture of ridge and face routes offering typical Alpine terrain. The best looking of these peaks lay directly above our camp, so we did not need to ski to it. During the ascent, by its fine NE ridge, we were temporarily held up by a broken crampon which was repaired with a length of prusik cord to enable a cold-footed continuation by its owner.

On 31 July five of us climbed one of the peaks by two different routes, one a ridge and the other an ice face. At the same time, the other three members made an exploratory ski tour across the glacier to its northern edge to view down onto the Kristian glacier. From there they skied south-west, then south for some kilometres, climbing two snow summits as firsts, before returning to camp while the rest of us descended our mountain. All these summits lay on the crest line overlooking the Pourquoi-pas to the south. They all gave extensive views, from Schweizerland in the west, to Mont Forel and the ice cap in the north-west, then along other ranges running across the northern skyline to Sekstjernen with glimpses beyond into the Kronprins Frederiks Bjerge. South and east, past the Pourquoi-pas glacier, stretched the KIV Steenstrup Braeer systems feeding out into the iceberg-studded Denmark Strait.

We had hoped to complete this phase of the expedition by making a tra-verse of the high snow arêtes of P.2300 on the opposite edge of the glacier. However, the ski-touring party reported a major sérac dislocation in the far end of the ridge, invisible from our camp, which would be a great obstacle to a possible descent. Perhaps we could try an out-and-return attempt? In the event, on the night in question the weather signs did not look promising, with heavy grey cloud piling up in the southern and western skies. We had had a very good opening week and had run down our rations of food, so we opted to return to base to re-stock and rest.

Very early on 1st August we skied away downhill to the east and by 3.30am had located the marker pole left on our supply depot down on the Pourquoi-pas. We re-set our camp and rested while talking over our future plans. The pulks were reloaded for an intended move in the pre-dawn hours of 2 August. At 1am the sky was leaden and down to the west the mountains were swathed in thick cloud. By 3am snow began to fall and we decided to stay put: this was just as well as the storm intensified. It snowed or rained for the whole of 2 and 3 August, and half 4 August, confining us to our tents and sleeping-bags. Our decision to move back to base had been vindicated, allowing us access to food and fuel.

The long depressing hours were spent asleep or reading, but we longed for a return to activity. In the afternoon of the 4th, the cloud broke up and the sun reappeared. The camp was visited by a group of strikingly white Ivory Gulls. Everyone was busy, drying damp belongings and gathering together what we needed for further climbing.

Our earlier climbs had shown us a group of impressive higher mountains at the eastern end of the Pourquoi-pas. Two of them in particular looked very appealing objectives, the higher being a great fin of ice and rock over a high col and the other a fine white pyramid. We had thought to circumnavigate this massif, climbing where we could. Close study of the aerial photographs showed some potentially time-consuming crevassed zones on our proposed route, so we chose instead to make a return journey that would involve two new camps.

We added to our loads supplies to last for 12 days. In the evening of 4 August we stepped into our ski-bindings and hauled the pulks towards a distant nunatak projecting from the ice of the upper glacier. By midnight we had selected a camp site in the mouth of a side bay of the glacier and quickly had all the tents up.

Frustrated by the enforced idleness of the storm, two of us set off almost immediately to climb the nearest peak. This took about 2½ hours via a ridge of moss-decked rocks, then steepening ice slopes, leading to a snow dome. We followed a corniced edge to the highest point. Just beyond, on a rock shelf, sat a small cairn. On investigation, the cairn contained an aluminium canister holding a note left by the 'Schweizer Grønland Expedition 1966', dated 9 August 1966, with two names. We added a note of our own before replacing the canister inside the cairn. At 3.30am the sun rose as a bright red disc from behind the high mountains at the far edge of Sekstjernen, restoring colour to the landscape.

From the summit of 'Schneekuppe', so dubbed by the Swiss, we were able to scout access routes to the two high peaks we hoped to ascend. The approach to them would involve glacier complications and detours of which the map made no hint. We also spied a suitable area in which to site our next camp.

The following night and morning, the whole group of eight were thwarted in an attempt on a big snowy mountain two kilometres south of the camp. The impasse lay in the form of a very deep and wide crevasse cutting the slope for hundreds of metres with no possibility of forcing a crossing. We traversed the mountain flank for a half-kilometre or more, looking for alternative access, but conditions forced us to give it best. We descended, with some disappointment. Later in the day the weather dealt us another blow with rain out of the west. This rain became snow driven by strong wind which lasted through 6 August and on into the morning of the 7th – not the most conducive situation for team morale.

When the snow abated, the sun reasserted itself, producing a beautiful bow in the airborne ice crystals as it burned through the ground-mist. We held a 'conference', with some frank but amiable exchange of views. The outcome was a decision to move to a new camp from where the more experienced team members would attempt the two higher peaks, while others would seek less taxing objectives.

In beautiful evening light we hauled the pulks along the glacier, below a subsidiary ridge of small tops and icefalls, to a point some kilometres further east where we turned uphill to go back west onto the higher glacier shelf where we needed our camp. Just after midnight, as 8 August ushered itself in, we set up the tents at c1520m and slept soundly. This camp was blessed with a sweeping outlook across the whole of the huge Sekstjernen basin and further onto the fringes of the inland ice. Unfortunately, and significantly, it also caught the wind.

Cruelly, rain fell from 7pm onwards and stopped us from setting out. During 9 August the rain continued until a fall in temperature changed it to snow which, after 24 hours, lay as a deep cloak of powder. It was getting difficult to sustain our night-for-day regime.

On 10 August the Gregsons rose at 6am, tempted by the prospect of a good ski run in the now sunlit powder, and skinned uphill to find a suitable slope. We cut some passable linked telemark turns into the pristine snow, but a steeper gradient would have helped. To allow the snow to settle we chose to make a climb on one of the small triangular rock peaks on the nearby subsidiary ridge. Within a couple of hours six of us had climbed loose ledges onto a ramp line crossing the S face of the closest mountain and crowded onto its summit. It was another first ascent and we enjoyed our resumption of activity.

The next day we set out to try to climb the highest peak. Six of us were to form two ropes of three, while Alan Jones and Graham Harkness went off as an independent pair to look at another two summits further west. We wished them well, cautioning them to be wary of crevasses after the recent snowfall. In the course of the morning they had the satisfaction of making two first ascents, one of them a fine promontory over a drop to the Steenstrup Braeer [glaciers].

Meanwhile, in very cold conditions causing us to wear jackets and extra gloves, the remaining six of us were engaged in tackling the high fin of our chosen mountain. From the upper col, which took two hours to reach, this fin rose in a steep ice slope cut by an obvious crevasse, giving onto a ridge punctuated by projecting rocks. Three rope lengths on the 50° ice got us to the ridge where we used rock belay points for two pitches to the topmost blocks at c2400m, the highest summit in the vicinity. On a jutting ledge there stood a cairn. Nevertheless we had made a good climb and were rewarded with views from ocean to ice cap over range upon range of mountains stretching away in every direction.

The descent went well and back at camp we all shared in each other's sense of achievement. Alan and Graham had done splendidly and their pleasure was justly earned. Now the big white pyramid peak beckoned strongly; it lay before us all the time, asking to be climbed. If we could get up it, we would be happy to go back to base with a good 'tick list'.

At 11pm on 11 August, the starting time we had set, there was a fierce wind from the west. A shouted inter-tent conversation about wind-chill factors led to a postponement. By 4am on 12 August, when the sun ought to have shone, the tents were being blasted with spindrift with big drifts burying the pulks. We needed an estimated window of six hours to make an attempt. For my own part, I was willing to try in the less-than-ideal conditions, and Sandy agreed to come with me.

At 8.30am the wind still blew and the sky was overcast. No new snow appeared to have fallen – just redistribution of the spindrift. I discussed the proposed climb with the others. Only Andrew Howick seemed keen, but lacked a partner. I preferred to climb just as a pair with Sandy; our long-term Alpine partnership would allow us the best chance of success. John Starbuck wavered over his decision and, anxious to be away, I set a 15 minute deadline time before going back to my own tent to put on extra clothing.

John opted against going, so Sandy and I hurried to set off. The others would wait for us, although we all realised that we would soon need to start our return journey to Pourquoi-pas base. After only 15 minutes the two of us reached the lee of the mountainside behind the camp, and from then on we were in calm air for the rest of the outing. The wind at the tents had been a very localised phenomenon.

We skied as far as we could, then continued on foot in deep snow, making one long detour to bypass a massive crevasse. Our aim was to get onto the N ridge of the mountain, a narrow arête firing directly to the pyramid apex. We stopped to put on crampons before passing through a hollow filled with knee-deep powder to seek a crossing of the bergschrund arcing along the slope. By a deep blue gap there was a solid-looking bridge which we could use. We cut a knee-step in the upper lip to gain a lodging on the firmer ice above to reach the ridge. Here we placed an ice piton and left a marker sling for our return. Fondly, we had thought the ridge might permit more rapid progress, but to our dismay it was loaded with windslab. This caused our crampons to ball up dreadfully, making balance precarious. After going over a corniced hump we reached a broader section of ridge, but the going was so arduous that we actually took off our crampons. Higher up the arête narrowed down, so we put them back on again. We left our sacks where the terminal crest began.

We climbed first on the left side, then crossed to the right. The exposure became more and more apparent. To the left the NE face plunged down icy buttresses for six or seven hundred metres. On the right the W flank was a sheer sweep of steep ice below our feet. We progressed on a short rope, with axe and hammer shafts driven into the very crest of the ridge, while kicking hard through the soft top layer to get our points into the ice beneath. As this arête was not corniced we were constantly looking directly down the inhospitable NE face. Gradually we approached the top, the ridge easing slightly, until at 2pm we arrived at the summit, almost four hours out from camp. We yelled to the others below who, on seeing our arrival, fired off a mini-flare. Neither signal was heard or seen by those for whom it was intended! There was a cairn (any climber would be drawn towards such a peak) – but we were too concerned over the coming descent to be disappointed.

Going down called on all our experience of Alpine terrain. Security lay more in mutual trust than anything else. Having kicked good footings into the ridge flank, the first narrow section was not too bad, apart from breaking steps where a couple of transverse crevasses cut through the crest. After we had picked up our sacks things got more wearing. Every so often the snow settled with sickening creaks, and we struggled with our balled-up crampons. Minor slides broke away from our feet causing heart-in-mouth moments. I think that if we had set off one big break-away on the way up we would have retreated. Re-crossing the corniced hump was very nerve-racking and we were both in a state of high tension by the time we got back to the ice peg above the bergschrund crossing. The peg was loose and the marker sling had thawed into the ice, so we repositioned them together with a back-up screw. Sandy went down to prod the snow-bridge and belay once back over it. I followed down in turn, treading lightly onto its softened folds, before stepping across onto safer, easier ground.

We were heartily relieved to be off the hazardous snow of the arête, having taken two hours to come down from the top. Taking off our crampons we plodded through the wet afternoon snow to our skis and pushed them slowly downhill towards the tents and the congratulations of our friends. They had kindly prepared drinks and a meal for us. We were very tired and wanted to sleep for a while before continuing, with the others, through the night to get back to base to prepare for our flight out. This journey was interrupted by one mishap: skiing down very difficult snow in which only step turns would work, I took a heavy, twisting fall after catching an edge. The impact caused my pulk's tow-bar to break free from its mounting, allowing the heavily-laden pulk to career off down the mountain on its own, leaving me in a bruised heap on the ice. After about half a kilometre the pulk slid to a halt without finding any crevasses. Our two engineers, John Starbuck and Graham Harkness, effected a repair and the journey was resumed.

With increasing weariness we covered the last kilometres back to base camp, reaching it at about 2.30am on 13 August. Most of us were sated for now, but Andrew Howick and John Starbuck made one more climb in an eight-hour round trip in the very early morning hours of 14 August, while Alan Jones and Graham Harkness made a final tour in search of flowers and rock samples.

The flight out was an impressive finale to our expedition, and by 16 August we were all cleaned up and celebrating in Reykjavik. We felt it had been a successful and rewarding trip – between us we had climbed fourteen peaks and tops of which ten had been first ascents. But the problem with 'once-in-a-lifetime' experiences is that they can become addictive, so already some of us are thinking 'Why not go back again?'

**Summary**: Karabiner Mountaineering Club Greenland Expedition 1994, 22 July – 18 August.

*Team members*:
Jim Gregson (leader), Sandra Gregson, Alan Jones, Graham Harkness, Andrew Howick, John Starbuck, Lucy Walker, Paul Walker.

*Peaks climbed*:

| Peak 1 (25.7.94) | 66°37'N, 35°43'W, | c1500m | 1st ascent (E ridge) |
|---|---|---|---|
| Peak 2 (28.7.94) | 66°42'30"N, 35°50'W, | c2200m | 1st ascent (NW ridge) |
| Peak 3 (29.7.94) | 66°43'N, 35°46'W, | c2100m | 1st ascent (N ridge) |
| Peak 4 (30.7.94) | 66°43'N, 35°44'W | c2180m | 1st ascent (NE ridge) |
| Peak 5 (31.7.94) | 66°43'N, 35°47'W | c2080m | 1st ascent (E face) |
| Peak 6 (31.7.94) | 66°42'30"N, 35°53'W | c2000m | 1st ascent (N flank) |
| Peak 7 (31.7.94) | 66°42'30"N, 35°52'W | c2000m | 1st ascent (N flank) |

| Peak 8 (5.8.94) | 66°40'N, 35°34'W | c2090m (Note in cairn) | 1st British ascent |
| Peak 9 (10.8.94) | 66°41'N, 35°32'W | c1650m | 1st ascent (W ridge/S face) |
| Peak 10 (11.8.94) | 66°40'N, 35°31'W | c2400m (Cairn) | Probably 1st British ascent (W flank/NE ridge) |
| Peak 11 (11.8.94) | 66°39'N, 35°34'30"W | c2000m | 1st ascent (NE flank) |
| Peak 12 (11.8.94) | 66°39'30"N, 35°34'30"W | c1990m | 1st ascent (E flank) |
| Peak 13 (12.8.94) | 66°40'N, 35°28'W | c2370m (Cairn) | Probably 1st British ascent (N ridge) |
| Peak 14 (14.8.94) | 66°38'N, 35°42'W | c1800m (Cairn) | Probably 1st British ascent (N ridge) |

*Note*: All positions are approximated from maps at a scale of 1:250 000. Heights were taken from readings by Thommen altimeter or were based on estimates.

*Maps*: 66 Ø.1 Steenstrup Braeer and 66 Ø.2 Schweizerland in Grønland, 1:250 000 Series (Geodaetisk Institut, Danmark)

BIBLIOGRAPHY

F Spencer Chapman, *Watkins' Last Expedition*. Chatto and Windus, 1934.
Noel Dilly, 'East Greenland: Kristians glacier area, 1968' in *AJ74*, 276-281, 1969.
Derek Fordham, 'East Greenland: Kangerdlugssuatsiaq fjord area, 1968' in *AJ74*, 282-284, 1969.
Derek Fordham, 'Kristians glacier area' in *AJ75*, 240-242, 1970.
Erik Hoff, 'Mountaineering in Greenland 1870-1966' in *Mountain World 1966/67*. The Swiss Foundation for Alpine Research, 1968.
Erik Hoff, 'Mountaineering in Greenland' in *American Alpine Journal 22, Issue 53*, 1979.
J M Scott, *Gino Watkins*. Hodder, 1935.

ACKNOWLEDGEMENTS

The expedition team would like to acknowledge with thanks the support of our patron The Lord Hunt of Llanfairwaterdine. We are also grateful for support and grant aid provided by the Mount Everest Foundation, the British Mountaineering Council and the Gino Watkins Memorial Fund.

# New Directions

ED DOUGLAS

# Protect and Survive

Pinned to the noticeboard in my office is a photograph taken at the Pen y Gwryd in 1993. A group of friends have gathered by the door and are looking with some resignation towards a bank of photographers just in front of them. There is little about this group of pensioners, beyond the inclusion of one or two Nepalese faces, that would seem remarkable except for the almost tangible impression that they have shared a great part of their lives together, and the story of each one of them is inextricably woven into those of all the others.

They could be trades unionists, or an angling club, but that's not what counts. The importance of the photograph is the comradeship that so obviously binds them. John Hunt wrote after the first ascent of Everest that, 'If there is a deeper and more lasting message behind our venture than the mere ephemeral sensation of a physical feat, I believe this to be the value of comradeship and the many virtues which combine to create it.' Of course, the world rarely lives up to such ideals but their occasional reiteration does nobody any harm.

This was also very much the message given by the team that made the first ascent of Everest during the celebrations of its fortieth anniversary, although at times you would have been hard pressed to recognise that fact. Not that there was any shortage of coverage, but rather that the interest dwelt elsewhere. Instead the newspapers concentrated on how the mountain was now climbed routinely – although that was conveniently put aside when Rebecca Stephens made the first ascent by a British woman – and how it was also a trash heap. The impression given was that somehow, since the new Elizabethan age of innocence, mountaineering had slid into a trough of mediocrity and indifference. The sub-text, rather crudely drawn, was that this slide reflected some national collapse led by the familial upheavals of the House of Windsor. Thus the full gamut of tabloid interest – sex, death and royalty – was squeezed out.

For the majority of those climbers who bother to think about such things, comment from the opinionated but ill-informed is easily brushed aside. But do they have a point? Have we maltreated the mountains we supposedly love? Has the sport become a cipher for ambition rather than teamwork and comradeship? Sometimes you feel that the challenges of John Hunt's youth were more straightforward; the good guys wore white hats and the bad guys black. Nobody, it seems, wears hats – or helmets for that matter – at all these days.

Superficially, there is evidence that we have lost some of the integrity of 1953. There are parts of the world that have suffered from the influx of mountaineers, not least Everest itself. The sport is commercially viable now, offering a route for professionals as well as amateurs, with the attendant need for publicity and reputation. Expeditions themselves are run as businesses, crags become holiday resorts.

And yet the brilliant and compelling quality of climbing mountains for personal satisfaction, to be in the company of friends, to develop an interest in the world around us, is just the same. The notion that Everest is somehow reduced by our activity whether good or ill is obvious nonsense. The scraps of litter that garnish our sport's greatest icon, the tiny number of people that have struggled up its bulk make not the slightest bit of difference to Everest's challenge any more than its first ascent did. Nor have the people changed that much, although I suppose you could make an argument that the immediate post-war generation were physically and mentally tougher than the current bunch. But Paul Pritchard, Andy Parkin, Dick Renshaw, Dougal Haston and Don Whillans – plucked pretty much at random from the last forty years of British alpinism – have all pushed the limits of the possible and so all have a great deal in common in terms of motivation and ability.

Whillans battling his way up the Central Pillar of Frêney, Haston slugging it out with the Eiger, Renshaw doing the same but in more committing style, Parkin bringing new technical standards to the steep north faces, Pritchard realising Chouinard's dream of superalpinism in Patagonia and Baffin – modern mountaineers are probably a bit fitter, certainly better equipped, but the thing that fires them to take the next step into the unknown is pretty much standard issue. Scratch the surface of glossy presentation with which each great leap forward is greeted and you quickly discover that the sport is more organic than hierarchical. One era is no better than another. Mummery and Messner, Bonington and Béghin, their business is the same. It's only when you include personality and style that differences emerge.

If this were the whole story then mountaineering would continue serenely on the same course ad infinitum. The trouble is that once something gets momentum, it's very hard to bring back. This is happening with climbing and it's got very little to do with those at the front of the pack. The issue is the pack itself. There seems to be an almost exponential growth in the numbers taking up the sport and very few of those who help influence its direction have even begun to understand where that growth in interest will take us.

Personally, I think it's groovy that a lot more people are having as good a time as I am, although I must be honest and confess that I would rather they did it somewhere else. But the increase is presenting us with challenges as great as the ones we climb. Whereas before we were a quirky minority, now we are an interest group. While our tiny numbers used to leave little impact, now there are complaints that we wreck the place. Where before our heroes had their egos regularly deflated in the pub, now they have fan clubs.

There are some who see this as a shame. I think it's great simply because it's different and exciting but that doesn't mean that we can afford to ignore the new responsibilities that it demands. There is an inherent rebellious streak in climbers which is worth preserving but tends to provide an excuse for avoiding unpalatable truths. We have to share the hills with so many other interests and unless we acknowledge the need for compromise then we might find ourselves in trouble. Already in Europe and the United States, climbers are being excluded because of the impact we have on the environment. I am not suggesting that we are necessarily in the wrong – the reverse is often the case – but unless we provide positive reasons why we should enjoy the same levels of access as we have in the past then we will only have ourselves to blame when it all goes wrong.

Already there are moves to strengthen links between the UIAA and the International Mountain Society. This co-operation between mountaineering and conservation interests could become one of the most positive forces in the future. Who can better defend the mountain environment than those who love it as we do? This has to be reflected in the way we conduct ourselves. It means taking responsibility for our trash, giving up time to solve access problems, agreeing to reasonable demands from landowners. We have the opportunity to earn respect not just for 'the more ephemeral sensation of a physical feat' but for what we put back. The new commercial strength of mountain sports – and I would include skiing in that bracket – offers us the chance to influence these changes. Equipment manufacturers have to recognise that their increasing market carries with it responsibilities to the arena their customers frequent. Already Patagonia has tried to move in this direction, Chris Brasher has put aside profits for conservation work and numerous companies offer clothes that are environmentally more acceptable. It is up to us to see that this trend is continued.

In the same way, our purchasing power can affect the lives of the people who live among the mountains we climb in. Doug Scott has argued forcefully for some time that we have a responsibility to protect the social welfare of the poorer countries we travel through. Ensuring that porters are reasonably paid and treated is only the beginning. We should be aware of how the poorer countries we visit are developing in every aspect, not just those that affect us directly.

When John Hunt arrived in Kathmandu in 1953 there were few cars and no roads. Now there are more than 70,000 vehicles plaguing the city with terrible pollution. Mountaineers were at the vanguard of such changes and we shouldn't absent ourselves now. There are a number of high-profile mountaineers involved in this debate but little attempt has been made to harness the voting and commercial power of millions of mountaineers all over the world.

We have an obvious if depressing precedent on our doorstep. The climbers who helped awaken interest in the Alps could not have foreseen the changes that would transform them into the tourist processing plant of today. Many who visit now resent the style of the development but there are scores of mountain ranges which will face the same kind of problems in the future. At least we have the benefit of hindsight with which to protect them.

This growing interest and respect for the mountain environment is beginning to affect the ethics of our sport. The retro-bolting of many crags in Europe seems a *fait accompli*, but there is growing opposition to an extension of that practice to the mountains. Climbers like Royal Robbins, Catherine Destivelle and Paul Pritchard have all publicly doubted the practice of retro-bolting and inevitably this concern will extend to the broad majority of alpinists who are reluctant to see their achievements devalued. We would be horrified at the retro-bolting of climbs like *Spiral Stairs* on Dinas Cromlech, but there are bolts on the Cosmiques Arête of the Aiguille du Midi. *Right Wall* with ten bolts would no doubt become doubly popular, but there would be outrage. Why then is the South Face of the Midi smothered in the shiny little blighters? It is not a question of trying to force ethics on other countries, but rather a request for some kind of debate before it's too late.

No climber could expect to find Rébuffat's classic as he did, but for the route to be emasculated by a bolt gun is unnecessary – it's safe enough already – and robs future generations of the same pleasure that we have enjoyed. Of course there are thousands of routes in the Alps most of which see few repeats but does that really offer an excuse for what is happening on the standard classics?

There is so much that is new and impressive in modern climbing that reports of the sport's demise seem to have been grossly exaggerated. While there may be something of a hiatus currently underway on the world's highest peaks, the level of exploration, new routing and hard repeats elsewhere continues and increases. Technical standards in the last ten years have soared both in summer and winter and it is only logical that this practice should be extended to the big mountains. The prospect is mouth-watering. And far from John Hunt's world of comradeship being lost to ambition, it seems that we are on the verge of a major change in the Himalaya too, as ordinary climbers finally discover that the roof of the world isn't reserved for the élite. But we mustn't wreck the place.

DUNCAN TUNSTALL

# Climbing in the Ecrins

The quantity and quality of high-standard rock climbs now available in all areas of the Alps is astounding. Many of the areas are well known – Chamonix, the Bregaglia, the Sella Pass area of the Dolomites, Sanetsch and, of course, Handeg. All offer routes of high quality and perfect rock. There is only one problem with these areas and that is that they are too popular. Fortunately, for those of us who value solitude in the mountains, there are still regions in the Alps that provide routes of equal standing to the above but, for reasons not entirely understood, do not attract the crowds. One of the best kept secrets in British climbing circles is that some of the finest rock climbing in the Alps is now to be found in the Ecrins massif where many of the climbs stand comparison with anything that Chamonix or the Bregaglia have to offer. The quality of the rock is more than adequate on most routes, although the odd slightly suspect pitch may add a spice of adventure. This factor has given the range an unfair reputation for looseness which, when combined with a lack of téléphériques, has been effective in keeping the crowds away.

A brief summary follows of the best of the granite climbing in the Ecrins massif. But first I feel I ought to say something about the use of bolts. This is a difficult subject and many words have already been expended on it. My own views are simple: the high mountains, like our own small cliffs, are no place for bolts. Having said that, I have to admit that most of the recent developments in the Ecrins make use of bolt protection. Some of the routes are fully bolted, some have equipped belays, while others are in a more traditional state. Except in a few of the more alarming examples, I have avoided making any comments on the relative use/misuse of bolts on any particular route. However, I do think that, in general, the Ecrins has been overbolted and I applaud the stance taken by the National Park to try to limit this activity.

Many of the routes described in this article are not in the AC guidebook and anyone visiting the area should supplement the latter with Jean-Michel Cambon's topo guide *L'Oisans Nouveau Est Arrivé*. It employs an innovative star system to indicate the relative amount of fixed gear present on any route. This system is very helpful and ensures that wherever you place yourself on the 'sport climber/traditional Alpinist' continuum you will find routes to your taste. I have taken the liberty of adopting the following system of stars to give an impression of the amount of fixed protection currently in use on Ecrins routes:

\*          Denotes a fully bolted sport route. A rack of Quick draws should be sufficient to protect the route.

\*\*        Indicates that bolt belays are provided, plus the odd peg/bolt on sections difficult to protect with traditional protection. A full rack should be carried.

\*\*\*      Implies a traditional Alpine route with little fixed protection. Expect fewer pegs than on comparable Chamonix routes. A full rack, including pegs, should be carried.

\*\*\*\*    Four stars signifies a true challenge.

The Ecrins needs no introduction to regular readers of the *Alpine Journal*. Ailefroide is arguably the most picturesque of the main centres and is a good place to start. There are three venues of interest to the rock climber: the cliffs surrounding the campsite, ideal for the true crag rat, the Aiguille de Sialouze for the more discerning climbers who prefer their cragging in a mountain setting, and the faces above the Glacier Noir, for those who value solitude and ambience enough to undertake a stiff walk.

There are an incredible seven sectors within 30 minutes walk of the campsite – sufficient, indeed, to warrant a local climbing guide. All are fully equipped and there are over 100 routes, from 20-metre sport climbs to 12-pitch routes. Grades vary from 3 to 8a (or possibly, by now, even harder). The rock and the climbing are generally of high quality, with many good friction slabs and several steeper face climbs. These routes are in no way related to Alpinism and, for my taste, the routes are rather anonymous. The Tête de la Draye arguably has the best sport routes. Of the longer routes, the *Fissure d'Ailefroide*\*\* (5) will appeal to some and *Palavar les Flots*\* (5+, 1990) is very popular.

More appealing are the routes on the Aiguille de Sialouze (3576m). This is easily reached from the Refuge du Sélé. The main attraction is the SW face, a 400m slab of perfect granite. There are nine routes on the face, many of which are outstanding. For the aspiring TD leader *Super Pilou*\*\* (TD– 5+, 1984) would be a fine choice in that this is one of the few Ecrins mountain routes of that grade on good rock. *L'Attaque a Main Armée*\* (ED 6c/7a, 1985), *Jour de Colère*\*\* (ED 7a, 1984) and *Ventre à Terre*\* (TD+ 6a, 1985) are all recommended for the well honed.

Having acclimatised on the Sialouze it will undoubtedly be necessary to make a visit to Glacier Noir. Park the car at the Refuge Cézanne and take the obvious path north. After 30 minutes the path divides and the accompanying crowds will head right, to the Refuge du Glacier Blanc and the *voie normal* of the Barre des Ecrins. Instead, walk alone up the moraine of the Glacier Noir into the oppressive coomb at its head. Here the walls are big. To the south are three major north faces: the Pelvoux (3946m), the Pic Sans Nom (3914m) and the Ailefroide (3953m). To the north lies the S face of the Barre des Ecrins (4101m). All four faces are over 1000m in height. The latter is the most amenable, with both the Arête Rouge and the

South Pillar offering classic routes to the highest peak in the range. The South Pillar** (1100m, TD V+, 1944), after an easy start, gives 400m of enjoyable and exposed climbing up the Bastion, climaxing in an overhanging crack to reach the Miroir and easy ground to the top. A combination of some suspect rock and the long descent of the N face makes this a fine expedition.

The N faces opposite have even more to offer those with an inclination for adventure. The Pic Sans Nom is the main attraction. The modern Alpinist, for whom summits for their own sake are not important, will be attracted by the Pilier de Gauche. This sports two 500m routes in the modern idiom: *Magic Stones* ** (TD+ 6a, 1983) and *l'Aurore Nucléaire* ** (ED 6b, 1986), the latter taking a stunning line up a very compact piece of rock. Descent is by 15 abseils down the line of *l'Aurore*.. Traditionalists will prefer to bag the summit and will therefore choose to pit their talents against either the *Russenberger* (ED– 6a,1950) or the *Directe de Droite* by J M Cambon (ED– 6a, 1975). Both get the coveted three star rating! Those who cannot resist the urge to don crampons will be drawn to either Boivin's *Raie des Fesses* **** (1000m, ED+, 1976) on the Pic Sans Nom or Cambon's *Pilier des Séracs* **** (1000m, TD+, 1981) on the Pointe Forestière. With their four stars, both appear worthy of serious attention.

Although it is possible to cross the massif easily on foot, the crag rat will opt to drive over the Col de Lauteret to La Bérarde. En route it is worth spending a few days in La Grave. From here one can take a leisurely stroll up the beautiful Clot des Cavales valley to the isolated Refuge du Lac du Pavé – an ideal base from which to attempt the 900m *Devies-Gervasutti* on Pic Gaspard (3883m). This is probably one of Gervasutti's least frequented routes and a classic. At TD 6a and attracting the magic three star rating, it should appeal to many. Less traditional, but offering bold climbing on excellent rock, are *Traffic* * (200m, TD+ 6b, 1988) on the E face of Pic Nord des Cavales (3362m) and the short routes on Pointe Emma (3344m) *l'Aurore Naissante* ** (200m TD+ 6b, 1988) and *Eurydice* ** (ED– 6b, 1989).

The remaining cliffs are more easily approached from La Bérarde. The campsite there reminds me of a disused airfield but has the advantages of being at 1800m and giving reasonable access to many good mountain rock climbs. Like Ailefroide, there has been considerable development of the local roadside crags which now sport over 30 routes of between four and ten pitches. The main sectors are the Tête de la Maye, Tête Blanche, the Encoula slabs and the recently opened Grande Rochaille. There are also several one-pitch sport crags and good bouldering just above the campsite on the path to the Refuge Carrelet. The routes tend to be of a uniform quality and most lack something from the point of view of character. They are a useful way to keep fit and are nearly always in condition. I would definitely recommend an afternoon on the first five pitches of *Maye O Niaise* * (ED 6b, 1991) which gives several pitches of outstanding wall climbing only 20 minutes from the road. From the top of the wall it is possible to escape right or meander up another five pitches to the summit on good but disjointed climbing.

Of the lower mountain crags, both the Aiguille Dibona (3130m) and the Pic Nord des Cavales (3362m) are well known. The former has had several fine routes ruined by retro-bolting, as well as several new additions. *Visite Obligatoire** (TD+ 6a, 1988) stands out as the best of the new crop, but watch out for the crowds. Pic Nord des Cavales would be as popular if it were not for the steep approach: like the Cromlech only longer. However, those that make the effort will be well rewarded by having a fine cliff to themselves. Particularly impressive is the exposed traverse on *La Fureur de Vivre** (ED– 6b, 1988).

As well as the good climbing, one would be hard pressed not to notice the outstanding views offered by this small but well placed peak. It is a fine spot from which to admire the S face of La Meije (3982m). This has to be one of the Alps' great cliffs, whose friendly aspect gives fine rock climbing for five months of the year. The architecture is magnificent, with a continuous wall of yellow granite spreading all the way from the deep notch of the Col de la Meije to the Col du Pavé. The wall is topped by a series of massive towers, the largest being the stately Grand Pic. The Promontoire thrusts down into the Etançons glacier, offering a compelling line to the Glacier Carré. This remote glacier and the fading snow patches on the Fauteuil des Allemands add definition to the face. It may take four hours of uphill slog to get there but few will not think it a worthwhile effort. There are at least 15 routes on the wall, most of them of the highest quality. The Promontoire hut makes an excellent base and you will be more popular with the warden if you book first and remember to carry water. The best plan is to go for several days and aim to climb a couple of routes, returning to the hut before reaching the summit and then continuing the great traverse to the Aigle hut and La Grave.

Just 20 minutes from the hut lies the very amenable SW face. It only catches the sun from 10am so there is ample justification for a healthy lie in, subject of course to your being able to sleep through the mass exodus at 3am by those attempting the traverse. Both the *Voie de Marseilles**** (500m, TD 6a, 1966) and *l'Horreur du Bide** (ED 6c, 1987) provide good quality routes and quick descents back to the hut.

To the far right of the face, beyond the Zsigmondy Couloir, stands the Face Sud d'Arrêts with its prominent Central Bastion. Here the imaginatively named *Bastion Central*** (500m, TD 5+, 1969) provides a fine traditional route, while *L'épinard Hallucinogène*** (500m ED– 6b, 1984) takes you through some enormous roofs (A0) to some fine free climbing on the walls above. Purists on either route will follow 300m of easier climbing to the *Troisième Doigt* before finishing the traverse, while the norm now is to bail out at the top of the Bastion and make the 15 abseils needed to reach sacks left at the foot of the face.

Sandwiched between the Promontoire and the Bastion lies the massive Grand Pic de la Meije. This 800m wall holds Pierre Alain's 1935 master-piece *South Face Direct*\*\* (TD V). This landmark route forges its way up the right side of the face, requiring inspired and devious route-finding to keep technical difficulties down to an acceptable level. Most parties will get lost at some time on the upper face. To its left stand two modern neigh-bours: *La Chevauchée des Vacheskiripent*\*\* (800m, ED 7a, 1986), one of the current test pieces requiring a competent party to complete it in one day, and the fine *Le Dossier du Fauteuil*\*\* (800m, ED– 6b/c, 1986). This follows the prominent crack line in the centre of the face and boasts a real gritstone special: a 30m overhanging jamming crack at about E2 5c. The rest of the route provides sustained balance climbing on steep slabs at 5-6a right to the summit. Those wishing to complete the traverse should bivvy at the good sites at the foot of the Glacier Carré. To return to the hut, a descent is made of the Promontoire route, for which axes and crampons should be carried. Apparently it is possible to descend the face by 24 abseils! Good luck.

After satiating yourself on these sunny walls, you might feel the urge once again to enter the shadows to gather the full Ecrins experience. The N side of the Meije offers several fine options, and indeed one can hardly ignore the *Gervasutti route*\*\*\* on the NW face of the Ailefroide, 3953m (1100m, TD+ 6, 1936) , probably the most coveted of all the big classic rock routes in the massif. If these are not in condition, and by now your fingertips are worn through, perhaps you should investigate some of the fine limestone cliffs in the region or even the many traditional mountain-eering routes.

# The Alpinists

They stalk the campsite
in drab cags, like cranes
in shorts, scouring the sky
for signs to be off and up
on the rising pressure.

They have packed sacs in the rain,
included a sunhat, some tat and
a secret bit of line
that comes in handy
for only they know what.

They leave saying little,
suppressing even their own
inner questions with the imperative
of confidence.  They leave late
with only half a hill to climb

to the hut or an open bivi
just above it and the old
teamwork of tasks:  water,
a wind-shelter wall, sweeping
sharp stones and alarm setting.

Down in the valley after dark
wine and conversation construct
a campsite cosiness against
regret, guilt, envy, the loss
of those who know they live too low.

They return still in harness
willing to talk to whoever
needs advice, encouragement,
direction.  Now the mountains
seem to speak through them.

*Terry Gifford*

'The Alpinists' was written after the Alpine Club/Climbers' Club/ABMSAC meets
at Ailefroide and Courmayeur in July/August 1994.

# The End of 'The Golden Age'

PETER BERG

# The Eagle's Nest

A Victorian mountaineer and his summer home in the Alps

*(Plates 69–71)*

Sir Alfred Wills is chiefly remembered today for his ascent of the Wetterhorn in September 1854, said to have marked the start of the Golden Age of mountaineering. He was one of the original members of the Alpine Club, and at the General Meeting following his death in 1912, the President, making the announcement, said that Sir Alfred Wills's ' ... alpine life is part of the early history of the Club, and is to be found in the pages of *Peaks, Passes and Glaciers*, in the volumes of the *Alpine Journal,* and in those two charming alpine classics *Wanderings among the High Alps* and *The Eagle's Nest in the Valley of Sixt.*'[1]

Wills was born in 1828, the son of a successful Birmingham solicitor, educated at non-conformist schools and University College, London, where he obtained the highest honours in classics, mathematics and law. He was called to the Bar in 1851, took silk in 1872, and was made a judge and knighted in 1884. The best-known trial over which he presided was that of Oscar Wilde in 1895: ' ... the worst case I have ever tried,' he declared in his summing-up. He was made a member of the Privy Council in 1905 and devoted his closing years to the affairs of what was to become Southampton University. His first marriage produced two children, and the second, after the death of his first wife, five more. Further details of his life may be found in an extensive obituary in the *Alpine Journal,*[2] and in the Alpine Club Register,[3] but the facts sketched above serve to show what Ronald W Clark described as 'in many ways the laboratory specimen of the early Victorian mountaineer'[4] – a man rising to the top of his profession, but willing to devote a couple of months every year to the mountains.

The ascent of the Wetterhorn was Wills's first major peak, his earlier summers in the Alps having been concerned only with cols and passes: his ambition to attempt higher things was the result of meeting the Chamonix guide Auguste Balmat, whom Professor Forbes had brought to England during the winter of 1853. Wills was newly married, and the visit to Grindelwald came at the end of a honeymoon which had included a night on the Mer de Glace as an introduction for his wife to the joys of the high mountains. Here, though, Lucy remained in the village, while her husband, accompanied by Balmat and three other guides and a porter, headed for the Wetterhorn.

It was not the first ascent – the mountain had been climbed three times before, though never from the Grindelwald side – but there were two factors which distinguished this expedition: it had no scientific purpose, and there was an element of sporting competition about it.  There were no porters bearing heavy theodolites or devices for measuring the depth of the snow – just an iron sheet carried by one of the guides to be planted as a 'flagge' on the summit.  And the competition appeared in the shape of two local chamois hunters[5] who thought they would try to save the honour of Grindelwald by beating the foreign party to the top: in the event, after threats of fisticuffs from Balmat, the parties joined forces and continued climbing together with good humour all round.  The route to the summit ridge lay up a rocky arête:

> At length, we came to a very singular formation.  Standing out from a nearly perpendicular wall of rock were a series of thin parallel wedges of rock, planted, with the thin edge upwards, at right angles to the body of the mountain, and separated from one another by deep intervening clefts and hollows ... presenting, at the top, a rough and jagged ridge, forty or fifty feet long, by which we must pass to reach the plateau which lay just beyond ... It was nervous work;  a good head, a stout heart, a steady hand and foot were needed.[6]

Those who have climbed the Wetterhorn by this route will recognise from Wills's description, in *Wanderings among the High Alps*, first published in 1856, the upper section of the arête that bears his name, the Willsgrätli – a permanent reminder of the role of this man in encouraging Alpine adventure.  Wills and his family are also remembered with affection in the Giffre valley in France, and hikers on the GR5, heading southwards towards Chamonix, may make a stop at the Refuge Alfred Wills below the Col d'Anterne, high above the family chalet.

My own interest in Wills started with finding a battered copy of his book *The Eagle's Nest* in a pile of Victorian mountaineering literature lent by a friend.  It is a highly readable book with a strong romantic appeal.  The author's descriptions of finding, in the Alps of Haute Savoie, the site for a chalet, negotiations for purchase and the role of his young wife in designing the house she was not to survive to see completed, speak to us clearly over the century-and-a-half since they were written. The book obviously had the same appeal for Wills's contemporaries: a second edition was called for within six weeks of its first appearance.  The binding is attractive, cloth with elaborate gilt foliage on the cover surrounding a medallion of an eagle with young sitting on a nest.  The dedication is to Lucy, who died in 1860: 'To the memory of a gentle, loving, and most accomplished wife ... these pages concerning scenes and plans which, however fascinating in themselves, derived their chief interest in my eyes from the hope that we should often again enjoy them together, are dedicated.'

Wills was captivated by the place the first time he saw it:

> It was in the month of August 1857 that I first saw the Plateau des
> Fonds. I was descending from the summit of the Buet in company
> with Balmat and an English friend.[7] The scenery struck us as un-
> common in character and unique in beauty, and as we stood at the
> edge of the level ground, it passed through my mind what a glorious
> site it would be for a chalet. A day or two afterwards we both wished
> to revisit the spot, for we could neither of us call to mind in our
> Alpine experiences a view that had pleased us equally. Finding that
> our second visit did but strengthen our impressions of the rare beauty
> of the scenery, the passing thought of the former day returned, and
> began to assume the character of a definite wish.[8]

The land was owned by the commune of Sixt, and initial negotiations
were promising, but when Wills returned after a week away, local opposition, led by the Curé, had hardened against him:

> I found on my return to Sixt that no stone had been left unturned to
> get a majority in the council to take the high conservative view of
> the question. There would be a protestant crusade in the valley;
> domestic purity would suffer even more severely than religious
> orthodoxy;  one intruder would give rise to another, and their
> 'montagnes' (sufficient for many times the number of cattle at
> present pastured upon them) would be cut up into building patches
> to satisfy the vagaries of English taste;  then the cattle and goats
> would stray over the land of this English aristocrat, who would im-
> pound them and refuse to release them except upon payment of
> exorbitant compensation;  besides, it was all nonsense about his
> wanting to build a place for autumn recreation;  would he be likely
> to come a thousand miles from home for such a purpose? The fact
> was, he had found the vein of gold ore Jacques Balmat had failed to
> discover;  and their forests – the pride and wealth of the valley –
> would be destroyed to find fuel for his smelting furnaces – or if not
> that, he wanted to build an hotel, or some similar abomination;
> and why should they be condemned to have their valley overrun by
> foreigners, like that of Chamouni?[9]

An extremely hostile meeting of the Sixt council followed, and at this
point Wills thought the matter closed but, encouraged by a local lawyer,
he pursued his request with higher authorities, ultimately to the Minister
of the Interior at Turin (until 1860, Savoy belonged to Piedmont). In
July 1858, the plot of land in the Vallée des Fonds was his.

Wills returned with his wife that August to a tumultuous welcome –
astounding considering the hostility which had surrounded his previous

visit: a brass band played beneath their hotel balcony at Samoëns, a deputation greeted them on the road to Sixt and a salute was fired in the Gorge des Tines! Permission to set up a saw-mill and a lime-kiln was granted without the slightest opposition, and requests for timber, stone and sand met with immediate positive response. Lucy was equally enchanted by the valley, and she – sole architect for the project – and her husband marked out the position of the chalet. Wills notes that the contractor pronounced that her scale-drawings were good enough to work from, and it was agreed that work should begin in the following spring. She also wrote the following lines 'to be carved, after the Swiss fashion, along the base of the galleries:

> A wanderer I: I left my much-loved home,
> O'er plain and hill, 'mid ice and snows to roam;
> Through many a land my wandering feet have strayed,
> Yet here, at length, content my feet have stayed.[10]

Wills was unable to visit Sixt in 1859, but was 'obliged to trust implicitly, as I may safely do', in the competence of the contractor, under the supervision of Balmat, trust in whom, as it turned out, was seriously misplaced.

The book tells us no more about the Eagle's Nest, nothing of its completion nor of the excitement of the first stay in it. Perhaps this had something to do with Lucy's death in April 1860.

In the summer of 1992 I walked up the track from Sixt to the Vallée des Fonds to discover that the chalet is, indeed, still there, in a superb position above the Giffre facing the Pointe de Salles. It has seen better times, however, and looked a little sad on a wet and misty day, windows boarded up, with a rusty corrugated iron roof replacing the original wooden shingles. Enquiry at the refuge revealed that the Wills family had sold the chalet long ago, and that it was now owned by a Mme Lucas who lived in Paris but walked up to the valley every summer in spite of being well on in years.

That might have been the end of the story as far as I was concerned, but then I discovered that a fellow AC member, Bill Norton, was a great-grandson of Sir Alfred Wills, and he was able to tell me that one of his cousins, John Wills, had been in regular contact with Mme Lucas and would give me her address in Paris. A short letter from me produced a long reply from her, with a warm welcome to visit her at the chalet the following summer. This I did, and spent a fascinating couple of hours with her. It turned out that Denise Lucas is half English and is the widow of an Englishman with whom she had a book business – which, in her eighties, she still runs – and that they had bought the chalet in 1958. The interior of the Eagle's Nest is just as interesting as the exterior; built around a grand central staircase, it is altogether on a more imposing scale than the usual Alpine chalet. My appetite for finding out more about the history of the place was whetted still further.

John Wills had also told me that he was working on his great-grandfather's correspondence, making abstracts for the family. A visit to him in Norwich gave me a sight of 27 leather-bound volumes – a mammoth task, well in hand with three volumes of abstracts already issued, as well as a volume of letters between Alfred Wills and his father printed verbatim, edited by John's cousin David Wills. Equally fascinating were books of photographs of the Eagle's Nest and its surroundings: full-plate records of life there in its heyday.

Bill Norton also put me in touch with another cousin, Peter Norton, who visited the Eagle's Nest for the first time in 1922 at the age of nine, and had many tales to tell of pre-war visitors and climbs around the valley – 'there were giants in those days', he wrote in a letter inviting me to Sussex to look at the chalet archives. Here I found the *Livre des Voyageurs*, an imposing volume bound in green leather embossed with the eagle's nest motif and with a delightful pencil drawing of the chalet bordered by watercolours of local wild flowers as its frontispiece. There were also three volumes of Logs of the doings of the inhabitants and two copies of a history of the chalet written by Wills's eldest daughter Edith, as well as several more volumes of photographs.

This wealth of material gives remarkable insight into the leisure life of an English family in the Alps at that time, but there is altogether too much material to do justice to in one short article; it would be good if one day someone were to use it to write a book. For the present, we shall have to content ourselves with some glimpses.

One of the most significant features of Wills's mountaineering was his close relationship with one particular guide, Auguste Balmat; indeed, he was one of the first of the gentleman mountaineers to develop the close bond with his guide which was to be such an important feature of the Golden Age. By the time the Eagle's Nest was completed in 1860, Balmat was employed by Wills on a more or less exclusive basis. A letter from Geneva dated August 1861 to his fiancée Bertha Taylor mentions being assailed by a Prussian 'savant' who wanted to be taken to Sixt, and also desired the services of Balmat on Mont Blanc: both requests were refused.[11] Wills and Bertha were married that autumn and from this time on, the main source of information about the chalet is the *Short History*, compiled by Edith Sarah (Wills) Norton in the 1930s from letters between her father (AW) and her stepmother (BW) and her own old diaries.[12] Balmat's death is described at length.

Unusually for a guide, Balmat's responsibilities continued in the valley, and he was entrusted with Wills's business affairs in connection with the building of the Eagle's Nest, a period of 22 months when AW did not go abroad. In June 1862 Bertha, then about six months pregnant, together with Edith and Jack, the children of the first marriage, travelled ahead to the chalet – 'BW carried up in a *chaise à porteurs*'. Everywhere there were signs of Balmat's industry: plantings of English rhododendrons, holly, privet

* Sadly, Peter Norton died in March 1995

and many roses (none of which appear to survive today). When AW arrived in August, Balmat fell ill with what Edith describes as 'softening of the brain'. As the patient became worse, his sister Angélique came over from Chamonix to nurse him, prescribing an alarming regime of leeches, blisters, mustard poultices and heaps of bedclothes, moaning '*Pauvre Auguste*' over him from morning to night. Wills appears not to have been happy with this treatment. Edith continues: 'Although AW ordered the mustard to be locked up, Angélique got at it and his feet were tied up on a horrid mess of mustard and linseed – quite dry and hard – and then wrapped in a thick worsted jacket.' After Wills took over the nursing, Balmat 'improved a little, but his mind was completely gone and he did not recollect anything from hour to hour and talked much nonsense. Worse remained, for it transpired that his affairs were hopelessly entangled. He had borrowed money to lend to others but had nothing to show for it and was being pressed on every side for thousands of francs. Money sent him by AW had not been used to pay workmen, as intended, and AW had already paid £70 twice over, and was constantly finding out fresh delinquencies.' Worse still, it was found that Balmat had forged a bill for 4000 francs: Wills appears to have had to find the money so that Balmat would not be prosecuted, but took the view that the rest of his affairs were in such a muddle that it was best not to intervene. Balmat died at the Eagle's Nest on 27 September 1862 – his debts, estimated at over £500 (in money of the time), appear to have died with him. Edith ends her account of the year by mentioning the unexpected birth of a son to her stepmother in Paris on the way home to England. 'Poor BW! What a summer holiday!'

After Balmat's death, Wills's climbing exploits were chiefly devoted to his own neighbourhood, including two first ascents on the Pic de Tenneverge as well as occasional expeditions over the Col d'Anterne to the mountains around Chamonix, and to other parts of the Alps. The early volumes of the Log of the Eagle's Nest are missing, but Peter Norton remembered that there were at least a dozen routes in the Vallée des Fonds which were regularly climbed by visitors to the chalet. The rock of the lower slopes of Mont Buet is an extremely friable shale, a considerable challenge to those used, for example, to the solid granite of the Chamonix aiguilles, and the family became adept at dealing with what the rest of us would describe as 'bad rock'. Tom Longstaff, who frequently visited the Eagle's Nest between the wars, commented that the Norton family were very careful climbers: 'when they have finished with their hand-holds they always replace them'! Lieut-General E F Norton (father of Bill) said that it was an excellent training ground for the higher slopes of Mount Everest, training which he had put to good use when he reached a high point of 28,126ft while leading the 1924 expedition.

Photographs of the Eagle's Nest from the 1870s and 1880s show the chalet overflowing with visitors. A family group taken in about 1887 has Wills – wearing the new-fangled knickerbockers which he had described as 'a piece of foppery' a few years earlier – presiding over assorted children, grandchildren and servants, under a painted sign 'The Will's Arms – Good Beds'. Further beds were provided in the *Succursale*, and the *Buanderie* dealt with what must have been mountains of laundry. Both buildings have now disappeared. Topographical features were all given names: for instance, 'Tent Wood' commemorated the spot where a darkroom was set up by a visiting photographer; the 'Via Salutis' was a path on which hard physical work helped Wills regain his health after a breakdown in 1871.

The summer visits to the chalet clearly brought Wills much satisfaction: in his summary of the 1891 season in the Visitors' Book, for example, he wrote: 'Our season has been a great and confirmed success. I do not know how to believe that I am in my 63rd year. Everything has gone well and happily, and things are thoroughly well ordered at the nest.' But time was marching on, and in 1902 he spent his last summer at the chalet, making a gift of it two years later to his daughter Edith, by then Mrs Edward Norton. Wills died on 9 August 1912, and thereafter the history of the chalet largely refers to the Norton family.

The First World War left the chalet unscathed. Edith notes that on arrival in July 1919 they 'found everything unchanged, and our old clothes dry and fit to put on after 5 years'. The family itself did not fare so well: Edith lost a son, Richard (R C Norton on the memorial in Sixt), as well as many friends and locals from the valley. Tragedy struck again in March 1933, when another son, Eric, was killed with a friend by an avalanche below the Col d'Anterne – the first (and only) serious accident in all the years the Wills/Norton family owned the chalet. Edith herself died at the Eagle's Nest in August1936 and was buried in the churchyard at Sixt. It had been her 55th summer at the chalet, and obituary notices in the local papers speak of her as a woman of unequalled simple generosity and kindness, much loved in the area.

The entry in the Log for 22 August 1939 – in the hand of Edith's eldest son, J H Norton – reads 'We leave in a state of great uncertainty with all the usual regrets'. These misgivings were well placed, for when JHN, with his brother E F Norton, returned in June 1946, for the first time after the War, he notes 'Chalet in an indescribable state of destruction and filth'. After a brief look inside they had to go up the valley to look at the wild flowers as an antidote to the shock. A caretaker had been paid throughout the War, but when the chalet was taken over by the Maquis there was little he could do. In 1947 it was decided to sell – the locals were 'sad and amazed' – and the following summer the chalet was let to a potential purchaser who was sufficiently serious to instal electric wiring at his own expense. Nothing came of this, and Norton family parties (including, for the first time, Bill) spent short holidays there in 1949 and 1953.

In 1956, 'Mr Charles Lucas of Librairie Charles Lucas St Cloud visited Sixt as a tourist with his wife and children. He heard that the chalet was for sale and went up and looked at it. Subsequently he came to England ...

to see JHN to negotiate purchase.' The final entry in the History, dated
1958, reads: 'Permission to sell was at last obtained from the Treasury, and
the Chalet became Lucas property on March 1st ... Sic transit'.

So ended an association with a British mountaineering family which had
lasted just one hundred years, but the Eagle's Nest still stands proudly at
the head of the Giffre valley as a monument to Sir Alfred Wills and his
successors as proof of their love for this part of France and their determination to make a successful summer home there.

REFERENCES AND NOTES

1   *AJ26*, 478, 1912.
2   *AJ27*, 47, 1913.
3   AC Register, ed. A L Mumm, 383.
4   Ronald W Clark, *The Victorian Mountaineers*. Batsford, 1953.
5   The 'two local chamois hunters' were Christian Almer (then aged 28)
    and his brother-in-law Ulrich Kaufmann, both later to become leading
    Grindelwald guides.  See also Note 7, p445, A W Moore, *The Alps in
    1864*, (Blackwell's edition 1939).
6   Sir Alfred Wills, *Wanderings among the High Alps*, 2nd edition.
    R Bentley, 278, 1858. (This book was dedicated to Auguste Balmat.)
7   A Mr Welby.
8   Sir Alfred Wills, *"The Eagle's Nest" in the Valley of Sixt; a summer home
    in the Alps; together with some excursions among the great glaciers*.
    2nd edition, Longman, 95, 1860.
9   Ibid, 102.
10  Ibid, Frontispiece.
11  *Letters from Alfred Wills to Bertha Taylor, 1860-61*, ed John Wills.
    Published privately.
12  *A Short History of the Eagle's Nest, compiled by E S Norton from
    Alfred Wills & Bertha Wills's letters & ESN's old diaries*.  MS *c*1935.

ACKNOWLEDGEMENTS

I would like to record a debt of gratitude to John and David Wills and to
Bill Norton and the late Peter Norton who gave me help, encouragement,
hospitality and access to family papers.

ALAN LYALL

# The Matterhorn Lithographs of 1865

## Gustave Doré and his links with Edward Whymper

(*Plates 79, 80*)

Gustave Doré's two large lithographs of the first ascent of the Matterhorn, showing the arrival at the summit and the accident, merit closer attention than they generally get as despite their faults they incorporate certain details that could only have come from Edward Whymper. Charles Gos appears to be the only writer who has considered them closely and he concluded[1] that Doré had either consulted some competent mountaineers, had met Whymper himself or corresponded with him or even that Whymper had perhaps submitted his own drawings.

Gos noticed how Doré's prints could be distinguished from the fantastic and ridiculous prints that other artists produced of the Matterhorn drama by their attention to precise detail. He was particularly intrigued by the similarity between the description of the accident which Whymper gave in the *Journal de Zermatt* article[2] in August 1895 and Doré's representation of the accident. But he could find nothing in Smythe's biography of Whymper nor in the biographies of Doré by Roosevelt and by Valmy-Baysse with which to answer the questions, did Doré ever see the Matterhorn? and did he know Whymper? Doré had been to Chamonix in 1853, Switzerland in 1854 and the Tyrol in 1860 but in the summer of 1865 he had taken a cure in Baden Baden.

Recent study of some letters kept by Whymper throws a good deal of light on the subject but it is first necessary to look at such other evidence as there is of co-operation or of a professional relationship between the two men whose artistic skills were to a large extent complementary. There is no doubt that they did meet at some stage as in the course of an article on Mountaineering Tragedies published in 1909[3] Whymper referred to the Croz subscription fund amounting to nearly £300 and added: 'That is not much for the life of a man Gustave Doré said to me, and I agreed with him.' This conversation, however, must have taken place long after the two prints were published on 1 October 1865, as the subscription fund was still open at that time.

We know that Doré provided the frontispiece to the third abridged edition of *Scrambles*, published in 1880. There had been a note in the *Alpine Journal* as early as November 1873,[4] stating that 'the principal portion of

Mr. E. Whymper's "Scrambles amongst the Alps" will reappear next season under the title of the "Ascent of the Matterhorn" with numerous fresh illustrations, amongst which will be a new frontispiece by M. Gustave Doré, and some Chamois subjects by Joseph Wolf. The work will not be reprinted in its original form.' The reason for the subsequent five-year delay in publishing the abridged edition is not apparent. The first edition of *Scrambles* is believed to have been delayed on account of the illustrations, which Whymper had to engrave in his spare time, but the additional ones in the third edition could hardly account for a five-year hitch. However, this aspect does merit further consideration in the light of an article by the Swiss art critics and historians Caroline Kesser and Peter Killer published in *Berge* in 1983[5] in which they draw attention to one of the plates in *Scrambles* 'The crags of the Matterhorn ... Aug. 10 1863'.[6] They suggest that this most splendid illustration has been produced by the parallel engraving technique which was characteristic of Gustave Doré but not typical of Whymper. They point out that in contrast to most of the other woodcuts in *Scrambles* it does not bear Whymper's name as the engraver and they consider it probable that Whymper relied on some Doré trained reproduction specialists. They suggest that Doré's contribution may indeed have gone much further in view of his co-operation in the third edition and, in the light of the correspondence referred to below, it seems probable that they are correct and that Gustave Doré was indebted to Whymper and did help him directly or indirectly to prepare a few of the illustrations for *Scrambles*.

An undated French newspaper cutting[7] that must be of early August 1865, probably the second week, refers to the crowd stopping outside the Montmartre premises of the publishers Goupil to admire G. Doré's two fine tinted drawings of the Matterhorn catastrophe (75cms by 40cms). The reporter states that he does not know if Doré went to the scene or if it comes from his imagination with the help of photographs of the Matterhorn but that the drawings will be available as prints before long.

It is doubtful whether Doré's original drawings had very much in common with the published prints (52cms by 39cms) apart from the crags in the background of the accident scene, and if they are still in existence they may be hardly recognisable for what they are. It is probable that Adams Reilly saw the original drawings in Montmartre on about 11 August on his way home from Zermatt and Chamonix, as on 23 August Whymper wrote in a letter[8] 'For several weeks past Messrs Goupil have exhibited in Paris two large drawings by Gustave Doré, one of the accident and the other of the summit of the mountain. At the same time they publicly announced that they were going to publish these drawings, which I have been informed by a friend are grossly inaccurate.' Adams Reilly had been in Zermatt from 18 July until the end of the month and would have been fully conversant with the circumstances of the accident. He went to see Whymper in London on 14 August to give him some French newspapers, when he probably told him of Doré's drawings.

On about 18 August Goupil's agent in London sent a letter to Whymper seeking information about him and about those who had accompanied him on the Matterhorn and also about the scene of the accident. The following day he called to see Whymper. Thereafter he seems to have written to the relatives of Hudson, Hadow and Douglas asking for a portrait that Doré could use. None of these letters appears to have survived but there is still in existence a letter of 23 August written by Hadow's father to Whymper which states:

'I have just been informed by Messrs Goupil that it is their intention to publish a print of the catastrophe of the "Matterhorn" and that you are going to supply the drawing for it, while I am actually asked to supply a likeness of my dear son for the picture.

'I can hardly say how much pain and distress such a proceeding would cause to ourselves and to Mrs. Hudson, who has written to us on the subject. I have no wish to interfere with parties who may wish to publish drawings of the scene of this sad accident, but they might surely spare the feelings of those relatives who have already suffered so much, and abstain from bringing forward again to notoriety the victims of this fatal occurrence.

'I venture therefore to hope that you will exert your influence with the publishers and the artist to omit from the design any attempted likeness of Mr. Hudson or of my son; their insertion could not in any way improve it, while it would be most distasteful to all the relatives and friends of the deceased. Glad indeed should we be if a veil could now be drawn over this distressing occurrence.'

Whymper despatched his reply the same day, 23 August, saying that Hadow had either been misinformed by Goupil, or else had misunderstood their communication inasmuch as it regarded him. He referred to the large drawings being exhibited in Paris for several weeks, to the announcement they were to be published and to being told they were grossly inaccurate. He sent Hadow Goupil's letter to him of 18 August 'by which you will see that I am a total stranger to their house' and he referred to his subsequent promise to give them a sketch of the spot, whilst declining to give them the slightest assistance in procuring the portraits.

'I greatly regret that anything I have done should have caused you the slightest pain or annoyance and I shall immediately withdraw my promise to help Messrs Goupil to produce a correct representation of the spot ... I am sorry to say that I believe it will be of no use to endeavour to prevent them publishing the drawings ...

'It gives me the greatest pain to see from the tenor of your letter you have been led to believe that the idea of publishing these drawings was more or less originated or helped by myself but I trust that you will no longer entertain any such idea as it is entirely without foundation ... '

Further correspondence from the agent confirms that Whymper wrote to them on 23 August stating that he could no longer lend his assistance, but Hadow's reply of 26 August indicated that he was now satisfied.

' ... I had no intention, nor do I now wish to interfere with your arrangements for supplying a correct sketch of the mountain or of the scene of this
lamentable catastrophe, but gathering from Messrs Goupil's letter that they
proposed to introduce portraits or attempted likeness into the sketch you
were to furnish, I ventured to solicit your influence to prevent that part of
the work being done, for the reasons which must be obvious to any person
of good taste ... '

Subsequently the agent wrote again to Whymper on 4 September saying
he had received a portrait of Lord Douglas 'but of course shall now not
make any use of it' and enclosing a lengthy letter in French addressed to
Whymper from Goupil. The letter is handwritten on both sides of two
sheets of thin paper, which the ink has soaked through, but with the exception
of a few words and phrases which seem unlikely to be of great significance
it can with difficulty be deciphered and translates as follows:

Goupil et Cie

Paris 1st Sep. 1865

Mr. Edward Whymper,
Sir,

   Our agent in London has told us of the kind reception you
gave initially to our request for information about the gentlemen
who accompanied you on the Matterhorn and also about yourself
and he told us at the same time of your plan to come to Paris so
that you could give Mr. Gustave Doré all the details he could
have need of to complete his drawings. Subsequently you have
let it be known to us that the parents of the victims of the
catastrophe on the 14th July were objecting to the execution of
Mr. Doré's drawings and to their reproduction, and in consequence you did not wish to participate in any way. You have
furthermore communicated to us some letters addressed to you
on the subject by Mrs. Hudson and by Mr. Hadow.

   One need only imagine oneself for a moment in the position
of these unfortunate parents to understand how the representation of this fatal occurrence would be very painful for them, yet
we do not believe it is possible not to proceed with this publication;
allow us, Sir, to make you the judge of our reasons.

   Mr. Gustave Doré was deeply impressed by the account you
gave of the catastrophe which all the newspapers then published
throughout the world. In three days he made his two drawings
and asked us to exhibit them to the public in our shop in the
Boulevard Montmartre; all Paris came to see and talked about
the drawings as much on account of the enterprise of the artist
as of the interest of the scenes that they depicted; the French
press reviewed the exhibition, as did the correspondents of foreign
newspapers. Faced with such a great success Mr. Doré's friends

urged him to reproduce the drawings and to publish them and we agreed to undertake the service. So it is, that Mr. Doré, wanting to complete his work by adding every possible true detail, asked us to enquire as to whether you would be willing to communicate information to him and during the time that you were replying to us at first favourably and subsequently when you were refusing us, the reproduction was undertaken and today it is almost finished. It is therefore no longer a question of abandoning a simple project; an accomplished work would have to be destroyed. But would destruction achieve anything? Obviously not, as one could not prevent the sad occurrence, that one would like to see forgotten, becoming the object of other publications whether in France or elsewhere.

We believe, Sir, that the only thing we can do is to accede to Mr. Hadow's request and refrain from any attempted likeness of the unfortunate victims. Our sole object having been to reproduce a work of great artistic merit we do not agree it could be supposed that we wanted to speculate on a scene of mourning. As for Mr. Gustave Doré, it would never have occurred to him that he could be criticised for putting his name to the representation of a drama whose last act, admittedly terrible and painful, was such a triumph of human will and energy – he was only concerned with the poetry and with the philosophy of the subject. Lastly, if the publication of these two drawings can be criticised, one would have to be equally critical of the accounts which newspapers have published and it would be necessary to prohibit representation of the deeds of war which make certain families glorious, but plunge them into mourning.

Sir, please excuse this very long pleading,

And please accept [etc]

Goupil et Cie

There is no further correspondence on the subject and one can only guess the subsequent developments. Whymper clearly had a professional interest in helping Doré and it may well be for this reason that he may have contemplated going to see him in Paris on the occasion he met Goupil's London agent. In any event it seems probable, in the light of the correspondence and in particular Hadow's satisfaction once the question of incorporating portraits had been excluded, when he had no wish to interfere with Whymper's arrangements for supplying 'a correct sketch of the mountain or of the scene of this lamentable catastrophe', that Whymper decided that there was no reason why he should not co-operate and provide two sketches. The ultimate prints are certainly not 'grossly inaccurate in almost every particular' and they contain details that no one but Whymper could have provided to Doré. The probability is that one sketch gave an approximate outline of the immediate approach to the summit, so far as Whymper could recollect it, and that it included the figures of Croz and himself but no one else, as the rest of the party would still have been some distance from the summit if they did not arrive there until about 10 minutes later, as Whymper wrote in his letter to *The Times*. Whatever the nature of Doré's original representation of the arrival at the summit and however accurate Whymper's drawing of the final peak may or may not have been, it will have been necessary for Doré to retain in the print some resemblance to his original drawing so as not to confuse or discourage his admirers and potential customers. Croz' axe corresponds with Whymper's drawing of Croz' axe in *Scrambles*[9] in contrast to Anderegg's axe,[10] and Whymper's stance on the Swiss summit has features in common with the drawing,[11] showing himself on the Italian summit.

But it is the representation of the fall of the four victims that can only have come from a sketch provided by Whymper. Old Peter Taugwalder may to some extent be Whymper's impression, although instead of hugging a large rock with both arms he just has one hand on it, but the silhouettes of Young Peter and of Whymper himself seem to be as much a part of Doré's background as the strange cliffs in the upper left-hand corner, which seem altogether out of place in the vicinity of the accident. Once again Doré would have had to relate the details provided by Whymper to his own original drawing which had excited such widespread public interest. The apparent demarcation between Whymper and Doré in the accident scene may be better appreciated by looking at a mirror image, when Whymper's foreground becomes even more realistic. It may even be that Doré incorporated a mirror image of Whymper's sketch in order to portray the falling climbers in front of his own existing background, but that is speculation. What is probable is that only a month after writing to *The Times* in August 1865 and some six years prior to his publishing *Scrambles* Whymper recorded his own pictorial impression of the actual accident and that this was incorporated by Doré into his own lithographed print. Doré seems never to have acknowledged publicly his debt to Whymper, nor did Whymper publish anything indicative of any contribution on his part. Nevertheless there would have been no great secrecy about his involvement and it is probable that his own immediate circle of friends knew that he had supplied Doré with two sketches. This may well explain the reference in Rev J M Elliott's letter of 25 July 1868 to his friend Wood describing the second ascent of the Matterhorn from Zermatt, to turning a corner at the base of the final peak. 'It is as unlike Whymper's picture as anything I have ever seen.' When Elliott's letter was first published in *The Field* in 1910 the Editor added a note:

'Mr. Whymper, to whom several references are made in Mr. Elliott's letter, informs us that he has no recollection of having shown or of having made any drawings at the point referred to by Mr. Elliott, who may possibly have had in his mind two drawings by Gustave Doré which were lithographed and circulated extensively, but had nothing to do with Mr. Whymper.'[12]

If Whymper was in fact responsible for the precise details in Doré's prints, mention should also be made of Ferdinand Hodler's two monumental paintings 'Aufstieg' and 'Absturz' ('Ascent' and 'Fall'), which were commissioned from him for the 1894 World Exhibition in Antwerp. Hodler's inspiration clearly came from Doré and his four falling climbers are undoubtedly the Whymper/Doré Matterhorn victims, to which Hodler added variations of his own. The 25ft high canvasses were subsequently cut into several sections and the surviving pieces which include the four victims are now displayed in the new Alpine Museum in Bern. In an article in *Die Alpen* in 1934[13] Werner Müller wrote of the two Hodler's:

'They are not pictures, they are not mere painted canvasses: they are monuments! Monuments to the many unknown heroes and conquerors of the mountains! Gravestones and rolls of honour for every victim of the mountains.'

### REFERENCES

1   C Gos, *Le Cervin, Vol 2*. Attinger (Neuchâtel), 195-196, 1948.
2   *Journal de Zermatt*, 25.8.1895. See *AJ45*, 322, 1933; or C Gos, *Ibid, Vol 1*. 107-111.
3   *The Strand Magazine 37*, 56, 1909.
4   *AJ6*, 320, 1873.
5   Caroline Kesser und Peter Killer, 'Maler sehen das Matterhorn' in *Berge*, 73, June 1983.
6   E Whymper, *Scrambles amongst the Alps*. John Murray (London), 175, 1871.
7   In the Whymper archives; almost certainly given to Whymper by Adams Reilly.
8   Letter to P D Hadow of 23 August cited on next page.
9   E Whymper, *Ibid*, 180.
10  *Ibid*, 193.
11  *Ibid*, 390.
12  J M Elliott, 'The Second Ascent of the Matterhorn by the East Face' in *AJ28*, 292 & 296, 1914.
13  Werner Müller, 'Ferdinand Hodler: "Aufstieg" und "Absturz"' in *Die Alpen 10*, 136 -140, 1934.

### ACKNOWLEDGEMENTS

I am grateful to Timothy Woodgate, Whymper's great-nephew, and to Robert Headland of the Scott Polar Research Institute, Cambridge for permission to quote from documents in the Whymper archives.

MICHAEL WARD

# Preparations for Everest
## Cho Oyu, London and Zermatt 1952

*This is the last in a series of four articles, in consecutive volumes of the* Alpine Journal, *describing some of the important events, both geographical and scientific, which preceded the first ascent of Everest in 1953.*

The 1952 Cho Oyu expedition was the first to combine mountain exploration with modern medical research in the field. It ensured that the preparations for the attempt on Everest in 1953 were correctly and scientifically based. The exploration carried out on this expedition filled in two large 'blanks on the map' of the Everest region: that of the N–S watershed/frontier range between the Tesi Lapcha pass in the south to the Nangpa La in the north and the Barun glacier and W side of the Makalu region. At the same time, the medical work accomplished by Griffith Pugh between the summer of 1951 and the autumn of 1952 solved the problem of 'the last thousand feet' of Everest. However, the inception of the 1952 Cho Oyu expedition was, to say the least, inauspicious and, at the time, it was considered a failure. In fact, nothing could have been further from the truth.

The expedition came about as a result of the Swiss obtaining permission to go to Everest in the Spring of 1952. The British were slow off the mark and attempts to mount a combined Swiss–UK expedition to Everest in 1952 not surprisingly failed; so, as an alternative, the British expedition to Cho Oyu, 30 miles west of Everest, was organised. It had two objectives: first, to obtain a nucleus of climbers for any future Everest attempt; second, to obtain information on every aspect of the effects of cold and altitude in the Himalaya, and to establish the most effective flow rates of oxygen, in both the open and closed circuit oxygen sets, for the purpose of putting a mountaineer on the summit of Everest.

The members of the 1951 expedition had already consulted Griffith Pugh and the Medical Research Council unofficially, before the Joint Himalayan Committee of the Alpine Club and the Royal Geographical Society (previously the Everest Committee) became involved in the project. It was the members of that party, rather than the Joint Himalayan Committee, who had asked Eric Shipton to join them as leader, and Shipton, in turn, who had insisted that the Alpine Club and RGS should be involved.[1] When the 1951 expedition returned to the UK, Pugh was asked to advise on diet for an Everest attempt. It was obvious to him that a much more radical approach to the Everest problem was needed. So when the Cho Oyu expedition was organised, Pugh suggested that he should continue his laboratory work, started in London in 1951, at altitude in the field, and for this he obtained a separate grant from the Royal Society.

Cho Oyu was chosen for the 1952 expedition because it was a high peak near to Everest, and Shipton and I had seen what we thought was a route on the southern, Nepalese side from a peak above Chhule, about 20 miles away, in November 1951. The northern, Tibetan, side was well known and had been photographed on the 1921 reconnaissance and visually inspected from the Nangpa La by Bourdillon and Murray in 1951. When Cho Oyu was initially surveyed from the north, the Survey of India allotted the symbols T.45 or M.1 to this peak and the 1921 party was the first to discover its correct name. 'Cho' means a deity or demon, whilst 'Yu' means turquoise. The letter 'O' may have been included because the name was misheard.

In 1951 we climbed the peak above Chhule, partly to continue the compass traverse that I was making west of Everest (the area east of Everest was already included on the Hinks–Milne map of 1933-45) and partly to find a pass into the Menlung–Gaurisankar basin from the Bhote Kosi valley. We wished to do this because on the quarter-inch Survey of India map there appeared to be an extra peak, later called Menlungtse, in a 'blank on the map', and we wanted to confirm the correct position of both Gaurisankar and the 'extra' peak. Historically, too, the area was interesting: Gaurisankar had been mistaken for Everest in the late 19th century, and Everest was called Gaurisankar in early *Alpine Journals*. In addition, Edmund Hillary and Earle Riddiford had inspected the south side of Gaurisankar by descending the Rolwaling valley a few days before we crossed into the Menlung basin. An account of the first exploration of the Menlung basin on the N side of Gaurisankar can be found in Shipton's book on the 1951 Everest reconnaissance.[2]

The members chosen by Shipton for the 1952 Cho Oyu expedition were Edmund Hillary, who had been on the 1951 reconnaissance, and George Lowe, Hillary's New Zealand climbing partner, with whom he had been on Mukut Parbat in 1951; Earle Riddiford, who had been on both Mukut Parbat and Everest in 1951; Tom Bourdillon, a member of the 1951 reconnaissance expedition; Charles Evans, who had been in Central Nepal in 1951 with Tilman (but who had not been able to come with us on the 1951 reconnaissance because of surgical commitments); Campbell Secord, who, independently, was pressing for a reconnaissance of the Nepalese side of Everest, had alerted the Joint Himalayan Committee to our plans in 1951 and had helped with the early organisation; Alfred Gregory and Ray Colledge, two well-known and experienced mountaineers from the north of England; and Dr Griffith Pugh who was to do the physiological research. W H Murray was not available. Unfortunately I was unable to join the party as I had to complete my national service in the RAMC; but I kept in touch with Shipton, Bourdillon and Pugh.[3,4]

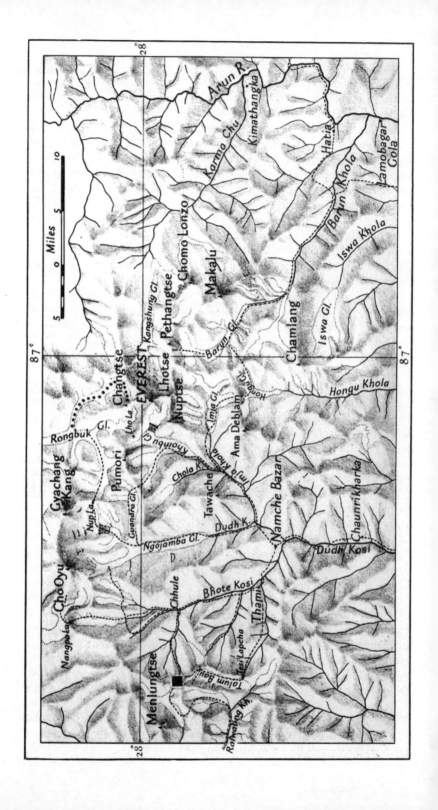

Before leaving the UK, Shipton went to Zurich to co-ordinate the approaches to Namche Bazar of the two expeditions. The Swiss came in from the west via Kathmandu and arrived 24 hours before the British–New Zealand party, who approached from the south via Jogbani. Pugh also spent some time in Switzerland testing out new methods of measuring oxygen consumption in the field at intermediate altitudes.

From Namche Bazar the British party went straight up the Bhote Kosi towards the Nangpa La. Evans and Gregory and two Sherpas turned east onto a ridge running south from Cho Oyu which divided the Bhote Kosi valley from the Ngojumba glacier which we had visited in 1951. Their main and most distressing finding was that there was no possibility of a route up the S face of Cho Oyu – it was too steep and too long. The only feasible alternative lay on the north side in Tibet. In the meantime, Hillary and Lowe climbed two peaks of 21,000ft to the west of the Nangpa La, and later another peak to the north, in Tibet. From these they had excellent views of a feasible route on Cho Oyu – from Tibet. Unfortunately, any serious attempt from Tibet posed considerable political problems. Because of the continuous passage of Sherpas over the Nangpa La to Tengri in South Tibet, the presence of a British party would soon be known to the Chinese in Tengri and it was very likely that an armed party would be sent up to investigate. Shipton himself would be viewed with considerable suspicion, for in early 1951 he had returned to the UK from his post as Consul in Kunming by 'escaping' down the Yangtse Kiang river and was, in any event, considered by the Chinese to be a spy because of his postings to Kashgar and Kunming. Moreover, he, together with Murray, Bourdillon and myself, had been captured inside Tibet in the Rongshar valley in the autumn of 1951, when we had bribed our way out.

The whole party discussed the situation over two days, 27-29 April, and finally came to the conclusion that to attempt a full-scale assault on Cho Oyu from Tibet would take about two weeks, and that politically this was too risky. Each member of the party, except Earle Riddiford, agreed that such an attempt should therefore be abandoned. Riddiford was in favour of launching an all-out attempt in spite of the political dangers, and when it was clear that this was not going to happen, he left the expedition and returned to New Zealand.

In spite of these difficulties, a partial reconnaissance was made of Cho Oyu and a light camp established at 21,000ft; from here Hillary and Lowe

*Left*
Map from Eric Shipton's article 'The Expedition to Cho Oyu' in the *Geographical Journal 119*, 1953.

■ The position of the 1952 physiology camp on the Menlung La.
The extra line of dots indicates the route up the East Rongbuk Glacier.

hoped to reach a considerable height and perhaps even get to the top. This was not to be, however; they stopped at some steep ice cliffs at 22,500ft but, having no back-up owing to illness, decided not to push it hard. Realising that a more sustained attempt would take time and possibly attract an investigation by Chinese soldiers, they decided to abandon the attempt.

No other really high peak was accessible. Gyachung Kang, from the south, looked too difficult, as did Menlungtse (in Tibet), and Gaurisankar was on the border. The decision was made, therefore, to carry out as much exploration as possible, whilst climbing peaks up to 22,000ft. Large areas of the Everest region had not been visited by the reconnaissance expedition of 1951, so there was still a genuine need for further exploration of the many unvisited peaks, valleys and glaciers before any map could be made, and already such a map was being considered in London. This also suited Shipton's temperament for he did not care for highly-structured expeditions. It was the paradox of 1952 that the Cho Oyu expedition involved both a highly-structured scientific investigation and a minimally-structured reconnaissance. It only worked because each group was kept separate.

The party now split into three groups. The first group consisted of just Hillary and Lowe who wanted to try an exciting but obviously over-ambitious project – to circumnavigate Everest by crossing the Nup La, travelling round to the Kangshung glacier, crossing into the Barun glacier and returning via the Hongu and Imja to Namche Bazar. Instead of making this circuit they decided to cross the Nup La and try to climb Changtse, a peak north of Everest, by its E ridge. The second group – Shipton, Gregory and Evans – explored the complex border range north of the Tesi Lapcha pass and south of the Nangpa La. It was planned that these two explorations were to be followed by the exploration of the Barun glacier and the W side of Makalu. Meanwhile, the third group – Pugh, Bourdillon, Secord and Colledge – carried out physiological studies on the Menlung La (20,000ft), a four-man party being the best number for Pugh's work.

## Crossing the Nup La and the attempt on Changtse
Shipton thought that crossing the Nup La would be so difficult that Hillary and Lowe would use up all their time doing this and that the likelihood of their getting into Tibet was remote. Even if they succeeded, it was thought unlikely that they would be discovered, as the lamas from the Rongbuk monastery did not normally ascend the Rongbuk glacier. However, by avoiding the lower icefall of the Ngojumba glacier, which had stopped us in 1951 (and which was very much more difficult than the Khumbu icefall), and by attacking the upper Nup La icefall from the west, Hillary and Lowe reached the Nup La pass in six days. Here they left a food dump for their return and descended the west and then the main Rongbuk glacier. They just managed to prevent their Sherpas paying a visit to the head lama at Rongbuk monastery and ascended the East Rongbuk glacier to the foot of the long and easy-looking E ridge of Changtse. As they had left their

crampons on the Nup La, preferring to take their weight in food, they could only ascend slowly by step-cutting and had to turn back at 22,000ft.

Returning to the Nup La they descended the Ngojumba glacier to its junction with the Guanara glacier and, ascending this, crossed by the pass we had used in 1951, to the Khumbu glacier where they visited the Swiss Base Camp at the foot of the Khumbu icefall. Finally, they descended towards Namche Bazar, where they joined up with Shipton.

## Exploration of the frontier ridge between the Tesi Lapcha and Nangpa La. The Tolam Bau glacier

Shipton, Evans and Gregory made a number of attempts to find another pass between the Bhote Kosi valley (leading to the Nangpa La) and the Menlung basin to the west. These all failed, showing how lucky we were to find the Menlung La in 1951.

The first attempt to find a pass north of the Menlung La was made west of Lunak. This failed, so the party crossed a snow col to the south and entered the Pangbuk basin, from which the Menlung La is crossed. They then descended the Bhote Kosi and turned west again by the Langmoche Khola. No way could be found over the frontier ridge here and neither could they discover a high snow plateau previously seen from the north. Returning to the Bhote Kosi again, they crossed the Tesi Lapcha pass and, on its far, W side, found a glacier, the Tolam Bau, coming in from the north. Ascending this, they came to the 'plateau' – a snowfield at the head of the Tolam Bau.

From this plateau they climbed a peak of 21,000ft and then a pass, hoping to cross into the Menlung. Unfortunately this led only into the Nangaon valley – a side valley of the Rolwaling. Neither did another pass further north give access to the Menlung basin. Finally they returned to Namche Bazar. Alf Gregory then returned home, whilst Shipton and Evans joined up with Hillary and Lowe for the Barun exploration.

The Tolam Bau glacier region was surveyed in 1955 by a Merseyside party led by Alfred Gregory, and a peak, Pangbuk, to the south of the Menlung La climbed by Bourdillon and Colledge in 1952 had a second ascent, by Dennis Davis. This complicated piece of country was therefore finally elucidated and the 1955 survey incorporated into the RGS map of 1961.

## Exploration of the Barun glacier and west side of Makalu

This large glacier system, which drains the west side of Makalu, the frontier ridge, Pethangtse, and the east side of the Hongu–Barun watershed, was discovered from photographs taken on the Houston–Westland 'Flight Over Everest' expedition in 1933. In 1951 Hillary and Shipton had viewed it from the Hongu watershed and wondered if it would be possible to descend it to the Arun valley, which marks the eastern boundary of the Everest group. Such a bold piece of exploration would fill in a large gap on the

Pugh's scientific work on Cho Oyu in 1952 may be summarised in the following table:

| Altitude problem of Everest | | Pugh's solution in 1952 |
|---|---|---|
| Hypoxia | Hallucinations Extreme shortness of breath (7-10 breaths per step). Extreme fatigue Slow rate of ascent | Adequate supplementary oxygen (4 litres/minute on open-circuit) |
| Dehydration | Extreme thirst Low urine output Fluid loss from lungs | 3 litres/day fluid intake |
| Starvation | Weight loss Loss of muscle | 3000k cal/day |
| Cold injury | Incipient hypo- thermia Frostbite | Increased climbing rate and therefore heat production Flexible modern clothing |
| Deterioration | Mental and physical | Sleeping oxygen: 1 litre/minute |

map to the east of Everest. It was to be the culminating journey of the 1952 expedition, passing from one river system to another, and was carried out in two stages. Firstly, it was necessary to find out whether it was possible to cross from the Hongu into the Barun and whether there were any pastures in the upper part of the Barun valley; pastures would indicate that the gorge into which the Barun glacier drained was passable by men, sheep, goats and yaks. Secondly, enough food needed to be carried over two passes, from the Imja to the Hongu and from the Hongu to the Barun, to supply the party for the descent to the Arun gorge. Shipton decided that Evans should first cross into the Hongu by the Ambu Lapcha pass (crossed in 1951), leave a dump of food at the Panch Pokhari lakes at the head of the Hongu glacier and, if possible, then cross into the upper Barun glacier and follow it down to the first grass pasture. Having confirmed whether or not herdsmen used the pastures, he would return to the Panch Pokhari lakes and wait for the main party.

This preliminary exploration was completed by Evans between the 1st and 12th June, and then he was joined by Shipton, Lowe and Hillary. On the Hongu–Barun watershed they climbed two peaks and then descended into the upper Barun glacier, where they turned north, reaching a pass on the Tibet–Nepal frontier to the west of Pethangtse. From here they looked down into the upper Kama valley and the Kangshung glacier, visited for the first time in 1921. (Pethangtse was later climed in 1954 by an Anglo–New Zealand party.) Returning down the Barun glacier they passed a number of yak and sheep herders who were astonished to see them. They were forced to avoid the Barun Khola gorge by climbing over a ridge, now called Shipton's Pass, and reached the Arun river on 20 June.

Here, with Da Tenzing and Annalu, Evans left the others at Hatia, crossed the Arun and went east and north up the Arun valley, reaching the Lumba Sumba Himal of NE Nepal. He then followed the Mewa Khola to Tapeljung and, crossing the grain of the country, reached Darjeeling by the Singalila Ridge. In the meantime, Hillary, Lowe and Shipton continued down the Arun gorge to the East Nepal border with India at Jogbani.

### Physiology camp on the Menlung La (20,000ft)[5]
Pugh set up this camp, with Bourdillon, Secord and Colledge, on 22 May and carried out a number of studies on a prepared track of a known height and steepness under identical climatic conditions.

His most important finding was that a four litres per minute flow rate of supplementary oxygen in the open-circuit sets was necessary both to compensate for the weight of the set *and* to give a boost to performance at extreme altitude. In effect, this would lower the altitude 'in the depths of the lungs' to 20-21,000ft. Only two litres per minute had been used on all previous Everest expeditions, and this explained their relatively slow rate of ascent and failure to gain the summit. Pugh emphasised this critically important point in his article about the 1953 expedition in the *Geographical Journal*.[6] In military terms it was as if, in 1953, a successful army had won a battle with twice the firepower of its predecessors. Yet no mention of this salient fact was made in subsequent books. This omission raised a significant number of eyebrows at a meeting[7] (attended by both Pugh and myself) held at the Royal Society in early 1954 which was chaired by Sir Bryan Mathews FRS, then Director of the Institute of Aviation Medicine at Farnborough, who had overall responsibility to the Joint Himalayan Committee for all the scientific aspects of the 1953 expedition.

At the end of the research period Bourdillon and Colledge made the first ascent of Pangbuk, 22,000ft, a striking peak to the south of the Menlung La. They then crossed into the Rolwaling valley and returned to Namche Bazar by the Tesi Lapcha pass.

On his return to the UK, Pugh was able to compare and contrast the performance of the Swiss and British–New Zealand parties who were in the field at exactly the same time. The Swiss, from the start, were very fit and active, suffering little or no gastro-intestinal and respiratory infection during the march-in. By contrast, the UK party suffered considerably because their public health precautions were rudimentary in the extreme and Pugh was rightly scathing about these. The Swiss reached the South Col at the same time as the UK party were abandoning Cho Oyu. Overall, the Swiss performance at altitude was much better than ours (though a few members of the Cho Oyu party, in particular Hillary and Lowe, came up to the Swiss standard). However, owing to a design fault, the Swiss oxygen sets, which had worked well at sea-level, could not cope with the vastly increased breathing rates at increased altitude and were virtually useless. This factor was critical to the Swiss failure on Everest in 1952. In addition, they became extremely dehydrated at high altitude owing to respiratory water loss – a factor for which they had not catered. It was exhaustion caused by these combined physiological and equipment defects, rather than any mountaineering or leadership problems, that stopped them reaching the summit.

It cannot be over-emphasised that the various *disorders* of altitude – oxygen lack, fatigue, hunger, extreme cold, dehydration,[8] lack of sleep – will, both separately and together, adversely affect the brain's 'higher centres' (the parts of the brain concerned with intelligence, co-ordination, decision-making, etc.) Unless each and every one of these factors is combated, as they were on Everest in 1953 with the scientific work, but *not* by the Swiss in 1952, then the odds against success are considerably lengthened.

The lessons to be learned from the Swiss failure were recognised by the Joint Himalayan Committee. All Pugh's recommendations were accepted and immediately put into effect on his return from Cho Oyu. Most of them, but not all, were completed by October 1952, when John Hunt took over as leader.

**London and Switzerland**

Because of the general dissatisfaction felt about the Cho Oyu expedition, Shipton's management had been called into question and this was compounded by a letter from one of the members of the Cho Oyu party who wrote to the Joint Himalayan Committee criticising Shipton and suggesting that he (the writer of the letter) should take his place as leader in 1953; but as the writer had been one of the least active members of the expedition, his missive was not taken very seriously. Eventually it was decided not to appoint Shipton as leader since it was clear that a successful Everest expedition would necessitate a large party and a highly structured and organised assault. Shipton had repeatedly indicated that he did not feel at home with that kind of expedition. Looking at the successful teams which he had led over the previous years – Nanda Devi in 1934, Everest in 1935, the two Karakoram expeditions in 1937 and 1939 respectively, and Everest again in 1951 – all had been reconnaissance-type undertakings. Shipton would have been very happy with the present-day lightweight alpine-style expeditions to the world's highest peaks.

All this decision-making took time and it was not until September 1952 that Charles Wylie took over as secretary and started the initial organisation for the 1953 expedition. Before this, and whilst still on Cho Oyu, Shipton had asked Alfred Gregory to find further possible members for the 1953 party. It was therefore arranged that Tony Streather, John Jackson, Jack Tucker and myself should join Alf Gregory in Zermatt at the end of August 1952. The weather was quite atrocious, but the Alphubel, Aletschhorn, Täschhorn and Weisshorn were climbed. An attempt on the Rimpfischhorn was abandoned because of massive snowfall and avalanche danger.

Tony Streather showed by far the best adaptation to altitude, having climbed the 25,264ft Tirich Mir and spent long periods in Chitral at altitude, but he was less technically adept than the rest of us. However, his later performance on K2, Kangchenjunga and Haramosh showed that he should really have been a member of our Everest team in 1953.

After the ascent of Everest the Mount Everest Foundation (MEF) was set up as a charitable trust, jointly managed by the Alpine Club and the Royal Geographical Society. Its creation was masterminded by Sir Edwin Herbert (Lord Tangley), then President of the Alpine Club. The present vigour and longevity of the MEF is largely the result of his expertise, foresight and drafting; it was his greatest gift to mountain exploration.

REFERENCES

1   M P Ward, 'The Exploration of the Nepalese Side of Everest' in AJ97, 113-221, 1992/93.
2   E E Shipton, *The Mount Everest Reconnaissance Expedition 1951*. Hodder & Stoughton, London, 1952.
3   E E Shipton, 'The Expedition to Cho Oyu', *Geographical Journal 119*, 129-139, 1953.
4   R C Evans, 'The Cho Oyu Expedition 1952' in AJ59, 9-18, 1953.
5   L G C E Pugh, *The British Himalayan Expedition to Cho Oyu, 1952*. Medical Research Council, London, 1952.
6   L G C E Pugh, 'Scientific Aspects of the Expedition to Mount Everest, 1953' in *Geographical Journal 120*, 183-192, 1954.
7   B Mathews, A discussion on 'The Physiology of Man at High Altitudes'. *Proceedings of the Royal Society. B. 143*,1-42,1954.
8   P Lloyd, 'Valedictory Address' in *AJ85*, 3-15, 1980.

ACKNOWLEDGEMENTS

I should like to thank Sir Charles Evans, Alfred Gregory, John Jackson, Peter Lloyd, George Lowe and Tony Streather for their help in writing this article.

## APPENDIX

In 1953 I took a detailed 'clinical' history from each climber who went above the South Col. These were completed as soon as possible, often within 30 minutes to an hour, after the climber's return to Camp IV at the head of the Western Cwm. The history that I obtained from Edmund Hillary on 30 May was concerned with the basic facts of oxygen flow rates, food and fluid intake, and how these affected climbing performance.

Of particular interest in this account are:

1 The fact that Hillary carried 63lbs from 27,300ft to 27,800ft. He was only able to do this because he increased his oxygen flow rate to 5 litres/minute. This would effectively have *decreased* the altitude 'in the depths of his lungs' from around 21,000ft at a flow rate of 4 litres/minute to the equivalent of a much lower altitude. As Hillary told me: 'It was like changing gear – everything went more easily.'

2 Hillary passed urine on the summit. This meant that he was *not* badly dehydrated, which was later confirmed by clinical examination in the Western Cwm. In fact he drank about 2250mls on 28 May and 3000mls on 29 May. This was close to the daily intake, 3000mls, recommended by Pugh.

3 Food intake over the whole assault period was not adequate, but over this short period it was of less importance than adequate fluid intake.

4 Sleeping oxygen at 1 litre/minute promoted sleep, produced a feeling of warmth and recovery from fatigue. Therefore it combated high-altitude deterioration.

It is difficult to fault any of the recommendations contained in Pugh's *Report on the British Himalayan Expedition to Cho Oyu,* published by the Medical Research Council in 1952.

## C A RUSSELL

# One Hundred Years Ago

(with extracts from the *Alpine Journal*)

*(Plates 74–78)*

The 'Ski' race which took place on the slopes above Clavadel was probably the first of its kind in Switzerland. The competitors were judiciously handicapped, and the result was a capital race. The Ladies' race also proved highly exciting. Mrs Maclaren, though only on skis for the second time went splendidly without falling until she got past the road, but being obliged to unfasten her skis they fled on their own account and went over a precipice to the bottom of the Sertig valley whence they were recovered by Dr A Conan Doyle and Dr Wynne.

The impetus given to the sport is chiefly due to Dr Conan Doyle, who has recently made several expeditions on skis.

Although the exceptionally cold weather which prevailed in many parts of the Alps during the opening weeks of 1895 did not deter the enthusiastic groups of skiers at Davos and other resorts very little winter climbing of note was recorded, even the most determined parties being confined to the lower peaks. In the Bernese Oberland the severe winter was followed by a spring 'so beautiful and warm that the vast mass of snow has very quickly melted away.' During the second half of April several climbers were able to benefit from this welcome change and a number of lengthy but successful expeditions, including ascents of the Wetterhorn and Jungfrau, was completed by guided parties.

After a short unsettled period conditions steadily improved and the mountaineering season coincided with one of the longest spells of perfect weather on record.

The summer of 1895 will be remembered as one of the dryest and hottest ever experienced in the Alps. From the middle of August to the beginning of October we believe there was not one day on which no climbing could take place, and this was certainly the case during the whole of September. On one day, when the weather was particularly good, as many as 23 tourists were at the top of the Matterhorn, amongst them being two English ladies. Towards the end of the season the rock peaks became extremely dangerous on account of falling stones, while the so called snow mountains presented everywhere slopes of hardest ice.

The magnificent weather experienced during the season provided exceptional climbing opportunities and many expeditions of note were recorded. In the Dauphiné two high cols were traversed, for the first time on each occasion, by Auguste Reynier and Claude Verne with Maximin and Casimir Gaspard and Joseph Turc: the Coup de Sabre below the W ridge of the Pic Sans Nom on 17 July and, on 20 July, the Brèche Joseph Turc – 'a narrow gap through which one man only can pass at a time, the crest itself being as sharp as the edge of a knife' – between the Pic Central and the E summit of the Meije. On 27 August, with Maximin Gaspard and Turc, Reynier completed the first traverse of the Brèche Maximin Gaspard, between the E summit of the Meije and the Pavé.

To the south in the Maritime Alps the first recorded ascent of the Cime de la Maledie, on the frontier ridge near Mont Clapier, was made on 23 July by a party which included Louis Maubert and the guide Jean Plent. In the Graian Alps the pinnacled S ridge of Mont Herbetet, which had been attempted by several strong parties, was finally climbed on 20 September by F W Oliver with Albert and Benedict Supersaxo.

In the Mont Blanc range on 14 July E Vassaux and L Wanner with Joseph Quinodoz and J Metrailler reached the summit of the Aiguille d'Argentière from the Col du Chardonnet by way of the unclimbed NW ridge. Later in the season, on 28 August, Evan Mackenzie, with Laurent Croux and César Ollier, made the first ascent of the SE ridge of Punta Innominata, between the Brouillard and Frêney glaciers. A few days before the Innominata ascent, on 24 August, a tragic event occurred after A C Roberts had climbed the Aiguille du Géant with Emile Rey, the great guide of Courmayeur. During the descent over broken ground at the base of the final peak Rey, who was unroped, fell to his death on the glacier below.

During such a long period of settled weather it was not surprising that many fine ridges were climbed in the Pennine Alps. At the head of the Arolla valley on 15 August W W Naismith, with Quinodoz, made the first ascent of the NNE ridge of Mont Collon. In the following month, on 6 September, a new route was completed by Gerald Arbuthnot and L C F Oppenheim who reached the N, higher summit of the neighbouring Mitre de l'Evêque by way of the E ridge, accompanied by Jean Maître and Joseph Georges. In the Zermatt district on 2 September E A Broome with Josef M Biner and Ambros Imboden made the first complete ascent[1] of the Schaligrat, the SW ridge of the Weisshorn. Between 16 August and 4 September several members of the Alpine Club including O G Jones with Elias Furrer and W E Davidson with Christian Klucker and Daniel Maquignaz followed the Domgrat, the high ridge connecting the Dom and the Täschhorn.

On 29 August a route of great historical interest was repeated when Davidson, during an ascent of the Matterhorn with Klucker and Maquignaz, made the third recorded traverse of the Galerie Carrel, the famous ledge high on the W face which had been crossed during the first ascent of the peak from the Italian side. Later in the year Davidson recalled[2] how, some 50 minutes after leaving the SW, Italian ridge, the party arrived

> ... at a place whence a ribbon of snow stretched, pretty continuously, along a band of rock, running towards the Z'Mutt arête. At this spot we found the cork of a wine tin. About 30 minutes after we had started on the Z'Mutt face and just beyond the hardest bit of the climb – as we made it – we came across an iron piton driven into the rock and shortly afterwards we found two more similar iron-spikes.

In a further comment Davidson, who had made a rising traverse to reach the ledge at a point some way across the face, added[3]

> I understand that Mummery, who had surveyed the 'Galerie' from near the 'fault' in the ledge close to the Z'Mutt arête, told Farrar[4] that it was so easy that one could stroll across it with an old umbrella! If he had tried he would, I fear, with unexpected precipitation, have arrived at a very different conclusion.

In the Bernese Oberland on 2 August C A Macdonald, with Christian Jossi and Peter Bernet, forced a route up the NW face of the Ebnefluh. Further east, in the Dolomites, a remarkable achievement was the first ascent of the Torre Delago, one of the Vajolet Towers, by Hermann Delago, solo, on 22 September. Other notable climbs were the first ascent of Punta dell' Ideale in the Brenta group by Carlo Garbari with Nino Pooli on 18 August and the ascent of the unclimbed NW face of the Civetta on 24 August by the Rev A G S Raynor and J S Phillimore with Antonio Dimai and Giovanni Siorpaes. Later in the year, on 4 December, Garbari and his party completed the first ascent under winter conditions of Cimone della Pala.

In the Caucasus exploration was continued by C T Dent and Hermann Woolley, who arrived in the central region in July, accompanied by Kaspar Maurer and Simon Moor. Although snow conditions were unfavourable they crossed a number of passes and on 2 August made the first ascent of Tsiteli (4277m). Another visitor to the range was W R Rickmers who in October, accompanied by Amilius Hacker, made several attempts to ascend the S, higher peak of Ushba (4710m), reaching a height of some 4100m on each occasion.

During the year two expeditions of note were undertaken in more distant ranges. In New Zealand E A FitzGerald, accompanied by C L Barrow and the guide Mattias Zurbriggen, arrived at the Hermitage Hotel on 4 January with the principal aim of reaching unclimbed summits in the Southern Alps. As the first ascent of Mount Cook (3764m) had been completed shortly before his arrival[5] FitzGerald turned his attention to other peaks in the region.

Finding that the Hotel was officially closed the party was obliged to set up tents nearby, Jack Clarke, one of the climbers who had reached the summit of Mount Cook, being engaged to act as porter and to look after the camp. Although their plans were frequently disrupted by bad weather and other difficulties including the unwelcome attentions of a cow which consumed considerable quantities of soap and flour FitzGerald and Zurbriggen, who both made extensive use of crampons, were able to make first ascents of several fine peaks: Mount Sealy (2639m) on 24 January with Barrow and Clarke; Mount Tasman (3500m) by way of the unclimbed Silberhorn (3309m) and the S ridge on 5 February with Clarke; Mount Haidinger (3068m), also with Clarke, on 8 February; and Mount Sefton (3159m) on 14 February. The ascent of the E ridge of Mount Sefton was a fine achievement and FitzGerald later recalled their narrow escape during the climb.

> Never have I in all my experience seen rocks in such a fearfully rotten condition as these, and Zurbriggen also agreed that in all his travels he had never seen anything to equal them. The slightest touch would at times dislodge tons. We had to go up a most fearfully steep arête to reach the summit, near which there occurred what was very nearly being a fatal accident, a large rock falling down, throwing me completely over, and cutting two strands of the rope that held me. Zurbriggen was very badly placed at this moment, and was all but torn from his foothold. Had we fallen here we should have come straight down 7,000 ft. to the Mueller Glacier.

FitzGerald and Zurbriggen also succeeded in crossing a pass in the Main Divide – FitzGerald's Pass – to reach the W coast before returning to their camp, accompanied by A P Harper the surveyor and mountain explorer, by way of the Fox and Franz Josef glaciers and Graham Saddle.

FitzGerald later described[6] how after departing for Christchurch with F F Tuckett, who had been visiting the range, he enjoyed a final glimpse of the mountains in the evening sun.

> The whole chain of great snowy peaks stood forth clearly against the crimson west, and was again mirrored in the placid lake at our feet. So peaceful was this evening scene, that, as I gazed, I

could scarcely realise that these white, glittering peaks had been the theatre of so much hardship, so much privation, and so much peril during the last few months. I felt amply rewarded, however, for the long marches and hazardous climbs, for the cold, the wet, and the general discomfort of my sojourn, by the closer knowledge that I had obtained of these majestic heights; these seemingly impregnable fastnesses of ice and rock; by the sights which had been unfurled before my eyes of the wonderful contrasting zones of glacier and vegetation on the west coast, unparalleled by all that I have yet seen or heard described in the extraordinary proximity in which one climatic region is brought to another.

On 14 March Zurbriggen, who had remained behind to strike camp, succeeded in making the second ascent of Mount Cook. Accompanied by Jack Adamson of the Hermitage to a height of some 3150m Zurbriggen continued the climb alone, reaching the summit by way of the NE ridge, now known as Zurbriggen's Ridge.

On 20 June A F Mummery, accompanied by J N Collie and Geoffrey Hastings but without guides, sailed for Bombay in the hope of realising one of his great ambitions – the ascent of Nanga Parbat (8125m) in the Punjab Himalaya.

After a camp had been established near Tarshing in the Rupal valley below the precipitous S face of the mountain it soon became apparent that any attempt to force a route up this face would have little prospect of success. The party therefore decided to cross the Mazeno Pass (5377m) and on 22 July camped in the Diamirai valley where Mummery identified a possible route up the NW, Diamirai face. Returning to the Rupal valley after an exhausting journey over the Mazeno Pass Mummery and his companions were 'revived and comforted by many bottles of Bass' and by the Hon C G Bruce who at Mummery's invitation had joined the party with two men from his regiment, the 5th Gurkha Rifles.

On 5 August, after helping to establish a base camp beside the Diamirai glacier, Bruce left to return to his regiment. Although the weather then deteriorated small camps were established up the lower part of the route and a snow peak of some 5800m was ascended on 11 August. Addressing the Alpine Club in the following year Collie recalled how during the climb

Mummery never felt the least fatigue. He led the whole way – sometimes in deep powdery snow; sometimes he had to cut steps for nearly an hour at a time. The pace was quite as fast as he ever went in the Alps, and we had climbed nearly 7,000ft. Certainly that day the rarified air had not the slightest effect on him.

On 19 and 20 August Mummery, accompanied by one of the Gurkhas, succeeded in climbing the ribs in the centre of the face to a height of more than 6000m – an outstanding exploit, far in advance of its time – before the illness of his companion forced a retreat. It was then decided that Collie and Hastings, taking a lower route, would move the base camp to the Rakhiot valley to enable the party to examine the N, Rakhiot face and that Mummery would attempt a direct crossing over a col at approximately 6200m. On 24 August Mummery and the two Gurkhas set out for the col but were never seen again.

In the Canadian Rockies exploration of the Lake Louise region was continued by P S Abbot, C E Fay and C S Thompson. Although forced by bad weather to abandon an attempt to climb Mount Lefroy (3423m) they succeeded, on 30 July, in making the first recorded ascent of Mount Hector (3394m).

At home several notable routes were followed for the first time. In Wales J M Archer Thomson and Harold Hughes made their celebrated ascent of Twll Du or the Devil's Kitchen, the cleft in the central cliff of Clogwyn y Geifr above Llyn Idwal. In March, taking advantage of the intense cold during the winter, they succeeded in cutting holds up the frozen waterfall with a hatchet borrowed from Ogwen Cottage. Later in the year they completed a number of new routes on Glyder Fawr including *Grey Rib*, led by Archer Thomson, and *Twisting Gully*, climbed by Hughes with H Edwards and J R Smith. In the Lake District on 14 April two fine routes were established on Dow Crag: *Intermediate Gully*, by a party which included Edward and John Hopkinson; and *Hopkinson's Crack*, led by Charles Hopkinson with O J Koecher. In Scotland Collie explored the NE face of Ben Nevis where on 12 April with Naismith, Gilbert Thomson and M W Travers he made the first ascent of Castle Ridge.

In the autumn considerable interest was aroused by the publication of the second volume, dealing with Wales and Ireland, of *Climbing in the British Isles*, the famous guidebook edited by W P Haskett Smith. Other books published during the year included Mummery's classic *My Climbs in the Alps and Caucasus*, which appeared shortly before he left for the Himalaya, and *The Alps from End to End*, the account by Sir Martin Conway[7] of his journey through the Alps in the previous season.

An important event in the history of the Alpine Club was the move from the Club's first permanent home in London at 8 St Martin's Place, Trafalgar Square to new premises at 23 Savile Row. Addressing the Club on 2 April the President, D W Freshfield, acknowledged that the old rooms were no longer adequate and explained that

> ... Our lease was near its end, but we had ground for hope that the Geographical Society might make itself a centre for kindred bodies, and might erect new premises, with rooms and a hall available for our purposes. That hope was unfulfilled. ...

The Committee was generally requested and expected to take action. The problem before it – to find, in a first-rate situation, a suitable hall at a moderate rent – seemed to me, I confess, even so lately as six weeks ago, a very difficult one. But everything comes to those who can wait. The exact premises we wanted suddenly came into the market.

On 7 May the Club met for the first time at the new premises, where an exhibition of paintings was held later in the year.

A charming little exhibition opens today in the new club-house of the Alpine Club, 23 Savile Row. The house itself really deserves a notice. It is such a delightful old rambling place, with circular staircase, pleasant rooms, and a good gallery, or rather lecture-room, in which the pictures are hung. ... It is a house that figured a good deal in the doings of society in the days of Horace Walpole. It stands at the far corner of the street, set across the narrow straight line of the row. When it was built last century, it was the tea house or garden retreat of Lord Burlington, who had it decorated after the style of his mansion at the other end of the grounds.

The premises in Savile Row were to be the Club's home for more than 40 years.[8]

This account is concluded with a recollection of Mummery, taken from the notice which appeared in the *Alpine Journal* later in the year.

Face to face with the giant Nanga Parbat Mr. Mummery wagered and lost. If the wager were blameworthy the result should not influence the apportionment of blame. Had he won, would the Alpine Club have censured? Assuredly not. The Himalayas have their victim – one worthy of their pre-eminence among the high places of the earth – but he too has his monument. So long as English rule abides in India, so long will those who from Gulmerg, in fair Kashmir, behold in the far north the glittering dome and spires of Nanga Parbat relate, as they wonder at its beauty, 'There Mummery was killed – the great climber!'

REFERENCES

1    A route up the SE face and the upper section of the ridge had been completed by W E Davidson, J W Hartley and H Seymour Hoare with Peter Rubi, Johann Jaun and Alois Pollinger on 6 September 1877.

2    W E Davidson to Edward Whymper, letter, 24 December 1895
     (Edward Whymper, *Scrambles Amongst the Alps*, 6th Edition.
     London, John Murray, 1936.  Appendix D).
3    Davidson to Whymper, letter, 10 February 1896 (ibid.).
4    Captain J P Farrar, President of the Alpine Club 1917-19.
5    The summit – now some ten metres lower (*AJ99*, 221, 1994) – had
     been reached by J M Clarke, T C Fyfe and George Graham on 25
     December 1894.
6    E A FitzGerald, *Climbs in the New Zealand Alps*.  London, T Fisher
     Unwin, 1896.
7    Shortly before the book was published Conway received a knight-
     hood in recognition of his work in the Karakoram three years earlier.
8    Until the end of 1936.  The building was demolished in 1937.

# Area Notes 1994

## COMPILED BY ROY RUDDLE

| | |
|---|---|
| Alps and Pyrenees | *Lindsay Griffin* |
| Russia and Central Asia | *José Luis Bermúdez &* |
| | *Paul Knott* |
| India | *Harish Kapadia* |
| Pakistan | *Lindsay Griffin &* |
| | *Paul Nunn* |
| Nepal | *Bill O'Connor* |
| North America | *H Adams Carter* |
| South America and Antarctica | *Chris Cheeseman* |
| Scottish Winter | *Simon Richardson* |
| Middle East | *Tony Howard* |

---

## LINDSAY GRIFFIN

# Alps and Pyrenees 1994

*This report looks at selected activity from the wealth of interesting ascents, both in terms of exploration and technical performance, that occurred throughout the Alpine chain last year. In preparing these notes Lindsay Griffin would like to acknowledge the assistance of Graham Dudley, Roan Fair, Frank Jourdan, Igor Koller, Mireille Lazarevitch, Giuseppe Miotti, Andy Parkin, Michel Piola, Franci Savenc, Hubert Schmitt, Hillary Sharp and Teresio Valsesia. He would welcome further information and any new route descriptions for publication in these pages at: 2 Top Sling, Tregarth, Bangor, Gwynedd LL57 4RL.*

### WINTER 1993-1994

After an exceptionally wet autumn the winter continued in the same vein with plenty of snow to keep the skiers happy but no truly settled spell until the end of the season. It was no surprise, therefore, that most of the important ascents were completed during March, when many of the classic faces and *'goulottes'* were found to be in better condition than in recent years. Several important winter condition ascents, taking place outside the official winter season (21 December - 20 March inclusive), have also been noted.

# Pyrenees

While winter conditions in the Pyrenees can often be exceptionally good, the strong influence of more maritime weather does not generally allow the long periods of stability that can occur in the Alps. However, many excellent couloirs can normally be found in climbable condition from December to June. For more information, the bible of modern ice climbing in the Pyrenees is *Pirineos, Hielo y Nieve* by Joan Quintana (Editions Pleniluni). Definitive guides to the Pyrenees have long been out of date.

**Pic du Midi d'Ossau** From 17-18 March Rémi Thivel made probably the first solo winter ascent of the hard classic rock climb, the original *N face route* on the **Embarradère Pillar** (ED2), first climbed in 1965 by P Bouchet and the well-known Ravier brothers.

**Balaitous** Manuel Alvarez, Manuel Anson and Isidoro Sanchez made the second ascent, in winter conditions, of the climb *Lézard Glace* (ED2) on the big N face. This 450m route has as its crux a magnificent 160m+ ice smear which falls down the quasi-vertical headwall.

**Vignemale** There was considerable activity on the prestigious N face with nearly all the major events involving climbers operating alone. On 29 November, Yan Raulet made the first solo ascent of the *Y Couloir* in full winter conditions (the 600m left branch of the famous *Gaube Couloir*, TD+/ ED1, with three quasi-vertical ice pitches). From 28 January to 1 February, 22-year-old Jérome Thinières soloed the legendary *Despiau/Luquet route* (a 13-pitch ED3). This was the first solo, first winter ascent and almost certainly the only repeat since its original ascent in the summer of 1969.

However, the most important ascent of the season was a new ice/mixed route on the N face of **Pique Longue** by Benoît Dandonneau, Christian Ravier and Rémi Thivel. *Les Délinquants de l'Inutile* follows the depression between the 1933 N face original route and the 1965 N spur and required a 25m section of A3 to gain a hanging icicle. Graded ED2 with one section of 90°, this 750m route took the talented trio a total climbing time of 21 hours on 24-25 March.

**Mallo de las Penas (2662m)** Close to the famous Ordesa National Park, Jimmy Santos and Julio Vinuales have climbed *Ruta del Bakalao*, a snow and ice climb (65°) on the N face. This face still holds considerable potential for new routes and is only one hour from the upper terminus of the Panicosa téléphérique.

**Gavarnie** There were a number of new additions to this famous ice-climbing arena plus some significant repeats; but probably the most widely publicised event took place from 3-5 March when Patrick Gabarrou and Spanish student Ferran Latorre made the first complete and continuous direct ascent of the Cirque. The pair started up Dominique Julien's 300m *Banzayous* in the middle of the lower tier but then moved left to climb a thin ice smear (55m 90° and christened *Superbanzayous*). They then continued up to the second tier and climbed the obvious icefall just to the right of the classic *Mitalogica*. *Saphir* gave 135m of new climbing and was graded V/5.

During the next two days the pair overcame the final 180m of the upper tier via an extremely taxing line close to the left side of the wall. *Alois* offers two pitches of A2/3 and 5+ to reach a stalactite, then three delicate pitches of VI/5. Five bolts were placed during the ascent.

**Picos de Vallhiverna** A new winter route was climbed on the vast NW face by Jordi Agusti and Miguel Roca. *Arcadia* (45°-70°) is a full 830m high but was completed in just over six hours.

**Pic de Canigou** A new route was created on the most easterly high summit of the Pyrenees by Oriol Garcia, Eduard Palma and Joan Vendrell when they climbed a couloir that ends well right of the summit (immediately right of the **Pointe Cruz**). The 200m route was mainly 45°-55° with one vertical section.

## Ecrins

Winter climbing in the Ecrins is a completely different activity to that practised in the much frequented Mont Blanc Massif. Long approaches through valleys that are deep, sunless, steep sided and generally avalanche prone mean that winter ascents are, understandably, relatively rare.

**L'Olan** Christian Mora made a lonely ascent of the *Directissima* on the NW face (Bouilloux/Wilmart 1977 start plus the Cambon/Francou 1981 finish at 6b and A3 or 6c all free). This was a significant second winter solo of one of the most demanding routes in the region (ED2/3).

**Dome de Neige des Ecrins** On 29 March Bruno Ravanat made the first solo ascent of the *Boivin/Diaferia/Vionet-Fuasset couloir* (1976 ED2) on the W face. The crux was found to be a 70m-90m vertical section leading to a difficult chockstone pitch.

**Pic Sans Nom.** A week prior to the ascent reported above, Ravanat also made a completely unroped solo of the other famous Boivin creation in the Ecrins, the narrow goulotte of the *Raie des Fesses* on the N face.

**Tête d'Aval de Montbrison** On the famous limestone S face above Vallouise, German Alpinist Frank Jourdan soloed the 500m *L'Epinaustère* (ED1/6b/A2) in a mere 3½ hours on 7 February. However, there was little snow on the face (this area is often sheltered from the winter storms by the bulk of the Massif des Ecrins) and the temperature was only –3°C.

## Mont Blanc Massif

**Mont Blanc du Tacul** Chamonix resident Stevie Haston (UK) and Laurence Gouault climbed a demanding ice route immediately right of the *Martinetti Pillar* in late March. The technical mixed terrain in the upper section was considered to be Scottish Grade 6/7. The 350m E couloir of the **Corne du Diable** (Lafaille 1985) was thoroughly re-equipped for a rappel descent and consequently became very popular. Lafaille returned with Françoise Aubert this February, reclimbed his route but added a direct finish through the rocks on the left to join the upper section of the right-hand couloir of the **Col du Diable**.

**Périades** Returning to one of his favourite haunts in recent years, the W side of the Périades, Gabarrou, this time with Jean-Sébastien Knoertzer, created the nine-pitch *San Sébastian*, a tremendous quasi-vertical ice runnel on the right of *Hello Captain*.

**Petites Jorasses** In late March Gabarrou and Latorre completed the last remaining major ice gully on the N face when they climbed the ephemeral line between the 1981 *Japanese route* on the NW pillar and the 1976 *Koller/ Stejskal route* on the left side of the W face. The terrain was very technical and often delicate, involving aid climbing up to A3 and many sections of thin and sometimes hollow ice, precariously covering the granite (70°-80°). The crux pitch took 3 hours and the route was later christened, rather aptly, *Omega*.

**Aiguille des Pèlerins** Another UK Chamonix resident, Andy Parkin, made the first solo ascent of the *North Face route*, originally climbed in winter conditions by Rab Carrington and Al Rouse in 1975 (ED2) and now something of a modern winter classic.

**Aiguille du Fou** François Bernard and Antoine Cayrol scored a notable coup here with the first winter ascent of the 1988 Colas/Grenier route, *Les Ailes du Desir* (6b A2 or 7c free), on 8-9 March. The climbers solved the access problem by reaching the foot of the route via paraglider.

**Aiguille de Blaitière** Prior to the start of the winter season, François Marsigny and Andy Parkin put up a new ice route just left of the *Brown/ Whillans route* on the W face (TD 85° and thin).

**Aiguille Verte** Arnaud Baudet, Antoine Cayrol and David Ravanel made the first ascent of a very fine 500m (c12 pitches) ice gully above the Argentière glacier leading up to the right of **Pointe Farrar** on the Grands Montets Ridge (TD–).

**Grande Rocheuse** On 16 February the German Alpinists Robert Jasper and Jorn Heller climbed a hard new alternative to the *NE Face Direct* (Bourges/Mizrahi 1975), which follows the prominent corner system immediately to the right of the steep section. *Too Late to say I'm Sorry* sported several very steep pitches of seriously thin ice without a glimmer of protection and warranted an overall grade of ED3.

Later, on 4 March, Thierry Braguier, Paul Cieslar and Ark Gasienico completed a narrow gully immediately to the left of the 1975 crux, the first half of which had been climbed previously by Autheman, Dellavolpe and Vimal to give *Visagel*. *Visagel/ Suite et Fin* is now 900m and TD+.

**Petit Dru** The W face was the scene of two great solitary efforts, although the receptions given to each were rather different. In a highly publicised and, by some, much criticised extravaganza, Marc Batard completed a new route, solo, on 16 March after a 10-day effort and on his third attempt. *Soutien aux SDF (Sans Domicile Fixe)* (A2 6a, most of the climbing was on aid) lies to the left of the French Directissima. A week later Hugues Beauzile, also on his third attempt, made a much quieter 10-day solo of the notorious

*Thomas Gross route*, which lies immediately right of the French Directissima. Despite reports of several repetitions since the first ascent in 1975, Beauzile found only Gross's original gear above the big roof.

**Les Droites** The N face, which has generally been in a poor state over the past few winters, often with large areas of black ice, was well covered with a fine mantle of névé. The hard *Brèche des Droites Finish* (or *Couloir Ginat*) was climbed a record number of times (including several solos). On 3 February, Baudet, Cayrol and Ravanel produced their second new route of the season (*Baptistoune* TD/TD+) when they climbed steep ice runnels above and a little to the right of the *Richard Cranium Memorial route* on the NW face of the W summit. In mid-March Robert Jasper, Malte Roeper and Jorg Steinsburger climbed the large rounded rock buttress to the right of the upper section of the *Brooks/Colton route*. This gave 11 hard independent pitches which were predominantly negotiated on aid (A2 and A3 with one section across a steep slab at A4, plus several sections of 5+ to 6a). The *Maria Callas Memorial route* is 1000m in length and graded ED3.

**Aiguilles Rouges** Marc Ravanel and Christophe Profit appear to have completed the first integral winter traverse of the Aiguilles Rouges, starting at the Col des Montets and finishing at the Brévent, with two bivouacs.

# Valais

**Matterhorn** An historic event took place here in March. Catherine Destivelle became the first woman to solo the three classic Great North Faces of the Alps in winter, when she completed Walter Bonatti's 1965 *Direct route* over four days in March. Destivelle was unable to progress any faster up the face than Bonatti and considered the 1965 route to be far in advance of its time.

**Monte Rosa** At the end of March, Gabarrou and Latorre claimed a hard new mixed route, *Dies Irae,* on the giant E face of the **Signalkuppe**. However, their line appears to coincide more or less exactly with that followed by the Slovenians, Matjaz Jamnik and Bojan Pockar, in June 1993. On the 1994 winter ascent the difficulties included a pitch of V in the lower section and several of IV+ and A1 in the upper, together with several very steep or vertical ice pitches. The Slovenians on the other hand, climbing in June, found ice pitches of only 65° maximum but rock of VII– and A2.

# Bregaglia/Bernina

Access to most of the major peaks in the Bregaglia is decidedly problematical in a snowy winter and the only ascents so far reported took place on relatively low altitude venues.

**Monte Qualido** On 11-12 March, Marco Marras and Nicola Tondini made the first winter ascent of *Galactica*, a 450m route on the huge E face with unavoidable difficulties of VII+ free and A1. Thomas Tivadar also completed a new seven-pitch route to the right of *Via il Chercio* on the lower wall of the **Precipizio degli Asteroidi** - the El Cap of the Mello Valley. Christened *Karma Mama*, it offers a number of sections of A1 and two of A2+, interspersed with free climbing up to VI+.

**Punta Kennedy** On the N face of the 2982m eastern foresummit local activists Fanchetti and Vannuccini climbed a 280m ice/mixed couloir which they named *Cirio*. This gave six pitches of often 'sensational' climbing at an overall standard of TD. In May the same pair returned to make the first ski descent of the NE face of the main summit.

# Dolomites

At the time of writing little information has been received on activity in the Dolomites during 1994. However, the two most important winter ascents appear to be the first solo of the *Mauro/Minuzzo Directissima* (500m/V/A2) on the **Cima Grande di Lavaredo** by Franco Perlotto, and a solo ascent of the *Aste/Susatti* (700m VI) on the NW face of the **Civetta** over four days in March by Marco Anghileri.

## THE SUMMER SEASON

June and July were months of generally excellent weather, with long sunny spells only infrequently broken by violent storms. However, in mid July the temperatures soared and once again the spring snow, with little real base owing to the recent succession of dry winters followed by hot summers, rapidly vanished. By the beginning of August most ice faces, notably those on peaks below 3800m - 4000m, had been transformed into the now familiar bare, black rock walls. August was rather unstable with plenty of dramatic thunderstorms, though daytime air quality was often excellent with little of the heat haze normally experienced during this period. Severe storms and snowfall down to 1400m precluded climbing for most of September, and extensive flooding at lower altitudes ensured that several hut approaches involving bridges needed some attention before this summer.

# Ecrins

**Linked ascents** Marc Charvet carried out one of the most impressive solo enchaînements of the year, when, starting from La Bérarde, he made a continuous figure-of-eight journey through the Massif which encompassed: the N couloir of the **Tête de l'Etret,** the NE couloir of **Les Bans**, the **Promontoire Hut** at the foot of La Meije, the Gravelotte couloir on the N face of **La Meije** plus the Meije traverse, the **Col du Diable**, the **Adele**

**Planchard Hut** (where he rested a day), the N couloir of the **Brèche de Tombe Murée,** the Chaud couloir on the **Trois Dents de Pelvoux,** the N couloir of the **Coup de Sabré** and back to La Bérarde via the Sélé Hut and Col de Sélé: a total of over 13,500m of ascent which took in most of the classic ice couloirs of the range in a 'limited' holiday from 6-10 July.

**L'Olan** On the very steep rock of the sunny SE face of the S shoulder, Remy Karle and Rolland Marie have put up possibly the most technically difficult route to date, *Surprenante Soirée* (350m ED2 excellent rock). Karle, amongst others, has now developed some of the excellent rock-climbing opportunities of the Valgaudemar and details are currently available from his small topo guide available in the valley.

**La Meije** The 1962 *Ginel/Renaud route,* the North Face Direct, had around 20 ascents last summer and now has virtually classic status. In mid-June excellent conditions allowed Jean-Christophe Moulin to create two new routes on the right side of the N face. With Gerard Vionnet-Fuasset he climbed the 600m *Pinuche,* a fairly direct line to the **Brèche du Glacier Carré** (D+ mixed) and two days later with three students from ENSA he created a far more demanding line on the right flank of the **Pic du Glacier Carré** called *Les Vacances de Monsieur Moulin* (ED2 mixed). On the opposite side of the mountain Jean-Michel Cambon, Pierre Chapoutot and Etienne Rol put up a new route on the SW face of the **Grand Doigt** which was subsequently repeated several times during the season. *Nous Partirons dans l'Invresse* lies to the left of the classic *Voie des Marseillais* and was graded TD. However, a somewhat regressive move occurred elsewhere on the S face. Chapoutot's 1969 route on the S face of the Third Tooth (*Central Bastion*) has always been thought a fine undertaking at 4 to 5+ (TD) but sparsely equipped by modern standards. In an attempt to make it more popular, Chapoutot returned 25 years after his first ascent and re-equipped all the main belay stances with bolts.

**Aiguille Est de Soreiller** On the SW face of this fine rock-climbing venue two new routes have been created to the right of Mazurka. Immediately right is *La Javades Bombes Atomiques* (D+) by Jean-Michel and Sylvain Cambon plus Pierre Chapoutot and Pascal Junique. Right again is *Courage, Fuyons* (TD+) by Junique.

**Tête du Rouget** Junique added an excellent new route to the 200m W face, in 1993, called *Version Original.* At TD– it offers excellent climbing at an accessible standard and had so many repetitions in 1994 that it could now almost be considered to have modern classic status.

**La Bérarde** A number of routes have been added to low-altitude venues around here. Up-to-date information can be obtained in topo format from the CAF Alpine Centre in the village.

**Ailefroide** Eight new routes were created in this popular area by Cambon, Chapoutot and friends. The heights vary from 200-350m and grades are largely in the 5-6b category. The new topo guide to the valley was due to appear in spring 1995. (*See article 'Climbing in the Ecrins', pages 199-203.*)

**Pic Jocelme** On 9 June Laurent Girouse soloed the NE couloir in 3½ hours from the Bans Hut and then promptly 'surfed' it on a snowboard back to the hut in one hour: tricky in the upper section as it is no more than five metres wide.

**Tête d'Aval de Montbrison** Local climbers, Christian Ferrera, René Mohamed and Fred Roux, added *Cristal Majeur* up the sensationally steep rock on the far right side of the wall (350m ED1).

# Mont Blanc Massif

A large proportion of the routes created in the Mont Blanc Massif this summer were of excellent quality and by the end of the season had already received numerous repetitions.

**Mont Blanc** Around 11am on 28 July, a large sérac fall from the flanks of the Dôme de Gouter swept a 300m wide section of the Petit Plateau on the *Grands Mulets route*, burying eleven climbers. Two were lucky to escape from the debris but the rest, five French and four Italian soldiers, died.

**Aiguille Croux** On 21 August, Manlio Motto and Michel Piola completed their project on the SE face, first begun with the late Romain Vogler in 1992. This nine-pitch offering, *La Legganda,* cuts through the middle of the initial ramp on the *Hurzeler/Ottoz* and has maximum difficulties of 7a+.

**Aiguille Noire de Peuterey** Two important new routes were put up on the W face early last summer by Manlio Motto and Patrick Gabarrou. A lengthy and complex approach has led to this area becoming increasingly neglected and nowadays all routes should be attempted early in the season to facilitate crossing the Frêney Glacier. On 22-23 June, the pair completed *L'Amitié Toujours* on **Pointe Welzenbach**, a 13-pitch route on excellent granite with two ropelengths of 6c; then from the 30 June-1 July they climbed *L'Equipée des Bras Caisses* on **Pointe Brendel** which in the upper section follows a superb line of cracks reminiscent of climbing on the Grand Cap (maximum difficulties of 6c+, again on excellent rock).

**Mont Maudit** The first completely free ascent of the original *Bertone/Zappelli route* on the SE face of the **Androsace Pillar** was made by the talented Courmayeur guide Giovanni Bassanini, with Massimo Datrino, on 3 July. Two pitches went at 7a and one at 7a+. The pair continued to the summit of Mont Maudit via the Frontier Ridge.

**Grand Capucin** Three events of note last summer. On 22 June, David Ravanel made the first solo ascent of the demanding *L'Echo des Alpages* (ED3/400m/7a 6b+ obl) in under six hours. The 1984 Boivin/Diafera/Moioli route, *Eau et Gaz a tous les Etages,* was finally climbed completely free by Stevie Haston at 7b+/7c using a Number 4 Camalot wedged alongside a paperback book for protection to give the required width in the wide crux crack. Equally impressive was Haston's first free ascent of Marco Pedrini's wildly exposed roof pitch *Panoramix,* a spectacular 25m problem left of the normal finish to *Gulliver's Travellers.* The grade was again thought to be 7b+/7c.

**Le Trident** Bassanini, climbing with Guido Azzaléa, has put up a new and very strenuous crack climb next to *Bonne Ethique* which he named *Indurain Tiene dos Huevos* (200 demanding metres with a crux of 7b).

**Pointe Adolphe Rey** After beavering away over the years since 1991, Jean-Claude Droyer at last made the first continuous, all-free ascent of the 22m crack on the W face called *Entrez dans la Légende* (solid 8a+).

**Grandes Jorasses** In the early half of the season there were three important ascents on the N face. Thierry Schmitter and Jan Van der Berg claimed the third ascent of Slavko Sveticic's hard mixed free and aid route, *Manitua,* on the left flank of the **Croz Spur** but they were rescued by helicopter after joining the *Classic 1935 route,* when Schmitter took a 30m fall. The well-known Slovenian alpinist, Slavko Sveticic, made the third ascent and first solo of Jean-Marc Boivin and Gerard Vionnet-Fuasset's 1987 route *Extreme Dream,* finding the crux one of the most demanding ice pitches that he had ever climbed. On 23 June Sveticic teamed up with Ivano Ghiradini to attempt the thin *'goulotte'* that lies between Pointes Marguerite and Young. After a bivouac 600m above the rimaye but below an ice smear that they first considered impossible, the weather deteriorated and the party decided to split. Sveticic traversed out right to gain the upper section of the 1968 *Polish route* and followed it to the summit, whilst Ghiradini continued direct, climbing the 'impossible' pitch and christening his new 850m line, which must rarely come into condition, *Rêve Ephémère d'Alpinist.*

**Aiguille de Leschaux** On 10 July, Gabarrou and Motto climbed a new line, *Mélange,* up the prominent steep rounded buttress on the left side of the 750m NE face (nine pitches on generally good rock but with some danger from falling ice: 5+ to 6b+/6b/obl).

**The Envers des Aiguilles** continues to be thought of as the Mecca of mountain cragging, and a recent initiative, funded by Petzl and assisted by Elisabeth Maeten (warden of the Envers Hut for many years), has led to the majority of the popular routes having their belays re-equipped with stainless steel bolts and chains.

**Pointe de Lépiney** To the right of the modern Piola classic on the E face, *Je t'ai Conquis, Je t'Adore,* Phillippe Batoux, Emmanuel Pelissier and Benoit Robert have created and equipped *Le Versant du Soleil.* This is a particularly sustained undertaking at 6c/6c+ reserved exclusively for those proficient on thin slabs, especially the 10th runout which presents some demanding climbing at 6c obl.

**Aiguille du Fou** On 14 June, Fred Gentet made the first solo ascent of the 1988 Colas/Grenier route, *Les Ailes du Desir,* in under eight hours.

**Aiguille de Blaitière** The lower section of the rather unfrequented 1937 classic, the SE ridge, traditionally avoided by gaining the crest above from the glacier basin to the right, was surprisingly still untouched until last summer. Motto and Piola rectified this omission on 4 September with the excellent outing *Magie d'Orient,* 'a modern climb at an accessible standard on fantastic rock (5+ with two points of aid or 6a+ free, plus a couple of fine rappels: nuts and Friends obligatory).

**Tour Verte**  Two more routes were added to the excellent rock of this popular tower next door to the Envers Hut. Slovenians Tomaz Jakofcic and Cerne Rok put up *Marmotte* which starts up the impressive dièdre situated between *Gagafou* and *Homologue Exceptionnel* (sustained at 5+ to 6b with a crux, the dièdre, of 7a). On the extremely steep crest of the S pillar, Motto and Piola created one of the most difficult climbs on the Envers side of the Aiguilles when they put up *Retour à la Montagne* (7c but so far only climbed with rest points).

**Aiguille de Roc**  There were two more additions to the 30 or so established routes on the E face. On 6 August Piola and Rémy Tucoulou climbed *La Dolce Vita* up the steep slabby wall left of *Pyramid* (close to *Eye in the Sky*). This is reported to be a brilliant 10-pitch route that looks virtually impossible from a distance but went at 6b/6b+ with two short sections of aid (7a free). It subsequently received a considerable amount of traffic during the rest of August.

Previously the same pair had added an independent finish to Piola's own 1991 route, *Charlotte for Ever* (5+/6a).

**Grands Charmoz - Pt 2704m**  Two more lines were added to the E face by the guru of this area, Olivier Ratheaux. On 22 July with Marc Ravanel he put up a variant to the 1988 Albrand/Ratheaux route which he christened *Itinéraire Bis* (TD+ 6b). *Association Malfaiteur* was added on 5 August with Christophe Bodin and Loic Rousselle. This is another fine 12-pitch crack climb (TD mainly 4 to 5+ with one move of 6a) on the left side of the face, only slightly marred by two sections of easy broken ground in the lower part.

**Charpoua Hut**  Over the last two years a new approach to the Charpoua Hut has been equipped and will form the first stage of the *Le Balcon de la Mer de Glace*, a 'high level' path which will allow competent hill-walkers (with a good head for heights and some experience of using crampons on dry glaciers) to circumnavigate the **Mer de Glace** in three days.

After descending the usual ladders onto the Mer de Glace, cross directly to the far side where a conspicuous painted triangle at the base of the Echelets marks the start of a set of ladders which lead up onto a previously old and disused track. This is followed under the base of the **Flammes de Pierre Ridge** (access to many of the modern climbs in this vicinity) and beneath the Charpoua Glacier to the hut.

**Monts Rouges du Triolet**  Manlio Motto created three more new routes on the sunny walls near to the Triolet (Dalmazzi) Hut - *Zucchero Amaro*, a five-pitch slab route on the SW face of the first Pointe south of the N summit and, on the SE face of Pt 3289m, *Profuno Proibito* (seven sustained pitches of 6a/6a+) and *Cristallina* (six pitches 6c+/6b/obl).

**Aiguille Sans Nom**  On 25 May Andy Parkin soloed a new route on the right side of the NW face. *Sans Nom/Sans Ame* (ED2/85°/5+/A2) lies to the right of the 1963 *Brown/Patey route* and involved hard mixed climbing to finish at the Brèche Sans Nom.

**Pointe du Domino** Pierre Biedermann and Benoît Kempf climbed directly up the crest of the monolithic N spur situated to the left of the classic 1945 *Charlet/Rébuffat route*. After an initial ten pitches of loose mixed ground (3 and 4) on the left flank of the spur, *Voie Kevin* (TD– 500m) continues with seven pitches of 4 and 5 up the monolith, all eminently protected with nuts and interspersed with excellent stances and belays

**Aiguille d'Argentière** Patrick Gabarrou and Maxime Lopez climbed directly up the NE spur of the Flèche Rousse from the Saleina glacier on 8 June to create *Tobi*, a fine mixed route but only recommended very early in the season. At least one British party, climbing the old classic ESE (Flèche Rousse) Ridge (AD), felt that prospective parties should be warned about the extent of loose rock now encountered on the ridge, probably due to reduced snow cover in recent years.

**Trient and Orny Huts** There is now a wealth of short but well-equipped rock routes on the excellent granite adjacent to both these huts. Details of all the routes are available 'on site' but remember that these venues are very popular with Swiss guides.

**Envers des Dorées Bivouac Hut** The Dent de Lys section of the Swiss Alpine Club have constructed a new hut on a rocky saddle at 2980m, approximately midway between the Pointe des Plines and the Trident (Aiguilles Dorées). Twelve places are available for reservation (Tel: 021 921 85 50) and the remaining 11 can be snapped up on a first come first served basis. Bring your own sleeping-bags and gas stove.

**Aiguilles Dorées** Throughout its 1.3km length the S side of this granite crest offers sumptuous rock climbing with certain routes on a par with the best in the Mont Blanc Massif. The **Aiguille de la Varappe,** which appears to be the Mecca of all established climbing on this wall, gained a new route to the right of the modern super-classic, *Eole Danza per Noi. C'est Mozart qu'on Assassiné* (Monnet/Piola) is a 10-pitch creation, sustained at 6a/6a+, which takes a fantastic series of cracks and dièdres that are easily protected with natural gear. *Le Sud, le Soleil, la Plage, les Palmiers...* on the **Aiguilles Penchées** was completed by the evergreen Piola/Strappazzon partnership to give a very enjoyable 10-pitch route (6b/c with three points of aid or 7a) finishing up the extraordinary crest of the Capucin des Dorées.

The same pair added *Le Vent des Errances* (eight pitches 6b with four points of aid or 6c) to the walls right of the classic S ridge of the **Aiguille Sans Nom** and visited the previously overlooked buttresses on the SE flank of the **Trident,** where they created *Coup de Bambou,* a three-pitch 6b on excellent rock.

**Aiguilles Rouges** On 4 August Ratheaux soloed the previously unclimbed SE faces of the **Aiguille Martin** (200m, AD, a few sections of 4) and **Aiguille de l'Encrenez** (PD 200m). However, his best contribution to this area came on 9 August when with Christophe Bodin he made the first ascent of the S dièdre of the **Aiguille de la Persévérance**. *Le Père Sévère* (300m D) is a delightful route with nine pitches from 3 to 5.

# Valais

Although only the Slovenians appear to have been innovatory on the big and nasty mixed faces, there is still plenty of scope in this vast range for new routes at all levels of difficulty.

**Breithorn** Bojan Pokar climbed two new and undoubtedly serious mixed lines on the NW face of the W summit. On 25 June with Peter Meznar he climbed *Karatanska* (ED1/1150m/VI–/80°) in nine hours, then returned on 5 August with Ziga Petric to put up *Black Panther* (ED2/1100m/VII-/85°) in 12 hours.

**Nadelhorn** On the E face, Petric and Pocker climbed a difficult line up the mixed ground on the left to create *November Rain* (ED2/750m/VI/A1/75°). The route was completed in eight hours on 28 November.

**Monte Sarezza (2820m)** Two short new routes (VI and VII–, on very sound rock) were recorded by L Formagnana and S Origone on the previously unclimbed W face of this modest summit close to the Testa Grigia.

**Gressoney/Valpelline** It may seem astonishing to think that in these days 'virgin' summits still remain in the Alps but the collection of wild rugged rock peaks that lie between the Gressoney and Ayas valleys still hold a few secrets. The first recorded ascent of the 2767m **Corno Maria** took place on 20 July when Roan Fair and Stephen Fox climbed the SW face/ridge. This was completed in 1¾ hours and had a section of III+. There was no trace of any human presence high on the mountain, although a large cairn was visible on a shoulder halfway up the N ridge. The same pair also made the first recorded ascent of the 2887m **Punta di Soleron** on 8 August. They climbed the NE face, which gave seven pitches up to III+ on good rock, then descended the NE ridge.

An even more esoteric but far less significant route was made on the 3236m rocky 'aiguille' of **Pointe Chanoux**, which lies several kilometres NE of the popular snowy pyramid of the **Becca de Luseney.** The NW face, which would probably resemble a steep and crumbling slag heap during the summer, was climbed at the beginning of October by Lindsay Griffin. A good covering of well-frozen snow allowed pleasantly easy mixed climbing to a steeper exit onto the N ridge about 50m below the summit.

# Bernese Oberland

**Eiger** The 1992 Anker/Piola route, *Chant Du Cygne,* more or less a direct ascent of the crest of the **Geneva Pillar,** has certainly evolved rapidly into the modern classic on this sector of the face, with numerous ascents in 1994. To the left, *La Sanction* (1000m/ED3/VIII), a 1988 Anker/Piola route following the line 'attempted' by a star-studded cast led by Clint Eastwood in the film 'The Eiger Sanction', received its second and third ascents last summer when it was climbed by an East European team and then, on 20-21 August, by Swiss alpinists Christophe Germiquet and Gino Merazzi.

# Ortler/Adamello

At the eastern end of the Central Alps exploration continues to be sporadic. Most rock is best avoided in the Ortler but there are plenty of classic ice faces, many at a reasonable standard. Recommended are various routes on the N face (400m D and TD) of the **Cima San Matteo** (3678m), NNW faces (400m AD+) of **Punta Cadini** (3524m) and **Monte Rosole** (3531m), NE (380m AD+) and NW (600m AD+) faces of **Monte Pasquale** (3553m), N face (200m AD-) of **Monte Cristallo** (3431m), NE (350m AD) and NW (300m D+) faces of the **Cima Trafoi** (3565m), N face (450m D) of the **Cima Vertana** (3554m), plus of course the more serious routes on the famous N faces of the Zebru (Königsspitze) peaks and Ortles.

As good quality granite becomes more scarce, the numerous venues of the Adamello Massif offer much potential, albeit with generally a long approach. On the SE fringes, S Bella, C Care and L Sauda have put up a new 350m route on the N face of the **Cima d'Arno** (VI) and at a much higher standard, the *Pilastro Martina* on the 2900m **Cornone di Blumone** (250m VIII+ or A3). Also on the Cornone is *Rufugio Tita Secchi*, a 450m, VI– up the S face by Ballerini and Quecchia in September.

Opened last year was the **Julius Payer Research Centre** just north of the main Adamello 'ice cap'. The Centre conveniently lies on one of the great high-level routes of the region, the Marchetti Trail and plans to exhibit a permanent exhibition on glaciers and the Alpine environment.

# Bregaglia/Bernina

There was plenty of activity here last summer, especially on the Italian side of the range where, despite the sad introduction of electric drills into the mountains, there is still a small but advanced group of pioneers putting up very lengthy new routes on impressive big walls with a minimal use of manually placed bolts.

**Punta Redescala** Perhaps the most important ascent of the season took place in the remote and still little frequented region of the Sasso Manduino Group at the far western end of the range. *Amici Miei* on the stupendous Pilastro del 'Rut' of the S face of Punta Redescala is a 20-pitch route on an 800m+ pillar put up by the Libera brothers. It has obligatory crux moves of VIII+ and a minimal number of bolts.

**Monte Qualido** On the E face local climber Paolo Cucchi made the first solo ascents of both *Artemisia* (600m VII+) and *Galactica* (450m VII+ and A1).

**Escudo del Qualido** This fine shield of compact slabs above Alpe Qualido was more or less untouched until August 1992. It now has five excellent routes on superb rock, the latest courtesy of Lecco climbers Sonia Brambati and Paolo Vitali. *Esperando El Sol* (250m) gives some sustained climbing at V to VII+ with a crux pitch (the third) at VIII–.

**Cima del Cavalcorte** Brambati, Carnati and Vitali have added another route to this superb watchtower. *Pilastro Giovanni Marmotte* gives 350m of bolt-protected VII+ and lies on the right side of the spectacular prow of the SE pillar.

**Piz Badile** A significant repeat was made of *Ringo Star* by John Ashbridge and Graham Dudley on 12 July. Access to the route had definitely altered owing to glacial recession, giving an initial half-pitch of smooth, wet and gravelly granite which, combined with the rimaye, formed the crux of the climb. Only a few ancient pegs were found in place and certain pitches were loose, but the overall ambience of the climbing was superb.

**Pizzo Cengalo** The Brambati/Vitali team climbed a very direct line on the SW face of the **S summit (Punta Angela)** in just five hours on 6 August. *Carosello* (320m VII VI obl) is reported to give varied climbing on sound granite. Eleven bolts were placed on belays allowing a rapid rappel descent from the summit of Punta Angela. This supersedes all previous rappel lines and will be greatly appreciated by climbers coming off the classic *Vinci route*. Several days later Gianluca Maspes made the second ascent and first solo in an astonishing time of 5½ hours from Bagni del Masino.

**Cima di Castello** Galbaiti, Maggioni, Cattaneo, Tanzi and Panzeri, have created a new 10-pitch line up the right side of the wonderful golden slab that forms the S face. *Mamma Luisa* (VII+ and bolt protected) starts more or less in the middle of the face and in the upper section follows the true crest of the S pillar avoided by the *British route*.

**Torrone Occidentale** On **Punta 2987m**, Gianluca Maspes with Stefano Righetti made the second ascent of the 1993 Motto/Predan/Vogler line *Complicazioni Collaterali* (350m: VIII/VII+ obl). They then followed this with *El Diablo* (VIII with three points of aid or VII/VII+ and A1 obl/a full range of nuts and Friends necessary) a sustained 10-pitch route which several climbers are already saying may well be one of the best routes in the entire range. On the remote SE face of the **Torrone,** the Brambati/Carnati/Vitali team have added *Ilinx* to the right of *Il Tempo del Broncio* on the **Siamesi Pillars** (350m VIII+ and A2 VII+ obl). Although there is still considerable scope for further climbing here, this sort of expedition is unfashionable, being at least a four-hour grind from the Mello Valley.

**Picco Luigi Amedeo** On the 'Grand Capucin' of the Bregaglia the Slovakian team of Igor Koller and Dino Kuran created *Denti del Granito* on the right side of the magnificent E face. They also made the first free ascent of the *Czechoslovakian route* (Ciernik/Placek 1980 VI and A2 but now VIII–). The route later received a first solo ascent by Paolo Cucchi. Oto Bajana and Mato Henger made the first free ascent of the ferocious *Electroshock* (Fazzini/Gianola/Riva 1989 370m originally VIII/VIII+ and A0, now IX).

**Passo di Gembré** Michele Comi, Daniele Fiorelli and Cristian Gianatti explored the 1km long granitic cliff that lies immediately west of the **Passo di Gembré** (3231m). The Italians put up one good five-pitch route with a crux of VII, but plenty of other fantastic cracklines remain.

JOSÉ LUIS BERMÚDEZ & PAUL KNOTT

# Russia and Central Asia 1992-94

*We would like to thank all those correspondents who have sent information, in particular Yevgeniy B Gippenreiter and Vladimir Shataev; Igor Revenko of the Kamchatka Ecology Institute; Anatoli Gvozdev; Sergei Kurgin of SibAlp, Novosibirsk; Kazbek Valiev of Khan Tengri mountain service, Almaty. We would welcome further reports and information, which should be sent via the Alpine Club.*

The demise of the Soviet Union has made the mountain ranges of the former Soviet Union easily accessible to Western climbers. It has also made it possible to report local mountaineering developments in more detail. Information is becoming more available to English speakers, with a number of guidebooks and maps now available in English, including Frith Maier's remarkably comprehensive *Trekking in Russia & Central Asia*. These Area Notes introduce the principal mountaineering areas and provide information about the most significant ascents accomplished by foreign and local climbers since the winter of 1991-92. The activities of local climbers diminished after the collapse of the Soviet Union, which left mountaineering prohibitively expensive, but they are now on the rise again.

## The Pamir

**General** The mountains of the Pamir are mainly located in Tajikistan, although the NE edges run into Kyrgyzstan and the S and E parts run into Afghanistan and China. The Pamir span 280km N-S and 420km E-W. The climbing is expeditionary in character. The NW part of the range contains three of the four 7000m peaks in the former Soviet Union: **Pik Lenin (7134m)**; **Pik Kommunizma (7495m)**; and **Pik Evgenii Korzhenevskoi (7105m)**. Most climbing activity has been based around the popular base camps for these mountains. The climbing season is July-August, with winter ascents taking place generally in February.

    **Access** The political situation in Tajikistan is rather unstable at the time of going to press. The traditional jumping-off point of Osh is not at all safe. Most expeditions have been using Tashkent. It is worth noting that many groups (both Russian and foreign) experienced difficulties with helicopter transport from Tashkent to NW Pamir during the summer of 1994. The problem seemed to be Tajik authorities banning Uzbek helicopters, and then Tajik helicopter prices being pushed up to extortionate levels.

**Summer 1992   Pik Kommunizma (7495m)** saw a fair amount of activity. The 1987 *Lunyakov route* (5B) on the left SE buttress received a second ascent from a Kazakhstan team led by P Vorobiev. Three teams, all from Kazakhstan, climbed the S ridge (5B) from the Bivachnyi glacier. The N face (5A) from the Valtera glacier was climbed by three climbers from St Petersburg led by Yuri Krasnoukhov. On **Pik Evgenii Korzhenevskoi (7105m)** the S rib (5A) received three ascents, while the 1984 *Markelov route* on the SW ridge (5B) was climbed by four climbers from Cheliabinsk led by E Nagovitsina.

The route judged the best in 1992 in the high-altitude class was on **Pik Russia (6875m)** on the E side of **Pik Kommunizma.** Five climbers led by A Ruchkin made the second ascent of the *Ilyinksky route* on the buttress of the SE face (6A). A Mikhailov and party climbed the NE face of **Pik Engels (6510m).** In the **Sauk-Jailyau massif** (E end of the Alai ridge) the Ekaterinburg mountaineering team made several important ascents, including the first ascent of the buttress on the N face (6A) of **Main Sauk-Jailyau (5120m)**, the second ascent of the W face on **SE Sauk-Jailyau** and a first ascent of the S face of **Krutaja Stena (3450m)**. In the southern Pamir A Mikhailov and party climbed the NE face of **Pik Engels.**

**Summer 1993**   On **Pik Kommunizma (7495m)** the S ridge (5B) was climbed, as was the N face (5A) from the Walter glacier. On **Evgenii Korzhenevskoi (7105m)** the *1980 route* on the Central Pillar of the W face (6A) was climbed by a team from Vladivostock led by G Shaferov.

**Winter 1993-94** The major event this winter was the first ski traverse of the Pamir range from SE to NW by Vadim Vasiljev and three companions. They took 30 days to cross the 480km between Murgab and Daraut-Kurgan. (*See article 'The Transpamirs Ski Expedition', pages 175-177.*)

**Summer 1994** A team from St Petersburg led by Yuri Krasnoukhov climbed the SW ridge of **Evgenii Korzhenevskoi (7105m).**

## The Pamir Alai

**General** The Pamir Alai is a range 700km long, N of the main Pamir and stretching further W. The principal ridges are the Alai, Zeravshan and Turkestan. The summits in the Pamir Alai are generally under 5500m in height. The Fansky mountains used to be the best known of the ranges of the Pamir Alai, lying 40km E of Samarkand and containing the highest summits of the Zeravshan ridge. Recently mountaineering attention has focused primarily on the eastern end of the Turkestan range which lies between the Fergana depression and the Zeravshan valleys, where there are 35 peaks over 5000m.

In the Fansky mountains the climbing generally consists of single-day alpine rock routes. Elsewhere in the Pamir Alai climbing has become more ambitious since the mid-1980s, particularly on the N side of the Turkestan ridge. The best known areas are the Laylak (Ak-Su) and Karavshin valleys, where numerous high quality rock and mixed routes have been put up on the granite faces. These areas are popular both among Russians and foreigners and research will be needed for those who want to escape the crowds. The climbing season is from mid-July to September.

**Access** Some areas in the Pamir Alai can be accessed by truck (from Samarkand), notably the Fansky mountains. So too can the Laylak (Ak-Su) valley in the Turkestan range, where the Alai mountaineering camp is still functioning (reached from Hudjand via Isfana). The Karavshin river region is most easily accessed by helicopter from Tashkent, as are the other regions of the Pamir Alai, like the Mynteke area.

**Publications** West Col have published a map of the Fansky mountains.

**Summer 1992** In the Karavshin gorge, a new route was climbed up the centre of the E face (6A) of **Kyrkchilta (4507m)**, by an Uzbek team led by O Grigoriev. They also made the second ascent of the left buttress of the E face (6A) on the same mountain. The **Kyrkchilta Peaks (4507m, 4300m and 4810m)** were traversed by some of the same climbers, this time led by A Kotelnikov. A different team from Uzbekistan, led by P Ann, made the first ascent of the SW face (5B) of **Pik Slesov (4240m)**. Three Spanish climbers (Gallego, Gomez and Seiquer) made the first ascent of the *Spanish Dihedral* (6B) on Slesov. A new route at 6B was put up on the NNE face of **Pik Gorniak (5013m)** by a team of five led by D Sidorov.

In the **Laylak** area Pavel Shabalin and Andrei Antonov spent nine days making the first two-man ascent of the 1982 *Troschinenko route* on the N face of **Ak-Su North (5217m)**.

**Summer 1993** In the Laylak gorge there was more activity on the N face of **Ak-Su North (5217m)**, with V Babanov and A Ruchkin from Omsk making the second ascent of the 1986 *Popov route* up the centre. It took them 14 days of work in bad weather. Pavel Shabalin, Andrei Antonov and N Medvedev made the second ascent of the 1984 *Moschnikov couloir*. A new route on the E face of **Little Iskander (4520m)** was climbed by a three-man Italian team including Fabrizio de Francesco.

In the **Karavshin** region, a new route on the E face (6B) of **Pik 4810** was put up by A Klenov and party from Ekaterinburg over five days. Two ascents were made of the E face (6B) on the same peak. A Klenov and three companions also climbed a new route on the right of the N face (6B) of **Pik Slesov (4240m)**. There were two more new routes on the N face of Slesov: by the cleft (6B) by S Khabibullin and S Tarasov from Ekaterinburg; and up the left side of the centre (6A) by S Semiletkin and V Lebedev. Semiletkin and party also made the second ascent of the *Spanish Dihedral* (6B). Also on Slesov, the *Morozov route* up the centre of the N face (6B) was climbed twice, including an ascent by the omnipresent Shabalin and Antonov. Two French expeditions were active here. A large group led by Luc Jourjon made a range of repeats and first ascents, including the first free ascent of the 1991 *French route* on **Pik Slesov** (by L Pouzadoux and F Pallendre). On the NE face of **Pik 4810** R Karle, D Dumont and E Guy climed a direct line at ED+ (6b French). A Franco-Russian team climbed *Voie Papillon* on the W face of **Pik 3850** (5b+ French ED). Their principal new route was *Le Paradis Artificiel* (ABO 6b A4) which was climbed using bolt belays between 16 July and 31 July. A smaller group of four French climbers (Serge Angelucci, Eric Frossard, Pierre Isosar and Jean-Christophe Moulin) were also very active in the region. They repeated the *Russian Directissima* (6B) on the SE face of **Pik 4520**, as well as climbing a new route on the face in three days. They climbed a new route, *Totem* (6B), on the W face of **Pik 3850**, to the left of the *Russian Direct* (6A). Jean-Christophe Moulin soloed a hard gully line on the N face of **Pik Pyramidalny (5509m).**

**Summer 1994** In the Laylak gorge, a British team (Clive Davis, Jerry Hadwin, Andy Lewington and Neil McAdie) repeated the NE Pillar (6A) of **Pik Admiral (5090m)**, although they did not reach the summit. They graded it at E2/A2 with about half the pitches climbed free (*see MEF Reports, ref. 94/30*).

In the **Karavshin** region a new route was put up on the centre of the left side of the NW face of **Pik 4810** by a Moscow team led by K Sakharov.

In August a team from Bylorussia led by Stas Shabunia climbed in the Mynteke valley in the **Matcha massif** (accessed by helicopter from Tashkent). They made four first ascents, including the NW rib (5B) of **Pik Rosich**); the W face (6A) of **Pik 5070**; the W face (6A) of **Pik Basilia (4708m)**; and the pillar of the S face of **Pik 4600**. They also made a route up the right side of the wall that bounds the E side of the Mynteke glacier, grading it at 6B.

# The Tien Shan

**General** Most of the 2500km-long Tien Shan range lies within Kyrgyzstan, with the fringes running into Kazakhstan, Uzbekistan and China. The best known area is the Central Tien Shan, which includes the world's most northerly 7000m peak, **Pobeda (7439m)** unless the nearby **Khan Tengri (6995m)** is given its alternative height of 7010m. This height for Khan Tengri is generally disregarded by locals. The many other ranges offer a variety of climbing on peaks up to 5000m and often have more settled weather than around the highest peaks. The usual summer climbing season is July-August, with winter ascents taking place in February.

**Access** The usual access points for the Tien Shan are Bishkek in Kyrgyzstan and Almaty in Kazakhstan. For parts of the Western Tien Shan, Tashkent is more convenient. Currently there are no active conflicts in any of the Tien Shan mountain areas. Special permits are required to enter some areas, particularly those adjacent to the China border. These should be obtained in the main towns.

**Central Tien Shan** The mountaineering camps on the Inylchek glacier continue, with increasing numbers of climbers now tackling peaks other than Pobeda and Khan Tengri. The area's popularity with foreign climbers has been increasing owing to rapid helicopter access and reasonable costs. However, modest peak fees have been introduced by the government of Kyrgyzstan and it is feared that these may increase in future years.

**Winter 1992** In February **Khan Tengri** received its first winter ascent, by a seven-strong Kazakhstan team including Vladimir Suviga and the late Valeri Khrishchaty. The usual route via the W rib was taken, with the main problem being extreme exposure to storm winds.

**Summer 1992** A considerable number of climbers from Russia, Kyrgyzstan and Ukraine made successful ascents of **Pobeda** via the usual *Dikiy Pass route*. A team from Ekaterinburg led by A Agafonov climbed a new route on the Right Pillar of the S ridge of **Sovetskaya Kyrgyzia (5660m)** at 5B. A German team led by Leo Baumgartner was the first to climb from the Proletarskiy Turist glacier (immediately W of the Dikiy glacier leading to Pobeda), in mid-September. Ascents were made of peaks **5100m** and **5200m**, in poor snow conditions.

**Summer 1993** Activity around the Inylchek glacier has been previously reported (*AJ99*, 273, 1994). Immediately south of its lower reaches, a British team led by Daniel Cousins travelled by truck and on foot to the Kan-Dzhailoo glacier. Ascents were made of **Nansen (5697m)**, **P 5016**, **P 4500** and **P 4894**.

**Summer 1994** A British-Ukrainian team led by Nick Williams attempted a number of new routes on peaks around the S Inylchek glacier including **Pogrebetsky (6527m)** and **Chapaev (6371m)**, but all were foiled by bad weather or conditions (*see MEF Reports, ref. 94/18*). A team of two from Kemerovo in Siberia climbed a new route R of the Sviridenko rock triangle on the S face of **Khan Tengri**. The mountain also received an ascent by a Japanese women's team led by Junko Tabei. Its difficult N face was attempted by a six-man team led by V Suvita. After eight days the climb was abandoned at 6100m owing to poor weather. As in 1993, there were several fatal accidents on the Semenovsky glacier leading to the W ridge.

**Kyrgyz Range** This range, a short distance S of Bishkek, is readily accessible by road and is a popular training ground for locals and Russians. The first Western visit was by George Lowe's party in 1976. The main areas are the Ala-Archa and Alamedin valleys, with the highest peak being **Semionov-Tien-Shansky (4875m)**. Other parts of the range are less frequented.

**Winter 1991/2** A winter ascent of the *Semiletkin route* on **Svobodnaya (Free) Korea (4740m)** was made by a Kazakhstan-based team. This was the first winter ascent of a 6B route, and the 4th ascent overall, taking many days to complete. In February 1994 a team of five from Krasnoyarsk led by V Balezin climbed the Right Pillar of the N face of **Svobodnaya Korea** at 5B. In July Balezin led a different team of five on the central SW face of the 5th tower of **Korona (4860m)** at 6A.

**Terskiy Alatau**  This extensive ridge S of the Issyk-Kul lake has several peaks topping 5000m.  In August 1993 a multi-national team including Nick Shea and Ian Steel from the UK climbed above the Karakol valley. Ascents were made of **Gastello (4145m)**, **Tulenina (4240m)**, and **G.T.O. (4245m)**, all likely to have been first foreign ascents although well established by Russians as training routes.  In the same area but previously unvisited by mountaineers is the isolated **Khrebet Borkoldoy** range.

**Summer 1994**  A British team including Philip Bartlett, Marion Elmes and Mike Parsons made nine first ascents of peaks between 4500m and 5000m. (*For full details see 'Hills, Horses and Hunger', pages 82-84.*)

**Western Tien Shan**  There are a number of reports of recent activity around the Oygaing valley in Uzbekistan, close to the borders of Kazakhstan and Kyrgyzstan. Although comparatively low in altitude, these mountains offer some hard and serious climbing. In July 1992 in the Maidantalski range a Tashkent team led by I Tukhvatullin climbed a new route on the N ridge of **Udacha (3500m)** at 5B. Earlier the same year a Uzbekistan team led by O Grigoriev made a winter ascent up the W face of **Pik 3980**, also at 5B.

**Summer 1993**  A team from the Oygaing mountaineering camp climbed a new route on the NW face at 6A. The first British teams were also active in the area. Stuart Gallagher and Ken Mosley climbed the E ridge of **Haskova (4220m)**, the NE ridge of **Profsoyus (3750m)** and, with Mike Gill and Keith Lambley, the E ridge of **Pamyat (4090m)**. Brian Swales teamed with Russian Valeri Pershin to climb a 300m rock wall overlooking the main valley. John Chadwick, Pete Holden, Dave McKinney and Chris Woodall attempted a new route on an 800m face.  In the Pskemsky range Mike Gill and Keith Lambley made a probable first ascent of **Pik 4360**.

# The Caucasus

**General**  The mountains of the Caucasus stretch for 1150 km from the Black Sea to the Caspian Sea, with the highest summits being **Elbrus (5642m)**, **Shkhara (5200m)**, **Dykh-Tau (5198m)** and **Koshtan-Tau (5150m)**. The range divides the states of the Russian Federation from Georgia. The climbing is Alpine rather than expeditionary in style, although routes tend to be longer and more serious than in the Alps. The best time to climb is July-August, when the weather is reasonably settled.

**Publications**  Friedrich Bender's *Classic Climbs in the Caucasus* (translated from the German) is available in the UK. It gives descriptions and topos for routes in the Bezingi and Elbrus regions. These are often outdated and unreliable and should be used with caution. West Col have issued transcriptions of Russian maps.  These are very expensive and not particularly good, but the best available at present. The history of climbing in the Caucasus is covered in *On the Edge of Europe* by Audrey Salkeld and José Luis Bermúdez.

**Access**   The Caucasus is best reached by plane from Moscow to Mineralnye Vodye or Nalchik (two hours). Trains from Moscow are not recommended for non-Russian speakers. The Caucasus is well provided with mountaineering camps set up in Soviet times. The principal ones are Bezingi, Shkhelda, Adyl-Su and Ullu-Tau. Almost all of these are still functioning and provide basic food and accommodation as well as co-ordinating rescue facilities. Exceptions include the Baksan camp (occupied by Russian border guards) and the Tseya and Torpedo camps which are occupied by refugees. Visitors to the Caucasus are advised to check that camps are open and arrange transport to them in advance. The only area in the Caucasus at all comparable to the Alps (with hotels etc) is the village of Terskol, the jumping off point for ascents of Elbrus.

The political situation in the Caucasus is unsettled. The dispute between Russia and Chechnya has made the Eastern Caucasus a no-go area, and it would be foolish in the extreme to plan a visit to the Georgian side of the range (eg Suanetia). The major mountains are in the Central Caucasus, which lies in Kabardina-Balkaria, currently the most stable of the Caucasian republics. The rule of law is not very clearcut in the Caucasus. Robbery and banditry do not raise eyebrows; nor is terrorist activity unknown. Various acts of sabotage took place at Mineralnye Vodye airport in the summer of 1994.

**Winter 1991-92**   In the Eastern Caucasus a team led by S Semiletkin made the first winter ascent of the *Samoded route* (5B) on Main Peak of **Erydag (3925m)**. In the Central Caucasus A Abromov's team from Moscow made a winter ascent of the S face of **Pik Free Spain (4200m).**

**Summer 1992**   The *Kustovsky route* on **Ushba South (4710m)** received its first alpine-style ascent by S Antonov and M Shtarkov (Moscow) between 4 and 9 August. The route is one of the hardest (6B) on Ushba, a traditional forcing ground.  In the Bezingi region the N face (6A) of **Krumkol (4860m)** was repeated by Andreyev and party. A visiting South African mountaineer, Martin Seegers, was killed by lightning descending **Gestola**. In the Abkhazian Chain (Western Caucasus) a team from the city of Dniepropetrovsk carried out a number of first ascents more exploratory than technical in nature. The Snegovoy and Bogosskiy ranges in the Eastern Caucasus were visited by a joint British/Ukraine expedition led by Paul Knott and Nick Drobotenko.

**Winter 1992-93**   The principal event was the first winter ascent of the *Kustovsky route* (6B) on the SW face of **Ushba South (4710m)** by a team from St Petersburg led by V Smirnov. The ascent took seven days and one member was killed in the Ushba icefall on descent. In Digoria (Eastern Caucasus) four climbers from Rostov led by A Moiseev put up a new route (5B) on the S face of **Galdor (4130m)**.

**Summer 1993**   The *Kustovsky route* on Ushba South was climbed again, by a team from Krasnodar. The Central Caucasus was visited by Mark Gray and Julian Eliot who climbed the *Abalakov route* on the N face of Nakra-Tau and made the first British ascent of the S face of **Pik Free Spain** by the *Sybartovich route* (5B).

**Winter 1993-94** G Melnikov and D Petrov (Elbrus mountaineering camp) traversed **Ushba** in February (5A). A five-man team from the Elbrus mountain rescue service led by V Avtomov climbed the N face (5B) of **Chatyn-Tau**. S Egorin led a team of five climbers from Vladikavkaz in a first ascent of the NW rib and N face (5B) of **Arkhon Malyi (3942m)**. A ski traverse of the Caucasus was attempted by a British party led by David Hamilton. (*For full details see 'Almost a Russian Haute Route', pages 178-182* .)

**Summer 1994** Two British parties visited the Bezingi region in the Central Caucasus. A party led by Will Edwards made the first British ascent of the N face (5A) of **Ullu-Auz-Bashi (4671m)** and climbed the *Tomaschek-Muller route* on the N rib (5B) of **Shkhara (5200m)**. J L Bermúdez and N Wilson spent seven days making the first British traverse from Shkhara to Jangi-Tau (5030m). (*For full details see 'Crab Crawl on the Bezingi Wall', pages 85-90.*)

## Siberia and the Russian Far East

**Altai** These mountains have been accessible for a number of years, and had several visits from British and other foreign climbers up to 1990. Attention has been focused on the Ak-Kem area of the **Katun Range**, although several ranges to the east also offer interesting climbing. Local climbers have been active for many years, and have made a number of winter ascents. The usual time for climbing, however, is July and August.

In the **North Chuyski Range**, there are routes up to 5B on peaks to 4000m. The Ak-Tru area is the most developed. In the **South Chuyski Range** the Iiktu area has routes up to 4A/B on peaks above 3900m (**Iiktu 3941m**), and to its east the area of **Pik Chuyski (3777m)** is little developed. Further east still, by the Mongolia border, are the formerly closed **Tapduair-Sailugem** and **Ashatin/Dabani-Har** ranges. It is also possible to cross via Tashanta into the Ulgi region of Mongolia, where there are several mountain chains.

**Summer 1993** A team from Krasnoyarsk led by V Balezin made the third ascent of a 6A route on the right-hand side of the E face of **20th October Peak.** In spring 1994 a new fifth category ice route in the Ak-Tru region was climbed by three pairs, taking advantage of frozen conditions. Also in the spring a party including S Kurgin and German B Brakus made the first ascents of **Besimyannaya (3480m)** at 3A/B and **Tobduair (3505m)** at 3/4. In the summer members of the Altai rescue service climbed a new route on **Kupol (3400m)** in the Ak-Tru region at 3A/B.

**Kamchatka** Most of the mountains of Kamchatka are volcanoes, of which around 30 are still active. All of the summits are said to have been reached. Most routes on these mountains do not exceed Russian 3B, except on **Kamen (4579m)** which has routes at 4A and 4B. Nevertheless the height gain, loose terrain and threat of eruption make ascents relatively serious. The most popular areas are the Klyuchevskaya region and near to Petropavlovsk-Kamchatskiy, both of which can be accessed by truck.

Despite normally adverse conditions there have been winter ascents of peaks including **Klyuchevskaya (4750m),** the highest peak in Kamchatka. The first winter ascent of **Kamen** was in April 1991 by Fedor Farberov and Alexey Boltanov. Farberov also made a ski descent of the peak in 1993.

Foreign visits to the region started in 1991, when **Klyuchevskaya** was climbed by Russian/Japanese teams. In summer 1994 groups from Japan and several European countries, including the first British groups, climbed Klyuchevskaya. Filter masks were worn to protect against noxious gases and, weeks later, Klyuchevskaya erupted. (*See MEF Reports, ref. 94/7*)

In the **Ganalskiy Range**, 100km from Petropavlovsk, technical routes up to 6A have been climbed in recent years by local climbers including Fedor Farberov and Sergey Panyukin. These walls, up to 500m in height, now have the hardest technical climbing in Kamchatka. Other walls in the area reportedly have similar potential. The range is accessible in one long day from the road.

**Cherskiy** The Cherskiy is one of several extensive ranges in Eastern Siberia. The central and most interesting part of the range, the **Buordakh Massif**, was visited by a British party led by Paul Knott in July-August 1994. (*See MEF Reports, ref. 94/16*)

# Russia and Ukraine

**Crimea** Although not alpine in character, Crimea's mountains have a number of limestone cliffs up to 500m. Some routes commonly take more than one day. Guidebooks are becoming available, including *Rocks near the Sea* by A N Shcherbakov, in both English and Russian. Crimea is currently part of Ukraine. It can be reached without first entering Russia, and has no access problems.

**Kola Peninsula** At the end of August 1993 a team from St Petersburg climbed two new routes in the Khibins mountains, near Kirovsk. The Central Pillar of the N face of **Bolshoi Woodyavrchorr (1068m)** was climbed at 5A by A Remenjuk and three others; the N face of **Tahtarvumchorr (1154m)** was climbed by D Timoshenko and three others at 5B.

HARISH KAPADIA

# India 1994

There were 154 expeditions to the Indian Himalaya this year. Out of these, 96 were Indian expeditions, 53 foreign and five were joint. A very heavy and late monsoon troubled expeditions from July until almost the end of September. Surprisingly, the monsoon was most severe in the Trans-Himalayan areas. Spiti had the worst weather in its history, while Ladakh and the Eastern Karakoram also had much rain, which is a rarity there.

**Peak Fees** A double royalty is now being enforced in Sikkim: $3500 for the IMF and $3500 for the Sikkim government. In addition, two liaison officers have to be engaged to represent these two authorities. Despite a range of discussions taking place in Delhi nobody seems to be able to persuade the Government to change its mind, but the change of Local Government in the recent election may finally change this draconian rule. There is also a possibility of all Indian peak fees increasing.

**Literature** The *Himalayan Journal*, which is published from Bombay, brought out its 50th volume in 1994. To mark the event the book *Environment Protection of the Himalaya* (edited by Aamir Ali) and a *Consolidated Index to the HJ Volumes 1 to 50* were published.

## Arunachal Pradesh

In October the Himalayan Mountaineering Institute, Darjeeling, celebrating its 40th anniversary, attempted **Kangto (7090m)**, which has no ascent recorded from the Indian side. They explored Kangto beyond Chokersum, but felt that it could be approached only across the international boundary, the McMahon Line. Not wanting to risk a dispute, they returned and climbed **Gorichen I (6488 m)** and **Gorichen East (6222 m)** by their E ridges.

## Sikkim

**Siniolchu (6887m)** On 28 May Vanja Furlan and Uros Rupar (Slovenia) climbed the N face and NW ridge of this beautiful peak on the Zemu glacier. At the same time a Japanese team were reconnoitring the the N face. An Indian Army expedition climbed **Kabru South (7317m)** in W Sikkim in mid-May and, between September and November, a Japanese expedition climbed **Twins (7350m)** in N Sikkim. Some of the summiters were evacuated with serious frostbite.

# Kumaon - Garhwal

**Chaukhamba II (7068m)** A four-man Korean expedition led by Kim Woong Sik attempted this virgin peak. For the first time the mountain was approached from the Gangotri glacier. They were beaten by stonefall and an equipment shortage after establishing Camp 3 (6200m). On **Chaturangi III (6304m)** A S Miller and R Weight reached 100m below the summit on 29 October.

**Yogeshwar (6678m)** A Spanish expedition approached from the Shyamvarna glacier and attempted the S ridge, but gave up owing to huge crevasses and very loose rocks. They climbed the nearby **Saife (6166m)** on 19 September from the Swetvarna glacier.

A Japanese expedition reached 6100m on the W face of **Bhagirathi I (6856m)** in bad weather. On 7 October they climbed **Bhagirathi II (6572m).**

**Peak 6504m** This unnamed peak SE of Bhagirathi II on the Gangotri glacier was reported to be climbed by an Indian team in mid-June.

**Bhagirathi III (6454m)** John Chapman, Vera Wong and Bazely Kynam Peter climbed the SW pillar on 11 September with two bivouacs.

The well-known Slovene pair Matjaz Jamnik and Silvo Karo attempted the W face of **Bhagirathi IV (6173m)** (rated by Doug Scott as one of the major problems of the Garhwal). After eleven attempts to climb the face they reached a high point of c5500m on 22 August. They stayed in the Bhagirathi Group for 36 days of which only 3 days were without rain or snow. (*Józef Nyka*)

**Meru (6450m)** A Spanish team reached the summit via the E face on 27 September. They also climbed **Shivling (6543m)** from the east on 10 October. Other teams tried the N ridge and W ridge of **Shivling** unsuccessfully in August and September.

A Swiss expedition attempted **Kedarnath (6940m)** during the monsoon season. They reached 6300m in July, when soft snow and rains stopped them. Four foreign expeditions attempted **Thalay Sagar (6904m)** unsuccessfully.

**Kedar Dome (6831m)** This high peak with easy accessibility has become a popular target in recent years. Many expeditions attempted it this year, including one led by John Cleare (UK). On another, Ms Sunita Hayanki (India) was killed in an avalanche. Janusz Golab (Poland) climbed the mountain by the normal route in 12 hours.

**Nanda Devi East (7434m)** Four expeditions made attempts via the Longstaff col on the S ridge. A Spanish team were successful on 27 June, as were Roger Payne and Julie-Ann Clyma on 6 October, making the first British/New Zealand ascent. (*See article 'Voyage to the Goddess', pages 52-56*.)

**Chandra Parbat I (6739 m)** An Australian team led by Darren Miller made the first ascent of this peak, via the SW ridge, on 21 September. **Chandra Parbat II (6728m)** has already been climbed.

**Lamchir West (5500m)** An American expedition from the National

Outdoor Leadership School, led by Krishnan Kutty, climbed the NW ridge on 25 May. On 30 May, eleven members made the first ascent of the snow-dome named **Nandakini (5600m)** by the NW face. In October another team from the same organisation attempted **Lamchir** and were successful on **Nandakini.**

**Trisul 1 (7120m)** Markus Ulrich and Randler Marues (Germany) climbed the W ridge, reaching the summit on 22 September. An Indian team reached 6400m on the western route.

**Trimukhi Parbat (6422m)** An Indian Army team from the 14 Punjab Regiment made the first ascent of this shapely, difficult peak in the Jadhganga valley on 27 June. They also climbed **Nandi (5795m)** and **Trimukhi Parbat E (6280 m).** This area was first explored by Dr J B Auden in 1939. **Nandi** and **Trimukhi Parbat East** were first climbed by Harish Kapadia and Monesh Devjani in 1990.

**Mandani (6193m)** On 18 September a team from Bengal was stopped 100m below the summit owing to a huge crevasse. Two teams from Bengal climbed **Gangotri I (6672m)** on 25 May and 5 June.

**Satopanth (7075m)** Paul Herrington (Ireland) summited via the N ridge on 8 October, as did members of Korean and Japanese expeditions (on 27 May and 24 September respectively).

**Mana NW (7092m)** A team from Bombay led by Suhas Kharde reached 6900m on this virgin peak in June. They were stopped by sustained bad weather. A joint Mongolian–Indian– Tibet Border Police team climbed the NE ridge of **Jaonli (6632m)** on 23 November. An Indian team from Calcutta reached 6800m on **Chaukhamba I (7138m)** in the spring, giving up owing to soft snow.

**Nilgiri Parbat (6474m)** A four-man team from Bombay reached 5640m on this peak at the head of the Khulia Garvia glacier, Central Garhwal, during May-June. On 7 June an Indian Army expedition summited from the Banke Gad valley, using a similar approach to Frank Smythe's 1937 first ascent.

**Traill's Pass (5400m)** This difficult high pass which divides the Pindari glacier and the Milam valley was crossed by an Indian team led by Anup Sah. It may have been the first crossing for 40 years.

Baba Manindra Paul, a physically handicapped *sadhu* turned mountaineer, led an expedition to **Abi Gamin (7355m)** in the Garhwal Himalaya and reached the summit on 30 August.

# Himachal Pradesh

**Rangrik Rang (6553m), Manirang (6593m), Mangla (5800m), Saponang (5836m)** and **Ghunsarang (5800m)** An Indian–British Expedition led by Chris Bonington and Harish Kapadia climbed these peaks in May-June. (*See 'A Truly Joint Venture', pages 57-64, and 'Manirang, 6593m', pages 65-70.*)

**Sesar Rang (6095m)** This lovely peak is situated on the watershed between the Tirung gad and Gyamithang gad in the East Kinnaur. It was climbed by a 13-man team from Bengal on 2 September.

In July 1994, a Delhi team attempted **Gya (6794m)** from the north. This was the first attempt to climb the mountain and the first attempt to approach it from the north (Chang Thang, Ladakh) side. Base Camp was reached after traversing a largely unexplored, treacherous gorge in three days. They were affected by an unprecedented spell of bad weather in Spiti that lasted 17 days. Abandoning plans to attempt a steep rock face, they attempted an elegant mixed line leading to a col near the summit on the serrated NE ridge. Their high point was 6500m.

**Shigri Parbat (6526m)** A British expedition climbed this high peak situated on the Lahul–Spiti divide. They approached from the Bara Shigri glacier and climbed the NW ridge. Three members, Adrian Langnado, Paul Hart and Bob Neubry reached the summit on 13 September. They later failed on **Peak 6310m** on the Bara Shigri glacier owing to poor snow. A Bengal team climbed **Peak 5792m** on this glacier on 30 September.

**Kullu Pumori (6553m)** This peak stands in the centre of the Bara Shigri glacier like a beautiful pyramid. A Bengal expedition climbed the SE ridge on 6 September.

A Japanese team climbed **CB 13 (6264m)** in Central Lahul on 7 August. During August an Indian team, led by Arun Samant, climbed seven peaks in the **Losar nala.** Six were first ascents. **Num Themga (6024m)** was the hardest. A British expedition led by Oliver Shergold made several first ascents in the **Parvati valley.** (*See MEF Reports, ref. 94/27*)

A Polish group climbed the S face of **Peak (6005m)** (near **KR 7**) on 21 August. A Japanese expedition climbed the E ridge of **KR 7 (6096m)** in rather poor weather, reaching the summit on 18 August and another Japanese expedition climbed the NE ridge of **CB 14 (6079m)** in mid-August. An RAF team reached 6250m on **Menthosa (6443m).** (*See MEF Reports, ref. 91/10*)

**Hanuman Tibba (5928m)** An Assam Adventure Foundation team attempted this peak. They were defeated by bad weather and poor snow conditions on 26 May. A team from Delhi, led by Surender Sonik were successful on 14 September.

An Indian team climbed **Fluted Peak (6159m)** on the Karcha nala on 20 August. A team from Bengal climbed **Chau Chau Kang Nilda (6303m)** in Spiti on 30 August. Unfortunately one member, Sambhu Nath Gosh, died from altitude sickness.

**Snow Cone (6225m)** This peak rises above the Layul col (formerly Gunther's col) on the Bara Shigri glacier. An Indian party led by Soumajit Roy reached the col and attempted the peak on 16 and 19 August. They failed to climb the peak on both occasions owing to poor weather.

**Akela Killa (CB 46, 6006m)** in the Kulti valley was climbed on 2 September by a team from Bangalore. A team from Calcutta climbed the lovely peak **Gangstang (6162m)** in Lahul. They approached from the Nisang valley and summited on 2 September. Two teams from Bengal climbed **Karcha Parbat (6270m)**, on 28 August and 28 September respectively.

**Dharamsura (6446m)** A team from Bombay were defeated by heavy snowfall and strong winds in early June. They climbed the nearby peak of **Angdu Ri (5945m)** on 16 June.

**Ali Ratni Tibba (5490m)** in the Manikaran spires/Malana glacier area was attempted by a four-man Indian expedition. The expedition rode to Manali on two Enfield motorcycles and attempted the Scottish 1964 first ascent route up the steep ramp on the W face. They reached *c* 5000m. The route remains probably the most classic line in the whole area.

## Jammu and Kashmir

**Hagshu (6330m)** Access to the Kishtwar area from the usual approaches of Jammu is restricted. People climbing in these areas have had to use a long approach via Lahul or Zanskar. A Spanish expedition approached the mountain over Umasi La, via Zanskar. They established Camp 1 at 5700m near the rock wall and attempted the S ridge and SW face. Bad weather defeated their attempts and the expedition gave up on 26 August. John Barry and Seb Mankelow reached *c*6000m on the N face in September. (*See MEF Reports, ref. 94/28*)

**Arjun (6200m)** A German expedition attempted the E ridge and reached a high point on 24 September, when bad weather caught up with them. The party had problems with their guides and porters.

**Nun (7135m)** A British-American team led by Al Burgess attempted the W ridge, but gave up after lots of new snow and avalanche danger. A Spanish expedition climbed the E ridge of **Kun (7087m)** on 21 August.

## LINDSAY GRIFFIN & PAUL NUNN
# Pakistan 1994

Last summer in the Karakoram was one of the hottest on record. From early June through to August, parts of the range received little precipitation and expeditions to the higher peaks were relatively successful. However, many were also beaten because the weather was *too* good, excessive heat causing problems such as lack of snow cover and considerable rockfall. Those operating at lower altitudes needed to choose their routes carefully and most found it only feasible to climb through the coldest hours of the night. The months of June and July form the peak season in the Karakoram and the majority of teams climbing in August reported the last really clear weather around the middle of the month. In total there were 50 expeditions from 17 countries. 17 of the 29 expeditions to 8000m peaks were successful, but only four of the other 21 expeditions (above 6000m) succeeded.

The Pakistan government are still reviewing a possible introduction of permits and guides/liaison officers for teams climbing below 6000m in unrestricted areas. The well-known Pakistan mountaineer, Nazir Sabir, was recently elected to the Northern Area Council, defeating a member of the Hunza royal family and another candidate with a large following. This should benefit not only visitors, whose needs he understands well, but also the people of Northern Pakistan.

**K2** Thirteen climbers summited from Pakistan and four from China. The most notable events last season involved Basque mountaineers, who succeeded in climbing K2 from both sides. In 1983 the SSE Spur had been climbed to near a junction with the Abruzzi Spur by Andy Parkin, Jean Afanassieff, Roger Baxter-Jones and Doug Scott. In 1994 a six-man Basque team made a conventional fixed rope ascent of this route, reaching the summit on 24 June. The summiters were Juanito Oiarzabal (leader), Alberto and Felix Inurrategi, Enrique de Pablo and the Catalan Juan Tomas.

A strong American-Polish trio, Carlos Buhler, Wojciech Kurtyka and Krzysztof Wielicki, gave up their attempt on the W face and turned their attention to the SSE Spur. Also on this line were British mountaineer, Bill Barker, Australian Michael Groom and Americans Bruce Burns and Steve Untch, from Dave Bridges's USA organised expedition, whose primary objective had been the NW ridge. They changed to the SSE Spur, climbing to the shoulder on 8 July where they met with the well-known New Zealander Rob Hall and Finnish mountaineer Veikka Gustafsson. Most of these climbers stopped at the Shoulder but the next day Buhler, Hall, Groom, Gustafsson and Wielicki went for the summit. Having climbed through the Bottleneck and on towards the summit ridge, fatigue and the lateness of the hour caused the majority to opt for retreat. However, Hall, who was the only person using supplementary oxygen, still felt fresh and decided to continue. Twenty minutes later he made a radio call from the summit which was relayed by satellite to New Zealand. With this ascent, Hall became the first New Zealand climber to reach the summit of K2. His subsequent ascent of Cho Oyu in October 1994 completed a remarkable achievement: he had climbed four of the World's six highest peaks in one year (including Lhotse and Everest). The first tragedy on the mountain occurred two days later. A large Ukrainian expedition to the Abruzzi Spur lost three members in one accident – Dmitri Ibragimzade, Aleksei Kharaldin and Aleksandr Parkhomenko. American Steve Untch died on 26 July when a fixed rope broke. Having summited on 23 July, he was descending to help Michael Groom who was in trouble.

On the Chinese side, Basque, Italian and Anglo-American expeditions were active. On the latter, Alan Hinkes reached a high point of c8250m. (*For full details see 'The North Side of K2', pages 71 to 74.*) Two members of the Basque team summited on 30 July. Late on 4 August, Atxo Apellaniz and Juanjo San Sebastian also reached the top, in fine weather. Unable to descend more than 200m before dark, they were forced to make a high unplanned bivouac. Over the following days San Sebastian was avalanched 400m, but he (and later de la Cruz and Portilla who mounted a rescue operation) helped Apellaniz (suffering from cerebral oedema) down to 6900m, where he died. San Sebastian's evacuation was further delayed by repeated but unfulfilled promises of a helicopter by the Chinese. Back in Spain he lost parts of seven fingers but, remarkably under the circumstances, kept all his toes intact. The Italian team, led by Arturo Bergamaschi, were beaten by technical difficulties at nearly 8500m, whilst attempting to finish directly up the unclimbed top section of the true North Ridge.

This was the first season in the history of K2 that the mountain was climbed from both sides and the total number of ascents now stands at 113, with a high figure of 38 deaths.

**Broad Peak (8051m)** The main event on the mountain, and possibly the most significant achievement throughout the whole of the Karakoram last season, occurred on the 9 July, when the well-known Mexican climber, Carlos Carsolio, soloed the previously unclimbed SW buttress in a single push of 40 hours from Base Camp. He encountered Grade V rock and ice up to 70°. His was only the third route to be opened to the main summit of Broad Peak which is his ninth eight-thousander.

Eleven expeditions battled it out on the Normal Route. 1995 regulations in Pakistan should see this number reduced to a maximum of six. Only eight climbers appear to have been successful, though this year's events prove, as has long been suspected, that some mountaineers who claim to reach the top of Broad Peak actually stop at the foresummit, an hour or more short of the summit. Hans Kammerlander (South Tyrol) reached the summit on 21 June and left several metres of red and purple-coloured rope attached to a firmly placed ski pole immediately below the highest point. On his return, he mentioned nothing of this and was able to discreetly quiz many of the subsequent 'summiters' to ascertain whether their claims were true or false. His (Czech) expedition was sponsored by the French perfume company Yves Rocher and made a relatively comprehensive clean-up of the mountain and Base Camp area, transporting 30 porter loads of non-burnable garbage back to Skardu. They were highly critical of the lack of co-operation shown by other teams whilst carrying out an onerous but necessary task.

A three-man Swedish team led by Goran Kropp, attempted a new route on the S spur leading to the S shoulder. The main difficulties of this line lie in the steep ground between 5200m-7000m which had previously defeated several expeditions, including one involving the dynamic Kukuczka/Kurtyka partnership. The Swedes were unable to get higher than 6500m and quickly turned to the fast deepening trench of the Normal Route.

On 25 June, Kropp reached the second foresummit with Mats Holmgren, Australian Andrew Lock and Austrian Martina Bauer (daughter of Willi Bauer). There are two foresummits on the ridge before the main 8047m top. The first (8011m) has a rocky top and a little cairn, the second (8017m) is more snowy. Kropp was unsatisfied with his own performance yet rumours suggest that some of the other climbers made him promise that in any future debriefing he would not argue with a statement that everyone reached the true summit. Back at Base Camp the Austrians celebrated their success, whilst Kropp prepared for a second attempt. On 2 July, the same day that three other Austrian climbers reached the foresummit but celebrated a full ascent, he made the true summit in a single 18-hour push from Base. In a subsequent report the Austrian climbers rescinded their claim, admitting reaching only the foresummit, except for Bauer who steadfastly refuses to alter her story and a scenario of events hotly disputed by Kropp and the Swedish press.

Three expeditions were successful on **Gasherbrum 1 (Hidden Peak)** via the Gasherbrum La (the technically easier southern slopes being currently banned owing to their proximity to the Indo-Pakistan war zone). On 4 August Jonathan Pratt made the first British ascent, followed, on the 12th, by expedition doctor Andrew Collins and Daniel Mazur (USA). A day later Pratt, with two others, participated in an all-night rescue of a Bosnian climber who had suffered a stroke on neighbouring Gasherbrum 2. The victim had lain in his tent for three days before being reached by the rescuers. He was dragged down to Base Camp from c6000m in a sledge constructed from two blue plastic barrels. The team were also active in a major clean-up, which not only covered all camps on Gasherbrum 1 and the communal Gasherbrum Base Camps but extended to Camps 1 and 2 on the route to Gasherbrum 2. Abandoned tents, rope and rubbish were brought down, burnt or carried out. For 33-year-old Mazur this was his third 8000m peak. 35-year-old Pratt has now reached the summit of eight Himalayan peaks including the two above and a couple of high 7000ers.

**Gasherbrum 2**   Five expeditions attempted the standard Austrian route on this popular 8000m peak. Two were successful. On the Chinese side Kurt Diemberger, Rollo Steffans and Dr Erica Prokosch explored the N side of **K2** and the E faces of **Broad Peak** and **Hidden Peak**. Steffans and Diemberger also reached 5700m on **Gasherbrum 2**'s N ridge.

**Gasherbrum 3 (7980m)**   A British Royal Artillery MA team of eight climbers (leader Patrick Hickie) reached a high point of 7330m in an attempt, foiled by bad weather, to make the second ascent – by the original route climbed in 1975 by the Polish team (Alison Chadwick, her husband Janusz Onyskiewicz, Wanda Rutkiewicz, and Krzysztof Zdzitowiecki) via the col between G2 and 3 and the SE face.

Spanish expeditions to **Chogolisa** and **Uli Biaho (6527m)** were unsuccessful. Tomoyuki Watanabe's four-man Japanese team failed on a new route low down and right of the Norwegian Pillar on **Great Trango Tower NE (6231m)** after six pitches. On **Trango Tower (6239m)** Ki Soo Hwang's four-man Korean expedition also failed. On **Trango Pulpit,** a 5800m feature on the S side of the **Great Trango Tower** above the Dunge glacier, Stefan Eberhard and Julie Styles completed a new 600m big wall up the lower face. After fixing the initial pitches, the rest of the route went capsule-style using five ropes. In eight days in August they climbed 13 pitches, the first nine free and the rest on aid. Bolts were placed at each belay (*Trango Dreaming* VI Australian 19 A3+).

Seemingly only one expedition (Spanish) went to **Nanga Parbat** in 1994. Three climbers summited on the standard Kinshofer route on the Diamir Face in June, but another, Antonio Lopez, died.

Edi Birnbacher and Martin Goggelmann (Germany) explored the Thaille valley. From the roadhead at Daltir they walked to Bukma turning NE into a side valley and establishing Base Camp at 4200m, below the snout of the glacier. The weather in this region, which borders the Aling glacier SW of the Masherbrum Group, appears to have been poor in August, with plenty of rain. However, the duo managed to make the first ascent of a 5300m foresummit of **Daltir Peak** (their name) via its E face. The climbing was mixed with 65° snow and ice plus Grade III rock, the latter loose and rotten. The pair note that for whatever reasons (military and infrastructure seem the most likely) there was considerable evidence of new road building into remote valleys. An all-women British expedition attempted several peaks on the Aling glacier (*see MEF Reports, ref. 94/21*).

Two young British climbers went to the Gondogoro glacier area, repeating routes done during last year's UIAA Expeditions Commission Youth meet. Neil McKay and Peter Winterbottom tried **Cholon** twice, reaching 100m-200m below the summit on the second attempt. On 4 September they repeated **Madzenspitze (5700m)** in a 20-hour round trip, giving magnificent views of the 8000m peaks.

At 7388m, **Ultar** above Karimabad in Hunza remains one of the highest unclimbed massifs in the world. It retained its aura of impregnability last summer by shrugging off another two expeditions. The British team first made a reconnaissance of the N side from the Gulmit glacier, then Crag Jones and Steve Reid reached 5800m on a similar line to that taken by Saunders and Sustad in 1991, whilst Julian Freeman-Attwood and Ed Webster opted for a longer but objectively safer route, which would hit the E ridge much further down, below an ill-defined subsidiary summit of a little over 6000m named **Sarujet Sar.** They reached 6000m. A large Japanese team tried the S ridge integral from Altit, an enormous proposition but with less objective danger than other previously attempted routes on the S face. Yozaburoh Kurosaki was killed when a fixed rope was severed by rockfall at c6300m. Ultar has now been attempted by over a dozen expeditions.

**Shispare (7611m)** In July a Japanese expedition repeated the original route from the Pasu glacier (second ascent of the mountain). On 7 August a German expedition using skis repeated **Pasu Peak (7295m)**, a long glacial expedition from the east.

**Momhil Sar (7343m)** defeated a five-man Spanish team who tried the unclimbed E ridge above the col connecting Momhil to Trivor. Like Hans Schell in 1964, they found it too difficult. Schell had then traversed out left to the easier S ridge to complete the ascent.

**Diran** attracted six expeditions in the summer of 1994. One is believed to have reached the S ridge from the Upper Bagrot glacier to avoid avalanche danger, an approach explored in 1954 by Rebitsch's expedition. The others used the normal N face/W ridge route. Jon Tinker's commercial expedition failed because of deep avalanche snow low on the N face in December. Dave Wilkinson, Bill Church, Brian Davison and Tony Park were active in the Hispar area (*see MEF Reports, ref. 94/36*).

**Laila (6985m)** N of **Haramosh** was attempted by a Japanese expedition. They tried the E ridge from the junction of the Haramosh and Chogolungma glaciers. They appear to have been stopped more from lack of fixing rope than from insurmountable difficulty or weather problems.

Brendan Murphy (Ireland) and Dave Wills (New Zealand), recipients of the Nick Estcourt award for 1994, tried the N ridge of **Latok 1 (7145m).** They commented upon rubbish from base camps contaminating even this relatively unvisited area (*see MEF Reports, ref. 94/42*).

In Chitral repeats were made of **Dirgol Zom (6788m)** by the E ridge, **Gul Lasht Zom (6665m)** and **Nobaisum Zom (7070m)**. Three British climbers, Annabelle Barker, Pru Cartwright and Margaret Clennett, visited Babu base camp (4960m), used to reach the north side of Tirich Mir, and visited the valley south of Bandok, noting climbing potential and some good granite. A British team led by Dave Wilson explored the Hindu Raj (*see MEF Reports, ref. 94/12*).

*Thanks are due to Xavier Eguskitza, Adrian Burgess, Edi Birnbacher, Geoff Birtles, Jim Curran, Julian Freeman-Attwood, Joakim Gronvik, Alan Hinkes, Daniel Mazur, Józef Nyka, Abdul Quddus, Imtaz Ali, Taleh Mohammad and Nazir Sabir for help in compiling these notes.*

# Nepal 1994

Overall the news from Nepal for 1994, like the curate's egg, is a mixture of good and bad ! Let's begin with the good news.

**Entry Visas** The price of a Nepalese visa came down on 1st July. A single entry visa now costs $15 for up to 15 days and $25 for up to 30 days. A double entry visa for not more than 30 days is now $40 and a multiple entry visa is $60 for 60 days or less. Visas may be extended for $1 per day – so there you have it, Nepal on a dollar a day. Tour and trek leaders can get a non-tourist visa which is valid for six to twelve months.

**Trekking Permits** Whilst on the subject of fees and permits, a Standard Trekking Permit to open areas costs $5 per person per week for the first four weeks and $10 after that. For Lower Dolpo and the Kangchenjunga region the price doubles. For Humla the cost is $90 per week. Manaslu is also $90 between September and November falling to $75 outside that period. For Upper Mustang and Dolpo the fee is a staggering $700 for the first 10 days plus $70 per day thereafter.

**Trekking Peak Permits** Thankfully the price for these remains stable. The fee for up to ten climbers is $300 for the twelve highest peaks and $150 for the remaining six. The permit enables you to spend one month at or above base camp. There is no restriction on what route you climb. You can extend this permit for two weeks at a cost of 25% of the original fee. Additional members cost $7.50 per day.

The bad news is there has been an increase in accidents, particularly on trekking peaks. On Pisang Peak in the Manang Himal a large DAV group were avalanched below the summit, resulting in the death of ten trekkers and one Sherpa. The accident highlights the problem of both large commercial trips and the name, or misnomer, 'trekking peaks'.

The Khumbu was much quieter this year with far fewer expeditions on the major summits. Post-monsoon 1993 saw 80 expeditions in Nepal whereas in Spring 1994 there were just 17.

**Ama Dablam, 6852m** A new and difficult route was climbed on the SE face by a Russian expedition. Best seen from near the Khare glacier below the Mingbo La, the face is a stunning triangle of rock and ice. It was climbed in good style without fixed ropes during a 7-day push. The summit was reached on the 28 April by Sergei Bogomolov, Vladimir Beshkirov, Dimitry Botev and Sergei Golubtsov.

**Baruntse, 7129m** A four-man Swiss team climbed the standard S ridge reaching the summit on 4 May. During April a Czech expedition climbed a variation of the 1983 Dutch route on the W face of the N summit above the Imja glacier. The Czech route appears to follow the Dutch line low down but climbs directly through rock bands to reach the N ridge at circa 6500m. They descended the Dutch route.

**Cho Oyu, 8201m** An international expedition led by Mal Duff was successful via the standard West Ridge route after approaching the mountain via the Nangpa La from Nepal to Tibet. From BC at 5000m and ABC at 5500m four further camps were established at 5900m, 6300m, 6800m and 7400m. On 8 May 1994 at 4am Mal Duff (UK), Neil Lindsey (UK), Clive Jones (NZ), José Delgado (Venezuela) and Sherpa Pasang Gombu reached the summit. The descent, which took several days, required great strength and concentration in rapidly deteriorating weather. (*Józef Nyka*)

**Dhaulagiri, 8167m** The success of the Italian–International expedition led by Marco Berti was marred by a fatal accident. Marco Bianchi and Christian Kuntner of Italy summited on 25 September accompanied by the Swiss Paul-Victor Amaudruz. Next day Raymond D Caughron (USA), Joao Garcia (Portugal), Józef Gozdzik (Italy) and Piotr Pustelnik (Poland) reached the summit. During the descent they met the Swiss Robert Bächler who gave up the attempt and descended, apparently suffering from high-altitude sickness. Some minutes later he slipped and fell to his death down the NE face. (*Józef Nyka*)

**Everest** 'Forty-one years on' doesn't have quite the same ring and to prove it there were only four expeditions in the Western Cwm compared with 15 in 1993. All teams summited with 37 climbers reaching the top.

A Japanese team led by Mitsyoshi Hongou climbed the South Pillar, first climbed by the Poles in 1980. Seven Sherpas and three members reached the summit on 8 and 13 May.

There were three commercial expeditions. One, an American environmental expedition led by Steven Goryl, put six on top including Sherpa Lobsang Janbu without bottled oxygen. Janbu had already summited in 1993 at the age of 20 without supplementary oxygen. This time he climbed the mountain wearing traditional Sherpa clothing (Bakhu). Brent Bishop, son of Barry Bishop who summited with the Americans in 1963, also reached the top. This expedition is said to have removed two tons of rubbish from the mountain, including 200 discarded oxygen bottles.

Another American expedition led by Tom Burleson put a total of ten on top. Pete Athans was a member of the party; this was his fourth ascent of the mountain.

A third American group, the 'Sagarmatha Clean Up Expedition' had a 100% success rate when all eight members and three Sherpas reached the summit. New Zealand Guide Rob Hall joined Athans in being the only non-Sherpas to have summited four times. In the summit party was Norwegian adventurer and non-climber Erling Kagge. Kagge claims to be the first person to have reached the 'Three Poles' under his own steam, although a South Korean has already laid claim to that one. Kagge claims, however, that the Korean did not begin his South Pole trip at the coast.

Post-monsoon, the British Mount Everest Medical Expedition, led by Dr Simon Currin, put two doctors, Charlie Hornsby and Roddy Kirkwood, with Sherpas Dorje and Dawa Temba, on the summit. (*See MEF Reports, Ref. 94/1*)

**Ganji Kang 7038m** This remote peak, close to the Tibetan border north of Manaslu, was climbed by a joint Japanese/Nepalese expedition. Not on the permitted list, the first ascent was made possible only by a joint expedition – an approach used with much success by the Japanese. The ascent, made in October, included five members from the Nepalese police.

**Langshisha Ri, 6427m** The greatest single adventure in Nepal during the 1994 post-monsoon season was that of the lone Slovenian climber Vanja Furlan who climbed the hitherto unconquered 1700m high NW face (WNW face) of the Langshisha Ri (6427m) in the Langtang Himal. Furlan set out on 7 October at 11.30am from BC at Langshisha Karki (4150m) without a sleeping-bag but with two 50m ropes. He bivouacked on a big sérac at 5820m. The steep upper part of the face offered ice of 65°-70° with 2 sections of 80°. On 8 October at 12 noon Furlan reached the summit. He graded the route ED, II-IV, V, 60°-80°. The descent was by the Japanese first ascent route (1982) on the S face, where 500m were covered by abseiling. Thus he completed the first traverse of the mountain. This was Furlan's second spectacular achievement this year: on 28 May he made the ascent of Siniolchu (6887m) in Sikkim. (*Józef Nyka*)

**Lhotse** A Swedish permit included several well-known names including Viesturs, Hall and Carlos Carsolio from Mexico. Having first climbed Cho Oyu, Carsolio flew into the Khumbu by helicopter on 7 May. On 9 May Swedish climbers Oskar Kihlborg and Mikael Reutersward climbed the mountain. On May 13 Carsolio climbed the W face and returned to BC within 24 hours. This was his eighth 8000er including the five highest summits. A week after climbing Everest, Hall and Viesturs reached the summit of Lhotse on 15 May. Climbing from Camp 4 on the Lhotse Face they reached the summit in 3 hours.

**Urkinmang 6151m** A Japanese expedition led by Tamotsu Ohnishi climbed a new route on the N face. A camp and over 2000ft of fixed rope were used to siege the face. Five Japanese and three Sherpas reached the summit. This delightful mountain between Dorji Lhakpa and Gangchempo is in the Jugal Himal and towers above Tilman's Col. The mountain was first climbed by the Japanese in 1964 from the south and there have since been several unofficial ascents.

# H ADAMS CARTER
# North America 1994

## Alaska

The most remarkable climbs done in Alaska in 1994 were two new ascents on the N buttress of Mt Hunter (4441m). This very difficult 1200m high buttress has for some years attracted climbers and had three routes on it, the most prized being the 1981 *Moonflower Buttress*. In 1994, Bill Belcourt and Randy Rackliff made this route's fourth ascent and two other strong parties failed.

In early May, Marc Twight and Scott Backes climbed six pitches on a route to the left of the Moonflower route, but backed off, feeling it was not appropriate for their speed-dependent style. At 1am on 15 May, they started up a line to the right of the Moonflower route. They climbed through four difficult rock bands and up ice as steep as 90° until finally at 6am on May 17 they surmounted the buttress and started up the NE ridge, which leads to the summit. They called their route *Deprivation*. The other new route, *Wall of Shadows*, was climbed by Michael Kennedy and Greg Child. It lies to the left of the Moonflower Buttress and to the right of the 1984 French route. This pair climbed in a more conventional fashion and spent two days fixing six ropes. The route follows ice runnels linked by serious rock pitches. On 25 May, Kennedy and Child set out with ten days' food and fuel. The climbing here was extremely hard; after the third bivouac, it took Child a whole day to climb two A4 pitches.

On **Mt McKinley (Denali)** Mark Aspery, Ron Bauer, Marcus Brown, Tahoe Rowland, Mike Vanderbeck and Tom Whalen made the first ascent of the entire 12-mile-long S buttress. Austrian Andreas Orgler and a companion climbed the W faces of **Eyetooth** and **Sugartooth** above the Ruth gorge. Jeff Apple Benowitz and Michael Litzow made the first ascent of the N ridge of **Mather**.

New routes were also climbed on **Stalagmite Spire, Flattop, Nevermore (Kichatna Spires), Mount Torbert (3479m) (Tordrillo Mountains)** and **Burkett** (SE Alaska).

## Canada

There was much activity on Baffin Island in the Canadian Arctic, in particular on the North Tower of Asgard, where Noel Craine, Paul Pritchard, Steve Quinlan and Jordi Tosas climbed *Hyperborea* (*see 'Hammering the Anvil', pages 47-51*).

A second remarkable ascent, made by Americans Chris Breemer and Brad Jarrett, was named *Valkyrie*. This line ascended the N face. The pair had only two days of really good weather, but persisted despite the extreme difficulties and reached the top in late July. A Swiss team attempted the W face between the two previously mentioned ascents, reaching halfway in miserable weather. Germans also made some fine new routes, in particular one they called *13 Pieces of Candy* which lies behind **Mt Breidablik**. Canadians Ben Webster, Claude Berube and François-Guy Thirvèrge climbed the SW face and ridge of **Mt Thor**.

Canadians were busy making new routes in **Yukon Territory.** Graham Rowbotham, Tony Hunter, Bob Koen and New Zealander Andrew Scrase climbed the E peak of **McArthur Peak (4308m)** by the S face. A new route on the NE face of **Pinnacle Peak (3714m)** was made by David Scott, Grant Streatham, Mark Austin and Mike Dare. John Chilton, Rich Prokaska and Jim Condon made the first ascent of **Atlantic Peak (4879m)**, which lies close to **Lucania.**

In the **Logan Mountains** of the North West Territories, Kurt Smith and Scott Cosgrove made the fourth ascent of **Proboscis**, by a hard new route on the SE face. Farther south, in late August, Greg Child, Greg Collum and Steve Maseoli climbed a long new route on **Mt Combatant** in the **Coast Range** of British Columbia. At the end of July, Gray Thompson, Steve Sheriff and Jon Turk made the first ascent of the W face of **Little Snowpatch Spire** in the **Bugaboos**. This seems to have been only the second ascent of the peak.

# Continental United States

In **Yosemite** the highlight was Lynn Hill's 23-hour free ascent of the *Nose* of **El Capitan** on 19-20 September, accompanied by Steve Sutton. Scott Franklin and Steve Schneider made a 13-hour free climb, the first, of the 23-pitch regular NW face of Half Dome.

On the *Muir Wall* Kurt Smith and Scott Cosgrove were cited by the Park Service for having used a power drill to place belay anchors in a Wilderness area after climbing 31 pitches of the 34 pitches free and then aiding to the top.

In the **SW Deserts**, Cameron Burns and Luke Laeser climbed a new route on the 500m E face of **Shiprock**. Climbing there is illegal except when permission is given by the Navajos. This was done and the pair spent many hours picking up tourist trash as a token of thanks.

Jeff Lowe has developed the art of ice climbing to a fine point. His ascent of *Octopussy* near Vail, Colorado was accomplished with the use of possibly the most advanced ice technique yet seen.

CHRIS CHEESEMAN

# South America and Antarctica 1994

*The author would like to thank Marcello Scanu, Franci Savenc and Daniel Lazo for their help in preparing these notes.*

Under the direction of the Union d'Alpissimo Association Montagna (UPAM), training courses for climbing competitions have been taking place in most of the Latin American countries, which may give rise to some interesting developments. Much of the exciting mountaineering activity in Latin America during 1994 has been achieved by alpinists moving fast and light and has been concentrated on Argentina. Anybody looking for a hill to climb in 1995 should get a copy of Jill Neate's *Mountaineering in the Andes*, available from the Expedition Advisory Service.

## Ecuador
A combined team from Britain and the Institutio Geografico Militar climbed **Chimborato** and **Cotopaxi** and surveyed these two mountains using GPS. As a result, **Chimborato** (the highest peak in Ecuador) was found to be 42m below the accepted height of 6310m and the new figure looks likely to become accepted. The accepted height of Cotopaxi and the GPS height were virtually the same. Also on Cotopaxi, no less than 52 climbers summited between 28 and 29 May!

## Peru
Contrary to popular rumour abounding in the previous year, there are no plans to introduce any peak fees or regulations to control mountaineering. Overall, the recent terrorist activity perpetrated by 'Sendero Luminoso' is diminishing, but particular care should still be exercised in the Cordillera Huayhuash area. The situation between Peru and Ecuador on the border is delicate, to say the least, with military activity taking place across the border. The weather in Peru seemed to be less predictable than normal.

Slovenians Kosiv and Kecuan completed a new route on the SW wall of **Artensorajo**. A new route on **Chashan Oeste** was completed via the narrow E ridge to the lower W summit (5701m). An Australian ascent of the ENE face of **Jangyranu (5630m)** is also reported on good granite rock.

## Bolivia
Matthew Wetherall, Simon Shercliff and Ben Reynolds mapped and explored the Bolivian Altiplano area and climbed **Huayana Potosi (6088m)** in generally good weather conditions (*see MEF Reports, ref 94/40*).

## Argentina

Many of the formerly 'classified' maps are now 'de-classified' and are available. Also, from the Argentine Geographic Military Institute, is a series of revised heights for a number of peaks, including Fitzroy and Cerro Torre. Elections are due in 1995, but the political situation appears unlikely to change a great deal. Better access and improved facilities are increasing the popularity of Argentina's mountain areas.

British climber Mike Turner led an expedition to attempt the **S Tower of Paine**, but was forced to modify his objectives in the light of poor weather conditions and bad conditions on the route itself. No further details are available at present.

A new Normal Route has been established on Aconcagua in an attempt to reduce the environmental impact of climbers in the area. The new route is called *Via de los Guias de Medoza* and is reported to be to the left of the *Filo Sur Oeste* at the same grade as the original route.

**Pissis (6875m)** Sverre Aarseth made a solo ascent of the W summit (27° 45' 17" S, 68° 47' 56" W). Base Camp was on the northern side, using a new approach from Copiapo. An altitude of 6895m (+/- 50m) was measured by GPS (WGS 84). There is a correction of −20m for reduction to the local spheroid.

A serious new route on **Cerro Torre**'s S face by Slovenian climbers Janez Jeglic, Marco Lukic and Miha Praprotnik called *What's Love Got To Do With It* in the Banana Crack area goes at ED4 with A4, technical VIII- and 90° ice. The 22-pitch ascent required a great deal of aid climbing, 770m of fixed rope and only four pitches were completed each day. Britain's Andy Parkin and François Martigny attempted a new route via a 750m ice couloir to the Col of Hope on 60° to 80° ice. After several delays the pair were forced to abandon the summit owing to deteriorating bad weather. The 750m ice route was named *Lost Times*. **Cerro Torre**'s second solo ascent was achieved on 11 February by New Zealander Atholl Whimp and the first Australian ascent was performed by Andrew Linblade.

José Chaverri and Teo Plaza missed the summit of **Cerro Stanhardt (2730m)** by its E face by only 40m. Their retreat was forced owing to severe injuries sustained by Plaza earlier in the climb. The 1200m-high wall gave difficult climbing of VI and VII with pitches of A1 and A2. Plaza was tragically swept to his death in an avalanche only a few months later. Chaverri was himself later involved in an accident whilst attempting **Torre Egger** by the E face.

**Torre de la Media Luna** saw a bold solo on a new line by Ermanno Salvaterra. *Rubio y Azur* is a 400m route starting to the right of the 1988 Italian attempt, following the prominent First Pillar. Casimiro Ferrari and Martin Ceballos climbed a new route on the E face of **Aguja Mermoz**, the exact line of which is not clear but is 650m in length with difficulties of V+ and A3.

An Austrian team led by Dr M Kremsner completed the first E–W traverse of Glacier Tyndall, claiming the first ascents of three modest peaks: **Cerro Reina Maria Theresa (1165m)**, **Cerro Trillizo Sur (1270m)** and **Cerro Matrimonio (1710m)**.

## Chile
This season's efforts in the **Paine** area were marred by three deaths in separate incidents. Apart from the notable Spanish activity, seen below, there was not a great deal of activity this year.

On the **Central Tower of Paine**, part of a strong eight-man Spanish team began a new line between *Magico Este* and *Belena de los Vientos*, completing 500m of this 1000m wall with only three out of the 15 pitches being climbed free (VII/VII+ A3). The team hopes to return and complete the route. Meanwhile, the other part of the team completed the second ascent of the Italian line *Magico Este* (VII A3).

## Tierra del Fuego
In December 1994 Doug Scott experienced his first taste of 'sea mountaineering' when he joined an expedition based on the yacht *Pelagic*. The skipper and principal owner of the yacht was the world-renowned sailor James (Skip) Novak from Chicago. From Punta Arenas they sailed due south down the Straits of Magellan towards the western end of the Cordillera Darwin range. On 8 December, with difficulty, they finally reached the summit (Alpine TD inf) of a *c*6000ft peak in the Cordon Navarro which they named *Mt Pelagic*, 'although,' as Doug Scott said, 'we cannot be sure it had not been climbed before by Jack Miller's American group during a remarkable visit in 1966'. The view from the summit revealed a wealth of unclimbed peaks, particularly in the area north of Agostini Fjord. Other members of the climbing party were Julian Freeman-Attwood and Francis McDermot.

## South Georgia
Eight members from the 1st Royal Irish Regiment made the first ascent of **Pt 2296ft** on the Lyall glacier, Georgia, giving a route of Alpine PD. Current information on walking and climbing can be found in the log at Grytriken's Whaling Museum. A significant degree of glacial recession is reported in this area.

## Antarctica
In January-February 1994 Skip Novak sailed to the Antarctic Peninsula with two teams who had both climbing and filming objectives. Heavy pack ice prevented any landing in Crystal Sound, but a landing was made instead on the small island of Duchaylard. Two first ascents were made: of **Mt Duff (1822ft)**, the highest peak on the island, via the W ridge and the S face (Scottish IV and V) and of **Mt Williams (4970ft)** on Anvers Island. (*See 'Antarctica: Voyage of the Pelagic', pages 75-81*)

SIMON RICHARDSON

# Scottish Winter 1993-94

Scottish winter climbers will remember the 1993/94 winter as one of the best in recent years. It was a record season with over 140 new routes reported, reflecting a sustained level of intense activity by an ever-increasing number of winter enthusiasts. In contrast to previous lean winters which focused attention on mixed climbs, this season saw the best ice conditions since 1986. Unfortunately, there were few periods of stable weather, an essential ingredient for success on long and difficult winter climbs, so there were only 50 new routes graded V and over, compared with nearly 70 during the more settled winter of 1986. Full details of the winter's routes can be found in the 1994 *Scottish Mountaineering Club Journal*, but a selection of the season's important repeats and significant first ascents are described below.

## Northern Highlands

On **Beinn Bhan** there was considerable activity in Coire nam Fhamhair, with the exciting 400m long expedition of *Die Riesenwand* (VI, 5) receiving several ascents. The most important event was the first free ascent of Mick Fowler and Phil Butler's *Great Overhanging Gully* (VI, 7) by Dave Hesleden and Chris Cartwright which had successfully intimidated several strong teams in recent years intent on a repeat. On the nearby **Meall Gorm**, Graeme Ettle and John Lyall found *Blue in the Face* (VI, 7) an unlikely mixed line up the wall to the left of Lobster Gully. Further inland on **Fuar Tholl**, Hesleden and Simon Richardson found the SE cliff in immaculate condition and added *Il Duce* (VII, 7), the much-fancied thin ice line to the left of *Tholl Gate*.

Further north in Torridon, Coire Dubh Mor on **Liathach** was the scene for the boldest new route of the winter when Hesleden and Cartwright climbed the prominent icefall between *Poacher's Fall* and *Test Department*. After a mixed entry pitch, Hesleden tensioned onto the icefall and made a precarious 25m lead up 80° ice only 1 to 2cm thick. Four more pitches up steep (but thicker!) ice then led to the top. *Foobarbundee* is graded VIII,7 and ranks alongside Fowler's *West Central Gully* on Beinn Eighe as the hardest ice climb in the country.

The secluded Coire Ghranda on **Beinn Dearg** came of age with six new IIIs and IVs by Andy Nisbet and Brian Davison. Eager to capitalise on the excellent conditions, Nisbet later indulged in a soloing spree resulting in five new grade IVs and over 600m of new climbing. Further north in **Coigach**, the *Fhidhleir's Nose Direct* (VII, 8) saw its third and fourth winter ascents over the cold and snowy New Year period. This compelling 300m-high feature is surrounded by sea on three sides and is rarely in condition. On **Quinag**, Roger Webb and Simon Steer made a winter ascent of *Raeburn's Route* on Barrel Buttress (V, 6), and in the far north on **Foinaven**, Neil Wilson took advantage of good ice on **Creag Dubh**, with four new routes in the vicinity of his 1992 route *Overseer*. The best addition was *Columbian Couloir* (V,5) climbed with José Luis Bermúdez.

## The Cairngorms

After the intense development of recent years, activity in the Northern Corries was fairly quiet, although three technical snowed-up rock routes were added to Coire an Lochain by Nisbet, Ettle, Bruce Goodlad and Jonathan Preston. The remote Garbh Choire Mor on **Braeriach** was the scene for the hardest addition in the Cairngorms when Nisbet succeeded on *Hot Lips* (VI, 7) on his third visit with Preston and Davison. Also of note was *Virago* (V, 6), the line of grooves and roofs between *She Devil's Buttress* and *Vulcan*, by Roger Everett and Richardson.

## Creag Meagaidh

The heavy January snowfall resulted in excellent ice build-up on The Pinnacle, and *The Fly Direct* (VII, 6) saw well over a dozen ascents and is now firmly established as one of Scotland's greatest ice climbs. Further right, Andy Perkins and Nick Woods added *White Knuckle Ride* (VI, 6), a steep thin ice pencil to the left of *Pinnacle Buttress Direct*.

## Ben Nevis

Excellent conditions drew the crowds, with routes such as *Astronomy* (VI, 5), *The Shield Direct* (VII, 7), *Gemini* (VI, 6) and *Waterfall Gully True Finish* (VI, 6), which have rarely been in condition over the past few winters, all seeing ascents. There were several new mixed routes with *Slanting Slit* (VI, 6) on Fives Wall by Mal Duff and Steve Greenhaugh, and *The Edge of Beyond* (V, 5) on the East Flank of Tower Ridge by Colin Stead and Doug Lang, being of particular note.

Visiting French guides Godefroy Perroux and François Damilano got the pick of the ice. Perroux and Jim Blyth climbed *Place your Bets* (VI, 6), the prominent icefall joining the slanting rake of *Wendigo*, whilst Damilano pieced together *The Roar of the Bull* (VII, 6), a tenuous line of ice smears between *The Bullroar* and *The Shadow* on Carn Dearg Buttress.

## Glen Coe

The most significant ascent was on the Rannoch Wall of **Buachaille Etive Mor** where Mark Garthwaite and Andy Clarke added *Fear of a Flat Planet* (VII, 8) - a very bold hooking exercise. On **Bidean**, Andy Cave and Duff climbed the sensationally steep *Un Poco Loco* (VII, 7) which climbs through the Arch left of *Crypt Route*.

## Southern Highlands

Big news here was the long-awaited second ascent of the compelling line of *Messiah* (VII, 7) on **Creag an Socach** by Hesleden and Cartwright in less than optimum conditions in early January. Heavy snow cover made the first two mixed pitches awkward, and the top icy groove was only thinly iced. The third ascent was made by Clarke and Garthwaite in February, who also made a winter ascent of *Punster's Crack* (VI, 8) on **The Cobbler**.

## Orkneys: The Old Man of Hoy

In autumn 1994 the Old Man of Hoy was climbed by Mike Banks, with Richard Sykes (aged 61) and Dave Parker. Just approaching his 72nd birthday, Mike established a new age record for the climb, beating his own previous age record which he won several years ago.

# A Note on the new Scottish Winter Grading System

In 1992 a two-tier system for grading Scottish winter climbs was introduced. This was a direct result of the dramatic increase in the popularity of Scottish winter climbing, and the surge in standards throughout the 1980s. The new system has gained widespread acceptance and is now used in all new Scottish guidebooks. It works in a similar way to summer E grades, with a Roman numeral encompassing the overall difficulty of the route including seriousness, protection, sustainedness and length. The second digit reflects the technical difficulty of the hardest pitch or crux sequence. It is not intended to use the system for multiple-pitch gradings.

Taken together, the two numbers can either capture the serious nature of a Ben Nevis ice climb, or the well protected technical intricacies of a Cairngorm mixed route. The new Scottish grades should not be confused with the French and Canadian two-tier systems, which grade ice climbs based on their technical difficulty, with an additional seriousness rating.

By adopting an open-ended scale, no downgrading of existing climbs has been necessary, and *Point Five Gully* on Ben Nevis is taken as the benchmark V, 5 ice climb. This great classic is relatively straightforward compared with many recent climbs, and some of the hardest Scottish winter routes, such as *The Needle* on the Shelter Stone, merit grades as high as VIII, 8.

The following table of benchmark routes and keynote grades illustrates how the system works. The benchmark routes are all well known or celebrated climbs and are representative of the main climbing areas.

SCOTTISH WINTER CLIMBS - REMOTE GRADES

| | Snowed-up Rock | Mixed | Ice Gullies | Thin Face | Ice |
|---|---|---|---|---|---|
| | Techniques mainly include torquing and use of frozen turf. Great care must be taken not to damage the rock with peg placements, axe and crampon scratches, etc. | Mainly turf, iced cracks or sections of thin ice. Normally less well protected than snowed-up rock routes | Classic Scottish gullies – mainly ice. | Typical of many Ben Nevis routes – thin ice or névé over steep open slabs. Often very bold with limited protection. | Icefalls or ice smears. Harder routes may involve thin brittle ice or free hanging sections. |
| IV, 3<br>IV, 4<br>IV, 5<br>IV, 6 | Fingers Ridge<br>Aladdin's Buttress Original<br>The Message | Tough Brown Traverse<br>Observatory Ridge<br>Route Major (Etchachan) | Green Gully<br>Emerald Gully<br>–<br>– | Brimstone Groove<br>Platform's Rib<br>–<br>– | Farenheit 451<br>The Screen<br>–<br>– |
| V, 4<br>V, 5<br>V, 6<br>V, 7 | Mitre Ridge<br>Savage Slit<br>Hooker's Corner | 1959 Face Route<br>Scorpion<br>Sticil Face | Zero Gully<br>Point Five Gully<br>–<br>– | Indicator Wall<br>Orion Direct<br>–<br>– | The Pumpkin<br>Poacher's Fall<br>–<br>– |
| VI, 5<br>VI, 6<br>VI, 7<br>VI, 8 | Parallel Buttress<br>Fallout Corner<br>Savage | Die Riesenwand<br>Tower Face of the Comb<br>Crypt | North Post Direct<br>Minus One Gully<br>–<br>– | Slav Route<br>Galactic Hitchhiker<br>–<br>– | Astral Highway<br>Mega Route X<br>–<br>– |
| VII, 6<br>VII, 7<br>VII, 8<br>VII, 9 | Central Grooves<br>Citadel<br>Ventricle | The White Elephant<br>The Shield Direct<br>Trail of Tears | The Fly Direct<br>West Central Gully<br>–<br>– | Pointless<br>The Ayatollah<br>–<br>– | The Shroud<br>Tubular Bells<br>–<br>– |

Simon Richardson
October 1994

TONY HOWARD

# Middle East 1994

## Oman

Since the publication of Alec MacDonald's guide to *Rock Climbing in Oman* (distributed by Cordee), and Alec's departure from the country, development has been taken over by Jerry Hadwin. He is currently (January 1995) rumoured to have set his sights on another major route on **Jebel Misht**'s 1500m S face, having added a route of his own to this huge wall earlier in 1994 at VS grade between The Nose and the SE Pillar.

## The United Arab Emirates

John Gregory and friends have been busy in recent years, in particular at **Ras Al Khaimah**, bordering the western edge of Mussandam. He writes:

'The United Arab Emirates has recently become a very popular holiday destination, possibly because sunshine is almost guaranteed for 12 months of the year. Very little rock climbing has been done so far, but there is vast potential for routes of up to 300m-400m on many of the walls in the various wadis. The rock is limestone and can vary from very solid to horribly loose.

'Some 300m routes have been done in **Wadi Bih** and another smaller crag has produced 30 routes that have all been documented. Once the routes have been climbed and the loose rock eliminated they have proved to be varied and of good quality. Some routes were done as straight leads and others were cleaned off first. We have used only natural protection. The grades are generally about VS with a few HVS, E1 and E2.

'The best places are in the north of the country between Ras Al Khaimah on the west coast and Dibba on the east coast, an area of mountains known as the **Ru'us Al Jibal**. They form part of the Musandam Peninsula which protrudes northwards to the Straights of Hormuz at the entrance to the Gulf. These mountains rise to 2000m and also provide excellent scope for walking. All the main peaks have been explored and have provided many interesting and demanding walks of up to 14 hours. Exploring is the operative word as it has been very much a question of trying a route and seeing what happens. Success in reaching a summit is never certain as there are many steep rock bands barring access.

'The best time to visit is between November and March. The daily temperatures drop to around 20° in January. There is always a chance of rain during these months, which can be very heavy at times but rarely lasts for more than a few hours and the rock and wadis dry very quickly.

'A local contact would be very useful as there are no maps or guidebooks available. Access to the mountains is usually by 4-wheel drive and these can be hired. There are some superb spots for camping and the lack of people and the peace of the wadis is one of the area's great attractions.'

## Yemen

Local politics continue in turmoil. Sandstone and limestone cliffs have been reported with apparently good potential, but little or no development. The Shibam area was visited by Newcastle University Exploration Society where they reported sandstone cliffs with 'varied climbing offering a wide range of grades, but with little natural protection'. Travel is currently possible but not easy (it depends on your chosen destination) and permission to visit and climb in remote areas is unlikely.

## Jordan

This continues to be the major destination and area of development for climbing and trekking – especially so now that the borders with Israel are open and flight costs are reduced by 50%! For £170 it is now possible to fly to Eilat, where a couple of taxi rides will take you into Wadi Rum. Conversely the influx of tourism has led to an unprecedented leap in prices in Jordan. To get to Petra now costs £20 instead of £3 (unless you use your navigational skills to locate one of the 'backways'!). Prices in Rum for 4-wheel drive and camels have risen by about 30%, so be prepared to bargain hard or to get a small group together to climb in the more remote places such as Barrah Canyon.

Rising costs however have not stopped development. The most important contributors in 1994 were Austrian climbers Albert Precht and Ziggi Brochlmeier. The big shady N wall of **Jebel Kharazeh** (450m, UIAA 6), rising from the narrow gloomy depths of the Canyon of Zernouk el Daber, typifies their bold and fast ascents. It was matched by a route of similar grade and length on the opposite canyon wall, ascending **Jebel um Ishrin**. They also added two more routes to their own Vulcanics Tower on **Jebel Rum** and Precht completed his 600th new route on the S ridge of **Draif al Muragh**, to the south of the Nassrani Towers.

Also in the area last spring, Di Taylor, Mick Shaw and I continued our relaxed search for more esoteric gems following someone's plea in the New Routes book for 'more short climbs'. In the easily accessible maze of ravines in Rakabat Canyon, we and a team headed by Geoff Hornby added five new routes with grades of 5, 5+ and 6A (French grades are used throughout). These two English teams also spent time exploring more remote corners. Out east of Barrah, Hornby's team found a new dome and added some 5+ slab routes, and to the SE Pete Bishops climbed *Freedom as a concept* (6A) up the first pitch of the still unclimbed horrendous gash left of Doug Scott's *Guelta Grooves*. Over on Burdah the same group added two 450m slab routes up the E face, at TD and TD inf, finishing at the summit, and two shorter climbs also on the E face slabs at 5+ and 6A in the area of *Orange sunshine*.

Meanwhile, we were sniffing around the domes of Abu Khsheibah with young Bedouin climber Atieeq Auda (proud owner of the fastest camel in the valley!). Ascents included *Macho Man and the Granny* (5), to the recently discovered dome of **Jebel Farata Shaib** and, facing it, *The Gorgon* (5+) to another new top - **Jebel Dugranji.**

On the next dome to the west, members of this group also added *Walking the Plank* (5+) to the top of **Jebel Ikhnaisser** up the obvious northern black slab.

French Guides, Wilf Colonna and Bernard Domench were once again in Rum in the autumn. They too added numerous two and three-pitch routes of good quality in the Abu Khsheibah area as well as in Rakabat and Barrah Canyons and out near Disi to the NW.

More recently, Atieeq Auda solved the long unanswered question of the south-western approach to **Jebel Rum**'s summit by guiding Julian McIntosh and Joy Shand to the top in December 1994, up the huge and obvious canyon S of *Sabbah's Route* - 'a great day out'.

On a more ominous note, four young Austrians spent a few days creating a bolted sports-climbing crag just 10 minutes walk from the Rest House. We, and most other climbers visiting Rum, feel that the area should be preserved as an adventure climbing area, not a bolted playground. We took the bolts out and removed the eyesore. There are infinite possibilities for new routing in 'free' style without creating bolted lines. Details of all these routes and others will be found in the New Routes book at Wadi Rum's Rest House and Campsite. The 1994 guide to *Treks and Climbs in Wadi Rum* is available from Cicerone Press.

# Mount Everest Foundation Expedition Reports 1994

## SUMMARISED BY BILL RUTHVEN

Each year, the Mount Everest Foundation supports a number of expeditions undertaking exploration in one form or another amongst the high mountains of the world. As well as 'Approval' – which in itself may have the effect of opening other purses – most expeditions also receive a grant, usually ranging between £200 and £1500. Whilst this only represents a small proportion of the overall cost of an expedition, the moral support and the promise of a few hundred pounds during the preparatory stages of an expedition can sometimes make the difference between it going and not going.

All that the MEF asks in return is a comprehensive report. Once received, copies are lodged in the Alpine Club Library, the Royal Geographical Society and the British Mountaineering Council where they are available for consultation by future expeditioners. The following notes are based on reports that have been received up to the end of January 1995, and are divided into geographical areas. In response to popular demand, the names of the leader and other members of each team are given this year for the first time.

## America – North

**94/17 Scottish Alaskan 1994** Chris Schiller (with Mark Sinclair). April-May 1994.

Plans to climb new routes on Mounts Crosson and Foraker were thwarted by unseasonal warm weather. With the snow failing to consolidate, severe avalanches resulted, and the highest point reached was 2830m on the S ridge of Mount Crosson.

## America – South

**94/24 British South Tower of Paine 1994** Mike Turner (with Martin Doyle, Oliver Sanders and Louise Thomas). December 1994-January 1995.

On finding their original objective snowed up, this team tackled the continually overhanging E face of Cuernos Norte (2400m). Despite large sections of disintegrating and exfoliating granite, in four weeks they achieved the first ascent of a 23-pitch 800m A3+ route, which they called *A fistful of dollars* after the recently imposed climbing charge of $800.

**94/40  Cambridge Geological Project – Bolivia '94**  Matthew Wetherall (with Ben Reynolds and Simon Shercliff).  July-September 1994.

The main object of this trip was to produce a 1:10,000 geological map of a 45 sq km area of Altiplano near the village of Jesus de Machaca, a task that was completed with great success.  At the end of their work they found time to visit the Cordillera Real and climbed Huayani Potosí (6088m)

# Greenland and Arctic Europe

**93/38  British Greenland 1993**  Stephen Jones (with Carl Holt, Jamie Miller and Peter Price-Thomas).  July-September 1993.

This team made a 640km W–E crossing of the Greenland Ice Cap from near Angmassalik to Sondre Stromfjord in 38 days. 'Upski' parachutes provided one very exhilarating day of 61km, but mostly it was hard work towing heavy pulks and averaging 16km.  The hardest part of all came at the end, when a severely crevassed area had to be traversed, and then loads up to 50kg backpacked down to the coast.

**94/3  North–South Greenland: Phase I**  Dr Phil Jumeau (with Brian Hull and John Sweeney).  July-August 1994.

Time constraints have prevented this team from tackling its ambitious project – a N–S Greenland traverse – in a single year, so the journey has been divided into two (unequal) phases.  The first one, of 680km between Sangmilek Fjord (near Angmassalik) and Narssarssuak was completed in 35 days during which time the team reached a maximum altitude of 2800m. Phase II, scheduled for 1996, will start in the north of the island and finish 1800km later at Angmassalik.

**94/13  Karabiner M C Greenland 1994**  Jim Gregson (with Sandra Gregson, Graham Harkness, Andrew Howick, Alan Jones, John Starbuck, Lucy Walker and Paul Walker).  July-August 1994

This mixed club team explored the area of Schweizerland adjacent to the Pourquoi-pas, Champs-Elysées and Kristian glaciers.  During their 22 days in the field, they climbed a total of 14 peaks or tops between 1500m and 2400m, of which 10 were first ascents and the others probably first British ascents. (*See article 'Probing the Pourquoi-Pas', pages 183-191.*)

**94/26  Cardiff University Greenland 1994**  Dr Gary Timms (with David Crease, Andrew Roberts, Matthew Roberts, Jonathan Rowe and Andrew Woodward).  July-August 1994.

Six scientists working in the Stauning Alps experienced mostly excellent weather, enabling them to carry out their work programme before attempting some new routes in the area.  They achieved the summit of Dunottar (2524m) by its N face, but abandoned the N ridge of Glamis at c2000m owing to very loose shattered rock.

**94/43 1994 Trans-Greenland**   Nigel Harling (with Mark Evans).   July-August 1994.

Reasonable weather conditions enabled the 533km crossing from Isertoq on the east coast to near Sondrestrojm on the west to be made in a very creditable 26 days.  Parachutes were used as sails when possible, and 200km were covered in three days when the wind was right.

**94/32 British Mount Asgard 1994**   Simon Yates (with Noel Craine, Keith Jones, Paul Pritchard and Steve Quinlan).   May-July 1994.

The approach to this 2011m peak in Baffin Island took so much longer than anticipated that the leader and Jones had to return home before getting to grips with it.  The other three, with a lone Catalonian, then climbed the very steep NW face of the mountain in a 12-day push by a new direct route which they named *Hyperborea*, and graded ABO sup, A4, E3, 6a. (*See article 'Hammering the Anvil', pages  47-51..*)

# Himalaya – China

**94/48 Yangtze Gorges Caves 1994**   Richard Bartrop (with Anthony Baker, Colin Boothroyd, David Checkley, Peter Francis, Philip Goodwin, Adrian Gregory, Brian Judd, Steven Openshaw, Paul Seddon, Kevin Senior, Dick Willis and a group of Chinese cave scientists).   August-September 1994.

A period of five weeks was spent exploring caves in Sichuan Province, central China.  Near the town of Xin Long they surveyed a cave that proved to have a depth of 931m and is hence the deepest known cave in China.  Further south, several other deep caves were explored but lack of time prevented these from being 'bottomed'.

# Himalaya – India

**93/35 Nilkantha Ninety-Three**   Duncan Tunstall (with Chris Pasteur).   September-October 1993.

Although 'only' 6596m high, this peak in the Garhwal has repulsed all parties to date.  This expedition was no more successful as, owing to Pasteur's poor acclimatisation, the attempt was abandoned at *c*5600m.

**94/10 RAF Menthosa 1994**   Kev Williams (with Steve Atkins, Adrian Birkett, Richard Cooper, Brendan Dunn, Jim Groark, Peter Higgins, Andrew Nundy, Richard Turvey, and Carl Vanderlee).   August-September 1994.

This team planned to explore the Chamba/Lahul area of India and climb Menthosa (6443m) by two different routes.  However, the mountain had changed dramatically, making the climbing far more technical than anticipated, so that they could not progress beyond 6257m.  The trip was not without its problems, as their trekking group abandoned them in appalling weather, and the leader suffered concussion after being struck by a large block of ice; fortunately he made a full recovery.

**94/27  Imperial College Hidden Garhwal**  Oliver Shergold (with David Edwards, Martin Jackson, Martin Shelley, Toby Shergold and Philip Wickens). August-October 1994.

This expedition had both scientific and mountaineering aims, and recorded great success in both. After setting up a long-term study into the impact that tourists and trekkers have on the mountain environment, they then turned their attention to making their own impact on unclimbed peaks. They achieved first ascents of Jung Minar (5680m) via its NE face, Pyramid Peak (6036m) via its N ridge and 'Peak A' (6200m) by its N and NW ridges. On Peak 6128 they climbed to the highest point yet reached, but came across an unclimbable section at 5750m.

**94/28  Hagshu North Face**  John Barry (with Seb Mankelow). August-September 1994.

The leader has had a love-hate relationship with this 6300m peak over many years, returning time after time in the hope of making the first ascent of its N face. This time, two weeks of non-stop snow and storm caused the attempt to be abandoned at *c*6000m.

**94/41  1994 British Nanda Devi East**  Julie-Ann Clyma (with Roger Payne). September-October 1994.

This very experienced team hoped to attempt a new route on the NW ridge of this 7434m peak, but an unusually dry season made this impractical. They therefore moved to the S ridge and succeeded in making the first British/New Zealand ascent of the route, the first ascent by a woman and the first ascent of the mountain in alpine style.  (*See article 'Voyage to the Goddess', pages 52-56.*)

**94/45  Indian British Kinnaur 1994**  Chris Bonington and Harish Kapadia (with Jim Curran, Jim Fotheringham, Graham Little, Jim Lowther and Paul Nunn from the UK and Pasang Bodh, Prakash Chand, Muslim Contractor, Khubram, Kaivan Mistry, Divyesh Muni and Suratram from India). May-July 1994.

A very strong team of British and Indian climbers linked up to explore and climb in the rarely visited Kinnaur–Kailash range. The first ascent of Rangrik Rang (6553m) was achieved, together with the third ascent of Manirang (6593m). First ascents were also made of Mangla (5800m), Saponang (5836m) and Ghunsarang (5800m).  (*See articles 'A Truly Joint Venture', pages 57-64, and 'Manirang, 6593m', pages 65-70.*)

# Himalaya – Nepal

**94/1  British Mount Everest Medical 1994**  Dr Simon Currin (with Angus Andrew, Arthur Collins, Charlie Hornsby, Roddy Kirkwood, Andrew Pollard, Ronnie Robb, John Sanders and Alison Hargreaves).  July-October 1994.

The majority of the team named above were doctors undertaking a comprehensive research programme into a wide range of altitude-related medical problems.  While they acted as guinea-pigs for each other, there was a hard core of climbers amongst them who hoped to reach the summit of Everest.  Using supplementary oxygen, Charlie Hornsby and Roddy Kirkwood (with Sherpas Dorje and Dawa Temba) were successful, but Alison Hargreaves had to abandon her oxygenless attempt at c8400m owing to high winds and the risk of frostbite.

**94/5  Upper Mustang (scientific)**  Professor Myra Shackley (with David Barlow, Rose Beddington, Philip Behrend, Tsewang Bista, Ben Gladstone, James Gladstone, Richard Keeler, Dave McAdam, Lhakpa Sherpa and Gary Weber).  April-May 1994.

This was a most unusual project undertaken by a mixed party of specialists to assess the impact that tourism is having on a Tibet-like trekking area of Nepal only opened up in 1991.  Backed by the Annapurna Conservation Area Project, the King of Mustang/Mustang Development Corporation and the Nepal Ministry of Tourism, their work (which included a survey with a view to setting up a GIS) will form the basis of a Management Structure for the future: currently no more than 2000 visitors per year are allowed.

**94/14  British Himlung**  Pete Hudd (with Ray Harris, Brian Ottewell and David McCarthy).  October-November 1994.

For the leader, this was a return to a 7126m peak on which he failed in 1992.  Unfortunately, history repeated itself and continuous snow and wind caused the attempt to be abandoned at c6400m on the W ridge.  However, this was the highest point that anyone had achieved on the S face/W ridge.

**94/20  British Chamar**  Rob Brown (with Steve Callen, Don Davies, Graeme Daly, Dave Hill, John Hudson, Sarah Keast, Mark McDermott, Boz Morris and Alison Wright, plus 3 climbing Sherpas).  October-November 1994.

The first party to climb this 7178m peak in the Sringi Himal of West Nepal was from New Zealand, but their ascent is not recognised by the Nepalese authorities.  This team hoped to make the first British (2nd overall) ascent, but porter problems extended the walk-in by a full week, and then the route proved to be much longer than had been anticipated.  As a result the highest point reached was 5500m.

**94/35 RAFMA Tilicho Peak 1994** Flt Lt Colin Scott (with Tom Barbour, Guy Beaumont, Andy Heathfield, Kev Hewkin, Nigel Hodgson, Rick Lay, Phil McLachlan, Tim Payne, Chris Rawling and Ian Singleton). September-October 1994.

After a light monsoon there was little snow on the unclimbed S face of this 7134m peak in the Annapurna region. As a result, the team faced very loose rock on pitches of VS and harder. Most were hit by falling rocks at some stage, and the leader fell some six metres when his abseil belays pulled out. The attempt was abandoned at 6600m.

# Karakoram – Pakistan

**94/4 Beusten Glacier 1994** George Armstrong (with Rob Lee, Iain Miller, Jeremy Parker, Ed Shackley and Sally Smith). July-August 1994.

One of the hottest summers ever recorded in this area melted much of the snow, making river crossings hazardous on the approach, and replacing névé with hard ice on the mountains: rock avalanches were also frequent. Nevertheless, the team achieved its objective of making the first ascent of a previously unnamed c6000m mountain (subsequently named 'Jog's Peak') by its 1000m S face at Scottish grade III/IV. They also repeated the original N ridge route on NASA Peak (c5640m).

**94/9 British Ultar 1994** Julian Freeman-Attwood (with Crag Jones, Steve Reid and Ed Webster). June-August 1994

The team hoped to make the first ascent of this 7388m peak in Hunza, possibly from the rarely attempted N side. This proved impractical owing to an extremely broken glacier, so they turned their attention to the south but were forced to abandon the attempt at c6000m owing to continuous enormous avalanches caused by the unusually warm weather.

**94/12 Cumbrian Hindu Raj** Dave Wilson (with Rich Davis, Mike Morphew, Rob Thomas, Maggie Worth and Steve Wrigley). July-August 1994

The Katchikani area of the Hindu Kush is restricted, so it had previously been visited by few (if any) Westerners. This team explored the Thalo glacier and made probably the first ascent of a 5441m peak which they called 'Salghira Zom' – Chitrali for 'Birthday Peak'.

**94/21 British Women's Karakoram 1994** Penny Clay (with Julie Carter, Wyn Clayton and Mary Twomey). July-August 1994.

Dangerous cornices and poor snow conditions prevented this team from actually standing on the summits of Mitre Peak (5945m) and Sceptre (5800m). However, on the former they reached c5900m after making the second British ascent of the W face, and on the latter reached c5400m on the unclimbed SW ridge. Their third objective, which they thought was Crown Peak, turned out to be a peak attempted by the RAF from the east and called Portcullis: the real Crown Peak remains unclimbed, and is situated several kilometres to the east, on a northerly extension of the Mitre–Sceptre ridge.

**94/36  British Hispar 1994**  Dave Wilkinson (with Bill Church, Brian Davison and Tony Park). July-August 1994.

This party planned to make first ascents from the Yengutz but once in the Hispar valley they decided to climb from the Garumbar glacier instead. From here, they climbed Uyumrung Sar (*c*5900) from the SE and then Trapezium (*c*5800m) from the west, both probably first ascents. An inaccuracy on the Leoman map caused confusion when the leader and Davison moved to Gilgit. They attempted what they thought was Khaitar (c5600m), when they were actually on the S ridge of South Twin (5700m): the climb was abandoned well short of the summit owing to lack of rock gear and bivouac equipment.

**94/38  Durham University Mountaineering Club Sim Gang Glacier 1994**  Richard Dixon (with Phil Birch, Nigel Crook, Chris May and Jeff Snoxell). July-September 1994.

After establishing an advanced Base Camp at the head of the Sim Gang glacier, this team picked an interesting but unnamed peak (*c*5800m), and in one day climbed to within 150m of its summit. At this point they were on a very narrow ridge of unstable boulders, so decided not to progress further. Any ideas of other routes had to be shelved when a bear raided their Base Camp, and ate all the food stored there.

**94/42  British Latok North Ridge 1994**  Dave Wills (with Brendan Murphy). August-September 1994.

Porter strikes plus injury and memory loss caused by falling rocks added to the more usual hazards experienced by this team attempting the first ascent of the N ridge of Latok I (7145m) in pure alpine style. In the end, these and almost continuous bad weather resulted in the climb being abandoned at *c*5600m.

# Central Asia and the Far East

**94/7  British Kamchatka Volcanoes**  John Town (with Huw Davies, Alyson Starling, Richard Wojtaszewski and 10 Russian climbers). July-August 1994.

Kamchatka, the most easterly extremity of Siberia, was closed until recently, so is little explored. This team achieved successful ascents of Avacha (1800m), Ushkovsky (3943m) and Klyuchevskaya (*c*4750m). All are volcanoes, the last being the highest active volcano in Europe and Asia and also the highest peak in NE Asia.

**94/16 Cherskiy Mountains** Paul Knott (with Michael Doyle, Simon Inger and John Kentish). July-August 1994.

As the first Westerners to visit these mountains in NE Siberia, this team had the area to itself and were able to achieve 7 first ascents of peaks approx 3000m high. A pencilled line on a 1:500,000 pilotage map was the only guidance that they had for their heavily laden 165km walk-out at the end of the climbing: this was accomplished in 9 days, just in time to catch their return flight.

**94/18 British/Ukranian Tien Shan 1994** Nick Williams (with Chris Bedford, Richard Cross, Mat Dickinson and Adam Jackson from the UK and Ukranians Anton Bykov, Igor Chaplinsky, Nikolay Gorunov, Sveta Lineva, Taras Metropan, Alik Petruk & Sasha Pyapun). July-August 1994.

This joint team hoped to achieve new routes from the South Inylchek glacier but experienced bad weather for most of the time that they were in the area. Continuous danger of rock and sérac fall prevented attempts on any of their declared objectives, but a brief respite at the end of the trip enabled them to climb Khan Tengri (6995m) by the normal route.

**94/30 British Admiral Peak** Neil McAdie (with Clive Davis, Jerry Hadwin and Andy Lewington). July-August 1994.

This team arrived in Base Camp a mere 15 hours after leaving London, to find that their intended route had already been climbed by a CIS party. Any alternative would have involved many days of big wall artificial climbing for which they were not prepared, so they decided to repeat the route. McAdie, Davis and Hadwin achieved the first direct British ascent of the 5090m mountain by means of the NE spur/E ridge.

# Book Reviews

## COMPILED BY GEOFFREY TEMPLEMAN

### Spirits of the Air
Kurt Diemberger
Translated from the German by Audrey Salkeld
*Hodder & Stoughton, 1994, pp304, £17.99*

After his evocative book *Summits and Secrets* (1971), which has inspired many fledgling climbers, and *The Endless Knot* (1991), his poignant account of the K2 tragedy, Kurt Diemberger has presented us with another auto-biographical volume (the title is taken from an Eskimo proverb), celebrating his life as mountaineer, cameraman and supreme gangrel. His technique is to give memory free rein to conjure up episodes from his past: the result is an exuberant kaleidoscope of events and adventures, in no chronological order and almost bewildering in its variety, descriptions of landscape and friends all over the world, intermixed with musings on the meaning of it all. (There is a useful chronology of his main climbs and expeditions at the end of the book, but no index.) Diemberger's flamboyant style is well maintained in Audrey Salkeld's translation and keeps the reader constantly entertained. He is adept at painting landscapes in words, and on the whole he avoids the dangers of travel-writer's hype.

It is not all mountaineering, by any means. He can be very amusing, for example in describing a 'romantic' adventure in Atlanta, where the Peachtree Plaza Hotel reminds him of the Guglia di Brenta, and there is plenty of excitement, in episodes such as a flight over the Austrian Alps, in a small plane when the engine has failed, or filming a wrestle with Friendly Margherita, the boa constrictor. Indeed Diemberger, the fortunate hedonist, claims that he has himself the stomach, and the eating habits, of the big snake – and, of course, his predilection for attractive female company is evident throughout.

The allure of Diemberger's narrative may not work for everyone, but there will be few able to resist the arch-romantic's spell entirely. For me the most appealing aspects of the book included Diemberger's love for plants and animals and all aspects of the natural world – his thrill at witnessing fiery eruptions of the volcano Stromboli, the green flash observed on Mauna Loa in Hawaii – and his feeling for mountain history. Thus, the chapter on Greenland not only brings out well the special fascination of climbing in that beautiful land, but presents a moving account of the last tragic expedition in 1930 of Alfred Wegener, the scientist and explorer best known as the originator of the theory of Continental Drift; this is a drama fully comparable to that of Scott of the Antarctic, yet one with which few British readers will be familiar.

These are old-fashioned interests and attitudes, no doubt, in a mountaineer of such accomplishments. And for many attention will focus primarily on Kurt's doings on the highest mountains of the world: exploration in the Hindu Kush, in *'Westalpenstil'* of course; the attempt on the Lhotse Ridge in 1974 which led to the first ascent of Shartse, an epic if ever there was one; the return to the eight-thousanders, with the ascents of Makalu, Everest and Gasherbrum II, after an interval of 18 years; filming and climbing with Julie Tullis (recounted much more fully in *The Endless Knot*); and finally, his current love-affair, movingly described, with the mysterious Shaksgam region and the hidden side of Broad Peak.

Kurt Diemberger returned to the highest mountains in 1978 against the advice of climbing friends and doctors. It is a strange form of hedonism which drives a man in middle age to abandon the pleasures of ordinary mortals, which he evidently enjoys so much, in order to brave high-altitude cough, sleepless nights in rattling tents and struggles with malfunctioning oxygen sets, in his renewed quest for extreme adventure on hard and dangerous 8000m peaks. In the last resort this remarkable man remains an enigma. But who can fathom the Spirits of the Air?

*Ernst Sondheimer*

### Hypoxia and Molecular Medicine
Ed John R Sutton, Charles S Houston, Geoffrey Coates
*Queen City Printer Inc, Burlington, Vermont, USA. 1993*

Oxygen is essential to man's existence. That is why the study of the fit man at altitude – who acts as a model for those at sea-level with chronic lung and heart conditions – is so important. It was also the reason why the eighth biennial Hypoxia symposium, held at Château Lake Louise, Canada, from 8 to 13 February 1993, was attended by scientists and mountaineers from all over the world. The meeting coincided with the 40th anniversary of the first ascent of Everest; it was therefore dedicated to our Honorary Member Dr Griffith Pugh who, by his work at the Medical Research Council in London and in the field in 1951 and 1952, was responsible, more than any other single individual, for this landmark achievement in both mountaineering and medicine.

In *Hypoxia and Molecular Medicine*, which is based on the proceedings at the eighth Hypoxia symposium, there are five articles from contributors from three continents describing Pugh's work on cold, altitude and exercise, and man's ability to adapt and counter the hostile environment of the high mountains. An article by J S Milledge covers Griffith Pugh's career, emphasising, in particular, two innovative aspects of his style of research: first, the importance that he placed on getting out into the field to complement the more controlled studies of the laboratory and environmental chamber; secondly, his belief that the best way to study the physiology of extreme environments was to take extreme examples. Thus Pugh studied the effects of altitude at 5-6000m rather than 2-4000m and for months rather than days. He also used 'Olympic' athletes, rather than those of 'club' standard. Milledge also emphasises that, although Pugh's work was always meticulously planned and organised, he could also seize opportunities when they arose. One such occasion was his study of a Nepalese pilgrim who had, over many years, developed an extraordinary tolerance to cold and who visited our camp on the Silver Hut expedition in the winter of 1960-61. This resulted in a unique paper and the first scientific investigation of a phenomenon which had previously been dismissed as an old wives' tale; Pugh showed it to be a reality. Milledge also lists over 90 papers that Pugh published.

There are sections on the autonomic nervous system and oxygen lack, as well as one on the effects of oxygen lack on the genes responsible for cell function. There are also sections on muscle function and fatigue, together with various aspects of mountain medicine.

Forty years ago, in 1953, a major discovery in genetics, the double helix, was made at Cambridge University, equal to that of Darwin's great theory of natural selection. This was the starting point of the present explosion in knowledge which has led to genetic fingerprinting and the emergence of molecular medicine. Alfred Tissiere, another Alpine Club member, was involved in this work at Cambridge University -- so involved that, despite being invited, he was unable to join the 1951 Reconnaissance Expedition to Everest.

Because of our increased understanding of biological principles, the last 40 years have seen unprecedented advances in both mountaineering and medicine. In 1953 these two great human endeavours were creatively linked by the encouragement and financial backing they received from the Medical Research Council of the UK. For this, both mountaineers and medical scientists should be profoundly grateful.

*Michael Ward*

### High Altitude Medicine and Physiology
Michael P Ward, James S Milledge, John B West
*Chapman & Hall Medical, 2nd edition, 1995, pp618, £69.00*

What is mountain sickness? How do we acclimatise? Why can't I sleep at altitude? What limits exercise performance at altitude? How was Messner able to reach the summit of Everest without supplementary oxygen? How much higher than Everest could a man climb without supplementary oxygen (if there were higher mountains!)? What is high altitude pulmonary edema? How should frostbite be treated? Should the oral contraceptive be used at altitude? Do extreme altitude climbers suffer brain damage?

The second edition of this magnificent, comprehensive textbook gives all the known answers to questions about what happens to man at altitude and sensible advice about the prevention and treatment of altitude-related illness. From historical literary references about mountain sickness to general anaesthesia at 4000m, from the hypoxic ventilatory response to sunburn, it is hard to think of a topic omitted. These three wise men of mountain medicine and physiology – Michael Ward, James Milledge and John West – have been gathering knowledge for their book since long before I was born. They have climbed and studied climbers for over a century between them and made a major contribution to the research which is the basis of current understanding and of their textbook. During the 1990s they have written learned papers on altitude-related topics, and have talked at international scientific meetings on the medicine and physiology of ascent to altitude. All three have managed to combine their high altitude medical expertise with distinguished low altitude careers as doctors both in research and healing.

*High Altitude Medicine and Physiology* is the leading textbook on the subject and is necessarily written in the rather specialised language used by high altitude physiologists and doctors. Some of the technical information is therefore inaccessible to the ordinary climber, since much of the immense detail presupposes a considerable background knowledge of physiology. However, there is so much in this book that all those interested in high altitude will find some useful information and should have access to it as the definitive reference text. I have referred several science students, general practitioners and expedition doctors to the first edition (1989) and all have found it helpful, whether they were doing a project for a psychology degree, planning a field study for an expedition or advising a patient with epilepsy about going on a trekking holiday. It is a reference book best dipped into. A cover-to-cover read, which the authors do not expect of their readers, has been quite an undertaking for the reviewer!

The authors begin with a fascinating chapter on the history of high altitude medicine and physiology which must have taken many hours of research in the Alpine Club Library archives and other sources. There is then a key chapter about the atmosphere and barometric pressure which sets the scene for a tour around the effects of ascent to altitude on ventilation, the cardio-vascular system, the blood, the transport of blood gases, and peripheral tissues. Exercise, performance limitation, and sleep at altitude are covered before a return to the systematic review with chapters on the gut, endocrine system, renal and central nervous system. A series of chapters covers altitude-related illness including clinical symptoms and signs, prevention and treatment. The next section details the effects of cold at altitude before two new practical chapters which discuss skiing and mountaineering accidents and injuries and the effects of solar radiation. A chapter on medical conditions at altitude is important as a reference for general practitioners whose patients, for example, might ask advice about diabetes and ascent to altitude. The book concludes with the lessons that altitude research teaches the sea-level doctor, including those treating patients with bronchitis and emphysema. The final chapter is an appendix for the would-be field researcher.

The second edition includes an update of relevant work published since the first edition. It cannot have been an easy task because, as the authors note in the preface, there were 1369 articles written about high altitude in the medical press between 1987 and 1993. Indeed, there is an increasing interest in high altitude medicine and a third edition by the turn of the century must be inevitable. The preface to the first edition, sadly omitted from the 1995 version, clearly explained the need for this textbook with the increasing interest in travel to high altitude and expressed the authors' hope that ' ... this book will make the high places of the world safer and thereby increase the pleasure to be gained for those who visit these regions of outstanding natural beauty.' Ward, Milledge and West have produced an updated text which will be used by doctors, climbers and their medical advisors everywhere and must go some way towards making the high mountains safer.

*Andrew J Pollard*

### Yankee Rock & Ice
### A History of Climbing in the Northeastern United States
Guy and Laura Waterman
*Stackpole Books, 1993, pp334, US$19.95*

Americans, generally speaking, came late to climbing. Until the turn of the century, 'the frontier' provided the challenges missing from civilized life. Most of the few American alpinists at that time had European connections and climbed over here or in the US West, paying little attention to the hills of the northeast. Like our mid-Victorian mountaineers they treated their home crags as no more than an amusing diversion, which could possibly keep one fit for more serious ventures. How different now. Home-grown American rock and ice climbers have for years been among the world's best, and American enthusiasm has animated both development of new equipment and the contrary movement towards clean climbing.

For anyone interested in these developments, or involved in climbing in the US Northeast, this book is absorbing. I must confess that my heart sank at the prospect of reading what promised to be a whole book of 'Area Notes', but the sinking feeling was quickly dissipated. Open it where you will, it is well written and interesting. It is more than a record of events; it puts the climbs and the climbers into perspective and identifies the main phases of development. It is particularly fascinating to anyone who knows the characters involved and recognises the styles and codes of behaviour described. No doubt there is room for disagreement with some of the analysis of events, but I found it convincing.

The accounts of the achievements of each generation are interleaved with anecdotes, thumb-nail sketches of character, observations on equipment and ethics, and brief interludes of personal experiences of the authors. This varied presentation masks the enormous labour, lasting ten years, and the scholarship needed for this admirable history, making it very enjoyable reading.

*Michael Westmacott*

**Hold the Heights.  The Foundations of Mountaineering**
Walt Unsworth
*Hodder & Stoughton, 1993, pp432, £19.99*

*Hold the Heights* is a broad history of mountaineering from the pen of the prolific and well-known mountaineering author Walt Unsworth. However, the book is much more than a mere historical sequence, because Unsworth also attempts to set the mountaineers and climbers in their social contexts. Historical texts can be dull but this extremely well-researched book holds one's interest from beginning to end.

The compass of the book is wide – both temporally and geographically. It commences in 1492, with Antoine de Ville's ascent of Mont Aiguille in the Vercors, and it describes many of the most important ascents up to that of Everest in 1953.  In geographical terms the book ranges all over the globe, from the Old World to the Americas, from Norway to New Zealand. In his preface, Unsworth describes the technique he has employed: 'It was plain from the start that a totally comprehensive coverage, even of the major personalities and events, would need several volumes, so I have adopted instead a concentric plan similar to the effect obtained by dropping a pebble in a pond.  The tightest ripples are those rings nearest the centre; then, as they spread out, they get wider but less well defined ... as the nineteenth century advances and spills into the twentieth, the circle widens and becomes more selective.'

Unsworth shows that the birth of mountaineering really took place in the second half of the 18th century and, for the next 100 years or so, largely involved the Alps.  However, as the 19th century progressed, both explorers and mountaineers were active much further afield, and Unsworth demonstrates how mountaineering spread from Europe to the far corners of the world. Sometimes this involved Europeans, such as Edward Whymper, who in 1880 made the ascent of Chimborazo and other volcanoes in Ecuador, and Norman Collie, who climbed in the Rockies at the turn of the century. Sometimes it involved indigenous climbers such as T C Fyfe, whose team of New Zealanders made the first undisputed ascent of Mount Cook in 1894.  Unsworth describes ascents, and the character of the mountaineers making them, in many of the major ranges including the Caucasus, Himalaya and  Karakoram, as well as the Alps.

There are many interesting facts in the book; for example, I now know how the Viereselgrat ('Four Asses Ridge') on the Dent Blanche acquired its name. Although I enjoyed the whole book, the two chapters I found most interesting were 'Fine Opportunity for Breaking One's Neck', in which Unsworth discusses climbing in Britain in the 19th century, and 'Nordwand', in which the philosophy and spectacular north face climbs of the 1930's Munich School are described. The many references provided are laudable – many a PhD thesis is not so well-endowed – and the book has a good index.

I did have several niggles. As a geographer, I like to see scales on maps, and two of the maps (Himalaya and Yosemite) were without them; moreover, the quality of the map of Canada and North America leaves something to be desired. All 24 pages of photographs are in black and white; a few in colour would have been an attractive addition. But it would be quite wrong to let a few minor imperfections deter one from reading such an excellent treatise.

Writing this book has obviously involved a mammoth amount of work and must have been a real labour of love. There is now potential for a second volume documenting the latter half of the 20th century. I wonder whether Walt Unsworth is considering this? I certainly hope so.

*Nigel Gates*

## The Great Himalayan Traverse – Kanchendzonga to Karakoram
S P Chamoli
*Vikas Publishing House Pvt Ltd, New Delhi, 1993, pp267, 395 Rupees*

As I first turned the pages of this book, the story seemed vaguely familiar. Then I realised it was another account of the nine month journey made by the New Zealanders Graeme Dingle and Peter Hillary in 1981. In their book *First Across the Roof of the World*, published in New Zealand in 1982, they described this journey as 'The First-Ever Traverse of the Himalayas – 5,000km from Sikkim to Pakistan'. Although conceived by the New Zealanders, it became in fact a joint Indo-New Zealand expedition sponsored by the Indian Mountaineering Foundation under the patronage of its president Shri Harish Sarin and Sir Edmund Hillary. Three Indians and five New Zealanders were involved, divided into a traverse team and a support team. The traverse team was usually the trio of Dingle, Hillary and Chewang Tashi, a tough 42-year-old instructor from the Himalayan Mountaineering Institute in Darjeeling. An excellent linguist, Tashi was born in Kathmandu of Tibetan parents.

The Indians were recruited at very short notice; the author S P Chamoli was from the Indo-Tibetan Border Police and was the nominal leader of the expedition, although mainly in the support team. He has subsequently participated in various rafting expeditions, including the Tsangpo gorge of the Brahmaputra, and is currently serving as Deputy Inspector General on deputation to the Sikkim Police. The two books therefore make an interesting contrast in content and style between the forthright New Zealanders and the sensitive devout Hindu; neither is of great literary merit. In fact, Chamoli's book, published in New Delhi, is sadly marred by poor proof-reading, eg 'the famous mountaineer Long Staff'.

With a motto of 'Move fast, eat little, sleep rough and think big', the traverse was almost as much a political triumph as a physical one. The role of the Indian Mountaineering Foundation was essential in obtaining the necessary permits to enter the Inner Line areas. At the country borders, it was not possible to follow the aesthetic mountain line – for example, across the Singalila ridge from Sikkim into Nepal, or across the so-called 'cease-fire line' in Kashmir from India to Pakistan. In the latter case, after jointly reaching Leh, the New Zealanders crossed at Amritsar, flew to Skardu and made the traditional trek up to Concordia and the foot of K2. The three Indians, unable to enter Pakistan, set their goal as the Karakoram Pass, 5575m, on the Chinese border, following a variant of the old Silk Route from Leh to Yarkand.

From Kangchenjunga to the Karakoram Pass in 250 days from 17 February to 25 October, they had trekked over 5000km, crossed three passes over 7000m, 38 between 4600m and 7000m, and about 60 between 3000m and 4500m. Whether on the traverse or in the support party, their achievement was magnificent:

'Days of early spring in Sikkim, cool and comfortable summer in central Nepal and days of monsoon rains and low mists in Himachal and Kumaon. Then the blue sky with cold winds of Karakoram.'

I wish I could have been with them.

*George Band*

## Mountain Environments and Geographic Information Systems
### Edited by Martin F Price and D Ian Heywood
*Taylor & Francis, 1994, pp309, £55.00*

The editors hope that this book will prove useful and interesting to the many people who live and work in mountain environments. However, its subject matter is difficult and sophisticated and, realistically, the book will probably only be useful to those with decision-making or research interests in those areas. The expression 'Geographic Information System' (GIS) is now commonly used; it describes a computer system and software on which stored spatial information can be manipulated and/or utilised for a variety of purposes. The editors believe that this book is the first to consider explicitly the use of GIS in mountain environments.

The first chapter is the most readable; it describes the special characteristics and complexity of mountain areas and how GIS can be used in such areas. Mountains, as the editors point out, are distributed across every continent and include a great diversity of environments, from the wettest to the driest, from hot to cold, and from sea level to the summit of Everest. Mountains and uplands comprise about one-fifth of the world's terrestrial surface. They are home to about one-tenth of the world's population and are directly or indirectly important for more than half. They supply natural resources – food, wood and minerals – to an even greater proportion. Moreover, they are at the upper end of most of the world's river catchments, providing water, nutrients and energy to those living both nearby and at distant locations downstream. Furthermore, they provide environments for recreation and tourism, together with centres of biodiversity and refugia for relict species and communities. They are of great spiritual and aesthetic significance to many people. The value of using GIS to model these complex mountain environments is discussed, together with its limitations.

The physical characteristic that best defines mountains is its three-dimensionality and this (as mountaineers know) produces contrasting environments at different elevations. However, superimposed on this altitudinal zonation are variations that derive from the aspect, slope and topography of a particular mountain or region. Therefore, the GIS used in these regions usually incorporate digital terrain models which permit the representation of their three-dimensional nature. This is essential because the local and micro-climatic variations strongly influence the biophysical components (air, water, soils, vegetation and fauna) of mountain environments and also influence patterns of housing, agriculture and recreation. It is also important that GIS should be able to identify areas likely to be affected by hazards such as avalanches, rockfalls, floods and forest fires, the distribution of which is affected by the complex interaction of local climates and human activities with soil, bedrock and vegetation characteristics. GIS must be capable of predicting how, when and where such events are likely to occur.

Used carefully, GIS can be a valuable technological tool for descriptive, analytical and evaluative purposes and can assist policy makers, planners and environmentalists at local, regional and national levels to develop strategies for the economic and ecological management of mountain environments.

The second chapter of the book considers terrain modelling for mountains and the remaining thirteen chapters are divided into four sections: 'Regional Resource Inventory and Planning' (five chapters), 'Evaluation of Natural Hazards' (two chapters), 'Research and Resource Management In and Around Protected Areas' (four chapters) and 'Simulation and Prediction, Vegetation and Climatic Change' (two chapters). These thirteen chapters describe case studies from five continents and consider topics from the traditional concerns of mountain scientists and resource managers to the increasingly critical issue of global climate change.

There are 39 contributors from many countries including Australia, Canada, Russia, Switzerland, UK and USA. However, with chapter titles like 'Form and Pattern in the Alpine Environment: an Integrated Approach to Spatial Analysis and Modelling in Glacier National Park, USA' (Chapter 10), many people may be put off. This is a pity because the book is an erudite and scholarly collection of papers. Without doubt, similar books will follow. Although the subject is complex, let's hope that they are more readable and have a more general application.

*Nigel Gates*

### At the Rising of the Moon
Dermot Somers
*Bâton-Wicks/Collins Press, 1994, pp208, £8.99*

*Mountains and Other Ghosts,* Dermot Somers' first collection of short stories, was well received in the climbing press. It also won some recognition from the wider reading public, which is unusual for a writer whose principal themes are mountains and mountaineering. His second volume, *At the Rising of the Moon,* has received an even warmer welcome from the climbing world, winning outright the 1994 Boardman Tasker Memorial Award. It is too early to say how it will fare in the real world.

The stories in the new volume are broader in scope and more ambitious than the earlier ones – partly, it seems, because Somers is trying to escape the tight categorisation of a 'mountaineering writer', and partly because he is experimenting both formally and linguistically. Some of the pieces are long and relatively complex in their structure, falling midway between short stories and novellas. The subject matter varies from tensions between a husband and wife expeditioning together in Nepal ('Lightning in the Dark'), to the final hours of a (presumably Republican) fugitive on a hill in Wicklow in 'The Fox'. Locations range from an unspecified Eastern European mountain area in 'Johann' to a remote island off Ireland's Atlantic coast.

In some of these stories, however, Somers shows a tendency to introduce levels of thematic complexity and symbolism which he is not capable of keeping under control. This is particularly so in 'Johann' which tries to deal simultaneously with the themes of devotion to political struggle, cowardice in the mountains, possessive love, betrayal (both sexual and political), the appeal of Fascistic nationalism, and so on. This is more than 38 pages can bear and makes for a rather exhausting and unsatisfying read. The most successful stories in this collection, like 'The Fox', are the simplest ones.

The greatness of the great short story writers, from Anton Chekhov to Raymond Carver, lies in their capacity for suggestion, for evoking the richness of lives and their interaction with a few strokes of the brush. The imagination of the reader is what does the work, filling the gaps between salient details. In much of this book, however, Somers goes in the opposite direction. He tends to over-analyse his characters, explaining exactly what motivates them and what their deepest beliefs are. The intention is to add psychological depth, but the result is the opposite. Characters who are made too transparent end up being flat and boring.

Certainly, there are places where Somers shows himself to be a skilful writer. The description in 'The Singer' of how Síle Connery's husband was killed is a case in point. The work is done indirectly, in a brief paragraph with a minimum of adjectives, and the effect is powerful. Comparable passages appear at intervals in the book. Unfortunately they are often submerged in prose that fails to convince through trying too hard to convince.

It will be interesting to see in what direction Somers moves after *At the Rising of the Moon*. At times it seems as if he would be happier writing novels. Certainly his short stories cannot keep on expanding, and in that sense a novel would be the logical next step. But in many ways I feel he would serve his talents better by trimming down rather than expanding, developing a leaner style with less explicit description and fewer adjectives. As Hemingway put it, 'The dignity of movement of an iceberg is due to only one-eighth of it being above water'. In both this and his earlier collection there are signs that Somers has the eye for a revealing situation and the sharpness of intellect to make a good short story writer, but he must resist the temptation to over-write.

*José Luis Bermúdez*

### Montañas del Sol: Guía de Ascensiones a las Montañas del Ecuador
Freddy Landázuri, Iván Rojas and Marcos Serrano
*Campo Abierto, Quito, Ecuador, 1994, pp148, in Spanish*

### Cotopaxi: la Montaña de Luz/the Mountain of Light
Freddy Landázuri
*Campo Abierto, Quito, Ecuador, 1994, pp191, in Spanish and English*

### Pioneros y Precursores del Andinismo Ecuatoriano
Abya Yala and Nuevos Horizontes, editors
*Abya Yala, Quito, Ecuador, 1994, pp282, in Spanish*

### En los Altos Andes del Ecuador
Hans Meyer
*Abya Yala, Quito, Ecuador, 1993, pp750, in Spanish*

Each of these four books deals with a different aspect of Ecuadorian mountains and mountaineering. *Montañas del Sol* is a guidebook, compiled by the editors of the local mountain journal *Campo Abierto*. The book provides a great amount of information about the Ecuadorian highlands in general, history of climbing, mountain weather and advice on medical matters. Its main part is a methodical description of the 40 major peaks of the country, ranging from Chimborazo to Reventador (3567m). For each mountain there appears location, climbing history, access, normal route and other routes. Illustrations, all in black and white, are complemented by line drawings showing routes and position of huts, where available. This is an efficient updated guidebook that will render good service.

The Cotopaxi work is a bilingual monograph of the favourite mountain of the Ecuadorians and describes everything that is known about the 5897m ice volcano. The book has illustrations on almost every other page. Sections on history of climbing and surveys of past eruptions are particularly interesting. After covering all main ascents and routes, the book comes to an end with a description of the perilous descent into the bottom pit of the active crater, done in 1979 by three local climbers.

The third work is a homage to Nicolás Martínez (1874-1934), the true pioneer of South American sportive climbing. He exhibited a climbing career that lasted 32 years; he made, among other important ascents, the third of Chimborazo (1911), the first of Illiniza Norte and a new route on Cotopaxi. It was he who coined the term andinismo, so widely used nowadays. Furthermore, he published four books dealing exclusively with climbs in Ecuador and this 1994 volume contains ten chapters excerpted from those four books, a total of 268 pages. Illustrations, all historical, were reproduced from Martínez's own collection. Good as this book is, one can only hope that Ecuadorian institutions will eventually reprint in full every one of Martínez's books.

The German explorer Hans Meyer (1858–1929) is well known for his first ascent of Kilimanjaro in 1889 (see *AJ94*, 170-174, 1989/90), but little is known about his glaciological and climbing activities in Ecuador in 1903. The fourth book listed above is the Spanish version of his *In den Hochanden von Ecuador* (Berlin, 1907). It includes all the illustrations of the German original, although reproductions are often quite weak. Meyer was an amazingly methodical and accurate writer, who spared no effort to record a tremendous amount of information, which he poured into his usually massive books. In Ecuador he was not so fortunate as in Africa, having ascended only Cotopaxi, but his descriptions of the Ecuadorian heights are the most exact to be found, in this respect surpassing even another methodical man, Edward Whymper himself.

These four books offer much useful information about the mountains and mountaineering of a country that is at present a favourite of climbers, trekkers and ecologists. Quantity-wise, these works also confirm the lead that Ecuadorian mountain writers have been keeping in South America for the last two decades.

*Evelio Echevarría*

## In Search of Limits
Mark Bles
*Hodder & Stoughton, 1994, pp272, £17.99*

## Alps 4000
Martin Moran
*David & Charles, 1994, pp288, £17.99*

Before the summer of 1993 there had been several highly motivated attempts to climb all the 4000m peaks of the Alps in one season. Some had opted for a continuous traverse with minimal outside help, others had taken advantage of every facility available. While any of these might have succeeded given enough fine weather, all had failed.

In good conditions, climbing a four-thousander generally requires mountaineering judgement and fitness rather than great technical ability, so the project had attracted competent, middle-grade mountaineers with a certain amount of time on their hands. It appeared that something more 'professional' was required. Apart from other considerations, a high degree of organisation, plus some strong support, seemed mandatory. Just the sort of exercise, you might say, that would appeal to the military's Adventure Training network. No surprise then to find that by April 1993 Mark Bles, an ex-SAS officer, was preparing to lead a party of young, enthusiastic, though not necessarily experienced, climbers from the Scots Guards and SAS Reserve in Operation ALP 4000.

Based in a well-appointed Swiss Army Headquarters in Brig and with a variety of transport plus other amenities to hand, the team hoped to pick off the four-thousanders at will, choosing their objective to match prevailing conditions and then nipping quickly back to Brig for women and boozing, army style. Starting with the easy Allalinhorn on 3 May, Bles, already an established author, recounts their adventures in a flowing, humorous style. There are plenty of anecdotes, written with the usual army-speak plus its associated collection of expletives, yet now and again we are introduced to a little philosophy or some harsh criticism. Bles is certainly not reticent in speaking his mind and although not totally removed from military life, he has long been out of the 'system' and is able to stand back and laugh at its idiosyncrasies.

In a style that has rather unfairly been associated with military groups, the Guards seemed to drop a lot of gear, took some potentially serious falls and relied almost entirely on 15 to 20-year-old guidebooks but generally managed to muddle through, growing in confidence as their fitness and ability improved. The main reason for defeat was the unusually poor weather throughout the summer. Unable to maintain a suitable schedule, the season ended with 'only' 48 summits climbed and 'the weather closed in for ever'. The lads may not have completed their target but you certainly get the impression that they thoroughly enjoyed their attempt. On 20 September, when Bles finally threw in the towel, he was 'certain that all the Alpine four-thousanders could be climbed by ordinary climbers in one year'. Little did he realise that just over a month earlier two British guides had completed the first non-stop traverse of 75 four-thousanders in just 52 days, scorning all motorised forms of transport and linking individual ascents by simply skiing, walking or cycling.

In common with the Scots Guards, Simon Jenkins and Martin Moran took the opportunity of using their project to raise money for charity. Here the similarity ends. While the soldiers indulged in a peak-bagging exercise, and there is certainly nothing wrong in that, Jenkins and Moran's dream was set on a much higher plane – an Alpine *super-enchaînement*.

Both were required to commit all their savings, plus substantial peak season loss of revenue, into this expensive project. However, in purely mountaineering terms, the end result, it could be argued, was extremely cost effective, the pair notching up more four-thousanders in one season than many Alpinists accomplish in a lifetime of visits.

How they achieved this considerable feat is told in *Alps 4000*. Superb organisation and very strong back-up was certainly present, and the project would have quickly floundered without it, but in the end this pair succeeded because a combined wealth of experience in the Alps and Himalaya allowed them to continue their programme in all but the most diabolical of conditions. Their technical competence and previous first-hand knowledge of a vast number of four-thousanders allowed many of the *Voie Normales* on the great Valaisannes peaks to be tackled in very taxing conditions. Non-standard routes occasionally provided a viable option when alternatives were judged impossibly time-consuming or dangerous.

The pair also developed the endurance to pedal continuously over long, steep road passes or, towards the completion of their odyssey, to link eleven Mont Blanc four-thousanders in a continuous 33-hour push from the Col du Géant to the Eccles Bivouac Huts. A loss of momentum might also have precipitated a loss of motivation and, perhaps inevitably, there were one or two occasions when the boat was pushed out hard, such as during the panic-stricken, hail-swept rush to the summit of the Dent du Géant whilst thunder reverberated across the Vallée Blanche.

Constant involvement with support parties, plus regular radio calls to family and friends in the valley, ensured that, despite the lack of other parties on the hill through periods of adverse weather, this was certainly not a lonely journey. Moran uses frequent diary extracts from his wife Joy (who monitors his progress from the family's motor-home in the valley), Jenkins and several others who played crucial roles in Alps 4000 to complement his own honestly written narrative. Thus we are privy to the feelings of all the main characters, their frustration, anger, emotional strain and personal failings, as well as the triumphs and tribulations of a two-man partnership trying single-mindedly to achieve a dream, yet plagued by doubts as progress continues to drop further behind schedule in the abysmally poor weather.

There are occasions when the writing becomes a little melodramatic but *Alps 4000* is overall a well-crafted book and was a worthy nomination for last year's Boardman-Tasker Award. It is also a useful reference source, containing a host of informative mountain shots and a series of excellent sketch-maps that are essential if we are to make true sense of the journey. (*In Search of Limits* runs to a very small selection of photos, sandwiched in the centre pages, and no maps – all for the same price.)

While *In Search of Limits* is a very entertaining read and may for that reason have a greater appeal to the uninformed public, *Alps 4000* is for the mountaineer. The two books, like the two projects, are on different levels. Few Alpinists will wish to repeat the voyage described in *Alps 4000* but most, reading Moran's fascinating account, will find renewed inspiration for Alpine climbing, and many tantalising ideas for much lesser journeys or *enchaînements* through our ever-popular European playground.

*Lindsay Griffin*

### Monte Bianco Volume 1
Gino Buscaini
*Club Alpino Italiano / Touring Club Italiano, 1994, pp512, c L60,000*

The last definitive guide to the western end of the Mont Blanc massif, Lucien Devies's *Volume 1 (Col de la Seigne to the Col du Géant)* of the famous French Vallot series, was already out of date by the time of its publication in the late 1970s. Since then we have witnessed a whole new wave of rock climbing, plus the addition of innumerable and often ephemeral *goulottes*. Today it seems that even the region's most prolific activists are not entirely sure what has or has not been climbed, so the task of writing a complete guide would appear to border on the impossible.

There was probably only one person, with the knowledge and available sources of research material, capable of doing the job, and the well-known Italian author Gino Buscaini spent a full three years producing what amounts to a masterpiece of photo-diagrams, topos, maps and text. OK, there are several errors (there are in any guide) but the wealth of information is staggering and includes a complete history of early repeats, first winter ascents, solos, etc. Grades are an interesting mixture of UIAA and French, a problem that will no doubt resolve itself in time as the more traditional yet rarely repeated hard routes are frequented by modern climbers. The old classics are described with the 'normally accepted' amount of aid after noting an all-free rating in the introduction.

For those requiring up-to-date information on the less frequented climbs, little known alternatives to more popular routes or glimpses of virgin lines still waiting to be explored, this is essential reading and continues the very high standard of production for which both the author and the CAI are justly famous.

*Lindsay Griffin*

**A Hard Day's Summer.  Six Classic North Faces Solo**
Alison Hargreaves
*Hodder & Stoughton, 1994, pp (x)+158, £16.99*

Anyone who attended one of Alison Hargreaves' lectures on her big six
Alpine North Face climbs last summer will be aware of the interest they
aroused.  It was a case of standing room only – and it was easy to see why.
Somehow it had seemed almost a foregone conclusion that such hard men
as Martin Moran and Simon Jenkins would succeed in their race up and
down all the 4000m peaks that same summer, but not quite so probable
that Alison Hargreaves, a slim, modest figure, would be successful in her
solo exploits on these classic north faces,  especially during a summer notorious for bad weather and with her husband and two small children waiting around below the crags for six months.  How wrong can you be?

The bad weather put paid to a hoped-for early start and it was June before the big climbs could be attempted.  The previous three months were
devoted to training climbs in sunny Les Calanques and the Ecrins.  All the
big climbs were snatched, at great speed, during gaps in the bad weather.
Whilst the author is her usual modest self in describing them, they were
indeed tremendous achievements and must have seemed incredible to
other climbers who had to watch this small figure hurtling upwards past
them.  For the record, each of the six was, I believe, the first solo ascent by
a woman, and the Eiger was a new route adjacent to the original Lauper
route. The other routes were the Shroud on the Grandes Jorasses, the Schmid
on the Matterhorn, the Cassin on the Badile, the Allain on the Dru, and
the Comice on the Cima Grande.  The author has, of course, climbed many
other north face routes, notably the original route on the Eiger North Face
in 1988, and she returned three months after the Cima Grande climb to
solo the Croz Spur on the Grandes Jorasses, but that climb is not covered
in the book.

As each face fell, it became apparent that it might be possible for her to
complete all six faces in under 24 hours' actual climbing time.  And so it
proved:  her times totalled 23½ hours.  Hence the title of the book.

As to the book itself, the writing, whilst not a literary treat, flows along
well enough, though it needs to be read as a tale of a family summer as well
as of great climbing exploits.  However, in some ways the book proves to be
a disappointment.  For £17 you get only 117 pages of text, plus assorted
appendices and eight pages of colour photos.  Perhaps it is rather unfair to
compare this with Martin Moran's book on the 4000m summits, but you
do get a lot more for your money with that one!  One final point – I should
think the sponsors must be very happy, as I can't recall seeing so many
brand names used in a narrative before.

These small gripes apart, I did enjoy reading this record of a very significant achievement.

*Geoffrey Templeman*

## No Place to Fall
### Superalpinism in the High Himalaya
Victor Saunders
*Hodder & Stoughton, 1994, pp176, £16.99*

Personal diaries frequently make provocative reading, especially when written expressly for publication. Diary-style is now a standard form of mountaineering literature (along with the expedition book, the autobiography, the scientific study, the guidebook, and the occasional psychological thriller). During intervals between trekking, servicing their bodies, and (occasional) climbing, mountaineers keep their diaries and take photographs. Mostly they write about each other. Fortunately, climbers are a fairly entertaining bunch.

After a motor accident, witnesses only rarely agree over the details. Similarly, the personal realities of these scribbling mountaineers are bound to be rather individual. The 'big questions', however, remain the same: Why do we do it? Which is better, a success on an 'easy' peak, or a near-success (ie, a failure?) on a harder one? And what constitutes success, anyway?

This book is the story of the contemporary Himalayan climber. It is a blend of three Alpine-style but Himalayan-scale expeditions, with a nice balance of success and failure, and washed down with sharp wit in abundance. The after-taste is rich and inspiring. Climbers are rarely considered 'normal' by the population at large, but even on the scale of climbers, the people in these stories appear somewhat mad. But how I yearn to be with them. Readers of this superb book may just for a moment believe that they too can be superhuman.

Saunders and Sustad wanted to traverse Makalu from north to south in 1989, but the local gods thought otherwise. Of the many climbers on Makalu that year, only Pierre Béghin was permitted to reach the summit. After a preliminary excursion with Andy Fanshawe up Yaupa Central (6300m), Saunders and Sustad made the first ascent of the W face of nearby peak Kangchungtse (7640m). The account of the climb is shrouded in a certain disorder, which Saunders appears to believe to be intrinsic to his life in the mountains. They set off for a day in the hills with less equipment and food than some of us would take for a day on Ben Nevis. After some complex route-finding and technical climbing, adverse snow conditions forced them away from the direct route, and they attained a 'South Summit' late in the evening. By then the weather had deteriorated, and they had to sleep in snow holes. They returned to their tent 46 hours after having left it. If only that butterfly had not stolen the compass ...

The Karakoram Highway is five kilometres away from the summit of Ultar (7388m), in both the horizontal and vertical directions. The SE face of Ultar sports a giant Hidden Pillar which was Saunders' major target in 1991. In the classical tradition of high-altitude climbing, it was a problem to get to the bottom of the route. At last, at the end of August, they set out for a week of night climbing, but in order to avoid avalanches rather than proctors. Overcoming a series of difficulties with determination and courage, they arrived within spitting distance of the summit ridge. 'We felt optimistic about the weather ... and about our chances. But our optimism was horribly misplaced. By 11.00 a.m. the next morning, we knew our climb was over. Not only that, we would be lucky to make it down alive.' An unforeseen circumstance forced an emergency exit, down a line fraught with rock- and water-fall. On this occasion, the climbers survived without major incident. By retreating, they left the virgin summit undefended against a group of multi-roped Japanese climbers led by Tsuneo Hasegawa. Such is the way of the world. Hasegawa and Hoshino died in an avalanche a few weeks later.

Now the joint Indian British Panch Chuli expedition (1992) was quite another thing. Organised by Harish Kapadia and Chris Bonington, and with high-tech support by courtesy of the latter, this trip was doomed to success. Peaks were bagged by Indian and British alike, but at some cost. Saunders and friends spent a whole week on Rajrambha (6537m). Their glorious traverse of the watershed extended for miles of 'silver ridge', with its cornices and 'faithless film of powder'. Meanwhile, Bonington and Little put up a new route on the W ridge of Panch Chuli II, while an Indian team reached the same summit by the SW ridge.

Was it really an afterthought to take a look at the unclimbed Panch Chulis round the corner? Panch Chuli V (6437m) seemed the obvious choice in this seductive set, with her relative availability and easy summit ridge. The truth was otherwise. After two days in the presence of falling blocks of ice, the team arrived at a col at the foot of the South Ridge. Here Bonington stayed while the rest of the party extended itself to the summit, on a journey over steep rock and ice. It was on the descent, early next day, that Venables' abseil peg joined its master prematurely. This was no place to fall. You must read Saunders' moving account of the sequel, accompanied by some of the most compelling photographs in the book.

*No Place to Fall* is a superb and beautiful account of modern Himalayan climbing, laced with wit and intelligence, and laying bare the exquisite pains and rewards of the 'high life'. In the best diarist tradition of Samuel Pepys and Alan Clark, Victor Saunders is a critical observer of his surroundings and fellows, and thereby of himself. Through his eyes and pen, we travel to magic places, and back again. No, it is not a poem in prose, but rather a travel book, and sometimes even a sitcom. Combining three stories in one set of covers is a threat to continuity, but spares the reader an all-night sitting. Some additional photographs would have helped this reader to follow the routes.

There is more to an expedition than simply climbing. There is also dialogue. One of the morals of this book is: always take at least two mathematicians, one botanist, one geologist, and the tax inspector. Not only is the conversation enriched, but the skills of these individuals can even be useful. In particular, the mathematicians might disabuse the author of the belief that the outcome of an expedition depends on a strange conjunction of apparently insignificant events. More relevant than the scientific theory of *chaos* (which is often referred to in the book) is the theory of *self-organisation*. Roughly speaking, this theory suggests that individuals as highly motivated and physically capable as Saunders will always create their successes, whatever the intervening difficulties. As predicted by the Darwinian theory of evolution, individuals of this type are a rare breed. Their adventures make thrilling reading.

*Geoffrey Grimmett*

### Hands of a Climber. A Life of Colin Kirkus
Steve Dean
*The Ernest Press, 1993, pp (viii)+278, £15.95*

The definitive biography of Colin Kirkus (1910-1942) is an intensely re-searched study by Steve Dean, Derby town planner and rock climber.

To many British rock climbers today, Colin Kirkus is merely a name in the guidebooks, attached to routes characterised by boldness and a fine-ness of line exemplified by *Kirkus' Route* at Cwm Silin, its character pre-served to this day by a scarcity of protection. From 1930 until the outbreak of the Second World War, during which he was killed in a bombing raid over Bremen, Kirkus forged his way to the forefront of British climbing. He wrote one book (*Lets Go Climbing*), several guidebooks, and took part in a single Himalayan trip. He was passed over for several other expeditions, notably both the 1933 and 1936 Everest parties, doubtless because Caldy Grammar School and Liverpool College were less acceptable than Eton and Trinity. He was, after all, an insurance clerk, and not a member of the Alpine Club.

Steve Dean has tackled the difficult task of recording the life of a very private man. There are no hitherto unknown revelations here, but the fruits of solid research, aided by the survivors of the era who knew Colin Kirkus well and climbed with him, Jack Longland and A B Hargreaves in particu-lar. It is the meticulous detail of this book which will give it a lasting place in the library of British mountaineering. Kirkus's early life and exploits are followed with precision. There is an almost daily diary of his brief Alpine and Himalayan career (with Charles Warren and Marco Pallis in the Garhwal) and the accident on Ben Nevis in 1934 when Maurice Linnell was killed.

It is, however, this very detail which makes the book more a work of historical reference than a treasured glimpse into a private world. Colin Kirkus is portrayed as the honest, selfless, unassuming man he doubtless was. The skill of his hands is captured here but not, I fear, his soul.

*Charles Clarke*

## We Aspired:  The Last Innocent Americans
### Pete Sinclair
*Utah State University Press, 1993, pp232, £14.95*

This is not about an audacious new route on Denali in 1959 forced with
the total commitment of youth.  It is not about living a sixties' climber's life
on the road in and out of the company of Gary Hemming.  And it is not
about the pride, professionalism and eventual disillusionment of the ranger-
in-charge of rescue in Grand Teton National Park during a period when
the climbers' campground lost its innocence.  Although this remarkable
book does tell these stories, with the laconic humour learned of the American oral tradition and Chaucer, Faulkner and Cormac McCarthy, this book
is really about integrity.  Quietly, or wildly, or pragmatically, it creeps up
on the question of doing the right thing by your mates, or your heroes,
or the dead, or the rock.  It asks the question 'What is self-possession?'
I admire the maturity from which it looks back on a Bohemian climbing
life – and I want to quote lots.

The young hitch-hiking drop-out from Ivy League puritanism cannot
ask for charity and is, in fact, confronted with the dignity of the poor's
gener-osity.  So, too, amongst climbers who feed their partners while one
of them has work.  So when is clearing the unwanted debris of a fatality
'looting'?  So what has happened when the rangers-of-the-road hound out
Chouinard from the Tetons for a minor infringement?  So what is the future of climbing when the bolt has made all climbs possible?  These are the
shifts in the culture that this book softly charts and they are not confined to
the Tetons.  Let me quote only once and for our British rearguard action
against the crag-creeping bolt-plague of today:

> This is hard to describe in a way that doesn't sound silly, but after
> you've climbed in one area a lot, you have the feeling that the moun-
> tains tell you how they ought to be climbed.  You climb in a certain
> way because of the nature of the rock or terrain, the weather, the
> history and tradition of the place, and something of your own which
> asks for something more graceful than just surviving.  If it works you
> have done something beautiful.  When you've got that feeling, you've
> got the right way to do it.  You hear the mountain's message by how
> you feel ... To learn what was right meant that you humbled yourself
> not before Royal Robbins but before where he had been and how he
> got there and what he had learned in getting there.  These days there
> is talk of our need for an ethic of place.  That is precisely what we
> were about.

More than once this writer admits that he was wrong.  For a lead rescuer
that's a little unusual.  But this is an unusual book that is an honest, reflect-
ive odyssey out of an era of everyone knowing each other *and* the shared
codes, into the open recreational context of today, where we know what
will be the consequences of our choices with the bolt, the mobile telephone

or the helicopter. As Sinclair puts it, 'Innocence is what you leave in your wake when you know the story.' There's a lot of valuable innocence to be recovered from this one.

*Terry Gifford*

## Whensoever
### 50 years of the RAF Mountain Rescue Service 1943-1993
Frank Card
*The Ernest Press, 1993, pp (xii)+340, £17.95*

## The Black Cloud
I D S Thomson
*The Ernest Press, 1993, pp274, £9.99*

## Countdown to Rescue
Bob Maslen-Jones
*The Ernest Press, 1993, pp221, £9.95*

Over the years, there has been a small number of books on mountain rescue, notably by Gwen Moffatt and Hamish MacInnes. Now, within a short space of time, three more have appeared – not, perhaps, so surprising when you consider that Jack Baines of the Ernest Press was himself a member of the RAF Mountain Rescue Service for many years.

In *Whensoever* Frank Card tells the story of the Service from its rather ad hoc beginnings during the Second World War to its present-day efficient organisation, and of how it has changed from its original aims of searching for crashed aircrews, through giving assistance to those of the general public who have come to grief in the mountains, to such tragic modern-day happenings as the Lockerbie disaster. Most of the major call-outs are covered, not only in Wales, Scotland and the Peak District, but also in Cyprus, Turkey and the Far East where the RAFMRS was active. The book is beautifully produced, with numerous photographs, cartoons and maps, and is a worthy record of a magnificent service, which is constantly under threat at the present time.

*The Black Cloud* is a detailed account of seven Scottish mountain accidents which occurred between 1928 and 1966, four between 1928 and 1934, and the remaining three after 1951. Among the climbing fraternity the best known of these is the accident involving Colin Kirkus and Maurice Linnell on *The Castle* on Ben Nevis at Easter weekend 1934, in which Linnell was killed. The author has used existing newspaper accounts, coupled with interviews with people involved at the time, to bring a fresh look at many of these incidents.

In the final book, *Countdown to Rescue*, Bob Maslen-Jones recounts his personal experiences in mountain rescue work in Snowdonia over the past 15 years or so. Numerous incidents are covered and, in particular, the work of the Search and Rescue Dog Association.

*Geoffrey Templeman*

**Mount Everest Massif. Monograph-guide-chronicle**
Jan Kielkowski
*Explo, Gliwice, Poland, 1993, pp202, npq*

Jan Kielkowski has been issuing guides to Himalayan mountains for some years now, but his latest effort *Mount Everest Massif* has to be the best so far. Packed with information on routes and ascents, with numerous maps, and almost a hundred of the author's own drawings of peaks and faces, it embodies an incredible amount of work. I almost described the drawings as 'topo-diagrams', but that would have been inaccurate for, while clearly showing the lines of all the routes, they are far more than just diagrams. Look at the double-page spreads of the SW face of Everest and the upper part of the S face of Lhotse to see what I mean.

The book covers the complete Mount Everest massif, that is all peaks and passes on the ridges radiating out from Everest, Lhotse and Nuptse. Following a general introduction to the massif, a list of all expeditions to the area from 1921 to 1992 is given, with the nationality, leader and achievement of the team. Each peak or pass then receives a general description, with notes on nomenclature, followed by sections for each face or feature, with route descriptions where applicable and details of all attempts/ascents.

While this is obviously no ordinary guide (you won't roll up at the foot of Lhotse, open it, and say 'Let's try route 72'), it would be invaluable as an accompaniment to any Everest area expedition book you read; or, of course, for showing where the new route gaps are. Unfortunately, although the book is in English, I can't help you as to where you can purchase a copy.

*Geoffrey Templeman*

**Shadows on the Wasteland**
**Crossing Antarctica with Ranulph Fiennes**
Mike Stroud
*Jonathan Cape, 1993, pp (x)+182, £14.99*

Everyone must know by now the story of the Ran Fiennes/Mike Stroud crossing of Antarctica in 1992/93: 1350 miles, 95 days, completely unsupported, starting off by pulling nearly 500lbs each on sledges, and ending with a pick-up on the Ross ice shelf, when it would have been suicide to continue over the floating ice to the open sea.

This is Stroud's version of that journey, dwelling mainly on the relationship evident in the sub-title. You would, after all, need a pretty vivid imagination to write at great length about the scenery in Antarctica; the weather, the conditions, your health and relationship with your companions are everything. When there are only two of you, the relationship must be even more intense! The Press made a great play of the animosity that developed between the two men, but this book sets the record straight; at least from

Stroud's point of view! The two men were not strangers, either to each other or to harsh conditions, as they had been together in similar-style attempts on the North Pole; but this time irritation between the two was never far away. As far as can be ascertained, Stroud relates this fairly and, in the process, has written a very readable book.

They apparently finished the expedition the best of friends and, although he got rather rattled again by some of the statements Fiennes made in his lectures, Stroud finishes the book by saying: 'If the opportunity were to come again to step out of life and visit other planets, there is no question as to whom I would wish for a companion. I would go with Ran.'

*Geoffrey Templeman*

### The Illustrated Library of the Earth: Mountains
Edited by J D Ives
*Rodale Press, Emmaus USA, $35*

Mountains is the second volume in a series of which *Oceans & Islands* has already appeared. A glossy 'coffee-table' book with superb illustrations and an authoritative text, it provides a nice complement to the plainer *State of the World's Mountains* (reviewed in *AJ98*, 297, 1993) with which it shares some of the same distinguished contributors. In contrast to the latter, it is arranged by topics, drawing illustrative examples from different regions of the world. First it describes the tectonic, volcanic and erosional backgrounds to mountain formation and decay, with spectacular photos of volcanoes and glaciation, and clear diagrams of plate tectonics and vulcanism. The special characteristics of mountain weather are described, together with its effects on the surrounding lowlands and the effects of hypoxia on humans. Next are the plants and animals that live in the mountains, naturally picking out and illustrating spectacular examples such as giant lobelias, giant puyas and giant condors.

The last third of the book deals with mountain people and their way of life, emphasising first the extreme upland inhabitants of Tibet and the Andes, then those that gain their livelihood from farming the slopes, together with some of the problems and controversies that have arisen from this. Brief glances at mountains in Greek mythology, Tibetan Buddhism and the yeti are followed by consideration of those outsiders who exploit mountains in various ways, for mining, damming, skiing and climbing, usually damaging the environment in the process. A final chapter summarises in a few pages the essentials of Mountain Agenda's case for conservation and careful development. One very striking full-page photo is wrongly captioned; can you spot it?

*Henry Osmaston*

(Adapted with the permission of the publishers, Butterworth Heineman Ltd, from a review first published in *Global Environmental Change*.)

## Arka Tagh.  The Mysterious Mountains
William Holgate
*The Ernest Press, 1994, pp (6)+154, £15.95*

The Arka Tagh, the mountain range featured in this book, lies on the borders of Tibet and Xinjiang, with the arid Taklamakan Desert to the north and the Tibetan Plateau to the south.  The author decided to visit this area, one of the most isolated places on earth, and follow in the footsteps of Dutreuil de Rhins (1893), St George Littledale (1895), and Sven Hedin (1896).  It took him ten years (and one unofficial attempt when he was arrested and deported) to obtain Chinese consent and finally to make the journey, travelling with one British companion, Tim Martin, and with Huang Min Min as co-leader. The journey could only be achieved as a joint expedition, as had been the case with the Chinese–American expedition to Ulugh Mustagh, the highest peak in the range, in 1985.

While early explorers had been forced to contend with physical danger from local tribesmen, this trip was bedevilled by the bureaucratic muddle and general inefficiency of Huang, although most of Huang's subordinates did their best to help and seemed to dislike him as much as the author did. Anyway, a small party of eight men, nineteen camels and a dog completed a round trip of over 300 miles, although not all the camels made it to the end.

There are no great mountaineering exploits here, but it is a well-told tale of travel in remote areas, in the Shipton/Tilman tradition.  However, trying to follow the route on the *Mountains of Central Asia* map proved to be almost impossible, as none of the names on the map are the same as those in the book.

*Geoffrey Templeman*

## Mountaineering in the Andes.  A Sourcebook for Climbers
Jill Neate
*Expedition Advisory Centre, RGS, 1994, pp (vi)+256, npq*

The last major work completed by Jill Neate before her tragic death in 1993 was this revised edition of her Andean sourcebook, first published in 1987 and now issued in soft cover book form.  This is the essential reference work for anyone contemplating climbing in or travelling through the Andean mountains.  For each country, region or range there is a general topographical introduction, a summary of climbing history, lists of peaks, and selected references where further studies can be made.  Add to this sketch maps of the areas described and details of local journals and organisations, and you get a mine of information, much of it available in English for the first time.  When Jill Neate died, the climbing community lost a major historian and bibliographer.

*Geoffrey Templeman*

## Among Mountains
Jim Crumley
*Mainstream, 1993, pp160, £14.99*

As Jim Crumley says: 'There has always been more to going to the mountains than mere mountaineering.' This book, like the eight others he has written, deals entirely with his native Scottish hills, and is a plea to take the time to pause and take in the whole mountain environment. Not for him the ticking-off of Munros in a group clad in bright-coloured anoraks, their shouts ringing round the hills. His themes are wildlife, the vanished inhabitants of the hills and glens, and conservation. Some of his previous books have been produced in collaboration with photographer Colin Baxter, but this one shows that he is more than competent to illustrate his own writings, and to add to the text with his own poems.

## In the Shadow of Denali
Jonathan Waterman
*Delta, 1994, pp (x)+246, pb, $11.95*

The author has lived and worked in the shadow of McKinley for many years, as a guide and as a rescue ranger in the Denali Park Service, and was also for a number of years an editor on *Climbing* magazine. He has had numerous articles published in mountaineering and outdoor publications, and brings a fine, polished style to this, his third book. Sub-titled *Life and Death on Alaska's Mt McKinley*, it tells the stories of many of his friends and companions on Alaskan adventures. Most of the American climbers active in the far north get a mention, plus a number of British ones, and the book ends with an appreciation of Mugs Stump. This is a fine piece of mountaineering writing.

## Environmental Protection of the Himalaya. A Mountaineers' View
Edited by Aamir Ali
*Indus Publishing Co, New Delhi, 1994, pp112, npq*

This special publication has been issued in celebration of the 50th volume of the *Himalayan Journal*. A 'postal symposium' was held amongst various members of the Himalayan Club and other authorities, and the book contains their edited replies. Following the editor's own introduction, there are 21 short essays covering many environmental problems: eg waste disposal, deforestation and fuel, tourism, litter, sociological damage, and many other aspects. The problems are well presented for all to see; the answers pose greater difficulties.

## Over the Himalaya
Koichiro Ohmori
*Diadem, 1994, £25.00*

This is the last book to be published under the Diadem imprint and is up to their usual high standard. It consists of 44 double-page aerial photographs of the main mountain groups in Nepal, all of exceptional clarity and mercifully free from the lurid sunrise/sunset effects beloved by so many Japanese photographers. The text is limited to brief topographical details, the author's thoughts on flying over the Himalaya, and photographic notes.

## Mountaineering.
### Catalogue of the Graham Brown and Lloyd Collections in the National Library of Scotland
*National Library of Scotland, 1994, pp (xviii) + 454, £15.00*

Two former prominent members of the Alpine Club donated books to the National Library of Scotland in Edinburgh. In 1958 R W Lloyd gave over 1650 volumes to the Library, and this was followed in 1965 by Professor T Graham Brown, who donated his entire library of some 20,000 items. This has made the National Library one of the chief centres in Europe for those wishing to study Alpinism and mountaineering in general. This hefty catalogue lists all the items contained in the two collections, but differs from the AC's own Library Catalogue in having its main section listed alphabetically by title, rather than by author. It is also not quite so detailed as the AC volume. Even though a number of the books included have nothing to do with mountaineering, this must still be a useful aid for bibliographical study.

## Trekking in Russia & Central Asia. A Traveller's Guide
Frith Maier
*Cordee/Mountaineers, 1994, pp370, £12.95*

This is a further volume in the series inaugurated by The Mountaineers, which has included *Trekking in Nepal* and *Trekking in Tibet*. All have been exemplary in the amount of factual detail provided, and have given excellent in-depth backgrounds to the culture, as well as the geography of the countries concerned. The present volume covers an enormous amount of ground, much of it completely unknown to the average traveller, including parts of the Urals, Pamirs, Caucasus, Siberia, Lake Baikal and the Crimean and Kamchatka Peninsulas.

The author, a native of Alaska, has spent the past ten years in exploratory mountain travel to the remotest parts of the former USSR including ascents of Peak Communism and Khan Tengri. Whilst the book is mainly concerned with trekking, it does also include guides to the ascents of Pobeda, Lenin and Korzhenevskiy as well as the above, plus opportunities for mountain biking, rafting, etc. One of the features of the book are the maps, drawn by a Russian map-maker and unique to this publication. This is certainly an indispensable guide for anyone contemplating travelling in this vast area, now that such a journey is permitted, if not easy.

The Alpine Club Library also received the following books during 1994:

**Exploring the Far North West of Scotland. A Walker's Guide to the Hills, Glens and Coastline of Wester Ross & Sutherland** Richard Gilbert. *Cordee, 1994, pp144, £12.95*

**On Foot in Snowdonia. The Best Hill Walks and Scrambles from Cadair Idris to the Carneddau** Bob Allen. *Michael Joseph, 1993, pp (xii)+228, £14.99*

**Short Walks in the Lake District. 60 Walks for Short Days, Wet Days – and with the family** Bob Allen. *Michael Joseph, 1994, pp224, £14.99*

**Britain's Highest Peaks. The Complete Illustrated Route Guide** Jeremy Ashcroft. *David & Charles, 1993, pp184, £19.99*

**Walking in the Harz Mountains. Including Walks from the Harz Narrow Gauge Railway** Fleur & Colin Speakman. *Cicerone, 1994, pp144, £7.99*

**Menlove** Jim Perrin. *The Ernest Press, 1993, pp (xii)+298, pb, £9.95*

**An Illustrated Guide to the Packhorse Bridges of the Lake District** Michael Hartwell. *The Ernest Press, 1994, pp132, £6.95*

**Ben Nevis. Rock and Ice Climbs** Simon Richardson, Alastair Walker, Robin Clothier. *SMC, 1994, pp (xii)+340, npq*

**Treks and Climbs in Wadi Rum, Jordan** Tony Howard. *Cicerone, 1994, pp192, £12.99*. Revised second edition

**Walks & Climbs in the Pyrenees** Kev Reynolds. *Cicerone, 1993, pp320, £14.99*. Third edition

**Northeast Outcrops. Including the Aberdeen, Moray & Banff sea cliffs, Deeside, Glen Clova & the Angus quarries** Compiled by Neil Morrison. *SMC, 1994, pp (x)+342, npq*

**The Hillwalker's Manual** Bill Birkett. *Cicerone, 1994, pp144, £7.99*

**Trekking in the Caucasus**  Yury Kolomiets & Aleksey Solovyev.
*Cicerone, 1994, pp248, £14.99*

**Exploring the Lakeland Fells. 32 Mountain Walks complete with Plan & Relief Maps**  Tom Lawton.  *Ward Lock, 1993, pp192, npq*

**Llanberis Pass**  Paul Williams.  *Climbers' Club, 1994, pp318, npq*

**100 Walks in the French Alps**  Terry March.
*Hodder & Stoughton, 1994, pp222, £15.99*

**Walking in the High Tatras (Slovakia & Poland). Including the Western Tatras in Poland and the White Tatras in Slovakia**
Colin Saunders & Renáta Nározná.  *Cicerone, 1994, pp234, £14.99*

**Selected Rock Climbs in Belgium & Luxembourg**  Chris Craggs.
*Cicerone, 1994, pp176, £12.99*

**Lowland Outcrops**  Tom Prentice & Grahame Nicoll.
*SMC, 1994, pp (xii)+367, npq*

**Lundy**  Gary Gibson & Paul Harrison.  *Climbers' Club, 1994, pp288, £12.95*

**Walking the Lakeland Round**  Tom Lawton.  *Ward Lock, 1994, pp176, £16.99*

**A Dry Ship to the Mountains. Down the Volga & Across the Caucasus in my Father's Footsteps**  Daniel Farson.
*Michael Joseph, 1994, pp (x)+246. £15.99*

**Altitude Illness. Prevention & Treatment**  Stephen Bezruchka.
*Cordee, 1994, pp96, £4.95*

**The Mountains of Turkey**  Karl Smith.  *Cicerone, 1994, pp176, £14.99*

**Walking the Watershed**  Dave Hewitt.  *Tacit, 1994, pp240, £7.99*

**Munros's Fables**  Grant Hutchison & Chris Tyler.  *Tacit, 1993, pp104, £5.99*

**Blind Corners. Adventures on Seven Continents**  Geoff Tabin.
*ICS Books, 1993, pp (xii)+196, $24.99*


The following books have been received and will be reviewed in next year's volume:  Harish Kapadia, **High Himalaya: Unknown Valleys**;  Gordon Stainforth, **The Cuillin**; Terry Gifford, **Orogenic Zones**.

# In Memoriam

COMPILED BY GEOFFREY TEMPLEMAN

| The Alpine Club Obituary | Year of Election | |
|---|---|---|
| Lewis Griffith Creswell Evans Pugh | HON | 1978 |
| Albrecht Robert von Leyden | | 1939 |
| Anthony David Machell Cox | | 1938 |
| Eleanor Winthrop Young | LAC | 1942 |
| James Waller | | 1936 |
| Kenneth Charles Pearson | | 1965 |
| Christopher Manfred Gravina | | 1960 |
| Alastair Lorimer Cram | | 1948 |
| Roderick Syme | | 1933 |
| Stephen A. Caswell | | 1993 |
| Donald Murray | | 1956 |
| Terris Moore | | 1934 |
| Enid Susie Smith | LAC | 1929 |
| Alexander Dougal Malcolm | | 1933 |
| John Travers Mends Gibson | | 1947 |
| Paul Arthur Fletcher | | 1950 |
| Frederick Llewellyn Jenkins | | 1954 |
| Richard Henry Hobhouse | | 1960 |

In addition to the above, an obituary is included for Louis Charles Baume, who died in 1993.

One further name I would like to mention is that of Barry Bishop who tragically died in a car accident at the age of 62. Although not currently a member, he had connections with the Club and had been a member of the American Alpine Club since 1952. In 1951, with Bradford Washburn, he made the first ascent of the West Buttress of Mt McKinley and in 1961, as the glaciologist and climatologist on Sir Edmund Hillary's scientific winter expedition, he made the first ascent of Ama Dablam. He was a member of the first American team to climb Mt Everest, summiting via the South Col with Lute Jerstad on 22 May 1963.

Finally, may I put in a request here that if any members feel they could write an obituary for a friend, please do not wait to be asked. Whilst I cannot promise that every contribution will be used, they will all be very gratefully received and preserved in the archives of the Club.

*Geoffrey Templeman*

# Lewis Griffith Cresswell Evans Pugh 1909–1994

Despite the fact that our Honorary Member, Dr Griffith Pugh, never considered himself to be a mountaineer, he made three major contributions to
mountaineering and to our knowledge of the mountain environment: firstly,
his solution of the problem of 'The Last Thousand Feet' of Everest leading to the successful first ascent in 1953; secondly, his organisation and
leadership of the Winter Physiology Party of the Silver Hut Expedition
1960-61 that wintered at 19,000ft in the Everest Region; and thirdly, his
successful investigation into the causes and prevention of deaths in the British Isles due to hypothermia .

Pugh was born on 30 November 1909, the son of a barrister. Between
1928 and 1931 he read Law at New College, Oxford but later changed to
medicine and spent a further three years at Oxford before qualifying at St
Thomas's Hospital in 1938. Whilst at University he raced in each of the
three skiing disciplines and was chosen for the British Olympic 18km cross-
country team of 1936, but because of injury could not compete. He also
climbed regularly in the Mont Blanc region and the Bernese Oberland.

In 1939 he was called up to serve in the RAMC. Posted to the Middle
East, he served in Greece, Palestine and Iran. In 1942 he received a tel-
egram from W J Riddell, with whom he had been a contemporary at
Harrow, asking him to join the newly formed Mountain and Snow Warfare Training School at the Cedars of Lebanon. There he spent the next
two years with W J Riddell who was in overall charge of both snow and
rock instruction. David Cox was Chief Instructor (Rock) and a New Zealander, John Carryer, was Chief Instructor (Snow).

This School had a number of functions: it acted as a leave centre, a
training centre for mountain troops and as a survival training unit. Pugh
had had no training as an exercise physiologist – a concept that did not
exist at that time in the British Armed Forces. Further, there was no general awareness that different physical tasks need different physical attributes
or indeed of the great diversity of human physical capability. He assessed
that the instructors at the School had the most appropriate physical characteristics and so they acted as yardsticks for the selection of personnel
who came to him from all over the Middle East, including the Long Range
Desert Group (now the SAS). Only 25-30% qualified for training and Pugh
had a special group who could be completely self-contained for up to eight
days, ski-mountaineering 20 miles a day. He regularly climbed on skis for
3-4000ft during a 12-hour day and this was continued for weeks on end.

The papers that he wrote during this period were incorporated in a series
of Army Training Manuals and, on discharge from the army, he joined the
staff of the Post-Graduate Medical School at Hammersmith. He stayed for
five years until the formation of the Medical Research Council's Unit of
Environmental Physiology (known as the Department of Human Physiology) where he was head of the Laboratory of Field Physiology.

Pugh's involvement with Everest started early in 1951, some months prior to Eric Shipton's appointment as leader of the Reconnaissance Expedition and over 18 months before John Hunt was made leader of the 1953 Expedition. During this period he launched a new era of high-altitude mountain exploration by providing it with a factual, scientific basis. Mountaineers followed what I would sum up as 'Pugh's Laws' to enable the first ascent of Everest and all the other 8000m peaks to be made within the next few years.

In 1957 Pugh was asked by Nello Pace of the University of California to join a physiological team working at Scott Base and associated with the Trans-Antarctic Expedition. He visited the American Base at the South Pole a number of times and did research into the warming effect of solar radiation, into carbon monoxide poisoning in tents and into tolerance to cold. It was here that, with Edmund Hillary, he conceived the idea of the Silver Hut Expedition 1960-61, using polar techniques to spend the winter at 19,000ft examining the stress of altitude on each part of the transport system of oxygen in humans. This produced new data not only on fundamental biological mechanisms but also, more significantly, on sea-level patients with heart and lung disease. In addition, by showing that the barometric pressure in the Himalaya was higher than expected, he demonstrated in theory that Everest could be climbed without supplementary oxygen. This theory was proved on Everest in 1978 by Habeler and Messner.

Later, in the 1960s, Pugh was asked to investigate deaths in young people from hypothermia in the British Isles. Because of his knowledge of fatigue in mountains he was able to do this very rapidly in a brilliant piece of research, and so saved many young lives.

Involved in the Mexico Olympics, he predicted correctly that the distance events would be slower at altitude, whilst owing to reduced air density, sprint events would be faster. Pugh always stressed the importance of field work to supplement laboratory and climatic chamber studies. He preferred to take extreme examples at 6000m rather than 4000m and for months rather than days. He also studied Olympic rather than club athletes.

Pugh was well known internationally and the Eighth International Hypoxia Symposium in 1993 in Canada (the year of the 40th anniversary of the first ascent of Everest) was appropriately dedicated to him in recognition of his work, which has remained the 'Gold Standard' to which others are compared and on which we build.

Pugh's tall athletic figure and bright red hair matched his highly individual style that gathered a garland of legends in his lifetime. With his dry sense of humour and love of life he was always a stimulating companion. His lasting contribution was that he saved many lives and, without self-interest, enabled others to win fame and glittering prizes. He will be remembered by his friends with great affection, amusement and gratitude.

*Michael Ward*

*W J Riddell writes:*
I think it is true to say that anyone who met Griffith Pugh, even casually, was impressed by him. When we first happened to coincide, as new boys at the same House at Harrow for the same first term in 1924, the odd eccentricity or two quickly manifested itself (and was totally impervious to teasing); Griffith stood out as someone very far removed from the commonplace and he remained a 'one off' throughout his 85-year-long life. Yet with all his enthusiasms, inventions and theories, coupled with his quiet, wry sense of humour and of the ridiculous, he could always count on a lot of admiring friends.

As a schoolboy he was eager and willing to apply his strength and enthusiasm to any sport or team game. He played football with his brain, ran well with his long legs and not many boys of any size were overjoyed to find themselves facing him in the Boxing Ring. Perhaps his major triumph was to win the coveted Silver Arrow trophy for marksmanship.

Of his professional life as a Doctor and Scientist a lot has been written elsewhere but much of his success as a Boffin was influenced and formed by his so-called holiday/hobby activities. It is to these activities that I have been asked to address this obituary. He had a boat and was devoted to sailing, but most of his friends soon discovered that an invitation to accompany him for a weekend's sailing often involved a challenge to disregard every appalling condition of wind and weather and interminable hours of being cold and soaked to the skin. I quickly became adept at finding excuses for not accepting such invitations!

Griffith's main athletic ability, however, emerged when, starting with school holidays, he fell under the challenging spell of the Swiss Alps and the then fast-growing sport of Alpine skiing and ski racing. Engelberg became his favourite resort where, with his analytical brain, he taught himself to become an excellent skier. In the late twenties and thirties ski lifts were few and far between and many of the glorious and demanding slopes of the Laub and Titlis could only be enjoyed by climbing on skins – and by the few who developed sound and flowing downhill technique and understood not a little about snowcraft. The young Pugh also became a fine cross-country skier. It was only an unlucky injury that prevented him from being in the British cross-country team and taking part in the 1936 Olympic Games at Garmisch Partenkirchen.

It was during the early stages of the Second World War, when Griffith and I had not seen each other for several years, that we once again happened to coincide. I was in the Middle East at the time when suddenly, quite out of the blue, I was landed with the huge task of starting up and running a new school high up in the Lebanese mountains to teach troops to be mobile on ski and to be self-sufficient in conditions of snow and extreme cold. Not the least of my problems was to find enough reasonably qualified instructors to cope with the large numbers of trainees that would be sent up regularly by GHQ in a few months' time. By the end of the first year things were running surprisingly well and I was asked by HQ in Cairo to go through voluminous lists of men known to be serving in the Middle East who had pre-war experience of skiing. My prize find was the name of Dr L G C Pugh, then serving in Teheran. We were both equally delighted when he was transferred and appeared at our HQ at the Cedars of Lebanon.

Captain Pugh was quickly to become a sort of ambient, free-ranging central pivot around which this physically arduous school very largely revolved for the following three years – winter and summer – during which period some 20,000 men of several nationalities underwent full training. Knowing something of his qualifications both medically and physiologically, and of his intense interest in the behaviour of the human body in all manner of difficult and unusual conditions, I am immensely proud of the fact that I was able to provide Griffith with a job for which he was ideally suited and with all the means and the power to put his many theories into practice. Working at altitudes between 6,000 and 10,000ft over some 100kms of a more or less 'private' mountain range, everything was there for him to use and monitor: ie suitable terrain of great variety, hundreds of volunteers, and all forms of weather and snow conditions from benign to violent.

'Pug', as he soon became known, tackled every single aspect of the school including methods of training on both snow and rock ... everything in fact, from tests to select suitable trainees, to diet, to physical fitness, to clothing and equipment, to load carrying, to improvements to ski bindings, to safety in general, to designing suitable lightweight tents and cooking utensils ... and so on. Everyone who crossed his path came to regard him with both respect and admiration – affection even – and yet with not a little apprehension about what tests he might next have in mind! But everyone knew full well that he never would ask for any effort he was not always ready to undertake himself.

Such were the beginnings of a distinguished career largely devoted to expert study of the manifold problems of the human body in extreme conditions of cold and altitude and effort, a career that was ultimately to lead to his important role in the 1953 conquest of Everest.

After the war Griffith was one of the main and most knowledgeable members of a committee formed by the War Office to compose the Military Training Manual entitled *Snow and Mountain Warfare*. Following this he became an active physiologist on the High Altitude Committee of the Medical Research Council in London and his wide range of experiments and knowledge led him to be chosen for the Everest team. Griffith always maintained that without his time in the Lebanon, which led to the MRC, Everest might well not have come his way; and he often told his friends that his years at the Cedars School gave him the happiest and most constructive time of his life.

Griffith's many friends and admirers greatly mourn the passing of this tall, angular 'one off' figure with his gentle eccentricities, his quiet dry humour – and his flaming red hair.

# Albrecht Robert von Leyden 1905-1994

Albrecht, long known to all his friends as 'Lolly', started climbing with his father and elder brother at the age of 15. His father had been elected to the Alpine Club in 1911, lost his membership because of the 1914-18 war and was re-elected in 1954 (Obit. *AJ69*, 177-180, 1964). Inflation in Germany in the twenties made it impossible for them to visit Switzerland or to employ guides. For several years they explored, unguided, the mountains of the Zillertal, Tauern, Stubai and Ötztaler Alps and other parts of Austria and Bavaria. They used to trek from one mountain hut to the next, carrying their own loads and climbing mountains on the way. In 1927 they made a short visit to the Engadine and traversed the Piz Kesch from the Needle to the summit. Albrecht climbed in the Zillertal again in 1930 with his father, sister and younger brother. He also climbed widely in the Bernina Alps before and after the Second World War with his friend and guide Kaspar Grass. Towards the end of his life he said that his favourite excursion was the Biancograt of the Piz Bernina.

I first met Lolly in 1938 when, during a week's holiday in Zermatt, four of us, with Herman Pollinger and Raphael Lochmatter, climbed the Matterhorn by the Zmutt ridge, the Obergabelhorn and the Weisshorn. In 1939 Lolly returned to Zermatt with Grass. They repeated the Zmutt ridge, climbed the Dent Blanche and the Zinalrothorn, encountered Zurcher and Knubel on Monte Rosa and arranged with them a joint climb of the Täschhorn by the Teufelsgrat. This was thwarted by the imminent outbreak of war. Grass, who was a reserve officer, departed to his post and Lolly made tracks for England. He had been elected to the Alpine Club in June 1939, proposed by C G Bruce and seconded by T G Longstaff.

As a young man Lolly had joined the firm of Agfa and was posted to Bombay in 1928. He made many friends there, both Europeans and Indians. His relations with members of the various races, creeds and castes in India was admirable and laid the foundations for his later commercial success. He believed intensely in principles of justice and fair play and showed himself to be liberal and compassionate. In 1938 he was granted British nationality but Nazi pressure forced his dismissal from the firm. At the eleventh hour he got his parents out of Germany to Bombay where they stayed for ten years. Predictably, Lolly found it hard to get a job in wartime England. Then a chance meeting with a director of the photographic firm Johnsons of Hendon led to a contract for him to open a branch in Bombay. By the end of the war he had built up a successful business with branches in other Indian cities.

In 1942 and 1943 Lolly made two reconnaissances of Bandarpunch (20,720ft), hitherto unclimbed. In October 1944 I was granted 28 days leave and accompanied him on his third visit. Our attempt to climb the mountain was defeated by black ice about 1000ft below the summit. We then made the first recorded ascent of Hanuman Peak, 18,200ft, (*AJ55*, 173-186, 1945-46). It was a totally joyful month, coming directly after five years of war. He later gave a talk with slides to the Alpine Club in which he suggested that Bandarpunch might be more readily climbed in June than in October. Bandarpunch was indeed climbed in June 1950 by Roy Greenwood, Tenzing Norgay and Tenzing's brother (*AJ69*, 201-210, 1964).

After his marriage in 1949 to Margit, a charming Swiss lady, a widow, Lolly devoted his life to her and the family and gave up climbing; but his love for the mountains remained undimmed. When the members of the 1953 Everest expedition arrived in Bombay, he effected swift passage through customs of the mountain of stores and baggage, with such success that two unexpected days of rest remained for the expedition. Charles Wylie later wrote to Margit, 'I think it was especially kind of you both to think of entertaining all of us like this when your husband has been working so hard for us for so long.' Wilfrid Noyce wrote of ' ... your super-human assistance and enormous hospitality. I really don't like to think how many days we should have been held up in Bombay but for you.'

After the war a merger with the Belgian firm Gaevert was made; in 1966 a second merger, with Agfa. Lolly continued for a year as general manager. Fate had indeed turned full circle. In 1967 he and Margit left India and lived happily in the chalet in Partenkirchen built by his father in the thirties. In 1969 Lolly was awarded the MBE for his work as Chairman of the Bombay Relief Association. After Margit's death in 1978 he moved, in 1982, to a flat in Luzern overlooking the lake and then spent the last two years of his life in a retired persons' home near Luzern.

He was a talented artist and painted hundreds of pictures in oils and water-colours, mostly of Indian, Himalayan and Alpine scenes. Some of his mountain paintings are especially evocative. He also painted numerous portraits. Perhaps the best of them is an excellent reconstruction of Graham Sutherland's controversial portrait of Winston Churchill, destroyed by order of Lady Churchill after her husband's death. Lolly, who held an intense admiration for Churchill, was deeply distressed by the picture's fate. He has described how, between 1979 and 1981, he searched for and found all the details he needed to reproduce the masterpiece. The painting took three months to complete – the same length of time that Sutherland had taken to paint the original. The portrait now hangs in the Churchill Room of the Carlton Club.

Lolly never lost his sense of fun nor his ability to raise the level of interest in those around him. Appropriately, the end of his life's journey held a moment of high enjoyment. At his funeral service in the chapel of the retirement home, his friend and neighbour, the flautist James Galway, played compositions by J S Bach, Gluck, Telemann and C P E Bach.

It may be of interest to readers of the *Alpine Journal* that Lolly's grandfather, Professor Ernst von Leyden, was a famous Berlin physician who attended the Emperor Frederick III, father of the Kaiser, throughout his fatal illness. A statue of the Professor still stands in Berlin and also a notable bronze memorial set up by grateful patients on the mountainside above Pontresina beside the zigzag path leading up towards the Segantini hut. Albrecht was a grandson fully worthy of such a man.

*Peter Wormald*

# Anthony David Machell Cox 1913-1994

David Cox was a mountaineer whose love of high and rocky places lasted a lifetime. The quality of this love shaped him and, through him, many others. The vocation, for such it was, started in his early 'teens. The family home was a prep' school near Yelverton and venturing out, often alone, David would make long expeditions over Dartmoor, scrambling on all the rocky tors within range, or bird-watching with his, slightly spartan, head-master-father. There was even an experimental abseil from the family roof. All these exploits were conscientiously written up in a growing array of diaries. In his first year at university he would record even the meteoro-logical details, the film he had just seen and the ground he had covered reading Cicero or Homer. Gradually the record becomes more mountain-centred and less earnest. David was never pompous or self-promoting. Increasingly there enters a touch of irony to salt the enthusiasm. It was this mixture of drive and ironic detachment which made powerful aims and modest self-assessments the characteristic qualities of both his moun-tain craft and of his scholarship.

I got to know David at Oxford in 1934. He had won a scholarship from Clifton to Hertford College two years before. He had already done severe climbs with John Hoyland in North Wales (Clogwyn du'r Arddu and Glyder Fach). He had missed a year, having had an unpleasant fall on Pontesford Rocks. Thereafter he carried a slight scar, symmetrical between two famously blue eyes. This is the only fall that I can remember; apart from one in 1947 when we were trying to cross the wrong col on the Frontier Ridge and I pulled him off. In 1934 he became Secretary, later President, of the OUMC. For a 21-year-old he had a strong sense of responsibility and of 'tradition'. Always an avid reader, he collected mountain books whenever he could. He would quote favoured and highly flavoured passages from the Abrahams or Andrews or from the Badminton Book to add colour to our own small epics. This fitted well into the slightly surreal scenario which prevailed when such friends as Low, Pullinger or Viney were around. David was learning more serious texts too: first the grist and grain of classical history; then he plunged into the likes of Stubbs' *Charters* and all that passes for 'modern' history at Oxford – ie up to about the 15th century. Crusader Castles, the Orders of Chivalry and medieval domestic and parish records were areas of interest. Castles, indeed, were part of his very last family holiday in Cyprus.

Pen y Pass, with all Geoffrey Young's contacts, was a place where the academic and the Alpine could mingle: a civilizing influence. We certainly felt privileged to be enjoying all this; more especially because in the 1930s the hills of Wales and Cumberland were wonderfully empty and unscarred. David climbed whenever study and money allowed, sometimes slightly against parental wishes: in Skye, in Wales, on Oxford Sundays with a hired car (not quite in line with University rules); or on the masonry bridges at Horsepath (good for fingers, risk of cow pats) or the great beech tree clump at Steeple Aston (red coats and hounds running below) or midnight among the All Souls pinnacles when David and a friend escaped the excesses of a bump supper. David's rumoured second ascent of the Radcliffe Camera, with Nully Kretschmer, may or may not have contributed favourably to his All Souls Fellowship.

David took his Alpine apprenticeship seriously though he did not, like his friend Wilfrid Noyce, have the benefit of a sustained period of hard climbing with an Alpine guide. Almost consciously he developed as a mountaineer on a steady learning curve: through the thirties, through the War (see his article on mountain warfare training in the Lebanon in *AJ97*, 191-197, 1992/93): and well into the 1950s. Altogether, I think he had 14 summer seasons in the Alps. This rising curve of competence went right up to his high point and near miss with Wilfrid Noyce on Machapuchare in the Spring of 1957 (see 'Climbing the Fish's Tail' in *AJ62*, 113-120, November 1957). I don't know how far he was considered for Everest. Family 'commitments' were part of the story and certainly he worked closely with the 1953 team and became close friends with most of them afterwards.

One further pre-war memory: Summer 1937. For four days we camped by Llyn Arddu and climbed, mainly on 'Cloggy' with Clare and Berridge Mallory, sharing the cooking and the reading of *Emma* between two tents; doing many of the existing climbs on that cliff and one new one – *Sunset Crack* – which David spotted over an evening brew-up. This was a forerunner of the more complex and severe West Buttress route, *Sheaf*, which he did (with Jock Campbell) at the end of his Commando training service. During that July of 1937 he was not able to come on the Caucasus expedition because he had a *viva* examination.

David gained First Class Honours both in (classical) Greats and in Modern History. In 1937 he was elected a Fellow of All Souls and, two years later, a Fellow of University College. For more than 30 years he was a loved and valued tutor there. Generations of graduates have spoken of his probing, questioning, anecdotal style in tutorials. After being Senior Tutor he was, for a time, Vice-Master under Lord Goodman. Much of his research was into the rich deposits of medieval domestic records of the College. He translated, ordered and interpreted for the benefit of a wider community and to the enrichment of his own teaching. He was a don in that Alpine/Academic tradition of 'Sligger' Urquhart and Cyril Bailey. As a historian, he was deeply interested in the detail and colour of real people; much less in the great trends of why? and whither? He published little but left his stamp on many learned and humane minds.

When David became Editor of the *Alpine Journal* (1962-1967) he was much more in tune with the gentle and generous tradition of Hal Tyndale than with other more acerbic predecessors. He was sufficiently close to the rising generation of committed British mountaineers to welcome their writings – up to a point. He firmly resisted the linguistic anarchy which characterised the effusions of the most fiery. But I doubt if he lost a friend through using the editorial pencil. As President (1971-1974) such strengths were also evident. His term of office saw the groundwork laid for the admission of women, the merger of the AC and the Ladies Alpine Club and the introduction of aspirant membership. Each of these potentially divisive measures was carried through with common-sense, the utmost good humour and no rancour whatsoever. It was so difficult to quarrel when he was around. His actual and metaphorical twinkle made it hard not to feel as good after a tense meeting as after his speech at a dinner. To the younger generation, both of the Alpine Club and the OUMC, he never appeared as an authority figure but more as a knowledgeable and wise older brother.

David Cox met his future wife, Gerardine Barstow, on a ski-touring trip in the Tyrol. They were both highly competent skiers in the style of the 1930s – skins uphill and stem-Christies down. They had three daughters, one of whom died after a serious, intermittent illness, the young mother of their first grandson. There were many good holidays in the hills and a variety of country pursuits around their 'Old Vicarage' in rural Oxfordshire. In 1958 David contracted a severe attack of polio after a short and strenuous Alpine holiday with Wilfrid Noyce and Anthony Rawlinson. He was left with permanently weakened arms and chest and this, in the end, was a factor in his final year of respiratory failure.

In their last few years David Cox and Kevin FitzGerald became particularly close friends. At a superficial level this was to do with the *Alpine Journal*, with mountain narratives, personalities and gossip. But behind that, there was something else. In the 1960s Kevin had reached a low point with drink-related depression; as some of his writings suggest. The new, deepening friendship helped to give him, despite his eventual blindness, 25 years of contented old age. So if you recall their rather baroque reminiscences in the inner bar at the P-y-G or the speeches of either at a dinner, you can also recall a very special kind of warmth and friendship which sustained them through hard times; and kindled others.

*Robin Hodgkin*


*John Hunt writes:*
It is now nearly 40 years since my last climb with David, who was stricken by polio after returning from the Alps in 1958; yet my memories of mountain occasions shared with him between 1943 and 1956 have remained, in vivid detail, over all that span of time. There were some great moments; they include the failures and frustrations which form part of every mountaineer's store of experience. There was one episode of tragedy, and one near disaster. There was also much fun. Always there was harmony between us. David was not a man of moods and I felt at ease in his company in all circumstances, from our very first meeting.

That meeting took place on a cold, wet and misty day early in 1943. I had just arrived in Braemar to join Frank Smythe's staff at the Commando Mountain and Snow Warfare Centre as its Chief Instructor. I lost no time in heading for the mountains to make contact with the various groups who, on that wintry afternoon, were engaged in the training programme. David, in his familiar khaki, fur-trimmed 'Parka' anorak, was doing his best to teach a group of dispirited soldiers the technique of stem turns on the narrow road at the Devil's Elbow, above Glen Shee; there was no lift in those days. That meeting marked the beginning of a friendship which grew from shared experience throughout the following 13 years, and remained close and constant until his death.

Of course, we both wanted to climb; at weekends we made a number of routes on the Creag an Dubh Loch, on Lochnagar and on the splendid Mitre Ridge in the Garbh Choire of Beinn a' Bhuird. The training courses included a period of rock climbing in Snowdonia for the eventual cliff landings of No 4 Commando at Dieppe. David and I lost no opportunities during breaks to climb together on those familiar crags. I recall a particularly fine day in the Arch Gully on Craig yr Ysfa (*Spiral* and *Gomorrah*).

After returning from Everest in 1953, my first climb, *Pigott's Climb* on Clogwyn du'r Arddu, was with David and Hamish Nicol. There followed three marvellous Alpine seasons, mainly shared with Wilf Noyce and sometimes with Michael Ward; some of the climbs we did have been recorded elsewhere. They remain vivid, across the gap of more than 30 years, as much for our companionship in some bivouac or mountain hut, as for the tensions and effort of the action.

I remember David, with a group of commando soldiers, as we huddled in darkness around a blazing log fire beneath the snow-laden pines of Rothiemurchus Forest. I recall him on the Brenva Ridge, above the Col Moore, nursing a petrol Primus on a flat stone between his knees, while Wilf, Michael Ward and I waited anxiously for the temperature to drop and the mists to disperse before venturing across those steep, ice-scoured couloirs to reach the foot of the *Sentinelle* on the Italian face of Mont Blanc. And there was a different kind of bivouac when, wedged uncomfortably in the Cheminée Fontaine, benighted during a traverse of the Requin by its E face and the *Voie Dibona*, Wilf Noyce, David and I shared the comforts of our meagre rations and, more importantly, of each others' warmth.

I recall a night on the Jungfrau when Robin Hodgkin, David and I practised prussiking off the beams of the Guggi hut after a day spent reconnoitring the hazards of the notorious Kühlauenen icefall. Next day, descending in a whiteout from the Silbersattel, Robin and I rescued David after he had fallen 60ft down a crevasse. I treasure especially the memory of an experience shared with David and Ernst Reiss of the 1956 Swiss Everest expedition. We spent a night in a cowshed, after Ernst had lost the way, in thick mist, to do a new route which he had made on the Gspaltenhorn. We nestled snugly in the straw, enjoying the warmth – but not the noise – of the bell-ringing cows in their stalls beneath us.

It was from those experiences, in action and repose, that I grew to love David for his coolness, steadiness and skill: for his warm humanity, his modesty, his sense of humour.

# Eleanor Winthrop Young 1897–1994

Eleanor Slingsby was born in 1897 at Carleton-in-Craven. Though she lived there for only her first fourteen years, for nearly a century she remained a staunch Daleswoman, richly endowed with what she called 'Yorkshire grit'. The course of her life was profoundly influenced by her close relationship with two legendary figures of mountaineering history, both writers of mountaineering classics – her father Cecil Slingsby and her husband Geoffrey Winthrop Young. With them she shared a devotion to the *High Hills* and to the *Northern Playground*.

In childhood her father introduced her to scrambling at Malham Cove and on neighbouring limestone crags. But it was not till 1921 that he took her to Norway, an experience which she found 'ecstatic'. Five years later she was back there celebrating the fiftieth anniversary of the first ascent of Skagastölstind, climbing it twice, once by the original route over the Slingsbybrae; then climbing other peaks with Norwegians and walking alone in the Jotunheim. She visited Norway again twice in her eighties, attending in 1976 the Skagastölstind centenary celebrations at Turtegrö, when her son Jocelin and two other Slingsby descendants repeated the ascent. She was on the committee of the Norwegian Mountaineering Club and wrote articles for their journal, as also for the Pinnacle and Fell and Rock Clubs. Len has her own special place in mountaineering history as co-founder and first president of the Pinnacle Club.

She first went to one of Geoffrey Young's Pen-y-Pass gatherings in 1910. And in April 1918, six months before the armistice, she married him. He had lost a leg, commanding an ambulance unit in Italy after the disastrous defeat of the Italian army at Caporetto. Len immediately devoted her energies not just to the restoration of his health but to helping him, step by step, in the remarkable achievement of creating a new legend as a mountaineer. Supported by her he gradually developed the technique that enabled him to make long and difficult expeditions, such as the Grépon and the Matterhorn, balancing at every move on his complicated peg-leg. Once, when he was in great difficulty alone on the top of Snowdon, Len, as if by magic, appeared out of the clouds and was able to help him safely down to Pen-y-Pass. Another time, when his leg broke down on Sty Head, she showed great strength and endurance in aiding Jocelin to support Geoffrey as he hopped on his good leg down to Wasdale Head.

When Geoffrey had doubts about reviving the Pen-y-Pass parties after the war, it was Len who encouraged him to start them again, and on all the post-war Easter gatherings she acted as an enthusiastic hostess, helpful to all, from veteran climber to shy beginner. In the twenties, when the Youngs were living in Cambridge, the Sunday Evenings in their attractive house in Bene't Place were memorable. It was the golden age of the Cambridge University Mountaineering Club, and among those who came there to be inspired by Geoffrey and vivaciously entertained by Len, were a host of budding mountaineers and explorers – Gino Watkins, Freddy Spencer Chapman, Bobby Chew, Peter Lloyd, Jack Longland, Charles Warren and many others ready to blossom in the Arctic, upon Everest and elsewhere. Here, as at Pen-y-Pass, with lively interest and friendliness Len helped us all to make the most of each other.

Her own achievement as a mountaineer was considerable. As she left no records, it is difficult to establish what she actually did. Throughout her active life she constantly enjoyed climbing on British rocks. In the Alps her activities were shaped by those of Geoffrey. Occasionally she accompanied him, notably in 1931, when a family party of Geoffrey, Len and Jocelin with Hans Brantschen as guide made a spectacular traverse of the Hohstock ridge. In the same part of the Oberland she made, without Geoffrey but again with Brantschen, the first ascent of a ridge of the southernmost of the Fusshörner. Her many climbs with guides included the Mönch. I only climbed once with her. It was in 1931 when Jack Longland and I, after following G.W.Y.'s footsteps up the Young-grat on the Breithorn, ascended the Rimpfischhorn with Len and Brantschen. Here I was able to appreciate her skill in moving on rock and ice with balance and rhythm, which she may have acquired when dancing was included in her early training for the stage at the Birmingham Repertory Theatre. On one occasion, hurrying back from Wales to Cambridge for a dress-rehearsal of 'Merrie England', she was seen practising her dancing steps in the train wearing climbing boots.

Those who knew Len will remember her for her enchanting vivacity and her love of people. She had time for everyone, young or old; and made them feel that they were of interest and importance. She communicated with them in fascinating conversational exchanges and slightly scatty letters and cards, written in her bold, wild and almost illegible hand. As her daughter Marcia put it, 'Len was fun'.

*Peter Bicknell*

## James Waller 1911–1994

During his boyhood, Jimmy Waller lived in the New Forest with his mother and step-father, both of them medical practitioners. Dr and Mrs Teasdale were, by chance, neighbours of Dr Tom Longstaff and his family and I have no doubt, from my own acquaintance with both of them at that time, that Tom exerted a powerful influence on the youthful Jimmy, inspiring in him a lasting enthusiasm for mountaineering. Jimmy first climbed with a guide, during a school holiday at Arolla in 1929 when he was 17. It was from this slight experience that, following his posting to a gunner regiment in India, he headed for Kashmir in 1932 where, from a base at Sonamark in the Sind valley, he made two spirited attempts on Thajawis Peak (15,928ft). Returning the following year, he climbed Buttress Peak from the Lidder valley and, in 1934, he attempted Nun with Jock Harrison, making the first ascent of White Needle (22,000ft).

By this time JW had raised his sights to the Karakoram giants, noting the existence of K36, later to be named Saltoro Kangri (25,400ft), in the East Karakoram. Little was known about it apart from a sighting by the Workmans which they had recorded in their tome *Two summers in the ice-wilds of eastern Karakoram*. With only a vague notion of its exact location and no knowledge of the approaches, JW set about organising his first major expedition. I was serving in Bengal on secondment to the Indian Police at that time, and was fortunate, through my contacts with the Himalayan Club, to receive an invitation to join him. The other members of the party were Rowland Brotherhood and Dr Stewart Carslaw, two RAF officers stationed at Quetta, neither of whom had any experience of mountaineering. The story is sufficiently recorded in the annals of the *Alpine Journal* and elsewhere. It was a classic example of a very lightweight expedition. We were fired by the burning enthusiasm and confidence of JW himself, and we very nearly made it to the top, with some miraculous escapes from avalanches and crevasses during a series of typical Karakoram storms. It was only 40 years later that Saltoro Kangri was climbed by a Japanese party. Among many vignettes in my memory, I retain the vision of JW's golden retriever Tony, roped with two hapless sheep, at the tail-end of one of the Balti caravans carrying our stores up the Likah glacier.

An interesting feature of the expedition was the novelty of our equipment. Apart from skis and racquettes, we used a sledge, and carried huge loads with a harness to which both a frontal and backpack were attached. All these unusual features derived from Jimmy's inventive genius. Our rations, devised by Jimmy's parents, weighed only 1¼lbs per man/day.

In 1936, in company with Rowland Brotherhood, JW enjoyed a very successful guided season based on Zermatt, climbing most of the great classic routes, including the Zmutt ridge on the Matterhorn.

Next year, having returned to his unit in India, he headed once again for the Kashmir Alps in company with a team of Sherpas. This time he succeeded in climbing Thajawis Peak, but was foiled by bad weather from another attempt on Nun. It was some compensation to climb Kolahoi by its easy E ridge.

1938 marked the zenith of Waller's climbing career: his attempt on Masherbrum (25,660ft) from the Hushe Nala. Once again I was invited to join him, but could not obtain leave from my duties in Bengal. This story, too, is well documented. It speaks much for the determination – the sheer guts – of JW and his companions (Jimmy Roberts, T Graham Brown, Robin Hodgkin and Jock Harrison) that such a lightweight expedition, slender on resources and experience, should arrive within a few hundred feet of the summit of another Karakoram giant. Moreover, they reconnoitred the southern approaches of Masherbrum fairly thoroughly and developed the 'correct' route which later, successful parties followed. Unfortunately their luck ran out on them, at great cost to Robin Hodgkin and Jock Harrison.

I met Jimmy only once more, briefly, during an official visit to Jersey in 1954. Though he had distinguished himself in the War and had keenly looked forward to it professionally, he was not by nature belligerent. For instance, he made several visits to Jawharlal Nehru in prison. As far as I know, he did not continue climbing. My memory of him is as a very young man, bursting with enthusiasm and ideas, strongly extrovert and self-confident, but modest about his mountaineering ability. JW was an excellent companion under the adverse circumstances we endured in 1935.

*John Hunt*

## Louis Charles Baume 1919-1993

Louis Baume died aged 74 in Katharine House Hospice, near Banbury, after a long illness most bravely borne.

Louis, of Swiss origin, belonged to the illustrious watchmaking family who had been pioneers in the horological industry since the early 19th century and who had established a London branch in 1844. Louis' father Alexandre Baume joined the firm from Switzerland in 1904.

Louis Baume, born in London, was educated at the Hall School, Hampstead and at Highgate School. He later graduated as Horloger Practicien at the École d'Horlogerie du Loclé in the Jura Neuchâtelois, after which he served an apprenticeship at the Longine watch factory. He joined the family firm in London in 1938.

It was during his times in Switzerland that Louis was able to extend his love of mountains, walking and skiing in the Jura and in 1939 making his first Alpine ascents: the Wetterhorn, the Mönch and the Jungfrau. The same year interrupted both his career and his further climbing when in September he volunteered for the army. After he was commissioned in the Royal Artillery he, along with his closest friend Charles Huntriss, later to become his brother-in-law, was posted to the Far East. They served both in Malaya and Singapore, suffering 3½ years as prisoners of the Japanese working on the infamous 'Railway of Death'.

During his captivity Louis, at the risk of severe penalty, kept a diary written on tissue paper and concealed in various places. The original and a transcription of this diary, a rare and meticulous record of Japanese captivity, are now valued additions to the archives of the Imperial War Museum. Remarkably, although both the victim and witness of much brutality, Louis retained no hatred for the Japanese, amongst whom he was subsequently to have many friends and business contacts.

Louis rejoined Baume & Co in London in 1946 as a partner and later as Joint Managing Director. He was also Chairman of the Swiss Watch Importers Association and for 20 years served on the Council of the British Horological Institute, being at one time Chairman. In 1951 Baume & Co were involved in the creation of the wildly imaginative Guinness Clock, a feature of the Festival of Britain Pleasure Garden.

After the war Louis returned to the Alps annually and in 1952 was elected to the Alpine Club with some 44 major ascents to his credit. Many of these climbs were with his older brother Pierre, also a member of the Alpine Club. Pierre was tragically killed in the air disaster at Oslo in 1963. Louis was also a member of the Swiss Alpine Club, and for some years both the Climbers' Club and the Yorkshire Ramblers' Club. He continued to climb in the Alps and other areas including Norway, the Julian Alps, Corsica and the Pyrenees as well as in Britain. His last overseas trip was to the Picos de Europa in northern Spain.

Louis' passion for the mountains was to extend to the polar regions when he joined the South Georgia Survey 1955–56, led by Duncan Carse. This was an unusually happy and successful expedition which, in six months of sledging and exploration, completed the survey of the island to a remarkable degree of accuracy and detail. A peak in South Georgia now bears his name, Mount Baume. It was as a fellow member of this expedition that I got to know Louis. We shared a tent on the first 60-day sledging journey. Being entombed together in an ever decreasing triangle of space in blizzards of up to seven days' duration is as good a test as any of friendship and, on his part, tolerance. Our harmony was never disturbed and Louis was then, as always, the perfect gentleman and remained a dear friend.

In 1967 Louis resigned all his directorships and changed the whole course of his life to pursue what was to become his dominating passion – books. He bought the stock of Thomas J Gaston of Chancery Lane and set up 'Gaston's Alpine Books', first in Harrow and later in Bloxham, Oxfordshire. He scoured this and other countries, haunting dealers and auction houses, adding to his stock a storehouse of treasures, unequalled in this country, the best of which he retained for his personal library. He had business dealings with collectors from 20 countries and he corresponded in five languages. He was to become one of the world's leading authorities on the literature of mountaineering, mountain travel and polar exploration, and his own personal collection was perhaps the finest in this country.

In addition, Louis was co-partner with Robin Collomb of Gaston West-Col Productions, publishing books and maps of interest to the mountaineer. One of their publications, researched and written by Louis, was *Sivalaya*, which chronicles the history of the fourteen Himalayan 8000 metre peaks. For some years he served on the Library Council of the Alpine Club, advising on the care and restoration of old and valuable books.

Louis was a man of immense integrity, both in his personal life and in his business affairs. He knew better than most the value of the books he bought and many a widow disposing of her husband's library had reason to be grateful for the scrupulous honesty of Louis Baume.

Louis was unmarried but his loss is much grieved by his sister Yvonne, his brother-in-law and his friends in many countries. My wife and I, who were near neighbours for many years, have fond memories of him; Louis' frequent company greatly enriched our lives.

*George B Spenceley*

74. E A FitzGerald (R), C L Barrow and Mattias Zurbriggen near the Hermitage, 1895.
(*Kinsey Collection, Alexander Turnbull Library, Wellington, NZ*) (p236)

79.  The Ascent of the Matterhorn, on July 14th 1865:  Arrival at the Summit.
(*Gustave Doré*)  (p215)

80.  The Ascent of the Matterhorn, on July 14th 1865:  The Fall.
     (*Gustave Doré*)  (p215)

81.  David Cox  (1913–1994).  (*John Cleare*)  (p332)

*Right*
82.  David Cox during the Second World War,
    probably in the Lebanon during his
    Commando training period.   (p332)

33. Eleanor Winthrop Young (1897–1994), in her 80s, at the foot of the Jostedalsbreen in Norway. (p336)

84.  Terris Moore (1908–1993) at 18,000ft on Mt McKinley in 1972.
     (*Bradford Washburn*)  (p341)

# Terris Moore  1908-1993

Terris Moore, who died at the age of 85 on 7 November 1993 after a massive heart attack, was the greatest American explorer/mountaineer of this century. He was also an extraordinary light plane pilot as well as Emeritus President of the University of Alaska.

Moore, Terry to his friends, was born in Haddonfield, New Jersey, on 11 April 1908 and attended schools in Philadelphia, Haddonfield and Cromwell, New York (Storm King) before entering and graduating from Williams College, where he captained the cross-country team and became an avid skier. After graduating from college he attended the Harvard Business School, from which he received two degrees: Master of Business Administration and Doctor of Commercial Science.

His mountain climbing had begun long before this time. In 1927 he had climbed Mt Chimborazo (20,702ft) in Ecuador, and then made the daring first ascent of 17,159ft Mt Sangay, an active volcano there. Three years later he joined the Harvard Mountaineering Club and also became a member of the American Alpine Club, connections which led to his making the first ascent of 16,400ft Mt Bona in Alaska with Allen Carpé, and the first unguided climb of Mt Robson, a dangerous ascent in the Canadian Rockies. These climbs led to his first ascent of 15,300ft Mt Fairweather in coastal Alaska, also with Carpé, and to his decision the following year to join an Explorers Club expedition to Minya Konka (now called Gongga Shan) in Sichuan, China, then rumoured to be the highest mountain in the world. Moore and Richard Burdsall ascended this very difficult mountain (which Burdsall and Arthur Emmons surveyed as 24,500ft high), and in so doing climbed several thousand feet higher than Americans had gone before. At the time, Moore was the outstanding American climber.

In 1933 Terry married Katrina Eaton Hinks and for two years taught at UCLA in California before settling in Boston as a financial consultant. Before the Second World War he had also become an experienced light plane pilot, but when he tried to enlist as a pilot in the Army Air Force, he was turned down as a physical risk. Instead he accepted an invitation to go to Washington as a consultant on clothing and equipment for troops experiencing arctic, winter or mountain conditions. In this capacity he tested items in various places and made the third ascent of Mt McKinley as a member of the Alaskan Test expedition in 1942.

After the war Moore became president of the New England Society of Natural History, and helped with its modernisation into the far more active Boston Museum of Science. Then, in 1939, he was asked to become the second president of the University of Alaska where he did a lot to make it a modern university. In his spare time he continued to establish world records for high-altitude landings. He also helped to establish the High Altitude Observatory on Mt Wrangel. Terry was much involved in flying rescue missions too, as I found when he gave up a trip East to search for a plane missing on a flight from the Seward glacier to Yakutat.

In the ensuing years Terry served as a member of the US Army Scientific Advisory Panel, and he and Katrina made frequent flights throughout northern and arctic Alaska and Canada, even helping with scientific work on the extreme northern tip of Greenland.

During his lifetime, Terris Moore received many honours from the US government, the Boston Museum of Science, the University of Alaska, the Explorers Club, the American Alpine Club, the Harvard Travellers Club, the Appalachian Mountain Club, and so on. He is survived by his wife Katrina, constant companion for over 50 years, his daughter (Katrina Moore Smathers), three grandchildren, one great-grandchild, and a sister (Marilyn Roland of Sun Valley, Idaho).

*Robert Bates*

# Donald Murray 1906–1994

Son of a country GP, Donald Murray lived in East Yorkshire all his life until a few weeks before he died in Cumbria. Educated at Uppingham School, Donald then joined the firm of J A Hewetson of Hull, hardwood dealers and manufacturers of flooring. He stayed with them throughout his working life, becoming managing director and a national expert on hardwoods.

In the early 1920s Donald began walking and climbing in the Pennines, Scotland and the Lake District and in 1928 joined the Fell and Rock Climbing Club, a club to which he devoted a tremendous amount of energy, becoming president in 1964. His presidency was marked by many changes and innovations in the organisation of club affairs, improvements which are still evident today.

An active climber all his life, Donald's experience was widespread both at home and abroad. He was particularly proud of his completion in 1929 of the ascent of the Three Peaks – Ben Nevis, Scafell Pike and Snowdon – within 24 hours, a feat which he repeated 50 years later in 36 hours, despite the handicap of two replacement hip joints.

Donald began climbing in the Alps in the late 1920s and accomplished many classic routes, accompanied for several seasons by the Swiss guide Alexander Pollinger of St Niklaus and later by the Austrian guide Franz Steindl, in the Dolomites, Austria and Switzerland. Donald joined the Alpine Club in 1956, the year in which he decided that, henceforth, he would explore, guideless, less frequented areas: the Julian Alps, the High Atlas, the Picos de Europa, the Encantados, and Corsica which he visited four or five times accompanied by his wife Nancy and a few Fell and Rock friends. The combination of Corsica's warm dry granite and its then uncrowded coastline was irresistible.

On retirement, Donald converted a long wheelbase Land Rover and, accompanied by Nancy, drove it to Nepal for his first trekking trip in the Himalaya. Other similar trips followed to Central America, the USA, Canada and Alaska.

Donald had a tremendous personality, bubbling with enthusiasm, energy and laughter: there was always a lot of noise whenever he was around. I have fond memories of him sandwiched between Tony Greenbank and myself and the pair of them laughing their way up a new route we discovered on the West Buttress of Sgumain during the 1958 Fell and Rock meet on Skye.

Advancing years prevented active participation on the hills but Donald still enjoyed visiting his favourite project, the Old Mill in Combe Ghyll, Borrowdale where, over the years, he had exercised his considerable crafts-man's skills by converting a broken-down sheep shelter into a highly desir-able private climbing hut.

Happily married for over 60 years, Donald is greatly missed by his family and many climbing friends.

I am greatly indebted to his daughter, Dr Janet O'Neill, for information on his early years.

*John Wilkinson*

## Christopher Manfred Gravina 1934–1994

A great early influence on Christopher Gravina and his brothers Michael and Timothy was their mother, who encouraged them in outdoor activi-ties, introducing them to the mountains of Wales, the Lake District and Switzerland, not just climbing, but also camping, canoeing, and sleeping in mountain huts or hay chalets.

At Marlborough College Chris developed an interest in running. He was in the school athletics team and won the mile in an annual athletics match. He also ran through the night the 18 miles to Stonehenge to see the sunrise on midsummer's day.

While he and his brother Michael were at school, they paddled in a can-vas-covered folding canoe along the Kennet and Avon Canal and down the Thames to London. This was several years before the annual Devizes to Westminster canoe race started. Christopher went to Iceland with the British Schools Exploring Society, where he used his hobby of radio to maintain contact with the outside world. After school he went to Canada and climbed in the Rockies. During one period of leave from National Service in the Royal Signals, he went skiing with his mother. Chris had not skied before, but after three days' instruction they went off ski touring and staying in mountain huts.

At Imperial College, London, Christopher not only obtained a degree but also spent much time with the college climbing club, climbing in Wales and the Alps. This culminated in an expedition to the Karakoram led by Eric Shipton and in 1960 Chris joined the Alpine Club. An important event for Chris at Imperial College was to meet Ann. After their marriage his work with Marconi took them both to various parts of the world in-cluding Ghana and Singapore. They finally returned and settled down in Essex, and Christopher started working for IBM computers.

A keen sailor, Chris spent much time sailing and racing in the Blackwater estuary. He enjoyed the challenge of racing, striving to get the best possible performance from his boat. Each successive boat he owned was faster and more uncomfortable than the previous one.

Several family holidays in the Lake District with Ann and their sons Robin and Richard rekindled his love of the fells. Thus in the early 1980s he started to develop a keen interest in fell running, perhaps a surprising hobby for one living in Essex! His love of mountains and general fitness made a good combination and he particularly enjoyed the challenge of the longer fell races and soon had his sights set firmly on the Bob Graham Round, which is a circular route 72 miles long over 42 of the highest peaks in the Lake District with a total ascent of 27,000ft to be completed in 24 hours. During 1984 and 1985 Chris made four unsuccessful attempts on this route. During one solo attempt, he first drove round the route leaving tins of rice pudding and apricots to be eaten on the way. He actually completed the course, but unfortunately took 25 hours, one hour over the limit.

In June 1986 he set off with two friends on yet another attempt, supported by family and friends. Each of the trio at some time had what Chris called 'a bit of a bad patch', an expression which I understand really meant total collapse. However, all three runners kept their minds fixed on the finish at Keswick, where at midnight they were welcomed into the Bob Graham Club: membership numbers 375, 376 and 377.

Chris fitted perfectly into the Bob Graham Club. At their annual dinner fantastic plans were discussed. Nothing was regarded as impossible, everything was worth trying. These ideas were, however, not just fantasies, they were usually carried out. Over the next few years Chris ran solo across Switzerland through the mountains, living on cheese and pasta. With friends from the Bob Graham Club he ran round Mont Blanc, and completed the Corsica High Route (which usually takes 14 days) in four days. Chris also ran some of the long-distance paths in the Dolomites and Pyrenees. In 1990 he ran the South Downs Way: 80 miles in 15 hours.

He ran many fell races and several times won the 50+ class. One year he came fourth in the British Fell Running Championship super-veteran class. He teamed up with several friends to take part in the Scottish Islands Race. This involved sailing from island to island and running up the highest mountain on each island. His knowledge of sailing obviously came in useful. Christopher set himself the task of climbing every hill in the Lake District over 2000ft high. He made a list of these hills and over a period of three years climbed them all.

In 1987 Chris persuaded his younger brother to partner him for the Karrimor Mountain Marathon, and this was the first of several mountain marathon events in which he took part. Those who accompanied him on Mountain Marathons soon learned that his legs were not only very fast, but also took up more than their share of a very small tent – a fact that Chris never seemed to notice! He was expert in lightweight camping, saving weight by leaving behind anything which *he* considered inessential. This might include cutting tent pegs in half and reducing their number. In gale force winds and sub-zero temperatures, his companion did not always share this enthusiasm. Chris loved these mountain marathons; he liked the challenge of finding routes across unknown terrain.

Not all his fell running events were successful. In the 1990 Ordnance Survey Lakes Race, he badly twisted his leg soon after the start. This slowed him down so much that he just exceeded the time limit for the 20-mile race. An X-ray later showed that the cause of his slowness was a broken fibula!

Possibly as a result of spending time in beautiful surroundings, he developed a talent for art and painting. Characteristically he threw himself energetically into the subject and produced some excellent water-colours; the quality of his work surprised many of us, showing much potential for the future.

Our sympathies go to his wife Ann and his two sons Robin and Richard. May his spirit run free where ever he is.

*Tim Gravina*

*M J Esten writes:*

Chris was my oldest friend in the Club. We were students together, and shared those happy days in the hills which, in youth, no doubt everyone thinks will continue for ever. He was the ultimate enthusiast: no matter what the subject, if it involved a bit of adventure, he would be there. We lost touch during our late twenties, so it is good to read, in Tim's account, of the many activities other than climbing that Chris characteristically threw himself into.

We did not meet again until some 25 years later, through the Alpine Club. Nothing had changed – there was the same Chris with all his old enthusiasms undimmed. Whatever the weather, he would want to be off, climbing, running, brisk walking – anything so long as it was done with gusto. Later we found ourselves on the AC Committee together. Chris, with his usual drive and energy, took over the running of the bar, advised the Club on computers and took on several other *ad hoc* jobs as well.

He was an enthusiast of so very many parts, and it is a cruel irony that he left us just as he was embarking on a planned, active retirement. As well as spending more time in the hills, he intended to paint more, and the last note that I received from him proposed that an exhibition of members' paintings be held at the Club House. This was duly organised and a large number of works, professional and amateur, including some of Chris's, were displayed. It is a fitting tribute to his many talents that, after a quick first look around the exhibition, I remarked to another member upon the water-colour which I thought to be the best, asking him to be so kind as to look in his catalogue and tell me something about it. It turned out to be one of Chris's.

# Alpine Club Notes

## OFFICERS AND COMMITTEE FOR 1995

| | |
|---|---|
| PRESIDENT | M H Westmacott |
| VICE PRESIDENTS | J S Cleare |
| | M A Fowler |
| HONORARY SECRETARY | Dr M J Esten |
| HONORARY TREASURER | J M C Evans |
| HONORARY LIBRARIAN | D J Lovatt |
| HONORARY EDITOR | Mrs J Merz |
| COMMITTEE ELECTIVE MEMBERS | J L Bermúdez |
| | J-A Clyma |
| | M W Fletcher |
| | M H Johnston |
| | S A Jones |
| | P Wickens |
| | E Douglas |
| | A J Hargreaves |
| | P J Knott |
| EXTRA COMMITTEE MEMBERS | R Lawford |
| | M F Baker |
| ACG REPRESENTATIVES | D Tunstall |
| | D Wills |

## OFFICE BEARERS

| | |
|---|---|
| LIBRARIAN EMERITUS | R Lawford |
| HONORARY ARCHIVIST | Miss L Gollancz |
| HONORARY ASSISTANT ARCHIVIST | Miss M Darvall |
| HONORARY ASSISTANT LIBRARIAN | R G Green |
| HONORARY KEEPER OF THE CLUB'S PICTURES ... | D J Lovatt |
| HONORARY KEEPER OF THE CLUB'S ARTEFACTS | R Lawford |
| CHAIRMAN OF THE FINANCE COMMITTEE | R F Morgan |
| CHAIRMAN OF THE HOUSE COMMITTEE | M H Johnston |
| CHAIRMAN OF THE LIBRARY COUNCIL | G C Band |
| CHAIRMAN OF THE MEMBERSHIP COMMITTEE | G D Hughes |
| CHAIRMAN OF THE PUBLICATIONS COMMITTEE | J N Slee-Smith |

## GENERAL MEETINGS OF THE ALPINE CLUB 1994

| | |
|---|---|
| 18 January | Mick Fowler, *Cerro Kishtwar* |
| 15 February | Stephen Venables, *Mountaineering in Five Continents* |
| 12-13 March | North Wales Meet and General Meeting |
| | S A Jones, *Crossing the Greenland Icecap* |
| 8 March | Nick Crane, *European Odyssey* |
| 12 April | Chris Bonington, *Greenland Revisited* |
| 10 May | Rannulph Fiennes, *Antarctic Crossing* |
| 13 September | Jim Curran, *Kinnaur* |
| 1-2 October | Lake District Meet and General Meeting |
| | Mike Banks, *Peak Bagging in Greenland* |
| 11 October | Luke Hughes, *Jostling in the Street* |
| 8 November | Mikhail Malakhov & Richard Weber, |
| | *North Pole Unsupported* |
| 12 November | Annual Symposium and Meet: Plas y Brenin, |
| | *The Mountains of Siberia and Turkestan* |
| 9 December | Annual General Meeting |
| | John Harding, *Turkish Ski Tours* |

The Annual London Dinner was held on 10 December at The Great Hall, St Bartholomew's Hospital. The principal guest was Dr Jürg Marmet, President of the Swiss Foundation for Alpine Research.

## CLIMBING MEETINGS 1994

| | |
|---|---|
| 20-21 February | ACG/AC Winter Meet, Glencoe |
| 6-7 March | North Wales Meet and General Meeting |
| 13-15 May | Derbyshire Meet |
| 23 July - 13 August | Joint Alpine Meet with the ABMSAC and CC: Ailefroide and Courmayeur |
| 1-9 September | Cornwall Meet - joint meet with CC at Bosigran |
| 1-2 October | Lake District Meet |

## HONOURS AND AWARDS

**Honours List**
Congratulations to Doug Scott who was awarded a CBE in 1994 for services to mountaineering.
Congratulations also to Charles Wylie who was awarded an OBE in 1995 for services to the Gurkhas.

**The King Albert I Memorial Awards**
The recipients of the first of these awards were announced on 14 June 1994. They were presented on 3 September to:

| | |
|---|---|
| John Hunt (Lord Hunt of Llanfairwaterdine) | Honorary Member, AC |
| Bradford Washburn | Honorary Member, AC |
| Wanda Rutkiewicz | (Posthumous) |

**The Boardman Tasker Memorial Award for Mountain Literature**
The 12th award ceremony was held at the Alpine Club on 19 October 1994. The judges were Paul Nunn (Chairman), Sheila Harrison and Joss Lynam. The winning book was *At the Rising of the Moon* by Dermot Somers (Bâton Wicks). Shortlisted were *We Aspired: The Last Innocent Americans* by Peter Sinclair (Utah University Press), *No Place to Fall* by Victor Saunders (Hodder & Stoughton), *Alps 4000* by Martin Moran (David and Charles) and *Among Mountains* by Jim Crumley (Mainstream Publishing).

## THE KING ALBERT I MEMORIAL FOUNDATION

King Albert I of the Belgians was killed in 1934 on a solitary rock climb at Marches-les-Dames in the valley of the Meuse. He possessed a deep love of mountains and had enjoyed a long climbing career in many parts of Switzerland and the Dolomites. Dr Walter Amstutz, an Honorary Member of the Alpine Club (and of the Groupe de Haute-Montagne and the Ski Club of Great Britain, also Honorary Chairman and co-founder of the Swiss Academic Ski Club, and a council member since 1942 of the Swiss Foundation for Alpine Research) had the privilege, when a student in 1929, to be King Albert's skiing companion in Mürren, and during four subsequent summer seasons he joined the King on his climbs in various regions of the Alps. Walter Amstutz, who was deeply moved by the King's death, determined to create a memorial to perpetuate the King's memory. Although assisted initially by friends, the entire initiative and responsibility for establishing what was to become the King Albert I Memorial Foundation rested with Dr Amstutz.

It was essential that the Foundation should be linked with mountains. The initial task was to find sponsors willing to support an appeal for funds. King Leopold III who succeeded his father headed the list of donors. From small beginnings in 1938 and thanks to generous contributions particularly from Belgian and Swiss donors, Walter Amstutz's goal of setting up a capital of one million Swiss Francs had finally been achieved. Whilst capital gains and interest should secure its future, the Foundation, which is currently administered by a board of four trustees under the presidency of Dr Amstutz, welcomes fresh donations from individuals and institutions. Various objectives, such as a benefit scheme for dependants of guides killed in the mountains, and a training centre in Mürren for young skiers and climbers, were considered before it was decided that the Foundation should be associated with an international Award to be conferred on persons or institutions who, through their outstanding feats and achievements, have made lasting contributions to an area related either directly or indirectly to the field of mountaineering  Eligibility would include special distinction in scientific and artistic fields and the protection of the mountain environment. The Award, comprising a gold medal and a diploma, is presented at intervals fixed by the board of trustees.

The Foundation, which has adopted as its motto a maxim of King Albert I, '*La Volonté, la Qualité maîtresse de l'Homme*', presented its first awards at a ceremony held at Castelmur in the Val Bregaglia on Saturday 3 September 1994. Those honoured to be the first recipients were Lord Hunt, Dr H Bradford Washburn, and Wanda Rutkiewicz (posthumously). The ceremony was attended by 33 invited guests from Switzerland, Belgium, Britain, the USA, Poland, Germany and Italy. The events began with an evening reception at the Palace Hotel St Moritz on Friday 2 September in an atmosphere which set the tone of friendly informality that prevailed through the various functions that followed. After an introductory address about the Foundation given by Dr Amstutz, it was interesting to speak to Wanda Rutkiewicz's sister Nina and her daughter who had come over from Germany, also to Count and Countess de Salis who live partly at the Palazzo Salis, their family seat in the Bregaglia, and partly in Wincanton, Somerset. Dinner followed at the Chesa Veglia in a setting steeped in Swiss tradition and complemented by good food and wine. This was hosted by the Commune and Tourist Office of St Moritz, whose director Dr Hans Danuser's after-dinner address provided a thumb-nail sketch of the growth of St Moritz as Switzerland's top ski resort with a resident population of 5500 and about 50,000 annual visitors, the English having played a large part in its early history by instituting the Cresta Run in 1885.

The following morning in beautiful weather we left St Moritz by coach, halting on the Maloja pass to view the hairpin descent into the lush and fertile vale of Bregaglia. Arriving at the 18th century Palazzo Castelmur outside the village of Stampa, we were entertained to some delightful singing by a group of schoolchildren from Bondo and Soglio. The Award ceremony was a solemn moment conducted in the ornate Sala dei Cavalieri of the Palazzo. The citations were read out in English by Dr Walter Amstutz who then invited the Countess de Salis to present the awards to Lord Hunt, Dr Bradford Washburn, and Mrs Nina Fies on behalf of her late sister Wanda Rutkiewicz. John Hunt's response of gratitude, in German, was movingly expressed, as were the expressions of thanks, in English, given by Dr Washburn and Nina Fies. After an aperitif hosted by the Bregaglia Tourist Office, we drove through rich chestnut forests to Soglio, where directly facing us were views of the Sciora group with Piz Cengalo and Piz Badile sharply outlined in the sparkling weather.

Lunch was held in the colourful garden of the Palazzo de Salis, originally built in 1650 and restored in 1701. An excellent meal was followed by a talk given by Albert Eggler. The keynote was personal and informal, illustrated by vignettes of each of the Award winners. Bradford Washburn replied in words full of human appeal and of humour, which seemed to match the mood perfectly. The 'official' proceedings concluded with the presentation by Dr Amstutz's daughter, Mrs Yvonne Gozon-Amstutz, of souvenir 'awards' to three of the trustees of the Foundation, Albert Eggler, Raoul Imseng and Dr Jürg Marmet, for contributing to the success of the occasion. It must have been a very satisfying moment personally for Dr Walter Amstutz, one in which his guests were pleased to share.

*Trevor Braham*


## THE ALPINE CLUB LIBRARY 1994

Several important developments have been considered in the five Council meetings during 1994.

At the end of 1993 it had been agreed in principle to computerise the catalogue system using a special Library package such as INMAGIC. Additional funds were being sought to pay for the computer hardware/software (£6400) and for the services of a professional cataloguer for, say, one year (£12,000) to load the 14-year backlog since the last published catalogue. Approaches over several months to charitable trusts and bodies, such as the British Library and the Foundation for Sport and the Arts, had proved unsuccessful, when the Pilgrim Trust came to our rescue in

November 1994 with a cheque for £6400 for which we are extremely grateful. This has now enabled us to order the equipment and at year's end it is being set up and we will start developing and loading the system using voluntary help.

Another area of concern has been the insurance of the collection which, with rising market values, is underinsured and does not provide special protection for the more valuable items. It was therefore agreed with the Club Committee that we should seek a range of quotes from our insurer for various levels of cover to protect the identified rarer books from the worst consequences of 'averaging' in the event of a claim. This required a comprehensive review of the more valuable books, which has been painstakingly carried out by the Honorary Librarian. This, in turn, led to a proposal, also agreed with the Club Committee, to dispose of several superfluous third or fourth copies of certain valuable books in order to create a readily available fund of some £25,000 to purchase desirable additions to the collection, which may come on the market at short notice, and for badly needed restoration of certain volumes.

No sooner had this policy been agreed than the unique archive of Col Howard Bury (leader of the 1921 Everest expedition), containing several items of extreme interest to the Club, came up for auction as a single lot in Dublin on 30 November. Although we were unsuccessful at the auction, the dealer who acquired the collection is being contacted to see whether any desired items would be available within our means.

The Himalayan Index is now being kept up to date by volunteers, notably Sally Holland, who has started to tap some of the less obvious sources of information. 2100 mountains, 3500 literature references and 4500 ascents or attempts are now recorded. In the course of 1995 the Index will be transferred to a modern database programme (Access), which will make it more attractive to foreign mountaineering associations.

The Library's investment portfolio, handled for us by Flemings, is oriented to provide income for about half of our annual operating expenses. Building on the success of the 1992 Appeal, a strategy to meet our future financial needs has been developed. This entails continuing efforts to seek renewal of expiring covenants and to encourage bequests, and a possible further approach during 1995 to senior members of the Club and to outside trusts, so that in the longer term our portfolio can be reoriented towards greater protection of capital, as well as providing sufficient income.

As always, the Library Council is greatly indebted to the core of volunteers supporting our professional Librarian, Margaret Eccleston. I thank them all, particularly Robert Lawford, Jerry Lovatt, Peter Ledeboer, John Peacock and Livia Gollancz, our Archivist, assisted by Margaret Darvall.

*George Band*
*Chairman of the Library Council*

## THE OXFORD MOUNTAINEERING LIBRARY

The Oxford Mountaineering Library, recently established within the School of Geography Library, is based on two collections: those of the Oxford University Mountaineering Club, and of the late Michael Roberts and his wife Janet Adam Smith, who had inherited many of the books from her father George Adam Smith (elected to the Alpine Club in 1886). When their son Adam Roberts, Professor of International Relations at Oxford, heard that the OUMC's books, formerly housed in David Cox's rooms in University College, and thereafter in various obscure cupboards, were in need of a new home, he suggested that the two collections should be joined to form the Oxford Mountaineering Library, and that it might be housed in the Library of the Geography School. Through the goodwill and enthusiasm of Professor Andrew Goudie and the Librarian, Linda Atkinson, this was realised, and the new Library was opened in December 1992, when David Cox and Janet Adam Smith spoke briefly about the collections.

The Oxford Mountaineering Library, which has a strong Alpine Club connection, contains books and journals on mountain travel and mountaineering in Britain, the Alps and beyond; it has already attracted gifts of books and of money which can be used for cataloguing, preservation and the purchase of books. It is open to all holders of the Bodleian card, so the books will be available to undergraduates who may find (as did David Cox and many others) that reading about mountains can inspire a wish to climb them.

Any AC member wishing to use the collection should get in touch with Linda Atkinson, Librarian of the School of Geography, Mansfield Road, Oxford OX1 3TB. (Tel. 01865-271919)

*Janet Adam Smith*

## ALPINE CLUB SYMPOSIUM 1994:
## THE MOUNTAINS OF SIBERIA AND TURKESTAN

A large audience of around 110 people attended the 1994 Symposium at Plas y Brenin and some 60 members and their guests stayed for the dinner afterwards. The successful Symposium was organised by John Temple, with help from Sheila Harrison.

**Opening Session**   Dr Yevgeniy B Gippenreiter, Master of Sport, Mountain Guide and Honorary Member of the Alpine Club, presented a geographical and historical background to mountaineering in the countries of the former Soviet Union (with the exception of the Caucasus which had been the subject of a previous Symposium). His overview was masterly and prepared the audience for the scale and variety of mountain scenery described in more detail in the subsequent talks.

**The Pre-Polar Urals**  Marian Elmes was about halfway through the Alpine 4000m tick list when a letter from a Siberian friend inspired a visit to the Urals. The area still being closed to Westerners, Marian had to be smuggled past officialdom disguised as a 'babushka'. Her cover was blown when the accompanying TV crew transmitted a live interview from the summit of Narodnaya, the highest point of the range. The setting was Arctic and very, very remote.

**Altai and Aksu**  Mick Fowler spoke about two areas displaying sharp contrasts: the Russian Altai was mainly a snow range culminating in Bieluka (4406m), while Aksu contained formidable granite peaks sharing some characteristics with both Yosemite and Baltoro. The informality of the Aksu trip was in complete contrast to the earlier one, glasnost having intervened, but Russian hospitality and the high standard of climbing were unchanged.

**The Cherskiy Mountains**  Paul Knott organised the first visit by Westerners to this, the central and highest section of a 1500km-long glaciated range in NE Siberia. Seven out of the ten mountains climbed by his party had not been climbed before and there were scores of unvisited summits left. Though not on an heroic scale, the mountains looked inviting in the low Arctic sunshine. Easy access by helicopter (at a realistic price) was followed by a formidable walk-out.

**Kyrgyzstan**  Pat Littlejohn had visited Kyrgyzstan to assess the climbing potential of a country more than five times the size of Switzerland. The mountains ranged from the 7000m-plus giants of the Tien Shan to unnamed, unclimbed Alpine-scale peaks not far from the airport.

**Kamchatka**  John Town demonstrated that this peninsula was a strong contender for the title 'Last Great Wilderness': he showed slides of geysers and glaciers, active volcanoes, forests, lakes and a savage coastline, which combined to produce some of Siberia's most spectacular scenery. The bad news was that the volcano John's party were climbing was dangerously active and unstable.

**Pamir and Fansky**  Doug Scott described trips to different countries and the political earthquakes following glasnost which had transformed the way in which mountaineering is organised. One shot in particular – of a 'political' meeting at 15,000ft complete with KGB minder in suit and black homberg – emphasised the change. The tensions generated between an anarchic group of young (in those days) British climbers and the structured Soviet system were vividly recalled.

*John Temple*

## THE EIGHTH INTERNATIONAL FESTIVAL
## OF MOUNTAINEERING LITERATURE
Bretton Hall, Yorkshire, 18 November 1994

It was billed as 'Three Women and a Diemberger' but it was Kurt Diemberger who, reading from his latest volume of autobiography *Spirits of the Air*, stole the show with the charm and timing of an experienced story-teller. The spirit of Diemberger's romantic approach to the mountains and to adventure connected with an audience who might have been sceptical about his words on the cold page. His books immediately sold out, despite extra boxes having been brought by Diemberger from one of his famous international 'depots' somewhere near Oldham.

Alison Hargreaves opened the proceedings with a reading from her first book, about an Alpine family camping holiday on which she kept slipping away to solo a North Face until she had climbed six, which is enough for any summer. Just as, in *Alpine Holidays*, Janet Adam Smith wrote about bog-myrtle and soldanelles as well as about peaks, passes and glaciers, so the modern female Alpinist describes, in *A Hard Day's Summer,* some international incidents at children's playgrounds dealt with by her husband.

Alison Osius, Senior Editor at *Climbing* magazine, had travelled from the USA to give a lecture on 'The Art of Profiling Climbers'. The magazine's investment in this type of feature, allowing at least five days' talking and climbing with a subject, is repaid by the professionalism of the subsequent redrafting and editing. The success, and to my mind also perhaps the limi-tation, of this process is that the personal judgement of the writer may become suspended. As a result, subjects tend to be happy with their profile since they are allowed to speak for themselves. Alison's gripping biogra-phy, *Second Ascent*, of the double amputee climber Hugh Herr, is a perfect example of her tact.

The third woman was the young poet Kym Martindale who had again accepted the challenge of writing three poems for the event. Her clear and confident delivery always commands attention, not least because she captures the experience of the ordinary climber (such as the guilt of not climbing on a Sunday) among a galaxy of Festival stars. Gordon Stainforth arrived fresh from winning the picture book prize at the first Banff Mountain Book Festival for *The Cuillin.* His talk gave some clues about the dedication and endurance that lay behind this inspirational book. Gordon had brought back from Banff the award won by Dermot Somers' collection of stories *At the Rising of the Moon.* Gordon presented the award to Dermot's publisher Ken Wilson. Since this book had also won the 1994 Boardman Tasker Memorial Award, and its author was away in Nepal, Joss Lynam came over from Dublin to read one of Dermot's vivid stories. Paul Nunn, chairman of the Boardman Tasker judges, read his adjudication address, which so convinced the audience that the usual rigorous debate was not forthcoming.

The winner of the Festival writing competition was declared by Harold Drasdo and Gordon Stainforth to be John Pennifold whose witty piece on a future access problem was read by Ian Smith and subsequently published in the December 1994 issue of *High* magazine.

*Terry Gifford*

*To receive details of future Festivals write to Terry Gifford, Bretton Hall College, West Bretton, Wakefield, W Yorks, WF4 4LG.*

## EQUIPPING CLIMBING ROUTES WITH BOLTS

Early in 1994 I attended a conference in Switzerland and talked to Swiss guides about their attitude towards bolting. Later in the year I had a short climbing holiday when I visited the Graue Wand, the Eldorado area near the St Gothard and other areas, all with Oswald Olz. All the climbs we did were protected by bolts. I asked various guides about this in a non-committal way and their response was entirely enthusiastic for the bolting to continue – they saw it only as an advantage, especially to their profession as guides. However, I was told by a very skilled female climber (not a guide) that in some valleys there was opposition to the Remy brothers moving in with bolt guns blazing.

After the conference I had enquired whether this was official CAS policy or the action of individuals. I was advised to write to Etienne Gross, Editor of *Die Alpen*, and in due course I received the following reply which I think all British climbers might find interesting:*

Redaktion Die Alpen, CH-3074 Muri, Switzerland

Mr Doug Scott                                                    14 June 1994
Chapel House, Low Cotehill
Near Carlisle
Cumbria, CA4 0EL, England

Dear Doug,

Thank you very much for your letter of 8th April 1994. I will try to consider your questions and to give you an appropriate statement in different chapters.

**The Swiss Alpine Club is open towards mountaineering**
First of all, the SAC does not consider itself as an institution determining the way to practise mountaineering. The SAC does not interfere in 'ethical' or 'ideological' arguments about 'correct' or 'incorrect' mountaineering and 'correct' or 'incorrect' forms of securing techniques (except for strictly technical matters concerning the quality level of security devices: the Club will recommend them accordingly).

---

\* NB All the words and phrases in italics were italicised in Etienne Gross's original letter.

Mountaineering (climbing included) is a sports discipline everyone may practise as they like; the SAC simply provides the appropriate infrastructure, ie courses, excursions, alpine huts/refuges and equipment if necessary etc.

**Equipping the routes**

Equipping the routes with fixed security devices (particularly with bolts) is an activity run primarily on *private initiative*. Indeed, individuals and groups with very different interests promote safety on a large scale: they may have a personal preference for a region or be authors of manuals, hut-keepers, course instructors, mountain guides, regional sections of the SAC or youth organisations (YO) belonging to them, associations of mountain guides etc. They secure the routes in a general sense – from climbing gardens up to major climbing itineraries. Anyone intending to improve the safety of regions with the best security devices presently available (eg bolts) will receive the necessary material, upon request, from the commission for sports climbing or the rescue commission of the SAC (note that the effort is not remunerated). After having completed the securing work, the author will establish a report according to the directives in effect.

**Scope of securing**

The SAC primarily supports securing activities in regions having the topographic features of climbing gardens, as well as on some classic routes (great and popular rock itineraries and particularly delicate and risky passages on alpine routes). The Club does so by giving the appropriate material. There is no pressure from the mountain guides or any third parties. Most of the securing work is realized without the support of the SAC (at least today). It is not known to what extent the regional sections of the SAC or their youth organizations secure the routes or encourage such activities; route safety is indeed an aspect concerning the individual sections and their YOs.

**Equipping the routes with fixed security devices: general approval**

Presently, the common tendency is that the SAC should reinforce its participation in terms of equipping the climbing routes. It does not mean, however, that any single climbing way (primarily in the alpine sector) should be equipped with bolts. As a matter of fact, *well and firmly secured routes are favoured and appreciated.* Anyone fixing the routes may therefore be certain to meet general *approval.*

There is no question that *a great majority of climbers will give preference to well and firmly secured routes*, that the *accident risk* will be significantly reduced and, should the occasion arise, the rescue operation facilitated accordingly.

**The development of climbing techniques**

With the constantly growing number of climbers achieving their training on indoor walls, the ability to fix additional security devices (such as chocks and friends) keeps decreasing (as did the 'art' of nailing up before). *The climbers therefore do and will expect more and more completely equipped routes.*

In that context, it must however be said that regarding most of the routes, even the very recent chock devices do not grant absolute safety and reliability (ie the complete elimination of accident risk).

The battery-operated and petrol-driven rock drills used today have given rise to entirely new securing techniques: indeed, *positioning bolts has become so simple that they have rapidly established themselves as the cheapest, easiest, most efficient and therefore universal security device.* That development, which has also largely promoted the popularity of climbing during the past few years, will continue just as other developments do. Most of the climbing routes will probably be secured some day, which would simply show that the chock devices are partially outdated, as they have been replaced by better and safer devices. *It is a very normal development: what is more effective replaces what is less effective.* And if an even faster, safer and more durable security device is invented, it will progressively succeed to the bolt.

**Climbing as a sports discipline, 'ethics' and 'ideology' in alpine sports**

Numerous texts on 'alpine ideology' have constantly been published in alpine magazines, discussing subjects such as 'correct' and 'incorrect' mountaineering, the controversy about the 'ethical' principles according to which mountaineering and climbing should be practised and developed etc. *Yet mountaineering (promoted to the top by the young) has hardly ever been significantly influenced by such arguments in practice, as it follows its own development and rules. What becomes established is what is most successful, reliable and efficient and suits best the needs of the majority.*

Mountaineering is a sports discipline. And sports *are practised as safely as possible* – with a major or minor risk remaining, according to the discipline. – Simultaneously, there is a tendency to practise it with a minimum of burden and problems in order to concentrate fully on its content (having fun or enjoying the performance by practising). Making additional efforts to get additional security does generally not fit into that concept, as the 'element of adventure' is not required there. It is up to everyone to find their personal 'adventure' in the content of their sports discipline. If the discipline – as practised at a particular stage – does not meet their expectations any more, the 'adventure' must be found elsewhere.

**Minimizing risks – a basic principle**

Eliminating the danger wherever possible – even when the risks are required (eg in alpine sports) – is the overall and permanent objective of humans and the purpose of all efforts. They illustrate a basic human tendency to be safe. Otherwise, ropes, bolts, chock devices, harnesses etc would never have been invented nor developed. Risk and adventure would have remained greatest with a hemp rope around the waist as the only security device (an adventure everyone may still experience by free-soloing). Alpine sports disciplines have always met the idea of a standstill at a certain point; but that idea has never succeeded and will never succeed, *as developments overtake it.*

**Conclusion**

– It may be possible to suppress the 'triumph of the bolt' in Britain for some time. It is up to British climbers. I would however question whether it is possible to disengage from a worldwide development in the long run.

– As for Switzerland and its neighbouring countries, I think that the bolt will establish itself as the presently most efficient security device. In fact, *the bolt has established itself as early as today.*

– Personally, I see no reason to fight in the name of some 'ethics' which are neither specified nor clearly delimited. Moreover, it is not consistent to suppress the development of security, whereas early alpinists have always favoured, required and encouraged such improvements. It is equally inconsistent to refuse a new security device which does seemingly not fit into a 'homemade' concept of 'ethics and adventure'.

Now, should we not rather start *questioning our own concept of 'ethics and adventure'*, as it is suddenly 'endangered' by a new security device? Would it not be more accurate to wonder why *we* have a problem with bolts? For there is an aspect which is easily forgotten: *only the person opposing the new security device has a problem with it.* The person using the new device has no problem with it. In other terms: is it not finally an attempt to shift a personal problem on others?

– The bolt is neither a topic nor a problem for the younger generation: *the bolt exists and they use it – what is all the talk about?*

– 'Ethics' which resist new developments are generally 'invented' by senior generations as a way to fight those new forms and to 'discipline' the young. If there is a problem with bolts – for Switzerland, I would say there is none – I think it is primarily **a *generation problem.***

I do not know whether my (personal) statement answers your questions, but it will certainly provide a basis for possible talks. We should however be aware that such discussions may well be an interesting and enriching experience, but that they will not influence the development any more, the bolts being a fact today. All we do is perhaps running after reality – a behaviour which I think is typical when it comes to alpine sports. Instead of recognizing and promoting new developments at an early stage, there is a tendency to suppress them by hiding behind fortifications such as 'old values', 'ethics' and further ideological traditions. It does not mean that anything should be thrown overboard. Traditions are important. They are part of development and act as its dynamic principle. They must, however, merge with progress and not be used as a means to hinder it whenever possible.

Yours sincerely,
Etienne Gross
Editor of the Swiss Alpine magazine *Die Alpen*


I understand from subsequent enquiry that this letter is in line with the generally held view in Switzerland, and Etienne Gross is happy to have his letter published.

... And all the time we thought that climbing was about protecting *our own* lives and facing up to the uncertainty of being able to do that.

*Doug Scott*


## COMPETITIONS IN MOUNTAIN AREAS

My article on this subject in the last *Alpine Journal* was based on a Report, entitled *UIAA Policy Towards Competitions in Mountain Areas*, which I presented to the UIAA General Assembly in October 1993. The UIAA endorsed that Report which tried to take a fresh approach towards these issues, covering the range of opinions involved and recognising the extent to which competitions in mountain areas already exist and are seen by some as beneficial to mountaineering.

In 1994 the Working Group on Competitions in Mountain Areas (in collaboration with the UIAA Commissions and member federations) has continued to analyse the extent and effects of mountain competitions; and has also arranged for assessments of the two current proposals for UIAA recognition, ie ski-alpinism and the annual speed climbing competition on Khan Tengri.

This work has tended to confirm the view that, at least on a technical level, it should be possible to establish UIAA criteria for the assessment of competitions, in consequence of which the UIAA could recognise or organise some competitions as meeting these criteria. We therefore see the way ahead more as a case by case approach, in which competitions proposed to the UIAA would be assessed as to whether or not they met the criteria, rather than as a rigid policy either for or against all mountain competitions.

Accordingly, the Working Group secured the approval of the 1994 AGM to a compromise under which the UIAA would issue Guidelines covering safety and environmental aspects of ski mountaineering, and possibly other, competitions and their impact on mountaineering or on the locality. It was further decided that the UIAA would formally recognise the existence of ski mountaineering races in member countries and of a representative organisation to co-ordinate the running of international competitions in Europe (who would be offered observer status in the UIAA on a reciprocal basis). The UIAA would also continue to monitor the development of ski mountaineering races and, so far as possible, other competitions.

In the case of the 1994 Khan Tengri competition, the Mountaineering Commission had two observers who went to the summit at the time; but their conclusion was that in its present form the race is not compatible with the proposed UIAA safety guidelines and could not therefore be recommended. Instead, the Central Asian federations interested in high-altitude competitions were to be asked collectively to make proposals to the UIAA as to the best way to proceed in the future.

It was recognised that a great deal of practical work would be required during 1995 in distinguishing between those competitions which were likely to be acceptable under the new Guidelines and those which would not be so, or which would need modification. Furthermore, it would be necessary to obtain legal advice on any possible potential UIAA liability for accidents which might occur at events associated with the UIAA.

It was also decided that the UIAA General Assembly might review the representation of organised competitive sports and its relationship with other relevant bodies again in the future, perhaps in 1997, by which time the UIAA would have sufficient knowledge and experience of the operation of competitive sports for its membership to be able to reach an informed decision on whether or not to take formal responsibility for mountain competitions of all kinds.

*Alan Blackshaw*

# Contributors

**GEORGE BAND** was the youngest member of the 1953 Everest team. In 1955 he made the first ascent (with Joe Brown) of Kangchenjunga, and subsequently climbed in Peru and the Caucasus. In 1991 he made the first ascent of Ngum Tang Gang III (5640m) in Bhutan. AC President 1987-89. Chairman of the Library Council from 1993.

**PETER BERG** is a retired scientist, now a freelance broadcaster and writer, representing Radio Sweden's English service in London, as well as writing on early music, food, mountaineering and sailing for various journals, and working on a book on an 18th century industrial spy.

**JOSÉ LUIS BERMÚDEZ** is a research fellow in the Faculty of Philosophy, University of Cambridge. He took up climbing too late and has been making up for lost time in the Alps, Himalaya and Caucasus. Co-author (with Audrey Salkeld) of *On the Edge of Europe: Mountaineering in the Caucasus.*

**CHRIS BONINGTON CBE**, whose distinguished career is well known, celebrated his 60th year by making the first ascent of Rangrik Rang (6553m) during the Indian British Kinnaur Expedition in 1994. He has climbed all over the world, written 12 books and worked on television and radio. His latest book, *Great Climbs,* was published in 1994.

**HAMISH BROWN** is a travel writer based in Scotland, when not wandering worldwide or making extended visits to Morocco. His latest book *From the Pennines to the Highlands. A Walking Route through the Scottish Borders* was published in 1992.

**PAUL CLARKE** is a management consultant who has lived and worked in East Africa since 1985. He is a former chairman of the Mountain Club of Kenya and author of *The Mountains of Kenya, A Walker's Guide.* In 1993 he was appointed by Kenya Wildlife Service to work with the warden of Mount Kenya to prepare a national park management plan.

**JULIE-ANN CLYMA** studied Physiology before moving to Britain from New Zealand in 1985. She has participated in nine expeditions, in the Southern Alps, Peru, Alaska, Pakistan, Nepal, the former Soviet Union and India, as well as the European Alps.

**ED DOUGLAS** was, until recently, editor of *Mountain Review* and writes on mountaineering for *The Guardian* and *The Observer*. When not pursuing this Walter Mittyish profession, he climbs in Britain and the Alps and has been known to surface in the United States and Alaska.

**EVELIO ECHEVARRÍA** was born in Santiago, Chile, and teaches Hispanic Literature at Colorado State University. He has climbed in North and South America, and has contributed numerous articles to Andean, North American and European journals.

**MARIAN ELMES** has climbed in the Alps, India, Central Asia and Norway. She has been on three expeditions to the CIS, including the long-forbidden Siberian wilderness of the Pre-Polar Urals. A keen rock-climber, she is rather ashamed to admit that she has completed all the Munros, many of them on ski.

**JULIAN FREEMAN-ATTWOOD** is a forestry manager who lives on the Shropshire/Welsh border. He has climbed in the Himalaya, Africa, the Antarctic and Sub-Antarctic, specialising in unclimbed peaks in little-known areas. He is becoming increasingly interested in sailing/mountaineering trips, having once part-owned Tilman's Pilot Cutter *Baroque*.

**TERRY GIFFORD** organises the International Festival of Mountaineering Literature at Bretton Hall College of Leeds University. His collections of poetry include *The Stone Spiral, Ten Letters to John Muir* and *Outcrops*.

**JIM GREGSON** is a teacher of Art. He has climbed extensively in the Alps since 1972. In recent years he has taken to Nordic ski-touring and ski-mountaineering in Scotland and Norway. He has been on two expeditions to Greenland.

**LINDSAY GRIFFIN** is a magazine editor/journalist living in North Wales. He pursues all aspects of climbing with undiminished enthusiasm but dwindling ability. Despite a love of exploratory visits to the Greater Ranges, he is drawn back to the Alps, especially the delightful northern Italian valleys where there still remains a wealth of little-known terrain.

**DAVID HAMILTON** earns a precarious living leading trekking and mountaineering expeditions to the world's great mountain ranges. He is a recent convert to the joys of ski mountaineering. His friends report that what he lacks in skiing technique he more than compensates for with enthusiasm. He is currently looking for his first 'proper' job (aged 33).

**J G R HARDING** is a solicitor (retired), but was formerly in the Colonial Service in South Arabia. He has climbed and skied extensively in Europe, Asia, Africa and Australia and in 1994 made the first winter traverse of Corsica's GR20.

**ALAN HINKES** has been going to the Himalaya for over 10 years. He has climbed four 8000ers, including two new routes on Shisha Pangma and the first British ascent of Manaslu. K2 has so far eluded him, but he is going back. Alan has an 11-year-old daughter Fiona. He is a British Mountain Guide (UIAGM) and technical consultant with Berghaus Ltd.

**TONY HOWARD**, a founding partner of Troll Safety Equipment, led the first ascent of Norway's Troll Wall in 1965. He wrote the guide to Romsdal. Expeditions include Arctic Norway and Canada, S Georgia, Greenland and desert mountains of Morocco, Algeria, Sudan, Iran, Egypt, Oman and Jordan where he wrote the guide to the mountains of Wadi Rum.

**HARISH KAPADIA** is a cloth merchant by profession. He has climbed and trekked in the Himalaya since 1960, with ascents up to 6800m. He is Honorary Editor of the *Himalayan Journal* and compiler of the *HC Newsletter*. In 1993 he was awarded the IMF's Gold Medal.

**PAUL KNOTT** started climbing at Bath University. He has climbed in the Alps, the Altai, the Tien Shan and the Caucasus. In 1994 he organised the first visit by Westerners to the Cherskiy Mountains in NE Siberia.

**JEFF LONG** lives and climbs in Boulder, Colorado. His latest book, *The Ascent*, won the 1993 Boardman Tasker Memorial Award and the American Alpine Club Literary Award. It dealt with an Everest expedition and larger themes of repression in Tibet. In November 1994 he returned to Tibet to reconnoitre for a medical clinic at Kharta in 1995.

**ALAN LYALL** is a retired solicitor, who has climbed or walked in Switzerland in each of the last 35 years. He has recently been carrying out some extensive research into the history of the first ascent of the Matterhorn.

**ROBERT NEW** is a property consultant living in Kota Kinabalu, where he designed and built the 4-man West Gurkha Hut at 12,600ft. He has climbed Mount Kinabalu approximately 50 times. As a student, he climbed in the French Alps and the Romsdal area of Norway and then extensively in East Africa. President of the Mountain Club of Uganda 1970-71.

**PAUL NUNN PhD** lectures in economic history at Sheffield. He has climbed for over 30 years in the Alps, Caucasus and Baffin Island and taken part in 15 expeditions to the Greater Ranges. His book *At the Sharp End* was published in 1988. AC Vice-President 1989-90, BMC President from 1994.

**BILL O'CONNOR** is a UIAGM mountain and ski guide who spends much of his time climbing and guiding abroad, with more than 30 summer Alpine seasons and 23 Himalayan expeditions in the bag. A one-time guidebook editor for the AC, he is the author of several books including a soon to be published volume on the Lake District where he lives.

**MICHAEL PEYRON** teaches English in Grenoble, France. He has climbed in the Moroccan Atlas and the French Alps since 1964, the recent emphasis having been as much on Berber studies as on ski-touring. He is currently preparing Vol 2 of a guidebook series on the French Pre-Alps. He holds the CAF's gold medal and is a past president of the Rabat section.

**JONATHAN PRATT** worked for several years as a mining engineer in the USA. Since 1986 he has climbed in N and S America, New Zealand and Africa and has taken part in 10 Himalayan expeditions. He has climbed Everest, K2 and, in 1994, Gasherbrum I (the first British ascent). He is the only Briton to have climbed the world's two highest mountains.

**PAUL PRITCHARD** has lived in North Wales for the last 9 years and has done many new routes on Gogarth, in the mountains and on slate. He has climbed on big walls in the Alps, Patagonia, Brazil, North America and the Himalaya. In 1994, with three companions, he climbed the NW face of Mt Asgard on Baffin Island.

**KEV REYNOLDS** has climbed in the Alps, Atlas, Caucasus, Turkey and extensively in the Pyrenees, and now makes an annual pilgrimage on trek in the Himalaya. A former Youth Hostel Warden, he is a freelance writer and lecturer.

**SIMON RICHARDSON** is a petroleum engineer based in Aberdeen. Experience gained climbing in the Alps, Andes, Himalaya and Alaska is put to good use most winter weekends whilst exploring and climbing in the Scottish Highlands.

**ROY RUDDLE** researches the psychology of virtual reality and finds that third world bureaucracy is sometimes too frustrating to enjoy. His favourite high mountain area is Alaska, where it is possible to arrange everything in advance by telephone and pay by credit card. Asst Editor from 1992.

**C A RUSSELL**, who formerly worked with a City bank, devotes much of his time to mountaineering and related activities. He has climbed in many regions of the Alps, in the Pyrenees, East Africa, North America and the Himalaya.

**BILL RUTHVEN** has been Hon Secretary of the Mount Everest Foundation since 1985. A keen traveller and photographer, he finds that MEF work now takes up at least 100% of his time, but remembers that in another life he was once an aeronautical engineer.

**DAWSON STELFOX MBE** is an architect and mountain guide who has climbed since 1976 in Europe, America and Asia. In 1993 he made both the first Irish ascent of Everest and the first British ascent of the North Ridge. He is currently Chairman of the Mountaineering Council of Ireland and of the UK Mountain Training Board.

**JULES STEWART** is a journalist who began climbing rather late in life. His first big challenge, aged 40, was Ecuador's Cotopaxi, a failed attempt which he repeated with success at 50. He has also climbed in the Alps and Nepal and took part in the 1992 University of Madrid expedition to Everest.

**JOHN TEMPLE** is a Yorkshireman, aged 60. Youthful struggles with gritstone are now supplemented, in retirement, by forays onto the sea cliffs and, broken limbs permitting, visits to the Alps, Caucasus and East Africa.

**GEOFFREY TEMPLEMAN,** a retired chartered surveyor, has greatly enjoyed being an Assistant Editor of the *AJ* for the past 19 years. A love of mountain literature is coupled with excursions into the hills which are becoming less and less energetic.

**JOHN TINKER** was born in 1959. He is a director of Out There Trekking Expeditions Ltd. He spends about six months a year in the Himalaya.

**DUNCAN TUNSTALL** is an energy Risk Manager. He has been climbing for many years and prefers to operate in some of the less well-known or fashionable ranges of the world. He has plans to continue wandering as long as work commitments permit.

**VADIM VASILJEV** was born in Leningrad in 1961 and has been climbing and skiing for over 20 years. After graduating from the Leningrad Electrical Engineering Institute in 1984, he spent six further years at the Institute researching acousto-optics. He now works for the Russian company VMB Travel as head of their adventure travel department.

**GRAEME WATSON** was born in East Africa and has travelled in the region widely. A former chairman of the Mountain Club of Kenya he spent a year in Mbeya in 1984, using the opportunity to explore the Southern Highlands, but in recent years has concentrated his efforts more on northern Tanzania from his base in Nairobi.

**MICHAEL WARD CBE MD FRCS** was Medical Officer on Everest in 1953. He is a consultant surgeon (retired) who has combined exploration in Nepal, Bhutan, Kun Lun and Tibet with high-altitude research. Honorary Member 1992

**CHARLES WARREN** is a consultant children's physician (retired). As a member of Marco Pallis's 1933 Gangotri expedition, and of the Everest expeditions in 1935, '36 and '37, he made several first ascents, including Kharta Changri (7056m) with Edward Kempson in 1935. He has also climbed in East and South Africa. Vice-President 1963, Honorary Member 1980.

# Index

## NOTES FOR CONTRIBUTORS

The *Alpine Journal* records all aspects of mountains and mountaineering, including expeditions, adventure, art, literature, geography, history, geology, medicine, ethics and the mountain environment.

**Articles** Contributions in English are invited. They should be sent to the **Hon Editor, Mrs J Merz, 14 Whitefield Close, Putney, London SW15 3SS.** Articles should be in the form of typed copy or on disk with accompanying hard copy. Their length should not exceed 3000 words without prior approval of the Editor **and may be edited or shortened at her discretion.** Authors are asked to keep a copy. It is regretted that the *Alpine Journal* is unable to offer a fee for articles published, but authors receive a complimentary copy of the issue of the *Alpine Journal* in which their article appears.

**Articles and book reviews should not have been published in substantially the same form by any other publication, nor subsequently be published elsewhere, without permission from the Editor.**

**Maps** These should be well researched, accurate, and finished ready for printing. They should show the most important place-names mentioned in the text. It is the authors' responsibility to get their maps redrawn if necessary. This can be arranged through the Editor if required.

**Photographs** Only top quality photographs will be accepted. Prints (any size) should be black and white, with glossy finish if possible, and with the author's name, in pencil, on the reverse side. Colour transparencies, in 35mm format or larger, should be originals (**not copies**).

**Captions** These should be listed **on a separate sheet** and should give title, author and approximate date when the photograph was taken.

**Copyright** It is the author's responsibility to obtain copyright clearance for both text and photographs, to pay any fees involved and to ensure that acknowledgements are in the form required by the copyright owner.

**Summaries** A brief summary should be included with all 'expedition' articles.

**Biographies** Authors are asked to provide a short biography, in not more than 50 words, listing the most noteworthy items in their climbing career and anything else they wish to mention.

**Deadline:   copy should reach the Editor by 1 January of the year of publication.**